Drawing on the all-encompassing worship of God in Isaiah 45:23 and contrasting this against the backdrop of the Roman cult of Augustus in the colony of Philippi, Surif shows how the apostle Paul encourages believers to orient their lives towards the coming universal worship of God and his Christ, who humbled himself and was exalted (Phil 2:6–11). It is a real delight to welcome the publication of this excellent, promising first monograph from a talented Indonesian New Testament scholar and teacher!

Markus Bockmuehl, PhD
Dean Ireland's Professor of the Exegesis of Holy Scripture,
University of Oxford, UK

This careful and theologically important study establishes that the universal eschatological worship of Christ serves as one of the keys to the message of Paul's letter to the Philippians. The importance of Isaiah's eschatological vision for Paul's understanding of Christ's role in God's ultimate plan for creation, the way Paul's message critically engages and undermines Roman imperial pretensions, and the practical relevance of Paul's eschatological vision for the ethical and spiritual lives of the believers in Philippi, are all explored and expounded in detail. As a whole, this study provides a valuable contribution to our understanding of Paul's theology as it is reflected in the letter to the Philippians.

Roy E. Ciampa, PhD
S. Louis and Ann W. Armstrong Chair of Religion,
Chair, Department of Biblical and Religious Studies,
Samford University, Birmingham, Alabama, USA

Surif is to be commended for effectively bringing to the fore the topic of eschatological worship, not just in the famous christological hymn of Paul's letter to the Philippians, but also the entire letter. Assiduously dovetailing the theme with the critical Jewish antecedents and the pervasive Roman imperial propaganda, Paul's parenetic goals are thereby cogently illuminated. I would not be surprised that readers will come away wondering silently, "Why didn't I see this before?" No stone is left unturned in this comprehensive account of the theme.

Huat Tan, PhD
Jew Testament,
ege, Singapore

The Universal Eschatological Worship of Jesus Christ in Paul's Letter to the Philippians

Surif

Langham

MONOGRAPHS

© 2021 Surif

Published 2021 by Langham Monographs
An imprint of Langham Publishing
www.langhampublishing.org

Langham Publishing and its imprints are a ministry of Langham Partnership

Langham Partnership
PO Box 296, Carlisle, Cumbria, CA3 9WZ, UK
www.langham.org

ISBNs:
978-1-83973-432-8 Print
978-1-83973-566-0 ePub
978-1-83973-567-7 Mobi
978-1-83973-568-4 PDF

British Library Cataloguing-in-Publication Data
A catalogue record for this book is available from the British Library

ISBN: 978-1-83973-432-8

Cover & Book Design: projectluz.com

Contents

Abbreviations ix

Chapter 1 1
Introduction
    1.1 Review of Scholarship 2
        1.1.1 Ernst Käsemann 3
        1.1.2 Ralph P. Martin 4
        1.1.3 Morna Hooker 4
        1.1.4 Larry W. Hurtado 5
        1.1.5 Stephen Fowl 6
        1.1.6 L. Gregory Bloomquist 7
        1.1.7 Peter Oakes 8
        1.1.8 Joseph H. Hellerman 10
        1.1.9 M. Sydney Park 10
        1.1.10 Sergio Rosell Nebreda 11
        1.1.11 Heiko Wojtkowiak 12
        1.1.12 Summary and Remarks 13
    1.2 Thesis 14
    1.3 The Terminology of Worship 15
    1.4 Methodology and Presentation 15

Chapter 2 19
The Universal Eschatological Worship of YHWH in Isaiah 45:23–24
    2.1 The Eschatological Worship of YHWH in Ancient Jewish
        Writings 20
        2.1.1 The Covenantal Notion 20
        2.1.2 The Visions of the Universal Worship of YHWH 23
        2.1.3 YHWH's Eschatological Reign 25
        2.1.4 The Transformation of the Worshippers of YHWH 29
        2.1.5 Summary 31
    2.2 The Universal Eschatological Worship of YHWH in Isaiah 31
        2.2.1 The Universal Eschatological Worship 32
        2.2.2 The Eschatological Reign of YHWH 36
        2.2.3 The Transformation of the Worshippers 40
        2.2.4 The Covenant Framework 42
        2.2.5 Summary 44

2.3 Reading Isaiah 45:23–24 44
    2.3.1 The Texts 45
    2.3.2 The Context 47
    2.3.3 The Universal Eschatological Worship of YHWH 48
    2.3.4 YHWH's Eschatological Reign and Salvation 50
    2.3.5 The Transformation of the Worshippers 52
    2.3.6 The Covenant Notion 53
2.4 Summary 55

Chapter 3 57
Paul's Reading of Isaiah 45:23
3.1 The Use of Isaiah 45:23 in 4Q215A – Time of Righteousness 58
    3.1.1 The Universal Eschatological Worship of the God of
    Israel 60
    3.1.2 The Eschatological Reign and Salvation of God 63
    3.1.3 The Motif of Holiness 65
    3.1.4 The Covenant Notion 67
    3.1.5 Synthesis 68
3.2 The Use of Isaiah 45:23 in the Aleinu Prayer 68
    3.2.1 The Universal Worship of God 70
    3.2.2 The Eschatological Reign of YHWH 71
    3.2.3 The Motif of Holiness 73
    3.2.4 The Covenant Notion 74
    3.2.5 Synthesis 74
3.3 The Use of Isaiah 45:23 in Romans 14:11 75
    3.3.1 The Universal Eschatological Worship 79
    3.3.2 YHWH's Eschatological Reign 80
    3.3.3 The Holiness Motif 82
    3.3.4 The Covenant Framework 84
3.4 Summary 86

Chapter 4 89
The Worship of Augustus in the City of Philippi
4.1 The Worship of Augustus in the Greco-Roman World 90
    4.1.1 The Roman Imperial Cult 90
    4.1.2 The Rise and Prominence of the Cult of Augustus 93
4.2 The Worship of Augustus in Philippi 95
    4.2.1 The Roman Philippi at the Time of Paul 95
    4.2.2 The Existence of the Cult of Augustus 100
    4.2.3 The Prominence of the Cult of Augustus 103
4.3 The Eschatological Significance of the Worship of Augustus 105

4.3.1 The Myth of the Golden Age in Antiquity 106
4.3.2 Virgil's Remaking of the Myth 107
4.3.3 The Imperial Version of the Golden Age...........................111
4.3.4 The Prevalence of the Mythical-Imperial Ideology...........114
4.3.5 The Worship of Augustus and the Golden Age
of Rome..117
4.4 Summary 118

Chapter 5 121
The Setting of Paul's Letter to the Philippians
5.1 The Integrity of the Letter 121
5.1.1 The External Evidence 122
5.1.2 The Internal Evidence 122
Excursus: The Epistolary Type and Rhetorical Structure 126
5.2 The Writer, the Recipients, and their Relationship 127
5.2.1 Paul, the Slave of Christ Jesus 127
5.2.2 The Church at Philippi..131
5.2.3 The *Koinonia* in the Gospel of Christ 137
5.3 The Addressed Problems 139
Excursus: The Cult of Augustus and the Civic Opposition
in Philippi 141
5.4 The Anti-Imperial Stance 146

Chapter 6 155
The Universal Worship of Christ in Philippians 2:6–11
6.1 Working Framework for Reading Philippians 2:6–11 156
6.1.1 The Context of Paul's Letter to the Philippians.................156
6.1.2 Philippians 2:6–11 as the Narratival Gospel of Jesus
Christ..158
6.1.3 The Reading of the Eschatological Narrative in Isaiah 160
6.1.4 Philippians 2:6–11 as a Polemic Against the
Imperial Narrative of Augustus 164
6.2 Philippians 2:10–11 as the Universal Worship of the
Messiah Jesus 167
6.2.1 Worship or Submission?...167
6.2.2 The Object of Worship..169
6.2.3 The Worshippers..174
6.2.4 The Event of Worship..176
6.3 The Significances of the Motif of Eschatological Worship
of Christ..177
6.3.1 Christology...178

6.3.2 Soteriology 183

6.3.3 Anti-Imperial Stance..188

6.3.4 Ethics...194

6.4 Summary 197

Chapter 7 199

The Function of Philippians 2:10–11

7.1 Paul's Eschatological Frame of Mind 200

7.1.1 Paul's Τοῦτο Φρονεῖν in 1:5–7 201

7.1.2 Paul's Τοῦτο Φρονεῖτε Exhortation in 2:5–11....................206

7.1.3 Paul's Τοῦτο Φρονῶμεν Exhortation in 3:4–15.................209

7.1.4 Synthesis 216

7.2 Reading Philippians 1:27–2:18 218

7.2.1 Paul's Rhetorical Strategy 218

7.2.2. The Pivotal Element of Paul's Eschatological Frame

of Mind 223

7.2.3 Synthesis 232

7.3 Reading Philippians 3:2–4:4...234

7.3.1 Paul's Rhetorical Strategy 235

7.3.2 The Pivotal Elements of Paul's Frame of Mind.................238

7.3.3 Synthesis 247

Chapter 8 249

Summary and Conclusion

Bibliography 255

Index of Names..279

Index of Scripture...281

Index of Ancient Texts and Literature 289

Abbreviations

ABD	*Achor Bible Dictionary*
AYBRL	Anchor Yale Bible Reference Library
BDAG	Walter Bauer, William F. Arndt, F. Wilbur Gingrich, and Frederick W. Danker. *Greek-English Lexicon of the New Testament and Other Early Christian Literature.*
BDF	Friedrich Blass, Albert Debrunner, and Robert W. Funk. *A Greek Grammar of the New Testament and Other Early Christian Literature.*
BCOTWP	Baker Commentary on the Old Testament Wisdom and Psalms
BECNT	Baker Exegetical Commentary on the New Testament
DJD	Discoveries in the Judean Desert
EDNT	*Exegetical Dictionary of the New Testament.*
FRLANT	Forschungen zur Religion und Literatur des Alten und Neuen Testaments
HCOT	Historical Commentary on the Old Testament
ICC	International Critical Commentary
JSJSup	Supplements to the Journal for the study of Judaism
JSNTSup	Journal for the Study of the New Testament Supplement Series
JSOTSup	Journal for the Study of the Old New Testament Supplement Series
LCL	Loeb Classical Library

LNTS	The Library of New Testament Studies
LSJ	Liddell, Henry George, Robert Scott, Hendry Stuart Jones. *A Greek-English Lexicon*
NAC	New American Commentary
NCBC	New Century Bible Commentary
NIBCNT	New International Biblical Commentary on the New Testament
NICNT	New International Commentary on the New Testament
NICOT	New International Commentary on the Old Testament
NIGTC	New International Greek Testament Commentary
NovTSup	Supplements Novum Testamentum
SNTSMS	Society for New Testament Studies Monograph Series
STDJ	Studies on the Texts of the Desert of Judah
TDNT	*Theological Dictionary of the New Testament*
THNTC	Two Horizons New Testament Commentary
WUNT	Wissenschaftliche Untersuchungen zum Neuen Testament

CHAPTER 1

Introduction

Philippians 2:6–11 continues to be a focal point of discussion in the recent studies of the New Testament. Notably, the discussions of this christological passage are divided into several loci. With regard to the composition, the discussions are centered on its authorship,[1] literary form,[2] and structure.[3] Concerning its content, the discussions focus on the background[4] and the nature of Christology in the passage.[5] Furthermore, in the last few decades, the anti-imperial nature of this passage is also hotly debated.[6] Finally, there is an arisen interest to discuss the rhetorical function of the passage in Paul's

---

1. The majority scholars hold the view of the non-Pauline composition. See Martin, *Hymn of Christ*. Having said this, there is also a growing opinion on the Pauline composition. See Hooker, "Philippians," 88–100; Fee, "Philippians," 29–46; Bockmuehl, *Philippians*.

2. Since Lohmeyer, *Kyrios Jesus*, Philippians 2:6–11 was generally regarded as a hymn of the earliest Christianity. This consensus, however, has been challenged recently. Various alternative opinions have been proposed in the last few decades. For a poem, see Hooker, "Philippians"; for an exalted-prose, see Fee, "Philippians"; for an encomiun, see Collins, "Psalms, Philippians," 361–72; for a hymnos, see Martin and Nash, "Philippians 2:6–11," 90–138.

3. For two strophes, which each consist of three three-line stanzas, see Lohmeyer, *Kyrios Jesus*; for three four-line stanzas, see Jeremias, "Zu Phil 2:7," 182–88; for six couplets, see Martin, *Hymn of Christ*; for three sentences, see Fee, "Philippians"; for two sentences, see Collins, "Psalms, Philippians."

4. Adam Christology in Dunn, *Christology in the Making*; wisdom Christology in Witherington III, *Paul's Narrative Thought*; the Isaianic servant of YHWH in Cerfaux, *Christ in the Theology*; divine hero Christology in Knox, "'Divine Hero' Christology," 229–49; pre-Christian Gnosticism in Käsemann, "Critical Analysis of Philippians," 45–88.

5. High Christology in Bauckham, "Worship of Jesus in Philippians," 128–39; Hurtado, "'Case Study,'" 83–107; low Christology in Dunn, *Christology in the Making*; Casey, *From Jewish Prophet*.

6. For anti-imperial reading, see Wright, "Paul's Gospel," 160–83; Oakes, "Re-Mapping the Universe," 301–22; Heen, "Phil 2:6–11," 125–54. For non anti-imperial reading, see Bryan, *Render to Caesar*; Kim, *Christ and Caesar*.

letter to the Philippians.[7] All this discussion has produced a great number of scholarly works in New Testament studies.[8]

Having said this, the lament of Larry J. Kreitzer in 1998 is felt to be still relevant:

> Perhaps the lion's share of scholarly attention has been so pre-occupied with the Christological implications of the hymn, most importantly the debate about preexistence . . ., *that the eschatological facet of the hymn has been neglected.* This is to be lamented, for it yields a one-dimensional interpretation of the hymn as it stands within the letter. Any persuasive exegesis of the Christological hymn must give due attention to the escha-tological perspective that underlies vv. 9–11.[9]

It is to respond to this lament that the present study is made. It intends to explore the eschatological significance of the second part of this christological passage, then to highlight its function in Paul's paraenetical discourses in his letter to the Philippians.

Before introducing the thesis of this study, it is necessary to outline past scholarly contributions on the function of Philippians 2:9–11 in its own literary context.

1.1 Review of Scholarship

While the self-abasement part of the christological passage in Philippians (2:6–8) befits Paul's exhortation in the letter, the exaltation part (2:9–11) appears to hang awkwardly. To solve this exegetical problem, numerous scholars in the last few decades have tried to establish more persuasively the rhetorical function of this exaltation part in the letter. Their opinions will be reviewed in this section. The presentation is not exhaustive but intends to highlight the development of thoughts on this issue in modern biblical scholarship. Ernst Käsemann's seminal article in 1950 is chosen as a starting point. Although in

---

7. For the kerygmatic reading, see Käsemann, "Critical Analysis of Philippians"; Martin, *Hymn of Christ.* For the ethical reading, see Hooker, "Philippians"; Hurtado, "Jesus as Lordly Example," 113–26; Fowl, *Story of Christ.*

8. This can be seen in the list of reference in Martin, *Hymn of Christ.*

9. Kreitzer, "When He at Last Is First," 113. The emphasis is mine.

the first half of the twentieth century some attention had been given to the exaltation of Jesus, it was this seminal article that led to scholarly scrutiny on its interpretation.

1.1.1 Ernst Käsemann

It was generally perceived in the first half of the twentieth century AD that the function of the christological passage in the letter to the Philippians was laid primarily for amplifying Christ's humble deeds in Paul's ethical exhortations. Accordingly, the imitation of Christ's humility is incentivized by God's reward, as it was with Christ. It was by Käsemann's seminal article in 1950 that the pendulum of interpretation swung to the opposite end.[10] This article powerfully asserts that the predominant force of this christological passage is not ethics, but eschatological soteriology. His interpretation is popularly labeled as the kerygmatic interpretation of Philippians 2:6–11. It vigorously argues that the passage presents Christ not as a perfect model to be imitated, but as the one who accomplished God's work of salvation.[11] His oft-quoted statement, Christ "ist Urbild nicht Vorbild" (Christ is an archetype and not a model),[12] summarizes his opinion on the role of this christological passage.

Consequently, the exaltation of Christ is not given as a reward for his noble ethics, but rather the heavenly enthronement that shifts all powers in the universe to him.[13] In this universal lordship, the role of this christological passage is clarified: because salvation means that sovereign authority has been handed to Christ, all Christians are called to live under the realm of his lordship.[14] The notion of obedience of believers is strongly emphasized, as he claims, "it becomes evident that the obedient one (Christ) is himself the author of the obedient ones (the church)," the proclamation of the lordship of the obedient one also "calls the Christian community . . . into obedience."[15]

---

10. Käsemann, "Critical Analysis of Philippians."
11. Käsemann, 52–53, 84–85.
12. Käsemann, 74.
13. Käsemann, 76–77.
14. Käsemann, 86–87.
15. Käsemann, 97.

1.1.2 Ralph P. Martin

Käsemann's treatment of Philippians 2:6–11 is notably isolated from its literary context. His view, however, has remarkable implications for how the function of the christological passage in Paul's letter to the Philippians should be perceived. This is demonstrated in Ralph P. Martin's seminal study in 1967.[16] Adopting Käsemann's interpretation, he maintains that Paul's intent in narrating this christological passage in his letter to the Philippians is not to call his readers to imitate Christ, but to live under his lordship, as he is now the Lord of the church.[17] God's exaltation of him, thus, does not imply any eschatological reward, given that in Philippians 2:4 this idea has been implicitly denied earlier "do not look to your own interest."[18] Rather, it becomes a part of God's eschatological scheme by which his lordship and salvation will be universally acknowledged. Its ethical impetus is exploited across the whole letter. The life of obedience under Christ's lordship is amplified in Paul's various exhortations (1:27; 2:2–4; 2:12–14), and it is presented in the lives of Timothy (2:19–24), Epaphroditus (2:25–30), and Paul (2:17; 3:8–21).[19]

1.1.3 Morna Hooker

While scholars generally agree with Käsemann's contention with regard to the salvific-eschatological thrust of Philippians 2:6–11, many have reservations about his rejection of the paradigmatic force of Christ's deed. In 1975 Morna Hooker provided a critical response to Käsemann's interpretation.[20] She argues that there is no need for a separation between Christ's salvific work and his ethical pattern in reading this christological passage.[21] Although in its original form and context this passage recites "the events which are the ground of salvation," it certainly has an ethical overtone in the context of Paul's letter to the Philippians.[22] In this letter, the readers are summoned to conform their acts to what they ought to be "in Christ" (2:5), and what the believers ought

---

16. Martin, *Hymn of Christ.*
17. Martin, 289–92. He establishes the lordship significance by reading the exhortation in 2:5 in conjunction with the universal confession of Christ in 2:11.
18. Martin, "Christology in the Prison," 199.
19. Martin, 98.
20. Hooker, "Philippians."
21. Hooker, 90–91.
22. Hooker, 90.

to be "in Christ" is precisely drawn from who Jesus is and what he has done, as it is presented in the christological passage.[23] While she adopts the view of the imitation of Christ,[24] in order to avoid the idea of "a strict imitation" or "copying an external pattern" the term "to conform" is employed.[25]

In this line of thought, she argues with regard to the significance of the exaltation part as follows: "Paul not only uses the so-called hymn, therefore, as the basis of his ethical appeal to the Philippians, but draws on its language in describing the goal of Christian life which he links with the Parousia."[26] She further emphasizes that the exaltation of Christ needs to be appreciated in the framework of the "interchange" between Christ and those in him – Christ became like us (i.e. he was made sin and being cursed) in order that we might share in what Christ is.[27] Accordingly, the exaltation of Christ anticipates the transformation of Christ's believers in 3:21. Her proposed scheme for the role of Philippians 2:9–11 can be defined as follows: as the lives of Christians conform to Christ, they will also become like him in the eschaton.[28] In this scheme, the obedience-vindication motif is noted.

1.1.4 Larry W. Hurtado

In 1984, Larry W. Hurtado produced a critical assessment of Käsemann's rejection of the ethical significance of Philippians 2:5–11[29] that basically argues that Christ's redemptive action indeed provides a pattern of behavior to be followed.[30] Following the example of Christ should be understood not as a strict imitation, but rather as *conformitas*[31] to him, that is to conform one's behavior to the pattern set by Christ's behavior. With regard to the role of

---

23. While accepting Käsemann's judgment that the phrase ἐν Χριστῷ Ἰησοῦ in 2:5 should be understood as Paul's usual phrase ἐν Χριστῷ, she interprets Philippians 2:5 as "have the mind of Christ Jesus." See Hooker, "Partner in the Gospel," 95.

24. Hooker, "Partner in the Gospel," 92–95.

25. Hooker, 91–92.

26. Hooker, "Philippians," 93.

27. Hooker, "Interchange in Christ," 13–25; "Philippians," 91–92; "Partner in the Gospel," 89–91.

28. Hooker, "Partner in the Gospel," 93, states "We suffer with him, Paul writes, in order that we may be glorified with him . . ."

29. Hurtado, "Jesus as Lordly Example."

30. Hurtado, 120–23.

31. Hurtado, 125.

the exaltation part, while accepting Käsemann's emphasis on the universal lordship of Christ in verses 9–11, he construes this motif as being used for demanding believers' obedience in conforming to the example set by Christ in verses 6–8. As "the one to whom his readers are summoned to conform is now the *kyrios*,"[32] Christ's deed becomes an authoritative example to be conformed to in the believers' life. In this respect, Hurtado's reading affirms the lordship-obedience motif, but with a demand for *conformitas* to the pattern set by Christ's deed.

1.1.5 Stephen Fowl

One important study on the rhetorical function of the christological passage in Philippians was done by Stephen Fowl in 1990.[33] The significance of this study is twofold: (1) an effort to situate the function of this christological passage in the literary and rhetorical context of Philippians; and (2) the function of the exaltation section in the context of Paul's argument is seriously considered.[34] In his view, the significance of this christological passage rests on the "down-up" pattern of Christ's story in which the exaltation is perceived as God's vindication of the obedient Christ.[35] This down-up story of Christ serves as a primary exemplar[36] from which its analogical relationship to various aspects of the situation of the Philippian church may be relevantly drawn.[37]

It is further argued in this study that the significance of the vindication of Christ should be defined within this analogical approach. As the case in 1:27–2:4, he argues as follows:

> To put the analogy crudely: if the Philippians will unite in a steadfast adherence to the gospel (which will entail the practice of the virtues in 2:2–4), even in the face of opposition, *then God will save them in the same way God saved the obedient, humiliated, and suffering* Christ in 2:6–11.[38]

---

32. Hurtado, 125.

33. Fowl, *Story of Christ*.

34. Fowl, 85.

35. See Fowl, "Christology and Ethics," 143n43.

36. Fowl defines *examplar* as "a concrete expression of a shared norm from which people can make analogical judgments about how they should live." Fowl, *Story of Christ*, 92–96.

37. Fowl, *Story of Christ*, 101.

38. Fowl, 95.

The same analogy is applied in Paul's exhortation in 2:12–18:

> If God were not at work among the Philippians, then the suffer-
> ing they will face at the hands of their opponents as a result of
> their steadfast faithfulness to the gospel would be senseless. In
> the same way as God worked to exalt the humiliated and obedi-
> ent Christ and vindicated his suffering, God will also work to
> bring about salvation "worked out" by the Philippians in obedi-
> ence to Paul's commands.[39]

In Paul's account of his life in Philippians 3, the humiliation-vindication[40] pattern of the story of Christ can be detected in verses 10–11 and verses 20–21.[41] Polemicizing against those walking as the enemies of the cross of Christ (vv. 18–19) who refuse the way of suffering, Paul emphasizes the ne-cessity to share in Christ's suffering (v. 10), as this is the way of life that God will vindicate (vv. 11, 20–21).[42] This reading is further developed in his article in 1998,[43] by adopting two studies on Philippians: (1) Loveday Alexander's proposal that Philippians is a family letter that seeks and offers assurance for the readers;[44] and (2) Wayne A. Meeks' suggestion that the exhortation in 2:5 intends to shape the practical reasoning of the Philippians readers.[45] In all, Fowl argues that in Philippians Paul calls the readers to conform their lives to Christ's death in the hope of his resurrection.[46]

1.1.6 L. Gregory Bloomquist

L. Gregory Bloomquist's study in 1993 primarily focuses on the role of suf-fering in Paul's letter to the Philippians,[47] but it gives brief notes on the function of 2:9–11 in the final pages of the book.[48] To him, the function of the presentation of Christ in 2:6–11 is neither ethical nor soteriological, but

---

39. Fowl, 97.
40. The terms humiliation-vindication and suffering-vindication are used interchangably.
41. Fowl, 91.
42. Fowl, 100–101.
43. Fowl, "Christology and Ethics," 140–53.
44. Alexander, "Hellenistic Letter-Forms," 87–101.
45. Meeks, "Man from Heaven," 329–36; Fowl, "Christology and Ethics," 145.
46. Fowl, "Christology and Ethics," 145.
47. Bloomquist, *Function of Suffering*.
48. Bloomquist, 195–96.

rhetorical, as it underscores the fact that vindication follows suffering.[49] In this respect, the theme of suffering is primarily used by Paul as "the occasion for his extended, eschatological confession of faith in God's grace to the servant, that is to those in whom the experiences of the Christ type are found."[50]

Although it is not explicitly stated, the exaltation of Christ has its counterpart in the eschatological victory in 3:11 and 3:20–21. In Philippians 3, Paul regards his suffering as part of the fulfillment of the Christ-type person, and thus he confidently expects his vindication (together with his co-workers and the Philippian Christians) as the case of Christ.[51] We can say, therefore, that Bloomquist's reading emphasizes the suffering-vindication motif, where the exaltation part provides an eschatological incentive for the Christ-type suffering believers in Philippi.

1.1.7 Peter Oakes

Peter Oakes's study on this christological passage in 2001 seeks to understand how the original readers of Philippians would have read the christological passage in Philippians in their own context.[52] The imperial backdrop of the Roman colony of Philippi notably shapes his interpretation of this passage. The event surrounding the enthronement of a new emperor serves as its background.[53] The significance of this christological passage is not religious, that is to oppose the imperial cults, but rather sociopolitical,[54] given that the passage presents Jesus Christ as "the symbolic head of Greco-Roman society."[55] Accordingly, the christological passage subversively moves the center of the universe from Caesar to Jesus Christ.[56] In this political framework, Oakes defines the significance of Philippians 2:6–11.

---

49. Bloomquist, 195.
50. Bloomquist, 196.
51. Bloomquist, 197.
52. Oakes, *Philippians*; "Re-Mapping the Universe," 301–22.
53. Oakes, "Re-Mapping the Universe," 319; *Philippians*, 133, 205.
54. Oakes, *Philippians*, 204–5.
55. Oakes, "Re-Mapping the Universe," 319–20.
56. Oakes, 319–21.

Oakes adopts Käsemann's interpretative keys,[57] but at the same time also defends the ethical significance of the obedience part, which is held by both Hooker and Hurtado:[58]

> They are bound to hear Christ's acts in verses 6–8 as exemplary. They are trying to think as someone in Christ's realm. Christ is their king. Christ lowers himself. They must be willing to lower themselves. Christ is obedient right to death. They will be obedient in this way if it is necessary.[59]

Having said this, he argues that the emphasis of the exaltation of Christ should not be on Christ's reward, as this notion is only implicitly present.[60] The exaltation mainly points to Christ's accession to lordship,[61] and thus this section concerns primarily the recognition of his universal lordship (vv. 10–11). In this enthronement scheme, the lordship of Christ leads to four ramifications: (1) with regard to authority, Christ has replaced the Roman emperor as the world's decisive power; (2) with regard to freedom, Christ has set all those in him free from the constraints imposed by the imperial society; (3) with regard to confidence, following Christ will surely lead to salvation (3:20–21); and (4) with regard to the church's view of itself, the victory and lordship of Christ de-marginalizes the status of all those in him, as this heavenly community belongs to the one in full authority.[62] Unfortunately, whether among the four there is one that is predominantly exploited by Paul in his rhetorical writing is not explored. That said, the general drift is regarded as clear: the Philippian Christians should regard the lordship of Christ as a source of security and encouragement for continuing their allegiance to Jesus despite all the oppression from imperial power.[63]

---

57. First, the phrase ἐν Χριστῷ Ἰησοῦ in 2:5 is read as Paul's technical term ἐν Χριστῷ. Second, the exaltation in 2:9 is understood as not a vindication, but the enthronement that changes the lordship of the universe. Oakes, *Philippians*, 188–89, 204–7.

58. Oakes, *Philippians*, 188.

59. Oakes, 189.

60. Oakes, 204. Furthermore, he argues that the reward should not be read against the scheme of God's vindication of the humble (pp. 203–4), but in the sense that as Christ is exalted as the universal lord, the status of Philippian believers will be also raised (p. 203).

61. Oakes, *Philippians*, 204.

62. Oakes, 205–7.

63. Oakes, "Re-Mapping the Universe," 320.

1.1.8 Joseph H. Hellerman

Joseph H. Hellerman's study on Philippians 2:6–11 in 2005 basically argues that this christological passage should be read against the cultural ethos of the Roman colony in Philippi.[64] Drawing on various inscriptions in Philippi, he concludes that the dominant culture of the Roman Philippi in the first century AD was *cursus honorum* that seeks self-honor in the society.[65] His reading of this christological passage is typical of Fowl's down-up story of Christ. Here, the deeds of Christ are regarded as *cursus pudorum* that stands against the *cursus honorum* culture of the Philippian society.[66] The role of the exaltation part is defined as follows: "God will fully vindicate all those who, like Jesus, use their status and power for the benefit of others in the community."[67]

Having said this, some differences are also noted. First, the immediate application of this hymn of Christ does not relate to the problem of suffering in 1:27–30, but the interpersonal relationship within the Philippian church (2:1–4, 12–18).[68] Accordingly, the emphasis is no more on suffering for Christ's sake, but the manner Jesus used his divine status. Second, God's vindication of Christ is understood as a reward.[69]

1.1.9 M. Sydney Park

Another study focusing on the function of the christological passage in Philippians, which is by M. Sydney Park, was published in 2007.[70] The study argues that the readers are called to imitate Christ's submission to God narrated in 2:6–8 because this way of life has been approved by God (2:9). Christ's deeds in 2:6–8 – that is his regarding the equality with God as something not to be exploited selfishly, but emptying himself, humbling himself, and his obedience to the point of death on the cross – are regarded as an expression of Christ's submission to God.[71] His submission does not only have a salvific effect, but it is also paradigmatic, as it establishes a norm for those who claim

---

64. Hellerman, *Reconstructing Honor.*
65. Hellerman, 62, 88–109.
66. Hellerman, 129–56.
67. Hellerman, 154.
68. Hellerman, 154.
69. Hellerman, 154–55.
70. Park, *Submission within the Godhead.*
71. Park, 118–24.

salvation in the name of Christ.[72] The application of this norm is demanded through various exhortations in 1:27–2:18 and 3:15–17[73] and reflected in the accounts of Timothy and Epaphroditus in 2:19–30 and Paul in 3:4–11.

As is the case in Fowl's study, the exaltation of Christ in 2:9 becomes an important element of Park's ethical reading. However, it does not operate within the framework of the humiliation/suffering-vindication motif that Fowl strongly contends.[74] Rather, adopting N. T. Wright's reading, she argues that this exaltation should be understood as the divine approval of Christ's submission.[75] This approval-exaltation schema, then, leads to the universal lordship of Christ that manifests God's eschatological salvation (cf. Isa 45:22–23) on the one hand, and demands the full submission of those who acclaim "Jesus Christ is Lord" on the other.[76] The former is amplified in Philippians 3:20–21. In this passage, Paul underlines that Christ's ability to subject all things will be exercised in the glorious transformation of believers.[77] Concerning the latter, as Christ's lordship is grounded in his selfless obedience, his leadership is never oppressive and coercive, but always invites the believers to imitate his submission to God.[78] In all, Christ's exaltation and lordship call the readers to imitate his submission to God, and at the same time provide an eschatological incentive of salvation for those who do so.

1.1.10 Sergio Rosell Nebreda

In 2011, the study on Philippians 2:6–11 from Sergio Rosell Nebreda was published.[79] He approaches this christological passage from a modern social scientific theory of Social Identity (SIT). The concern of this theory is on the person's self-concept "derived from his/her membership in a group."[80] Employing this approach, he argues that the christological passage intends

---

72. Park, 150.
73. Park, 150–51.
74. Park, 26–31.
75. Park, 30.
76. Park, 33–34.
77. Park, 151–52.
78. Park, 150.
79. Nebreda, *Christ Identity*.
80. Nebreda, 37.

to form a new social identity of the followers of Christ in Philippi,[81] that is their social identity is defined no longer in terms of ethnic origin and social merit, but by their association with Christ.[82] Those who have been identified with him will have a new orientation and standard of life set by this hymn.[83] In Nebreda's reading of Philippians 2:9–11, we detect that both the lordship-obedience and the humiliation-vindication motifs are at work. Concerning the former, the lordship of Christ is to be displayed by living according to a new set of values in the midst of the present crooked and perverted social system, so that they may shine in their holiness.[84] Concerning the latter, the humiliation-exaltation scheme is explicated as a path to be followed by those who confess Jesus Christ as their Lord.[85] As this Christ-hymn intends "to break through a system based on merit and honor (i.e., in power and status)," the idea of merit in the exaltation of Christ is logically rejected.[86]

1.1.11 Heiko Wojtkowiak

Finally, we need to add the study on Philippians 2:6–11 done by Heiko Wojtkowiak in 2012.[87] This study focuses on the ethical impetus of this christological passage in the context of the struggle of the church within the pagan imperial society of Philippi. To him, the point of conflict between the church and the society in Philippi (1:27–28; 2:15; 3:18) is not the Christians' proclamation of the gospel of Christ but their ethical conduct derived from this gospel.[88] He argues that the struggle and suffering of the church were driven by the fact that this gospel-like ethos was not only alien to the Roman society in Philippi but also contradicted its *mos maiorum* that praised the honor of persons.[89]

---

81. Nebreda, 278–86.
82. Nebreda, 344–45.
83. Nebreda, 333.
84. Nebreda, 336.
85. Nebreda, 346.
86. Nebreda, 331.
87. Wojtkowiak, *Christologie Und Ethik*.
88. Wojtkowiak, 120–31.
89. Wojtkowiak, 128–29, 149–57.

Adopting Christ's humility means suffering,[90] but this Christ-Psalm calls and encourages the church to continue to live up to this humility ethos.[91] Philippians 2:9–11, thus, provides an eschatological and soteriological motivation to the suffering church. This is briefly noted in 1:28, then fully developed in 3:20–21 where salvation is associated with the idea of the transformation of the body of Christians from humiliation to Christ's glory.[92]

1.1.12 Summary and Remarks

Risking oversimplifying the diversity of scholarly opinions on the function of Philippians 2:9–11, we group the scholarly opinions into two domains. The first emphasizes the lordship-obedience (κύριος-ὑπήκοος) scheme. This reading underlines the effect of Christ's lordship in 2:10–11 upon his believers. God's exaltation in 2:9 has established Jesus Christ as the Lord of all in 2:10–11. Although hitherto not all humans acknowledge this, those who currently call him "Savior" and "Lord" (3:20) are to offer their loyalty, obedience, and submission. If Christ's acts in 2:6–11 have a role in guiding Christian conduct, they then provide a pattern of obedience to be adopted by his believers. The second emphasizes the humiliation-vindication (ταπεινόω-ὑπερυψόω) scheme.[93] This reading regards Christ's kenosis in 2:6–8 and God's vindication of him in 2:9 as a pattern to be conformed to in the lives of Christ's believers. This exaltation is usually read in conjunction with the resurrection in 3:10–11 and the bodily transformation of believers in 3:20–21, so as to establish the idea of God's eschatological vindication for those currently adopting Christ's humility, obedience, and suffering.

As a result of the debate in the past between the kerygmatic and the ethical interpretations, these two schemes tend to stand in opposition rather than complementary to each other. The dichotomy has been generated by the fact that the correlation between the two schemes and Paul's ethical discourse

---

90. Wojtkowiak, 132–34, 231–50.

91. Wojtkowiak, 132–34, 164–66.

92. Wojtkowiak, 211.

93. One recent article that emphasizes the humiliation-exaltation scheme is Martin and Nash, "Philippians 2:6–11." This article basically argues that "Christ is honored for taking up what under each topos was conventionally considered shameful, and in place of what was considered honourable" (p. 135). Accordingly, Paul's inclusion of this *hymnos* in his letter is to support his instruction in 2:1–5: "those who did the same" (2:6–8) "will be exalted" (2:9–11) (p. 138).

in 1:27–2:18 is established in a rather implicit manner. A possible cause is the ambiguity of Paul's exhortation (τοῦτο φρονεῖτε ἐν ὑμῖν ὃ καὶ ἐν Χριστῷ Ἰησοῦ) in 2:5, which can be interpreted in favor of both the kerygmatic and the ethical readings.

It appears to us that to properly define the rhetorical function of Philippians 2:9–11 in the letter, not only must the ambiguity in reading 2:5 be resolved, but another coordinate needs also to be supplied. In this line of thought, the present study intends to unpack and highlight the significance of the motif of universal worship of Christ at the eschaton, which is depicted at the climactic end of the christological passage (vv. 10–11). Although this eschatological worship motif has been appreciated,[94] its theological and rhetorical significances in the letter have yet to be fully developed.

1.2 Thesis

This study claims that the motif of the universal worship of Christ at the eschaton in Philippians 2:10–11 has a pivotal role in both the christological passage and Paul's exhortations in his letter to the Philippians. This motif is derived from the biblical theme of the eschatological worship of YHWH, particularly the vision in Isaiah 45:22–24. In Philippians, this Isaianic vision is reworked to convey Paul's christological and eschatological conviction and to polemically respond to the imperial claim of the divinity of Augustus and the cultic veneration of him. These two dimensions (i.e. the Jewish and the Roman imperial) contribute to the significance of this eschatological worship motif in both the christological passage and the letter. This motif affirms Jesus, not Augustus, as the divine universal Lord, who has established God's eschatological reign and salvation, and who will demand accountability from all (cf. Rom 14:11). Accordingly, it calls Paul and his readers to be prepared for meeting God and his Messiah in this eschatological worship-judgment event (Phil 1:10–11; 2:10–11; 2:16). It is contended that the function of Philippians 2:9–11 in Paul's letter should be defined according to this rationale.

---

94. Hofius, *Der Christushymnus Philipper*, 41–55, 123–31; Kreitzer, *Jesus and God*, 114–17; Bauckham, "Worship of Jesus in Philippians," 128–39; Hurtado, "'Case Study,'" 83–107.

1.3 The Terminology of Worship

The term worship (noun) needs to be properly defined. The term denotes "an honor or reverence paid to a divine being or supernatural power."[95] It is always relational, as it expresses the superiority of the object of worship over the worshippers and performatively sustains their power over them.[96] In the ancient polytheistic matrix, worship was offered to the entities deemed to have possessed supernatural power. Such entities can be divine beings or human beings. In contrast, Jewish monotheism dictates that worship is to be offered exclusively to YHWH, the one and only God of Israel and all. Notably, in the Christian conviction, worship to this God is extended to his Messiah Jesus.

As a religious ritual, worship is perceived as sacred and regularly repeated cultic activities, which consist of stereotypical words (praising, praying, confessing, swearing), gestures (kneeling and bowing), and actions (dancing and offering sacrifice).[97] Accordingly, although there is no identical word for the term "worship" in both Hebrew and Greek languages, the idea of worship can be identified by these stereotypical words, gestures, and actions. In the letter to the Philippians, the idea of worship is evoked by various religious activities, such as εὐχαριστέω (1:3); δέησις (1:4); προσεύχομαι (1:9); σπένδω (2:17), θυσία (2:17), λειτουργία (2:17); λατρεύω (3:3); ὀσμή εὐωδίας (4:18). It is claimed in this study that in Philippians 2:10–11 worship is marked by πᾶν γόνυ κάμψη (the gesture of kneeling) and πᾶσα γλῶσσα ἐξομολογήσηται (the act of confession).

1.4 Methodology and Presentation

The study begins by analyzing the significance of the motif of eschatological worship in both Jewish and Roman imperial worldviews. In relation to the former, it will examine the significance of Jewish biblical visions of eschatological worship of YHWH, particularly the one in Isaiah 45:23. In relation to the latter, it will examine the mythical-imperial claim surrounding *divus* (the

---

95. In *Oxford English Dictionary*, 20:577, the verb "worship" means "to honor or to revere as supernatural being or power, or as a holy thing." In *Webster's Third New International Dictionary of the English Language*, 3:2647, worship is defined as "to honor or revere as a divine being or super natural power."

96. Aune, "Early Christian Worship," 974.

97. Aune, 974.

deified) Augustus and his cult in Philippi. Drawing upon some important insights from this examination, we will then investigate the significance of the motif of eschatological worship of Christ in Philippians, first of all, in the context of the christological passage (2:6–11), and later in the context of two major discourses in this letter (1:27–2:18; 3:2–4:4).

The presentation of this study follows closely the approach sketched above. The first two chapters are background studies of Philippians 2:10–11. Chapter 2 starts with the identification of some important tenets in various visions of eschatological worship of YHWH in Jewish Scriptures and the Second Temple writings. This provides us with an understanding of how Second Temple readers generally read various visions of the eschatological worship in Isaiah, particularly the one in 45:23. Following this, chapter 3 makes a comparison on how this Isaianic vision is interpreted in Romans 14:11 and two Second Temple writings (4Q215a – Time of Righteousness – and the Aleinu prayer), highlighting their similarities and differences. In chapter 4, the discussion will move from the Jewish background to the Roman imperial backdrop. First of all, it establishes that the cultic veneration of *divus* Augustus was already pervasively present in the Roman colony of Philippi at the time of Paul, and then unpacks the eschatological dimension of the imperial-Augustan ideology expressed in this cult.

Following the background study, the study investigates the significance of the depiction of the universal eschatological worship of Christ in Philippians 2:10–11. Chapter 5 establishes the general outlook of Paul's letter to the Philippians in which several pivotal issues that shape the reading of this letter are discussed: (1) the integrity of the letter; (2) the profile of the author and the recipients and their *koinonia* relationship; (3) the problems addressed in the letter; and (4) the anti-imperial stance in the letter. Chapter 6 develops our argument that Philippians 2:10–11 indeed depicts the universal worship of Christ at the eschaton, and then highlights its christological, soteriological, ethical, and anti-imperial ramifications. Chapter 7, then, situates the motif of the eschatological worship of Christ in Paul's letter to the Philippians, particularly in its two major paraenetical discourses (1:27–2:18 and 3:2–4:4), where it is generally appreciated that the christological passage has an important role in them.

Finally, chapter 8 will sum up the whole discussion on the motif of the universal worship of Christ in Paul's letter to the Philippians. Three elements are to be highlighted, namely its Jewish background, its Roman imperial foreground, and its rhetorical aim set by Paul's eschatological reasoning in the letter. We hope that this study will give a positive contribution to the understanding of the rhetorical function of this beautiful christological passage, particularly its exaltation part.

CHAPTER 2

The Universal Eschatological Worship of YHWH in Isaiah 45:23–24

The christological passage in Paul's letter to the Philippians ends with the depiction of the homage to Christ by all creatures in the triadic universe (2:10–11). It has been widely appreciated that this colossal picture of worship is inspired by the vision of the eschatological worship voiced in Isaiah 45:23.[1] For a greater appreciation of Paul's use of this Isaianic vision, it is necessary to read it within the Jewish eschatological matrix in antiquity. In doing so, we note that the theme of the universal worship of YHWH is not only voiced in Isaiah 45:23 but also in many parts of the book.[2] Moreover, similar themes are also voiced across the Old Testament (or the Hebrew Bible).[3] Finally, the theme is continually celebrated in the Second Temple era, as it is attested in many of the Second Temple writings.[4] All this demonstrates the prominence of this theme in many Jewish communities in Paul's era.

---

1. This has been noted in many contemporary commentaries, such as O'Brien, *Philippians*; Fee, *Philippians*; Bockmuehl, *Philippians*; Hansen, *Philippians*; Witherington III, *Philippians*; Cohick, *Philippians*.

2. Isa 2:2–4; 18:7; 19:19–25; 23:18; 24:14–16; 25:6–8; 56:1–8; 60:6–8; 66:18–24.

3. The theme can be found in Jer 3:17; 4:1–2; 12:6; 16:19–20; Ezek 20:40–41; Joel 2:32; Amos 9:11–12 LXX; Mic 4:1–4; Zeph 2:11; 3:9–10 LXX; Zech 2:14–15; 8:20–22; 14:16; Mal 1:11; 3:4; Pss 22:27–29; 86:8–10. The present study prefers to employ the term the Old Testament than the Hebrew Bible or the Jewish Scripture to highlight the relationship between the two testaments in the Christian Bible.

4. The theme is attested in Tob. 13:11; 14:6 OG[II]; Ps. Sol. 17:29–32; Sib. Or. 3:716–723, 772–775; The Animal Apocalypse (1 En. 90:29–33); the Book of Watchers (1 En. 10:21–22), the Parables of Enoch (1 En. 48:5; 61:8–9; 62:9).

Taking this into consideration, the present chapter intends to read the vision in Isaiah 45:23 within both the Isaianic eschatological thought and the larger ancient Jewish eschatological matrix. The discussion runs as follows. The first section delineates some pivotal tenets in the Jewish visions of the universal eschatological worship of YHWH that are commonly shared among the biblical and the Second Temple writings. The second section, then, draws the contour of this universal theme in the book of Isaiah by employing some pivotal tenets drawn in the first section. After doing these two preliminary observations, the study will scrutinize the vision in Isaiah 45:23. Hopefully this way of reading will produce valuable insights for understanding this Isaianic vision within the Jewish eschatological worldview.

2.1 The Eschatological Worship of YHWH in Ancient Jewish Writings

The wide distribution of the theme of the eschatological worship of YHWH in both the Old Testament and the Second Temple writings demonstrates its prominence in the ancient Jewish eschatological matrix. It can be justifiably said that pious Jewish people in the Second Temple era generally hoped that one day in the future their covenant God would be worshipped by all Israel and other nations. Within this general conviction, awareness needs to be made in reading biblical visions of worship. The visions notably arose from various historical and literary contexts and reflected various strands of thought in Judaism. So complex is this phenomenon that we can justifiably speak of visions in the plural. Having said this, given they are derived from the same biblical conviction, we also reasonably expect that the visions share some common and important tenets. As they contribute to the shaping of Paul's vision of the eschatological worship of Christ, these tenets are worth scrutiny.

2.1.1 The Covenantal Notion

The covenantal notion justifiably claims that all biblical visions of the eschatological worship of YHWH have a covenant framework as they all are grounded in the covenant relationship between Israel and her God. In the

Old Testament, YHWH often addresses Israel as "my people" (עַמִּי)[5] that recalls the Sinaitic covenant formula: "I will be your God and you will be my people" (see Lev 26:12).[6] The correlation between this covenantal identity and the vision of worship is demonstrated in the Sinaitic covenant proposal in Exodus 19:3–6:[7]

> The LORD called to him out of the mountain, saying, "Thus you
> shall say to the house of Jacob, and tell the people of Israel: 'You
> yourselves have seen what I did to the Egyptians, and how I bore
> you on eagles' wings and brought you to myself. Now, therefore,
> if you will indeed obey my voice and keep my covenant, you
> shall be *my treasured possession* [לִי סְגֻלָּה] among all peoples, for
> all the earth is mine; and you shall be to me *a kingdom of priests*
> [מַמְלֶכֶת כֹּהֲנִים] *and a holy nation* [וְגוֹי קָדוֹשׁ].' These are the words
> that you shall speak to the people of Israel."

The proposal more or less follows the order of the suzerainty treaty in ancient Near East practice: (1) a historical prologue in verse 4, (2) the obligation of a vassal nation in verse 5a, and (3) the blessing of the suzerain king in verses 5b–6.[8] This framework underlines that the suzerain king YHWH promises his future blessings and the vassal nation, Israel, is obligated to obey the covenant stipulations. In this ancient covenant framework, the correlation between Israel's covenant identity and the worship of YHWH should be discerned.

First, the phrase לִי סְגֻלָּה in verse 5 conveys the idea that the nation of Israel is YHWH's treasured people (cf. Deut 7:6; 14:2). This is notably reflected in the LXX translation, ἔσεσθέ μοι λαὸς περιούσιος. The identity is further amplified by the terms "kingdom of priests" (מַמְלֶכֶת כֹּהֲנִים) and "a holy nation" (גּוֹי קָדוֹשׁ). About the former, although the precise reading is debated,[9] its

---

5. The term עַמִּי (my people) frequently appears in the biblical writings that are prominent with a covenant theme, such as in Jeremiah (28x), Ezekiel (22x), Isaiah (22x), and Exodus (16x).

6. The covenant formula appears sixteen times in the Pentateuch and sixteen times in the prophetical writings. See Rendtorff, *Covenant Formula*, 13–14.

7. Emphasis and Hebrew words are added.

8. For the discussion of this treaty, see Levenson, *Sinai & Zion*, 26–32; McCarthy, *Treaty and Covenant*, 272–73.

9. Several proposals have been contended: (1) Israel is consecrated to God, (2) Israel is mediator among the nations, (3) Israel is ruled by priests, and (4) Israel is consecrated to God and ruled by priests. See Gowan, *Theology in Exodus*, 177.

worship notion remains clear that the nation of Israel is called to worship YHWH exclusively and wholeheartedly. About the latter, the phrase carries the idea of the separation of Israel from other nations due to her relationship with YHWH (cf. Lev 20:26). At the same time, it affirms Israel's calling to express his holiness (cf. Lev 19:2).[10] This is done by (1) worshipping YHWH exclusively (Exod 20:2–7); (2) maintaining ritual purities (Exod 20:8–11, 22–26; 22:28–31; 23:10–19); and (3) having a good moral conduct (Exod 20:12–17; 21:1–22:27; 23:1–9).[11] In all, this covenant identity calls the nation Israel to worship YHWH in holiness.

Second, as Israel's covenantal identity is located in the blessing section in this covenant proposal, the worshipping of YHWH in holiness should be regarded as his promised blessings waiting to be realized.[12] This envisioned reality is preconditioned by Israel's faithfulness to the covenant obligations (v. 5a).[13] The divine blueprint to make Israel the worshippers of YHWH is notably implemented shortly after the covenant proposal. Laws and instructions are given in Exodus 20–24; priests are instituted in Exodus 28–29 and 39; the tabernacle is constructed in Exodus 25–27, 30–31, 35–40. As it will be shown shortly, this future dimension provides a theological ground for the biblical visions of the eschatological worship of YHWH.

Finally, YHWH's claim "for all the earth is mine" (כי־לי כל־הארץ) in verse 5 has universal force, highlighting his kingship over the whole world. In the book of Psalms, he is depicted as the King not only of Israel but also all nations (47:3, 9; 67:4–5) and the whole universe (47:3, 8; 93:1–5; 97:1, 5; 103:19) including all gods (95:3; 96:4; 97:7–9).[14] His universal kingship can be understood either in a superlative or absolute sense. The former articulates the idea of the incomparability of YHWH among other gods (Exod 15:11; Pss 82:1–7; 95:3), while the latter claims him as the one and only God of the whole universe (Deut 4:39; Jer 10:2–10; Isa 44:9–20).[15] Provided Second Temple

---

10. Hartley, "Holy and Holiness," 420.

11. Balentine, *Torah's Vision*, 125–36; Gammie, *Holiness in Israel*, 32–34; Levenson, *Sinai & Zion*, 50–56.

12. Schramm, "Exodus 19," 334–43.

13. Balentine, *Torah's Vision*, 121–41; Schramm, "Exodus 19," 327–28.

14. Some biblical passages (Pss 47:2; 95:3; 99:1–3; Mal 1:14) employ the phrase מלך גדול (the great king) to associate YHWH with the monarch of the overlord empire.

15. Levenson, *Sinai & Zion*, 56–69.

Judaism was largely shaped by its monotheistic conviction, this clause was likely read in the absolute sense at that time. Accordingly, Israel's covenantal identity has a vocational dimension, namely to offer her priestly service to the world so that all nations will one day acknowledge YHWH as the only God and then worship him exclusively and wholeheartedly.[16]

In all, within the Sinaitic covenant framework (Exod 19:3–6) Israel's identity conveys both her present vocation and future destiny. The people of Israel are presently commanded to worship YHWH alone, and they all will one day worship him exclusively, wholeheartedly, and in holiness. As YHWH is the only true God, the identity of this nation has a vocational dimension, to lead all humankind to worship him alone. It is argued that this covenant framework forms a basic theological ground for various visions of universal eschatological worship of YHWH in the Old Testament and the Second Temple literature.

2.1.2 The Visions of the Universal Worship of YHWH

Although some visions exclude the participation of other nations in the eschatological worship of YHWH,[17] generally the biblical visions have a universal tone. In the Zion eschatological ideology, the city of Jerusalem will become the center for worshipping YHWH,[18] as YHWH has chosen this mount city to be his royal throne (or dwelling place) from where he will rule Israel and all nations (Isa 2:2–4; Mic 4:1–4).[19] Under this spatial ideology, three features of this eschatological worship are developed in the Old Testament writings. First, there will be religious pilgrimages of all nations to Jerusalem to join Israel in worshipping YHWH during her festivals (Isa 2:2–4; 66:23; Zech 2:1–15; 14:16).[20] In this regard, the worship of him is available to all nations through their incorporation into Israel's worship. Second, in these religious pilgrimages, many nations will also bring precious gifts as their holy offerings

---

16. Wright, "Covenant," 65; Balentine, *Torah's Vision*, 123–24; Levenson, *Sinai & Zion*, 31; Stuart, *Exodus*, 423.

17. Such as Ezek 20:40–44; 40–50; Joel 2:30–32. See Gowan, *Eschatology*, 42–46.

18. Tan, *Zion Traditions*, 23–51; Gowan, *Eschatology*, 4–20.

19. Gowan, *Eschatology*, 6–9.

20. Together with this, other motives are also detected, such as to listen to YHWH's instruction (Isa 2:2–4; Sib. Or. 3:16–23), to entreat YHWH's favor (Isa 56:7; Zech 8:20–22; Sib. Or. 3:16–23), to avoid YHWH's punishment (Zech 14:17–19), and to adopt Judaism (Jer 16:19–20; Sib. Or. 3:16–23).

(Isa 18:9; 60:5–7).[21] The gifts will be used for beautifying the temple and various cultic activities in it (Isa 23:17–18; 60:7; Hag 2:6–9).[22] Interestingly, some biblical passages portray the returned Israelites from their exile to Jerusalem as holy offerings to their covenant God (Ezek 20:41; Isa 60:9; 66:20; cf. Pss. Sol. 17:31). Finally, while Ezekiel (44:9) forbids any alien involvement in the eschatological temple, the book of Isaiah entertains the possibility of a gentile priesthood (56:6; 66:21).[23]

In some biblical texts, the scope of universality is notably extended beyond the realm of living human beings. Psalm 22:27–29, for example, seemingly includes the dead in the picture of the eschatological worship of YHWH.[24] The expression כל־יורדי עפר can be read as either "the dying person" or "the dead." The former is grounded in the assumption that biblical Psalms (Pss 6:5; 30:9; 88:10–12; 115:17) do not entertain the idea of post-mortem worship.[25] The latter finds support from the idea of the resurrection of the dead voiced in Isaiah 26:19 and Daniel 12:2.[26] Whatever the original meaning of this phrase, the idea that the end-time worship will include the resurrected dead is attested in the Second Temple writings, such as 1 Enoch (90:33). Moreover, the idea that YHWH is eternally worshipped by his angels is also attested in some biblical passages (Pss 103:20; 148:2; Isa 6:3). Along with this, the vision in Daniel 7:9–10 includes angelic beings as his worshippers.[27] The motif of end-time angelic worship is further developed in the Enochian corpus, such as in 1 Enoch 61:8–11.

Taken together, universalism is one prominent feature in the Jewish visions of worship. In consonance with Zion ideology, all nations will come to Jerusalem to join Israel's worship of YHWH, offering their precious gifts to him. Some of them will be appointed as his priests and Levites. Some biblical visions anticipate a much larger picture of this universal

---

21. The visit of the Queen of Sheba who brought her precious gifts for the construction of the Jerusalem Temple in 1 Kings 10 probably serves as a paradigm.

22. They include for rebuilding the Jerusalem Temple (Hag 2:6–9), beautifying it (Isa 60:7), sacrificial offerings in it (Isa 56:7; 60:7; Sib. Or. 3:772–5), and supporting the needs of the priests who serve there (Isa 23:17–18).

23. Blenkinsopp, *Isaiah 56–66*, 140; Oswalt, *Book of Isaiah*, 690; Koole, *Isaiah III*, 525.

24. See the discussion in Kraus, *Psalms 1–59*, 121.

25. Goldingay, *Psalms Volume 1*, 339.

26. Johnston, *Shades of Sheol*, 225.

27. Collins, *Daniel*, 301.

eschatological worship, the inclusion of the dead and the angelic beings as YHWH's worshippers.

2.1.3 YHWH's Eschatological Reign

Another important tenet of the visions of the eschatological worship of YHWH is the establishment of his eschatological reign. The Old Testament repeatedly underlines that the problem of worship in Israel is caused by her rejection of his kingship (Exod 32:7–10; Ps 95:6–11; Isa 1:4, 10–15; Mal 1:6–8). The historical assessment in Ezekiel 20 is concluded with the accusation that the nation persistently rebelled against their covenant God (Ezek 20:8, 13, 21, 31).[28] As a response, he expelled the nation from his holy land (Ezek 20:23; cf. 2 Kgs 24:13–17; 2 Chr 36:15–21; Jer 39:1–10). This theologically signifies that his rejection of Israel is due to her violation of their covenant relationship (Jer 25:4–11; Ezek 12:1–28).[29]

Having said this, a new hope is also given for the nation Israel. The biblical prophetical writings proclaim YHWH's renewal of his covenant (Jer 31:31–33; Ezek 16:30–33; Hos 2:23), and his commitment to solving Israel's problems through his eschatological reign over Israel (Isa 52:7–10; Ezek 20:33–44; Joel 2:28–32) and all nations (Isa 66:22–24; Jer 12:14–16; Zeph 2:11; 3:9; Zech 14:9). To Israel, his eschatological reign means the coming of her salvific restoration (Isa 40:10–11; 52:7–10). The universal worship of him, therefore, is their proper response to the establishment of his eschatological reign and salvation.

There are two important features of YHWH's eschatological reign, and they are briefly discussed below.

2.1.3.1 The Day of YHWH

The idea of YHWH's eschatological reign is often articulated by the term the day of YHWH (יום יהוה) in the Old Testament.[30] This phrase is derived from either the enthronement of YHWH as the king of Israel and the whole

---

28. Gammie, *Holiness in Israel*, 46.

29. Klein, *Israel in Exile*, 1–8.

30. This term is prominent in many biblical prophetical writings, such as in Isa 2:12; 13:6, 9; 22:5; 34:8; Jer 46:10; Lam 2:22; Ezek 7:19; 13:5; 30:3; Amos 5:18; Joel 1:5; 2:21; 3:4; 4:14; Obad 1:15; Zeph 1:8; 17, 18; 2:3; Zech 14:1; and Mal 4:1, 5.

world in the enthronement Psalms[31] or his victory over all his enemies in
the biblical holy war tradition.[32] In prophetic writings, the two ideas coexist
in portraying the establishment of YHWH's universal kingship on earth.[33]
On that day, all those rejecting his kingship will be judged or defeated. They
include the unrepentant Israel (Isa 1:24–25; Zeph 1:4–13), the unresponsive
gentile nations (Isa 66:15–18; Ezek 38–39; Mic 4:11–13; Joel 4:1–16; Zeph
2:8; Zech 14:1–15; Dan 7:9–12), and the gods of all nations (Isa 24:21; Zeph
2:11). In contrast, all the righteous and faithful Israel will enjoy the divine
salvation (Isa 66:20; Ezek 20:41; Joel 3:5; Dan 7:22).

The connection between the day of YHWH and the eschatological worship
of him can be played out in various schemes. First, on that day, all righteous
Israelites who faithfully worship YHWH will be saved (Joel 2:28–32). Second,
on that day, YHWH will judge both Israel and the nations. After this horrific
event, all righteous Israel and the repentant nations who survive from the
judgment will worship him (Isa 66:23–24; Zech 14:16; 1 En. 10:21–22 and
90:29–33). Finally, on that day, all will worship YHWH, then the righteous
among the Israelites will be saved, but wicked Israel and other nations will
be punished (1 En. 48:5; 61:8–9; 62:9).

2.1.3.2 *The Divine Eschatological Agent*

As the failure of national leadership greatly contributed to Israel's predicament, numerous biblical visions of worship correlate with the coming of an
eschatological agent who will restore YHWH's kingship and the worship of
him.[34] Three figures are worth noting.

One important strand of the eschatological visions in the Second Temple
period is the messianic expectation. In the Old Testament, the term משיח
refers to an anointed person who can be Israel's either king, priest, or prophet,
but the figure does not necessarily denote a future leader of the nation.[35] It

---

31. Mowinckel, *Psalms in Israel's Worship*, 106–92.

32. Rad, *Holy War*.

33. See the discussion in Cathcart, "Day of Yahweh," 84–85.

34. The figure of a king is noted in Mic 5:2–5; Isa 9:6–7; 11:1–9; 32:1–8; 33:17–24; Hag
2:22–23; Zech 4:6–8; 9:9–10, a priest in Zech 4:11–13, and a prophet in Isa 59:21; 61:1–4; Mal
4:5. See Block, "My Servant David," 22–49; Boda, "Figuring the Future," 47–74.

35. Jonge, "Messiah," 777.

was during the Second Temple era that the term became closely associated with the eschatological figure from YHWH.[36] The messianic expectation is biblically grounded, as a hope for a future righteous Davidic king has been persistently voiced by the prophetical writings in the pre-exilic era (Mic 5:2–5; Isa 11:1–9), the exilic era (Jer 23:5–6; Ezek 34:23–24), and the post-exilic era (Hag 2:22–23; Zech 9:9–10).[37] All this contributed to the flourishing of various messianic expectations in the Second Temple period.

Another eschatological figure is the "Servant of YHWH" (עבד יהוה) in Deutero-Isaiah. In Isaiah 52:13–53:12, he is depicted as being willing to suffer to the point of death for the sins of his people. In the Second Temple writings, the figure is celebrated as a messianic figure in the Christian circle. Given the absence of the figure in the Jewish writings outside this community – although he is regarded as the Messiah in the *Targum* of Isaiah[38] – its significance in the Second Temple eschatological hope is debated.[39] Martin Hengel and Daniel P. Bailey, however, have demonstrated that Isaiah 52–53 is not totally absent in the Second Temple writings.[40] They also strongly contend that Isaiah 51:5 and 52:14 are interpreted messianically in 1QIsaᵃ.[41] Their study provides support for positing a development of the messianic interpretation of the Isaianic servant of YHWH in the Second Temple Judaism.

The figure of "the Son of Man" (כבר אנש) in Daniel 7 is also worth noting. Daniel 7:13–14 depicts him as an eschatological figure who will receive homage from all nations. In the history of interpretation, various proposals

---

36. This is attested in Pss. Sol. 17:32; 18: 5, 7; some Qumran Texts (CD, 1QS, 1QSa, 1QSb, 1QM, 4Q161; 4Q174; 4Q175; 4Q252; 4Q285; 4Q376; 4Q458, 4Q51); 1 En. 48:10; 52:4; 4 Ezra 7:29–30; 12:32; and 2 Bar. 29:1; 30:1; 39:7; 40:1; 70:9; 72:2. See the discussion in Gener L. Davenport, "'Anointed of the Lord,'" 67–92; Evans, "Messiah in the Dead Sea," 86–88; Collins, *Scepter and the Star*, 21–51; Horbury, *Jewish Messianism*, 7–13.

37. Boda, "Figuring the Future," 35–74.

38. Horbury, *Jewish Messianism*, 33.

39. Hooker, *Jesus and the Servant*, 2–16; Collins, *Scepter and the Star*, 141–45.

40. The Servant motif can be detected in Dan 11–12, T. Mos. 10:9–11, 4Q491 frg.11i, 1 En. 62:5, 1QIsaa, and T. Benj. 3:8. See Hengel and Bailey, "Effective History," 75–146.

41. In the former case, while the MT has "my arms [זרעי] will judge the peoples," 1QIsaᵃ has "his arm [זרעו] will judge the peoples." Accordingly, the third person suffix (ו-) harks back to the Servant figure in 50:10. In the later case, while MT has משחת that can be translated as "so marred" or "so disfigured," 1QIsaaᵃ has משחתי that can be construed as *qal* perfect first person singular of משה with the meaning "I anointed." This indicates that not only should verse 14 be read as a continuation of the exaltation in verse 13, but also the idea of the Messiah is adumbrated by the verb משח. See Hengel and Bailey, "Effective History," 101–2.

have been made to define this unique figure, such as an exalted messianic figure, an angelic figure, and a collective symbol for God's people.[42] On the one hand, the installment of the Son of Man as YHWH's chosen king and the submission of all nations to him are typical of Psalms 2 and 110. On the other hand, the association of the figure with Israel is also made apparent in Daniel 7:18, 22. On balance, we think that the concept of *Rex pro Regno* is behind the description of the Son of Man in the book of Daniel.

A comparative reading of Daniel 7:13–14 amongst the texts represented by the MT, LXX, and *Theodotion* reveals an important dimension of the lordship of this messianic figure. His appearance in the cloud has a divine association,[43] and the term פלח, which connotes religious activity in the book of Daniel (3:12, 14, 17, 28; 6:17, 21), confirms this nuance.[44] This is further affirmed by the use of λατρεύω to translate this term in the LXX. The later Greek translation *Theodotion*, however, employs δουλεύω that mutes the religious nuance. Perhaps all this means that only some Jewish circles in the Second Temple era interpreted Daniel 7:14 as referring to the act of offering worship to the Son of Man.

The presentation of the Son of Man in 1 Enoch 37–71 reflects a further development of the worship notion in Daniel 7:13–14, as the Son of Man is identified as an individual (46:1–4) associated with the Messiah (48:10; 52:4).[45] He is somehow depicted as having a pre-existent state (48:2–3) and an eschatological role to exercise divine judgment (48:8–10).[46] What is striking is that the Son of Man will enjoy the worship that is uniquely God's (48:5):[47]

---

42. For messianic figure, see Rashi, *Sanh.* 98a. For the angelic figure, see Collins, *Apocalyptic Imagination*, 103. For the symbol of God's people, see Davies, *Daniel*, 100–07; Chiala and Boccaccini, "Son of Man," 156–59.

43. Exod 19:9; 34:5; Pss 18:11–12; 97:2; Zech 2:17 LXX. The imagery of YHWH's riding the clouds is noted in Pss 18:10; 104:3; Isa 19:1. See Meadowcroft, *Aramaic Daniel*, 223–28; Meadowcroft and Irwin, *Book of Daniel*, 121. In Ugarit texts, Baal is portrayed as "the rider of the clouds." See Collins, *Apocalyptic Imagination*, 101–02.

44. The Aramaic פלה can be used in both secular and religious senses. See *HALOT* 5:930. In Daniel, the latter is predominant. See Meadowcroft, *Aramaic Daniel*, 202–03.

45. VanderKam, "Righteous One," 149–91, argues that the writer combines the figure of the Son of Man in Daniel 7 and the servant of YHWH in Deutero-Isaiah.

46. Nickelsburg and VanderKam, *1 Enoch 2*, 174–76.

47. Bauckham, *Jesus and the God of Israel*, 169–72; Nickelsburg and VanderKam, *1 Enoch 2*, 172.

> All those who dwell upon the earth shall fall and worship before
>   *him* [the Son of Man];
>   they shall glorify, bless, and sing *the name of the* Lord *of the*
>   *Spirit.*[48]

Taken together, the vision of the worship of YHWH is inseparable from the realization of his eschatological reign over Israel and all nations. In the Jewish *theologoumenon*, YHWH is the one and only God who is faithful to his covenant with Israel despite her intransigence. On the day of YHWH, he will reclaim his universal kingship over Israel and all nations, and on that day, too, the righteous will be saved and the wicked punished. His eschatological agent will implement his universal dominion so that all nations will worship him alone. In some Jewish circles, this eschatological worship somehow extends to the worship of his agent.

2.1.4 The Transformation of the Worshippers of YHWH

Israel's covenant identity as both a kingdom of priests and a holy nation marks a close correlation between the worship of YHWH and his demand for holiness. Israel is to worship YHWH exclusively, to maintain ritual purity, and to live righteously.[49] In the biblical prophetic writings, the sins of Israel receive great attention. Some passages underline her failure to preserve ritual holiness (Ezek 20:13–24; 44:6–8; Mal 1:6–11), others emphasize her moral failure (Isa 1:21–23; Jer 1:1–11; Ezek 22:1–12; Amos 2:6–7; Mic 2:2; 7:1–6; Zeph 3:1–4; Zech 7:1–16)[50] and her idolatry (Jer 3:6–11; Ezek 20:1–32; Hos 2:1–13; Zeph 1:2–6). The last is regarded as the foremost obstacle in Israel's relationship with her covenant God. It is perceived as an abomination, which goes beyond ritual and moral faults. The book of Exodus provides a strong warning. The covenantal vision of worship (Exod 19:5–6) is followed not long after with the story of the Golden Calf (32:1–35) that depicts Israel as becoming a defiled nation right from its constitution.[51]

---

48. Cited from Issac, "1 (Ethiopic Apocalypse of) Enoch." The clarification is added.

49. See Haber, "*They Shall Purify Themselves*", 9–29.

50. For the discussion of "moral impurity," see Klawans, *Impurity and Sin*, 26–31.

51. In Exodus, after Israel's worship of the golden calf in (32:1–32), YHWH initially refused to bring Israel to the promised land (33:1–3) and his instruction to build the tabernacle (25:31) that would maintain their covenantal relationship was also suspended until the covenant renewal took place. See Hwang, "Turning the Tables," 577.

It is in response to Israel's lack of holiness that many visions of eschatological worship emphasize the aspect of holiness. The requirement of holiness is
applied to both Israel and the Gentiles who will join Israel's future worship.
Israel shall be purged and restored to holiness (Ezek 20:33–38; Zech 14:20–21;
cf. Pss. Sol. 17:26–27). YHWH will purify Jerusalem, as her representation,
as in the old days so that it will be called the city of righteousness, the city
of faithfulness (Isa 1:25–27), and the throne of God (Jer 3:17). The gentile
nations are also called to renounce their idolatries (Jer 16:19–20; cf. Sib. Or.
3:721–23) and to acknowledge him as the only God (Sib. Or. 3:720) who has
the power to save (Isa 45:21). They will seek his counsel and learn his law
(Isa 2:3). Through his instructions, they will have full knowledge of God that
will lead them into righteousness (4Q215a – Time of Righteousness frg.1 ii
lines 5–7).

In biblical visions, the transformative process takes on some interesting
features. Some biblical texts highlight that Israel will renounce her idolatries
and evil deeds, and this will be followed by the conversion of all nations (Isa
1–2; Jer 3:6–18; 4:1–2; 16:14–20 LXX; cf. Tob 13:11; 14:6–7; Pss. Sol. 17:31).
Isaiah 40–55 describes that both Israel and the gentile nations are called to
return to YHWH in response to YHWH's program of restoration and salvation. His eschatological judgment has a significant role in the transformative
process. Some texts highlight that the judgment will induce repentance or
conversion (Isa 1:24–31; 18:3–6; 19:14–17; 24:1–16; Jer 1:5–31; Zeph 3:8–13;
Joel 2:30–32), while other texts underline the termination effect of the divine
judgment by which the whole world will be cleansed from all kinds of unrighteousness (Isa 66:14–16; cf. 1 En. 10:20–22; 4Q215a).

The role of YHWH's eschatological agent in this transformative process
is noted in some writings. In Malachi (3:1–4), the eschatological messenger
of YHWH will purify the Levite priesthood. In Psalm of Solomon 17, the
coming of the eschatological Davidic Messiah will lead Israel (vv. 22, 26–28)
and other nations in righteousness (vv. 22, 29).[52] In the Parables of Enoch,
the eschatological transformation will be established through the divine judgment carried out by the messianic Son of Man (1 En. 48:10). He is depicted
as the staff for the righteous ones, the light of the nations, and the hopes of
the oppressed (v. 4; cf. Isa 42:6; 49:6). On the one hand, he will reveal divine

---

52. Davenport, "'Anointed of the Lord,'" 75–79.

wisdom to God's people and protect them from evil (v. 7), and on the other hand, he will judge and destroy all evildoers and oppressors (vv. 8–10).

Finally, the Old Testament also teaches that true holiness can be generated only by God's inward work within human beings. Jeremiah 31:33 envisions a new covenant that will not be like the Sinaitic covenant, because YHWH himself will inscribe his covenant laws on their hearts. Jeremiah (24:7; 32:39) and Ezekiel (11:19; 36:26–28) speak about one new heart given by YHWH to enable Israel to follow his laws. Ezekiel 36:27 also promises that God will put his Spirit within his people to cause them to walk according to his statutes. While Jeremiah and Ezekiel depict God's inward activity within eschatological Israel, Zephaniah 3:8–9 envisages YHWH's inner work within the nations. After the judgment, he will transform the speech of the nations into holiness so that they will be able to worship him, calling on his name and serving him in one accord.

2.1.5 Summary

It can be claimed that the universal eschatological worship of YHWH is a predominant theme in the Jewish eschatological worldview. A careful analysis of various visions of eschatological worship in the Old Testament and the Second Temple writings demonstrates that there are four common tenets in this theme. First, the visions are grounded in Israel's covenantal relationship with YHWH. Second, the eschatological worship of him has universal scope, as he is both the God of Israel and the whole creation. The visions notably invite all humankind to join Israel's covenantal worship. Third, this eschatological worship expresses a proper submission of Israel and all humankind to YHWH's eschatological reign and salvation. For the establishment of this divine kingship, an eschatological agent is envisaged in some of these visions. Fourth, as the eschatological worshippers, both Israel and all nations shall be made holy.

2.2 The Universal Eschatological Worship of YHWH in Isaiah

After capturing some important features of the universal eschatological worship of YHWH in Jewish ancient literature, now our attention turns to the contour of this theme in the prophetic writings under the name of Isaiah.

There are two reasons to do so. First, the book notably celebrates this theme (see Isa 2:2–4; 18:7; 19:19–25; 23:18; 24:14–16; 25:6–8; 45:23–24; 56:1–7; 60:6–8; 66:20–24). Second, since the book was enjoyed by various Jewish communities in the Second Temple period,[53] many Jews in this era must be familiar with the Isaianic theme of the eschatological worship of YHWH. Indeed, Paul's visions of worship in Romans 14:11 and Philippians 2:10–11 hearken back to the vision of worship in Isaiah.

In doing so, it is necessary to define how the book of Isaiah should be studied. The present study reads Isaiah holistically, as such a reading is closer to the way the Second Temple Jews read the book.[54] Scholars of the Old Testament generally appreciate that the formation of Isaiah took place from the eighth to the sixth century BC. Various authors and redactors had contributed to the formative process, and they are often labeled as Proto-Isaiah, Deutero-Isaiah, and Trito-Isaiah.[55] It is naturally expected, then, that the book flashes out discrete intentions and thoughts responding to different sets of political, social, and theological challenges in the history of Israel. Having said this, these diverse materials were carefully developed and arranged with a certain framework to shape its final form, and the later authors and editors seemingly redeveloped the ideas and materials upon the older existing thought and literary structure.[56] This affirms the unity and coherency of the materials of Isaiah, and thus it provides us a solid working ground to observe holistically the theme. To draw its contour, the study employs the four important tenets established in the previous section as its overarching framework.

2.2.1 The Universal Eschatological Worship

The observation starts with recognizing the theme of the universal eschatological worship of YHWH in the book of Isaiah. It is argued that the theme constantly appears in all three prophetic collections known as Proto-, Deutero-, and Trito-Isaiah. The theme is firstly introduced in Isaiah 2:2–4. During the

---

53. See the discussion in Blenkinsopp, *Opening the Sealed Book*; Watts, "Isaiah," 214–33.

54. Kugel, "Early Jewish Biblical Interpretation," 132.

55. The first collection (chapters 1–39), labelled as Proto-Isaiah, addresses the struggle of Jewish people in facing the expansion the Assyrian power in the late eighth century BC. The second collection (chapters 40–55), Deutero-Isaiah, addresses the struggle of the exiled Jews in the middle of sixth century BC. The third collection (chapters 56–66), Trito-Isaiah, addresses the struggle of the returned Jewish community in the late sixth century BC.

56. Stromberg, *Introduction to the Study of Isaiah*, 82–93.

political turmoil in the late eighth century BC the faith of Israel was facing a great challenge: would their covenant God able to save them from the coming destruction of the Assyrian military power?[57] In facing this political turmoil, Isaiah (2:5) summons the kingdom of Judah to walk faithfully in YHWH's light. The call is grounded in the previous prophetic vision in (2:2–4) that depicts the glorious eschatological future of Zion[58] as YHWH will reign universally from this mount city.[59] In response to his earthly kingship, many nations will stream to Zion. Their religious motive is noted in verse 3 by the use of עלה indicating that worship will take place on the top of the mountain where his temple is situated (cf. Ps 24:3).[60] The worship motive is further affirmed by the pilgrims' utterance that underlines both the openness of YHWH to instruct all nations and their willingness to walk in his way.

The theme of universal worship is repeatedly evoked in the oracles against the nations (Isa 13–23), but it is applied to some specific nations. YHWH's judgment against the Ethiopians (Isa 18:1–7) ends with their homage gifts brought to Zion.[61] After the completion of the divine judgment on Tyre, YHWH will visit and prosper this pagan city, and her wealth will be sent for the use of those serving in the Jerusalem temple (Isa 23:1–18).[62] In between these two visions, Isaiah 19 utters the worship of YHWH by the Egyptians. This nation experienced his judgment, but it does not aim for her total destruction. Instead, the judgment will generate the fear of YHWH, the adoption of Israel's faith, and then the worship of him in their homeland (vv. 1–19).

---

57. This historical setting is noted in Isaiah 7–8.

58. The opening clause, "it shall come to pass in the latter days" (והיה באחרית הימים; ὅτι ἔσται ἐν ταῖς ἐσχάταις ἡμέραις), points to Israel's glorious future, which will be totally different from her current gloomy state. The clause may speak simply a reference to a future time. See Sweeney, "Eschatology," 184–85. However, it can be justifiably regarded as an eschatological reference in the Old Testament category, as it speaks about the future significantly discontinuous from the present, and represents the culmination of YHWH's purposes and acts. See Gowan, *Eschatology*, xx; Martens, "Eschatology," 178.

59. The vision has its parallel in Micah 4:1–3, and it is re-voiced in many other Jewish writings, both in the Old Testament (Jer 3:17; 16:19; Zech 2:14–17; 8:20–22; 14:16) and in the Second Temple writings (Tob 14:6–7; Pss. Sol. 17:29–32).

60. The term עלה is a technical term for the pilgrimage to the sanctuary, although the meaning of this verb should be overstressed. See Wildberger, *Isaiah 1–12*, 90; Williamson, *Isaiah 1–5*, 182–83.

61. In all three appearances in the OT, the term שי always refers to the gift to God. See Grisanti, "שי," 97. In Gen 4:4, δῶρον refers to cultic offering. See Muraoka, *Greek-English Lexicon*, 138.

62. Wildberger, *Isaiah 13–27*, 437.

The theme also appears in Isaiah 24 that begins with the depiction of YHWH's judgment upon the earth, because all of its inhabitants have transgressed his laws and broken his everlasting covenant. In the midst of the universal desolation, unidentified people from all parts of the earth will raise voice giving glory to him (vv. 14–16). Similar to the one in Isaiah 19, the worship in Isaiah 24 is offered not in Jerusalem, but in their homelands.

In Isaiah 40–55, the theme of universal eschatological worship is noted in 45:23–24, particularly by the divine statement: "to me every knee shall bow, every tongue shall swear allegiance." A detailed discussion of this passage is set in the third section. It suffices here to make some important points. Addressing the struggle of the Israelites in Babylonian exile, Isaiah 45 declares the imminent coming of YHWH's salvation. All peoples (both Israel and other nations) are called to respond his eschatological reign by leaving their gods and then turning to him for their salvation. This salvific message is affirmed with the divine commitment to make into the reality that one day all nations will submit to him worshipfully.

Isaiah 56–66 notably celebrates this theme of worship. The material starts with the vision in 56:1–7 that the newly rebuilt Jerusalem Temple will open to all nations, and thus it will be called "a house of prayer for all peoples." Foreigners who adopt Israel's faith faithfully and obediently are welcomed into his temple to offer their worship. At the center, Isaiah 60:1–9 envisions that all nations will come to Jerusalem to pay homage to YHWH, bringing precious gifts to beautify his temple and to be offered upon its altar. They also will bring back the children of Israel from the exile, and thus picturing the coming of Israel's salvation. The ending section depicts that the survivors of YHWH's judgment,[63] having witnessed his glory (or judgment), will be sent back to their homeland to bring all the Israelites back to Jerusalem (66:15–21). In this context, the idea of universal worship is manifested powerfully. The returned Israel are pictured as holy offerings from the gentile nations to YHWH. Continuing this priestly language, some of the survivors of the nations will be pointed as priests and Levites to serve in his temple. The book, then, concludes with a grand vision of universal worship in Isaiah 66:22–24

---

63. The "survivors" is better understood not as the remnant of Israel, but the non-Israelites. See Koole, *Isaiah III*, 519–20.

that in the eschatological transformed world, all humankind will come to Jerusalem to worship YHWH.

This short observation demonstrates that Isaiah celebrates the theme of the universal eschatological worship of YHWH. The book not only opens and ends with a grand vision of worshipping YHWH by all nations, but many of its parts also voice out this very theme. All this affirms the dominance of this theme. Moreover, some elements of this universal worship can be drawn properly. In the eschatological future, all nations will stream to Jerusalem to worship YHWH in his mount temple. In doing so, they will bring precious gifts as holy offerings to the God of Israel. In the post-exilic context, their gifts will include the returning Jews from the exile. The acceptance of YHWH to their worship is openly declared in Isaiah 56:1–7 and 66:20–24. Many foreigners will worship in the Jerusalem Temple, and therefore it shall be called a house of prayer for all peoples. Some of them will be chosen as his priests and Levites to serve in this eschatological temple.

We note that some scholars raise their doubts on whether the nations' homage to YHWH in Isaiah depicts their religious devotion to him.[64] Some argue that the homage in Isaiah 18, 23, 45, and 60 speaks more of the recognition of his sovereign power rather than the religious devotion to him,[65] and that the worshippers in Isaiah 19 and 24 are actually the exilic Israelites.[66]

In response to their contentions, it can be argued that reading Corpus Isaiah holistically strongly affirms that the homage by all nations in the disputed texts should be understood as the religious devotion to YHWH. The opening and the concluding sections of the book are crucial to this reading.[67] Isaiah 1–2 shapes the orientation of the readers by pointing out the heart of Israel's spiritual problem: their worship has been regarded as defiled due to their sinful behaviors (1:10–15). Hence, a complete transformation of this nation is required to restore her relationship with YHWH. The divine program of restoration in Isaiah 1 highlights the transformation of Jerusalem

---

64. Kaminsky and Stewart, "God of All," 152–56.

65. See Brueggemann, *Isaiah 1–39*, 154–55; Roberts, *First Isaiah*, 250; Kaminsky and Stewart, "God of All," 152–55.

66. Brueggemann, *Isaiah 1–39*, 162, 193. Indeed, the LXX identifies the worshippers in Isaiah 18:7 as the dispersed Israel. See Baer, *When We All Go Home*, 199–276.

67. For this framework see the discussion in Shultz, "Nationalism and Universalism," 128–32, 143.

from the defiled and sinful city to the faithful and righteous city (1:21–31). Proceeding her restoration, Isaiah 2:2–4 envisions that in the future Jerusalem will be the cult center par excellence not only for Israel but also all nations. Coupling with this opening orientation is the concluding section in Isaiah 65–66 where hope for YHWH's eschatological salvation is robustly voiced out (65:17–25 and 66:18–24). They are closely related. The recreation of the world in Isaiah 65:17–25 apparently focuses on the restoration of Jerusalem, which apparently employs the paradisaic imagery in Isaiah 11:6–9. This recreation motif establishes Mount Zion as the center of the earth to where all humankind should come to meet their true God (2:2–4). The concluding remark "the new heavens and the new earth" in 66:22–24 evokes this very idea: in this newly restored world, all humankind, joining the religious festival of Israel (Sabbath and the New Moon), will come to worship YHWH. It is in the opening-closing scheme various expressions of the universal homage to YHWH across Isaiah should be understood.

2.2.2 The Eschatological Reign of YHWH

The book of Isaiah celebrates YHWH's eschatological dominion on earth.[68] He is depicted as the Great King who rules Israel, all nations, and the whole creation.[69] His kingship, however, was persistently challenged by Israel and other nations.[70] In response to their oppositions, the book loudly voices out the establishment of his rule on earth in the eschatological future.[71] This thrust is noted by the phrase "in the latter days" (באחרית הימים) in 2:2 and "on that day" (ביום), which occurs almost sixty times across the book. Many discourses marked by the term convey the idea of "the day of YHWH," the

---

68. Isa 2:2–4; 6:1–5; 19:16–25; 24:1–25; 33:1–24; 41:21; 43:15; 52:7; 62:1–3; 60:10–16; 66:22–24.

69. Isa 6:1–5 portrays YHWH as the mighty King sitting on his supreme throne, filling his temple with his glory, and surrounded by his seraphim who proclaim his incomparable unique holiness, to underline his royal supremacy and the readiness to exercise his eschatological kingship on earth (vv. 11–13). See the discussion in Abernethy, *Book of Isaiah*, 14–28. For his rule over Israel, see Isa 4:2–6; 52:7–10; for his rule over other nations, see Isa 2:2–4; 19:23–25; 45:20–25; 66:23–24; for his rule over the whole creation, see Isa 6:1–3; 24:21–23; 45:12, 18; 64:1–2.

70. For Israel's rebelion, see Isa 1:2–9; 5:1–2, 7; 9:7–9; 30:1–5; 42:18–25; 44:9–20; 46:3–13; 56:9–57:13; 58:1–12; for other nations', see Isa 10:5–11; 14:13–14; 24:5.

71. Abernethy, *Book of Isaiah*, 50–52, 81–82, 111–18.

day he will judge his opponents and thus save his righteous people.[72] It can be said, therefore, the universal worship of YHWH in Isaiah responds to the establishment of his kingship on earth.

The establishment of YHWH's universal kingship is firstly displayed in Isaiah 2:2–4 that depicts his universal reign from Mount Zion and then strongly affirmed in 6:1–5 that describes him as the Great King of all.[73] His eschatological reign is exercised through the divine judgments against the nations in Isaiah 13–23, which comes into its climax in Isaiah 24 that depicts his judgment upon all nations and their gods (vv. 21–23).[74] Isaiah 28–33 also speaks both his coming reign by which he will be exalted in Jerusalem and fills the city with his justice, righteousness, wisdom, and knowledge (33:5–6). All of his people, then, will see how this Great King in his beauty will save them (33:17, 20–22).[75]

The pre-exilic hope above, however, is trampled by the destruction of Jerusalem and her temple, and the exile of the nation of Israel, which is perceived as YHWH's abandonment of his people. In response to this theological crisis, Isaiah 40–55 envisions the glorious return of the Great King of Israel to Jerusalem (40:1–11; 52:7–10).[76] The hope is further endorsed by the Isaianic monotheistic faith that exalts him as the only true God (43:10; 44:6–8) and downgrades the gods of other nations as wooden and metal idols (44:9–20) that have no power to save (45:20; 46:1–2).[77]

Isaiah 56–66 deals with the post exilic situation where Israel's restoration had been challenged by social injustice and unrighteousness (56:1; 57:1–2; 58:2; 59:9, 14), irresponsible leaders (56:9–12), and idolatries (57:3–13) in the homeland. In response to these iniquities, Isaiah gives a strong warning that the warrior King of Israel will come to Zion to repay all the sinful deeds committed by the rebellious people (59:15–20; cf. 42:13). His punishment will produce a great fear across the earth, and nations will come to Zion in

---

72. For punishing Israel, see Isa 1:11–17; 13:6–13; 23:21–23; 34:8–15. For punishing other nations, see Isa 25:1–12; 27:6–13; 40:9–11; 52:1–10.

73. Abernethy, *Book of Isaiah*, 14–22.

74. Berges, "Kingship and Servanthood," 165–67; Abernethy, *Book of Isaiah*, 33–34.

75. Berges, 167–68; Abernethy, 39–46.

76. Abernethy, *Book of Isaiah*, 54–66.

77. Monotheism in Deutero-Isaiah has a strong polemical thrust. YHWH is compared not with the idols, but with the idol-makers. See the discussion in MacDonald, "Monotheism and Isaiah," 43–61, particularly 52–54, 59.

submission to his order (60:1–3). Finally, the book ends with the depiction of YHWH coming to judge the ingathering nations in Jerusalem (66:15–24). The survivors will gather again in this city to offer their worshipful submission to his kingship in his newly created order.

YHWH's eschatological reign will be ushered by various eschatological agents. Isaiah 1–39 envisions an ideal Davidic ruler who will rule with justice and righteousness to bring blissful peace in the land. Isaiah 7:14 speaks about a child, whose name is Immanuel, to signal the end of the current political turmoil and the coming blissful peace in Judah. Reading in conjunction with the vision in 9:1–7, it is logically assumed that the child is the future great ruler who will usher the blissful peace in the land. Isaiah 11:1–10 further identifies him as a descendant of David.[78] In contrast to the current leadership, the prophet envisions that this eschatological ruler will reign by the spirit of YHWH to establish justice and righteousness on earth. This is further affirmed by Isaiah 16:5 and 32:1–5 that depicts that a newly Davidic ruler will rule with justice and righteousness.[79]

A link can be made between the establishment of YHWH's eschatological dominion in 2:2–4 and the sovereignty of Davidic ruler in 11:1–10: (1) both speak of the coming of the glorious eschatological age (2:2; cf. 11:10); (2) both depict the creation of a peaceful world (2:4; cf. 11:6–9a); and (3) both underline this peace is caused by YHWH's revelation (his laws in 2:3; cf. his knowledge in 11:9b) and by the justice and righteous rule from Jerusalem (2:4; cf. 11:3–5).[80] All this implies that the divine eschatological reign will be carried by a future Davidic ruler. It is also worth noting that Isaiah 1–39 boldly proclaims YHWH as the King (מלך; 6:5; 33:17, 22), and avoids to entitle the envisioned ruler with this royal designation.[81] This infers that YHWH is always the real King of Israel, and all the Davidic rulers are his royal servants to carry out his rule on earth.

Isaiah 40–55 raises up some other figures to establish the divine kingship on earth: the servant of YHWH in 42:1–7; 49:1–6; 50:4–9; 52:13–53:12 and the Persian king Cyrus in 44:28–45:13. The precise identification of the servant is

78. Williamson, *Variations on a Theme*, 30–56; Abernethy, *Book of Isaiah*, 121–35.

79. Williamson, 56–72; Abernethy, 133–35.

80. For the link between Isaiah 2:2–4 and 11:9–10, see the discussion in Roberts, *First Isaiah*, 182.

81. Berges, "Kingship and Servanthood," 163.

still debated, whether the figure should be understood as a community (the whole Israel, or the righteous remnants of the nation) or as an individual (the Persian king Cyrus, or the Davidic king, or the prophet).[82]

While in the past the Servant Songs are often read in isolation from its current literary context, the present study observes all the figures synchronically. YHWH's servant is, first, inducted in Isaiah 41:8–9 where the figure is associated with the nation Israel. YHWH, in Deutero-Isaiah, is the King (43:15; 44:6), and the nation Israel is his servant. The servant role is elaborated in 42:1–7, that is to bring forth justice to all the nations to accomplish his appointed role as a covenant to the people and a light to the nations. The role is notably grounded in YHWH's promises to Abraham and Jacob (cf. Gen 12:3; 28:14) and the Sinaitic covenant (Exod 19:6). In fulfilling this mission, he is empowered by YHWH's Spirit like the ruler envisioned in Isaiah 11:2. The motif of "YHWH's Spirit resting upon him" implies the royal status of the servant, Israel (cf. Isa 11:2).

Having said this, Isaiah 42:19–25 depicts that the nation expected to open the blind eyes has turned to be blind and deaf and experienced great humiliation in the exile. In response to this dilemma, YHWH plans to save and restore this humiliated servant nation. He appoints the Persian king to subdue all nations in order to open the door of salvation for Israel and to rebuild Jerusalem together with her holy temple (44:28–45:13). Following up this salvific program, another servant vision is uttered, that is in 49:1–6. The reappearance of the motif of "a light to the nations" indicates its close correlation with the servant in Isaiah 42:1–7.

Should the figure in this passage be associated with the nation Israel or to an individual? There are a few good reasons to assume the latter: (1) Isaiah 44:5 speaks of individual pertaining to YHWH's belonging of the servant; (2) while Isaiah 49:3 associates the servant with Israel, it also declares that his main role is to restore the survival of this nation; (3) Isaiah 50:10 notably echoes the envisioned Davidic ruler in 11:2–5 by describing that the servant will rule by his mouth; and (4) Isaiah 52:13–53:12 discloses further that the servant will suffer greatly due to the transgression of YHWH's people before enjoying his vindication. All this affirms that the servant in Isaiah 49–55 is

---

82. Lindsey, *Servant Songs*, 9–17.

better associated with an individual, namely a future leader of the nation Israel who will follow up Cyrus's ministry.[83]

Isaiah 56–66 envisions another eschatological agent. The center part of this collection, Isaiah 60–62, depicts YHWH's eschatological light as having come upon Jerusalem, and it calls many nations to come in submission to his kingship, which is also perceived as salvation to many exiled Israel (60:1–16). Following this coming of salvation, Isaiah 61:1–3 depicts a royal prophetical agent. Like the royal Davidic ruler and the royal servant, the Spirit of YHWH also rests upon him (cf. 11:2; 42:1; 48:16). Like gentile king Cyrus, he is anointed by YHWH. His ministry is notably through his speech. However, instead of judging the nations, his mission is to proclaim the good news of Israel's salvation as the eschatological reign of YHWH has come to this nation.[84]

2.2.3 The Transformation of the Worshippers

It has been observed that the worship of YHWH demands holiness, and this expectation is also voiced in Isaiah. Across the book, the God of Israel is referred to as the Holy One of Israel, and the most explicit depiction of his holiness is in Isaiah 6:1–6 where King YHWH *Sebaoth* is praised with triple holy (קדש) by the seraphim.[85] While YHWH's triple holy is in the metaphysical category, in 5:16 the divine holy nature is closely connected with his righteous act.[86] Hence, when the prophet faced the absolute holiness of YHWH, he realized his own depravity (6:3–5). This shows that YHWH's holiness has a moral dimension.

In the book of Isaiah YHWH's holiness stands, first of all, against the sins of his own people, Israel. The nation is accused as being unfaithful and rebellious to YHWH by despising him, worshipping idols, and practicing magics.[87] Their leaders are also charged with lacking faith in YHWH's delivering power.[88] They both greatly impact her moral behavior. The city of Jerusalem, as

---

83. Abernethy, *Book of Isaiah*, 147.

84. Abernethy, 160–69.

85. The phrase the Holy One of Israel occurs in Isa 1:4; 17:7; 29:19; 37:23; 41:14; 55:5; 60:9.

86. Goldingay, "Theology of Isaiah," 171–73.

87. Isa 1:2–4, 21; 2:6–8; 3:8, 24; 8:6; 28:12; 29:15.

88. Isa 7:1–13; 22:11; 30:1 and 31:1.

the representation of the nation Israel, is pictured as both an unfaithful and unrighteous city (1:21–23).[89]

The book of Isaiah strongly highlights that worshippers will become what they worship. The Israelites will be transformed into holiness when they continue worshipping the Holy One of Israel wholeheartedly, but they will become blind and deaf (Isa 6:9–10; 42:17–20; 43:8; 44:17–18) when they worship idols who cannot see and hear (cf. Ps 115:4–6).[90] Isaiah clearly relates Israel's sinful behaviors of the preexilic Israelites to her spiritual handicap.[91] This obstruction continued among the exiled people[92] and caused them to commit idolatry (Isa 44:9, 18–20) and fail to appreciate YHWH's coming salvation. Despite the good news of their deliverance (40:9), they were living in fear and despair (41:10, 13; 43:1, 5; 44:2, 8; 51:13). This spiritual paralysis persisted even among the returning Israel (56:10; 64:4; 65:12), and caused them to fall back to their old behaviors of worshipping foreign idols, artificial religious acts, and doing all kinds of wickedness and oppression.[93]

YHWH's holiness also stands against the sins of other nations. Some passages highlight their oppression toward Israel, such as 13:11, 18:1–6, and 24:28–32. Having said this, the dominant picture of their sins is notably their haughtiness before the God of Israel, which is perceived as provoking his authoritative reign (10:5–19; 13:11; 14:12–23; 16:16; 23:1–9; 37:23–29).[94]

In response to both the sins of Israel and all other nations, Isaiah reveals YHWH's plan to restore the holiness of his people and to humble all other nations. The vision of the universal worship in 2:1–4 comes only after YHWH's restoration of Israel's holiness in 1:24–31. The idea of the day of YHWH in Isaiah is worth noting. It describes YHWH's plan to judge all people and even destroy the whole earth due to their sins (2:6–11; 13:11; 24:1–13). However, the judgment does not intend to a total destruction. In facing this horrific day, the Israelites are called to cast away their idols, to put off their evil deed, and

---

89. For the correlation between unfaithfulness and unrighteousness, see the discussion in Leclerc, *Yahweh Is Exalted*, 40–42.

90. Beale, *We Become What We Worship*, 36–64.

91. Isa 6:9–10; 28:7–13; 29:9–14; 30:9–11. See Smith, "Spiritual Blindness," 166–74.

92. Isa 42:18–20, 23; 43:8; 44:18.

93. For the first, see Isa 57:1–13 cf. 2:6–11; for the second, see 58:3–5; cf. 1:11–15; for the last, see 59:1–13 cf. 1:21–23.

94. Hamborg, "Reasons for Judgement," 155–56.

to learn good deeds and justice (1:16–20; 58:1–59:21). All other nations are also expected to humbly submit to YHWH's sovereign rule (18:7; 23:17–18; 45:23–24; 60:3–8) joining Israel to learn and obey his laws (2:3; 56:1–7).

One important observation needs to be made with regard to the role of the servant of YHWH in restoring the holiness of his people. Isaiah 52:7–12 proclaims the imminent coming of YHWH's eschatological reign and salvation, then calls Israel to purify herself to worship him. This is immediately followed by the servant account who is depicted as being highly exalted after experiencing extreme humiliation (52:13–53:12). To be sure, this suffering is endured in obedience to the divine will of bearing the sins of Israel. By his sacrificial service, many shall be declared righteous before YHWH. One possible background for such a nexus of ideas is the priestly teaching of the Day of Atonement (Lev 16).[95] The significance of the servant account in Isaiah 52–53 is that the sacrificial role is carried out not by a chosen animal, but YHWH's appointed servant. In the first century AD, this motif was picked up in many New Testament writings.

2.2.4 The Covenant Framework

The biblical vision of the universal worship of YHWH is grounded in Israel's covenant with her God at Sinai (Exod 19:3–6). In Isaiah this covenant framework is enlarged with a universal outlook. In order to appreciate this, the covenant notion of this prophetical book needs to be elaborated.

The book of Isaiah utilizes the term "covenant" (ברית) in defining Israel's unique relationship with YHWH. The term occurs twelve times, nine of which speak about Israel's relationship with him.[96] This covenant relationship can be easily detected in the way Israel's and YHWH's identities are described: YHWH is the parent (father and mother) and Israel is his/her children;[97] YHWH is the husband and Israel is his wife;[98] YHWH is the farmer and Israel

---

95. Walton, Matthews, and Chavalas, *IVP Bible Background*, 634.

96. In Isaiah, the term appears in various expressions: (1) "eternal covenant" (24:5; 55:3; 61:8); (2) YHWH's servant as "a covenant for the people" (42:6; 49:8); (3) "covenant of peace" (54:10); and (4) "my covenant" (56:4, 6; 59:21).

97. Isa 1:2–4; 44:24; 45:11; 63:8.

98. Isa 54:5–7.

his vineyard;[99] YHWH is the creator and Israel the work of his hands;[100] and YHWH is the God of Israel, the Holy One of Israel, and the King of Israel while Israel is his people. While all of this identity is pregnant with covenant thrust, the last deserves more attention.

Across the book of Isaiah YHWH often calls Israel "my people" (עַמִּי), which strongly adumbrates the covenant formula "You are my people and I am your God."[101] Coupled with this identity, the book calls YHWH the God of Israel/Jacob (אלהי ישראל),[102] the Holy One of Israel/Jacob (קדוש ישראל),[103] and the King of Israel (מלך ישראל).[104] The first adumbrates Jacob's covenant (Gen 28:18–22), and certainly the Sinaitic covenant. The second highlights not only the unapproachable holiness of YHWH but also his unique relationship with Israel that is made possible only by their covenant. The last evokes the Sinaitic covenant proposal that identifies YHWH as the king and Israel as his vassal nation.[105] In all, both the identities of Israel and YHWH in Isaiah have a covenant thrust.

It has been noted that Israel's covenant itself has universal trust, where all other nations will receive blessing through YHWH's people. This universal outlook is made louder in the book of Isaiah. In Isaiah 19:25, YHWH declares the Egyptians as his people, and Assyria the work of his hands to support their worship of him. Isaiah 56:3 utters further that all foreigners will not be separated from his people Israel in worshipping YHWH in his new Jerusalem temple.

The extension phenomenon can be also detected in the idea of covenant (ברית) in the book of Isaiah. The covenant in Isaiah 24:5 and 54:10 notably echoes the Noachic universal covenant. The role of YHWH's servant as "a

---

99. Isa 5:1–7.

100. Isa 29:23; 45:11.

101. Isa 1:3; 3:12, 15; 5:13; 10:2; 22:4; 26:11; 32:18; 40:1; 47:6; 51:4; 52:4–6; 63:8; 65:10, 22.

102. Isa 29:23; 45:15.

103. Isa 1:4; 5:19, 24; 10:20; 12:6; 17:7; 29:19, 30:11–12, 15; 31:1; 37:23; 41:14, 16, 20; 43:3, 14; 47:4; 48:17; 49:7; 54:5; 55:5; 60:9, 14.

104. Isa 44:6; cf. 6:5; 33:17, 22; 41:21; 43:15.

105. The God of Israel/Jacob adumbrates Jacob's covenant (Gen 28:18–22), and certainly the Sinaitic covenant (Exod 19–24). The Holy One of Israel/Jacob highlights not only the unapproachable holiness of YHWH (6:3, 5), but also his unique relationship with Israel that is made possible only by their covenant. The King of Israel recalls the Sinaitic covenant proposal that identifies Israel as YHWH's vassal nation. See the discussion in Roberts, "Isaiah," 136; Brueggemann, Isaiah 1–39, 16; Kratz, "Israel," 106.

covenant for the people" in Isaiah 42:6 and 49:6 certainly has a universal thrust. As the book celebrates the figure of Jacob-Israel,[106] these two passages adumbrate YHWH's covenant with Jacob in Genesis 28:13–22, particularly the promise in verse 14, "in you and your offspring shall all the families of the earth be blessed." Finally, while the covenant in Isaiah 56:4–6 is rooted in the Sinaitic covenant,[107] they also go beyond this old covenant as in the eschatological era the covenant will embrace eunuchs and gentile nations to be YHWH's people.

2.2.5 Summary

Our observation on the book of Isaiah reveals that the book of Isaiah indeed celebrates the theme of the universal worship of YHWH. The major picture of this universal worship is that one day in the future all nations will join Israel's worship during the festival of YHWH offering their precious gifts in the Jerusalem Temple. This theme is grounded in YHWH's covenant with Israel, which is extended to all nations. This universal thrust gains support from the Isaianic monotheistic claim that the God of Israel is also the one and only God of the whole creation. The universal worship of him in Isaiah, thus, is an expression of humble submission from all humankind to the establishment of his dominion on earth. His kingship means judgment to all of his enemies, but salvation to those on his side. Some eschatological figures are to carry out his universal rule. In response, both Israel and all other nations are called to leave all of their idols and sinful conducts, and then to turn to YHWH by walking according to his ways.

2.3 Reading Isaiah 45:23–24

After drawing the contour of four important tenets in the theme of the universal eschatological worship of YHWH in the book of Isaiah, a close examination now is given to the vision in Isaiah 45:23–24.

---

106. Isa 2:3, 5, 6; 8:17; 9:8; 10:20–21; 14:1; 17:4; 27:6, 9, 29:22–23; 40:27; 41:8; 41:14, 21, 24; 43:1, 22, 28; 44:1, 2, 5, 21, 23; 45:19; 46:3; 48:1, 12, 49:5, 6, 26; 58:14, 20; 60:16; 65.

107. Cf. the observation of Sabbath with Exod 31:12–14.

2.3.1 The Texts

The book of Isaiah was originally written in Hebrew and then translated into other languages (Greek, Aramaic, and Syriac) in antiquity. In the Second Temple period, Isaiah 45:23–24 was available in two languages: (1) the Hebrew text, which is represented by the Masoretic Text from the ninth century AD (hereafter MT) and the Qumran Text from the second century BC (hereafter QT; 1QIsaᵃ and 4QIsaᵇ); (2) the Greek text, which is represented by the Septuagint (hereafter LXX). Although *Targum Isaiah* is also very ancient, this Aramaic translation was produced in the rabbinic era.[108] To start the observation the MT, QT, and LXX texts are presented below for clarity:

MT	בי נשבעתי יצא מפי צדקה דבר ולא ישוב כי־לי תכרע כל־ברך תשבע כל־לשון:
	אך ביהוה **לי אמר** צדקות ועז עדיו יבוא ויבשו כל הנחרים בו:
QT (1QIsaᵃ)	בי נשבעתי יצא מפי צדקה דבר ולא ישוב כי־לי תכרע כל־ברך תשבע כל־לשון:
	אך ביהוה **ליא יאמר** צדקות ועז עדיו יבוא ויבשו כל הנחרים בו:

---

108. The discovery of some fragments of Targumin among the Dead Sea Scrolls, such as Leviticus in 4Q156 and Job in 11Q10 and 4Q157, indicates that at least some of the OT writings had been availabe in the Aramaic language by the first century AD. Given that Paul was regularly in contact with synagogues (Acts 13:14), he might be familiar with the Aramaic paraphrases of Hebrew Scripture. Having said this, the general scholarly assessment of the present Targum of Isaiah is that this written translation was produced in the rabbinic era. The editorial work had been started in Palestine during the Tannaitic period (AD 70–135) and its process was completed in Babylonia during the Amoraic period (fourth century AD). For this reason, the analysis of Isaiah *Tg. Isa* 45:23–24 is excluded in our study. See Flesher, McCracken, and Chilton, *Targums*, 174–75. The rabbinic exegetical framework is notably reflected in the translation of Isaiah 45:23–24:

במימרי קיימית נפק מן קדמי בזכו פתגם ולא יבטל ארי קדמי תכרע כל ברך תקיים כל לישן:
ברם **במימרא** דיוי עלי אמר לאיתאה זכוון ותקוף **במימריה** יודון ויבהתון בטעוותהון **כל עממיא** דהוו מתגרן בעמיה:

Two things should be noted. First, the use of the term מימר (*memra*). Second, the phrase כל הנחרים בו (those who stood against YHWH) is interpreted as כל עממיא דהוו מתגרן בעמיה (those who stood against YHWH's people), which reflects the negative Jewish sentiment after the destruction of Jerusalem and its temple by the Roman army in AD 70. See Chilton, *Isaiah Targum*, xv.

LXX	κατ' ἐμαυτοῦ ὀμνύω ἦ μὴν ἐξελεύσεται ἐκ τοῦ στόματός μου δικαιοσύνη οἱ λόγοι μου οὐκ ἀποστραφήσονται ὅτι ἐμοὶ κάμψει πᾶν γόνυ καὶ ἐξομολογήσεται (or ὀμεῖται)[109] πᾶσα γλῶσσα τῷ θεῷ λέγων δικαιοσύνη καὶ δόξα πρὸς αὐτὸν ἥξουσιν καὶ αἰσχυνθήσονται πάντες οἱ ἀφορίζοντες ἑαυτούς

There are some differences between the Hebrew text and the Greek text in reading Isaiah 45:23–24. First, in the Hebrew text, the whole statement in verse 24 is uttered by an unidentified speaker. The MT has אמר לי (one says), and the 1QIsaᵃ has ליא יאמר (it shall be said). In the Greek text (LXX), the utterance in verse 24 becomes the confession of every tongue (ἐξομολογήσεται) in verse 23. This is evinced by (1) the use of the participle λέγων in translating the Hebrew אמר לי or ליא יאמר and (2) the omission of אך ביהוה.

Second, in the Greek text, the phrase πρὸς αὐτὸν ἥξουσιν is usually construed as part of the previous statement: λέγων δικαιοσύνη καὶ δόξα πρὸς αὐτὸν ἥξουσιν. Thus, the translation runs as follows: "saying, 'righteousness and glory will come to him.'"[110] In our opinion, the phrase is better construed as being part of the subsequent clause πρὸς αὐτὸν ἥξουσιν καὶ αἰσχυνθήσονται πάντες οἱ ἀφορίζοντες ἑαυτούς, as this is the case in the Hebrew text (עדיו יבוא in the MT and עדיו יבואו in 1QIsaᵃ). The translation, then, should runs as this: "to him will come and be ashamed all who stand against him." In this conjecture, the content of the confession (ἐξομολογέω) to God is simply this: λέγων δικαιοσύνη καὶ δόξα (saying, "Righteousness and Glory!").

Third, there are two variants in the LXX translation of תשבע כל־לשון. The translation ἐξομολογήσεται πᾶσα γλῶσσα τῷ θεῷ, is in agreement with both Romans 14:11 and Philippians 2:11, while the translation ὀμεῖται πᾶσα γλῶσσα τὸν θεὸν is closer to the MT. There are two possible explanations for this. The first variant represents the original reading, and thus it was appropriated by Paul in his letters. Alternatively, the second variant represents the original reading, and thus the first variant is a later interpolation based on Paul's citation and allusion.[111] The present study inclines to the first option. The acclamation δικαιοσύνη καὶ δόξα (righteousness and glory) is closer not

---

109. The verb ἐξομολογήσεται is attested in A, Q*, Sc, and ὀμεῖται is in B, S*, the *Lucian* and *Catenan* recensions.

110. This reading is adopted in *NETS*.

111. See the discussion in Kreitzer, *Jesus and God in Paul's Eschatology*, 115–17, 226n80.

to an oath, but confessional praise. It is also easier to construe Paul as following closely his Greek *Vorlage* than replacing ὀμεῖται with ἐξομολογήσεται in citing Isaiah 45:23 LXX.

2.3.2 The Context

It is necessary to observe the historical and literary context of this Isaianic vision. Concerning the former, it is a general opinion that Yesaya 40–55 spoke to the nation Israel in the Babylonian exile.[112] The appearance of the historical figure of Cyrus in Isaiah 44:28 and 45:1 not only strengthens the consensus but also draws the historical background of the vision, which is the rise of the Persian king to overthrow the Babylonian supremacy in the middle of the sixth century BC.

Concerning the latter, the present study locates the vision within one unified oracle of Isaiah 44:24–45:25. As scholars have noted, the subject raised in this oracle is different from the previous and subsequent ones,[113] as it focuses on one dominant theme, the establishment of YHWH's kingship and salvation through Cyrus.[114] Following Baltzer, we divide the discourse into four smaller units as follows:

(1) Isaiah 44:24–45:8 declares YHWH's plan to raise King Cyrus as his agent to establish his eschatological reign and salvation.

(2) Isaiah 45:9–13 confronts Israel's objection to his salvific plan.

(3) Isaiah 45:14–17 draws the picture of YHWH's kingship over the nations.

(4) Isaiah 45:18–25 claims that YHWH is the only God, Creator, and Savior to whom Israel and all nations should turn and worship in submission to his kingship for their salvation.[115]

In all, the historical and literary context of Isaiah 44:28–45:25 relates to YHWH's eschatological plan to save the nation Israel from her exile through the rise of Cyrus's supremacy. With this in mind, we now examine Isaiah 4:23–24. To do so, the four major tenets of the Isaianic theme of the eschatological worship of YHWH will guide the analysis.

---

112. Stromberg, *Introduction to the Study of Isaiah*, 27–36.

113. Baltzer, *Deutero-Isaiah*, 209.

114. Baltzer, 209–10.

115. Baltzer, x–xi.

2.3.3 The Universal Eschatological Worship of YHWH

In Isaiah 45:23–24, the idea of worship is conveyed by the words כרע/κάμπτω and שבע/ἐξομολογέω. The former denotes the bodily gesture of "bending down" or "bowing down" that expresses humility before YHWH.[116] The latter connotes a public oath of allegiance to him. The LXX translates the verb שבע (to swear) as ἐξομολογέω (to praise confessionally), and thus it gives a stronger worship notion.[117] This notion finds support from several statements in the oracle. The statement "*to me* (לִי) every knee shall bow and every tongue shall swear (or confess)" indicates that the object of the homage is the God of Israel.[118] Moreover, this homage polemically responds to the idolatry of the nations (45:20). Although it mentions only once in the present oracle, both the preceding and the subsequent oracles thoroughly deal with this matter (44:9–20; 46:1–13). Finally, Isaiah 45:14 highlights the acknowledgment that there is no other God besides YHWH by other nations.

Having said this, this worshipful homage does not eliminate the idea of submission. The verb שבע in the MT expresses the idea of swearing of loyalty that conveys the idea of submission.[119] This is enforced further by the coming of YHWH's reign and salvation through his gentile messiah Cyrus (45:1–13). In balance, the homage is an act of submissive worship, which is common in ancient Near Eastern culture.

The scope of this submissive worship is notably universal. The word כל/πᾶς points back to all the nations bringing their homage gifts to Israel and YHWH in verse 14, the survivors of the nations in verse 20, and all those from the ends of the earth in verse 22. This universal scope is supported by the theological claim in Isaiah 40–55 that YHWH is the only true God of Israel and of all nations,[120] which is professed in 44:28–45:25. The oracle identifies YHWH as both the covenantal God of Israel and the creator of the whole universe (45:3–4, 11–12, 18). Indeed, the statements such as "I am YHWH,

---

116. See William, "כרע," *NIDOTTE* 2:727–28; for κάμπτω, see Danker, Bauer, and Arndt, "Κάμπτω," BDAG, 507.

117. Hofius, "Ἐξομολογέω," *EDNT* 2:8–9.

118. Here, לי harks back to הלוא אני יהוה in verse 21.

119. Goldingay and Payne, *Isaiah 40–55*, 60; Bauckham, "Worship of Jesus in Philippians," 128.

120. This has been widely appreciated, although the nature of the Isaianic monotheism is still debated. See the discussion in MacDonald, "Monotheism and Isaiah," 43–61; Bauckham, *Jesus and the God of Israel*, 82–94.

and there is no other, besides me, there is no God" and "Was it not I, YHWH? And there is no other god besides me," make a strong claim that YHWH is the only true God[121] and deny the existence of other divine beings professed in polytheistic ancient Near Eastern culture (vv. 5, 21).[122] This conviction establishes the God of Israel as the only Savior, while all other deities are depreciated merely as idols that have no ability to save (vv. 15, 20–21). In this respect, the vision of universal worship of Yhwh is a cultic application of the Isaianic monotheistic conviction.

This universal worship has an eschatological dimension. The future orientation of the vision is noted by the use of the *qal* imperfect of כרע and *niphal* imperfect of שבע in the MT, or the future indicative of κάμπτω and ἐξομολογέω in the LXX.[123] The phrase בי נשבעתי (MT) or κατ' ἐμαυτοῦ ὀμνύω (LXX) expresses the divine commitment to fulfill the promise.[124] In this oracle, YHWH claims himself as the only God, and therefore there is no other power that can stop the realization of this eschatological vision.

The eschatological thrust of this universal worship is further affirmed by situating the vision in the larger context of the book. Reading the vision in its literary context (Isa 44:24–45:25) the readers will expect its fulfillment during Cyrus's hegemony. However, it is worth noting that the vision is one of many visions voiced in the book of Isaiah to anticipate the grand vision of the universal eschatological worship of YHWH, as the book is opened and ended with such great visions of worship (2:2–4 and 66:22–24). Hence, the readers would naturally hope this vision of worship will be fulfilled in the eschatological future.

2.3.4 YHWH's Eschatological Reign and Salvation

This vision of worship also needs to be appreciated in connection with the establishment of YHWH's universal eschatological reign on earth. We have noted that in the book of Isaiah, he is claimed as the great King of Israel who

---

121. Paul, *Isaiah 40–66*, 229.

122. Baltzer, *Deutero-Isaiah*, 166.

123. Although these forms can be read as imperative, the future nuance is stronger given the vision of worship in Isaiah 45:23–24 is uttered as divine promise to be realized. See Goldingay, *Message of Isaiah 40–55*, 295.

124. There is no Hebrew word for "to promise." The verb שבע (to swear) is used to articulate this idea. Goldingay, *Message of Isaiah 40–55*, 296.

rules not only Israel but also all nations. In Deutero-Isaiah, his universal dominion is heightened by the prophet's monotheistic claim that the only God of Israel is also the creator of the whole universe whose authority is incontestable. This theological conviction is accentuated in the present oracle. The Holy One of Israel is claimed to be the only God (vv. 5–6) responsible for the creation of the heavens, the earth, and all humankind, and therefore he has all right and power to rule them all (vv. 8, 12, 18).[125]

In verses 18–25, YHWH's kingship is presented by the divine royal court imagery.[126] The great King of Israel sits on his royal throne, and the survivors of the nations are gathered in the divine court to present their case. Claiming himself as the only righteous God and Savior, he summons all nations turning to him for their salvation. This salvific call is assured by his commitment to establishing his universal kingship on earth so that all nations will submissively worship him.[127] Failure to respond to this divine invitation, therefore, will have a dreadful consequence. In this respect, the vision of worship is voiced in the context of YHWH exercising his universal kingship, anchored in Israel's monotheistic conviction, and secured by the divine commitment to carry out his eschatological plan of salvation.

The prophetic oracle also reveals the way YHWH establishes his salvific kingship. The great King of Israel who fully controls the whole universe chooses the gentile king Cyrus (כּוֹרֶשׁ/Κῦρος) to be his earthly agent to carry out his plan (45:1–8). His hegemony over the whole world, therefore, carries out two divine objectives, to restore the royal city Jerusalem including her holy temple (44:28; 45:13) and to set the Israelites free from their current exile (45:13, 17).

There is still an ongoing debate on whether the phrase "to you" (עליך) in 45:14 should refer to Israel-Jerusalem or Cyrus.[128] The new rising power of Cyrus certainly demands the tributes from all of his subjects, and Isaiah 43:3 depicts that YHWH will give Egypt, Cush, and Seba as ransom payments to redeem Israel. As Isaiah 44:28–45:3, 13 speak about this gentile king, it is expected that verse 14 speaks about the homage of other nations

---

125. Baltzer, *Deutero-Isaiah*, 226–31, 236.

126. Baltzer, 248.

127. Baltzer, 248–50.

128. Noted in Baltzer, 238–40; Goldingay and Payne, *Isaiah 40–55*, 43–44.

to king Cyrus. Having said this, in the phrase "to you" (עָלֶיךָ), the preposition עַל is suffixed with the second person in feminine form, and this makes the conjecture above become rather awkward. It is worth noting that verse 13 also speaks about the city Jerusalem and the people of Israel, which are commonly addressed in feminine form. As the present oracle speaks their restoration (44:28 and 45:13), and other parts of the book also envision that their restoration will include the tribute of other nations, including Egypt, Cush, and Sheba. Hence, the tribute and homage in Isaiah 45 can be offered to the nation of Israel.

In the present study, these two conjectures are welcomed for two reasons. First, both affirm that the homage gifts relate to the confession that YHWH is the only God. Second, in Isaiah 40–55, both Cyrus and Israel are pictured as eschatological agents to carry out his glory, and thus both deserve honorific homage (cf. Ps 72:10). Having said this, the difference between the two is also clear concerning the time of fulfillment. The former expects the immediate realization, the latter speaks of a more distant future one.

Opposition to this way of salvation is noted in verses 9–11. Among the Israelites in the exile, some held strong nationalistic sentiment and refuted this way of salvation.[129] Their objection is responded to with the divine claim that, as the maker of both Israel and the whole universe, YHHW has every right to do so (vv. 11–13). The metaphors of potter-clay and parent-child underline that as his creation, Israel should not challenge the Creator's will. YHWH's plan to establish his kingdom, thus, remains unchallenged. What all humankind should do is to acknowledge him as the only God, to turn to him as the only Savior, and to worshipfully submit to his universal kingship (vv. 14, 22–23).

The Isaianic vision of worship is situated in the historical context of the rise of Persian worldwide hegemony under king Cyrus in 559–530 BC. This gentile king is ordained to deliver Israel and rebuild Jerusalem and its temple. However, the history of Israel confirms only the partial fulfillment of Cyrus's tasks. While he successfully defeated Babylonia in 539 BC, only a small number of the Israelites did return to their homeland. While the rebuilding of the temple was started shortly after their arrival, its completion took place only in 515 BC. The city also remained an unsafe habitat until the middle of the

---

129. Brueggemann, *Isaiah 40–66*, 78; cf. Goldingay and Payne, *Isaiah 40–55*, 33–34.

fifth century BC. Hence, this post-exilic condition has failed to satisfy the expectation raised in Isaiah 45 that all nations shall come to acknowledge and worship YHWH as their God and Savior.

The vision, therefore, should be read against the backdrop provided by the larger framework of the book.[130] Isaiah 11:1–9 speaks of an ideal king who will establish peace on earth. Through this eschatological agent, the whole world will be covered by the knowledge of YHWH. Isaiah 33:17–24 also describes an ideal king who will establish the divine earthly kingship. Indeed, Isaiah 40–55 envisions not only the figure of Cyrus but also the servant of YHWH who will carry out his salvific mission.[131] Hence, as the vision had not been fully realized during the reign of Cyrus and even in the post-exilic era, the faithful remnants of Israel continued to wait for its fulfillment. The beginning and closing visions of the book of Isaiah indeed call for this eschatological hope.

2.3.5 The Transformation of the Worshippers

In Isaiah, YHWH is called frequently called the Holy One of Israel, and this identity has a purgative notion, underlining that YHWH is going to make his worshippers as holy as he is. In Isaiah 45, this holiness expectation is also accentuated.

In the present oracle, Israel's sin appears in the form of nationalistic sentiment. His way of salvation, using the gentile king to be his eschatological agent, is challenged by some exilic Israelites (45:9–11).[132] Israel's lacking faith and spiritual handicap certainly contribute to her inability to appreciate this way of salvation. In response, verses 11–13 warn any children of Israel not to challenge YHWH concerning his way of salvation. He is the creator of both Israel and the whole universe, and thus he holds all authority to carry out his way of saving this nation. Instead of resisting him, they are called to humbly and earnestly seek him (v. 19).

One kind of the sins that strongly provokes YHWH is their haughtiness against him. In the present oracle, this relates to the trust in the gods that cannot save, which is perceived as idolatry. Idolatry is a dominant struggle of

---

130. In Isaiah, the universal eschatological worship of YHWH serves as a unifying theme. See Begg, "Peoples and the Worship," 35–55; Schultz, "Nationalism and Universalism," 122–44.

131. Watts, *Isaiah 34–66*, 708.

132. Brueggemann, *Isaiah 40–66*, 78–77.

the Israelites not only in the past but also in the present, as many of them lost their faith in the foreign lands. Against this religious condition, the notion of holiness in this worship vision needs to be appreciated. While other nations and many among the Israelites professed the supremacy of Marduk, the chief god of the Persian Empire, Isaiah despises all foreign gods as merely human-made idols. The foolishness of worshipping them is certainly accentuated in this oracle.[133] These gods are pictured as powerless idols that are unable to save (v. 20). Hence, in the end, all who put trust and hope in them will be put into shame and confusion (v. 16). To Isaiah, the only way to their salvation is to acknowledge YHWH as the only God and Savior, to admit their foolishness in worshipping other gods, and then to turn to him in seeking salvation (vv. 15, 16, 22). In other words, both Israel and all other nations are called to renounce their past idolatries and worship YHWH exclusively and wholeheartedly. Certainly, such a transformation of Israel and gentile nations is only the first step to recover their relationship to the universal creator. In the larger context of Isaiah, both are called to faithfully worshipping him and to live out their obedience to his laws (56:1–7; 58:1–59:21).

2.3.6 The Covenant Notion

The term covenant (ברית) does not appear in Isaiah 44:24–45:25, but its idea undoubtedly presents. In this prophetic oracle, both the metaphors of potter-potteries and parent-children underline that the offsprings of Jacob/Israel uniquely belong to YHWH. On the one hand, YHWH is identified, therefore, as the God of Israel and the Holy One of Israel. On the other hand, Israel is his servant, his chosen ones, his children, and the work of his hand. All of these identities underlines the covenant relationship between YHWH and the nation Israel.

This prophetic oracle notably focuses on what the God of Israel is doing on behalf of his covenant people. The identification of YHWH as Israel's Redeemer in Isaiah 44:24 recalls the story of how YHWH redeemed Israel from Egyptian slavery in the past (Deut 7:8), and now it introduces his plan

---

133. Deutero-Isaiah indeed proscribes all kinds of idol worship (40:18–20; 41: 21–24; 44:9–28; 45:16, 20; 46:1–7). For the idol polemic in Deutero-Isaiah, see MacDonald, "Monotheism and Isaiah," 52–54.

to redeem again his people from the Babylonian bondage.[134] The verb גאל (to redeem) carries an idea that Israel belonged to YHWH, and due to her sins the nation had been sold (cf. 50:1), but now, in his mercy, the nation is bought back by him.[135] To Israel, this redemption also means the forgiveness of their past sins and the coming of their future salvation. All this establishes YHWH to be Israel's true Redeemer and Savior (44:24; 45:15, 21). His redemptive-salvific act is grounded in his faithfulness to the covenant with Israel, and for this, he is acclaimed as the righteous God (45:21).[136]

The extension of YHWH's covenant to other nations, which is detected in Isaiah 2, 19, 56, and 66, can be appreciated in this oracle too. The universal outlook of the oracle is made apparent by claiming YHWH as the creator of both Israel and the whole universe. This establishes him to be the only God who owns and governs the whole universe. This monotheistic claim provides a strong theological rationale for utilizing the gentile king to bring his eschatological salvation. The ordination of Cyrus certainly has a nationalistic interest, as he is to restore Jerusalem and set Israel free from the Babylonian bondage (vv. 4, 13).[137] At the same time, this ordination also welcomes the participation of gentile nations in YHWH's redemptive work in the history of Israel. Together with the monotheistic outlook of Isaiah 40–55, it gives support to the inclusion of other nations in Israel's covenant framework. Such a phenomenon is noted earlier in 19:25 and it will appear again later in 56:1–7. The present oracle provides theological reasoning on how YHWH's covenant blessing will flow from Israel to all humankind. All nations can be included within YHWH's covenant with Israel when they disassociate themselves from their former idols, acknowledge the God of Israel as the only true God, and then turn to him to receive his salvation (vv. 14–16, 20–24).

---

134. Niskanen, "Yhwh as Father," 401–2.

135. Baltzer, *Deutero-Isaiah*, 158.

136. For the covenantal notion of "righteousness" in Isaiah 40–55, see Oswalt, *Holy One of Israel*, 59–72.

137. While the universal outlook is quite apparent, Isaiah never loses its nationalistic thrust and commitment. Shultz, "Nationalism and Universalism," 142–44.

2.4 Summary

As Philippians 2:10–11 alludes to Isaiah 45:23 LXX, for a better appreciation of its significance this chapter investigates this Isaianic vision within
the Jewish eschatological matrix provided by the Old Testament the Second
Temple literature and certainly by the book of Isaiah itself. In doing so, the
study draws four important common tenets of the vision, namely YHWH's
covenant with Israel, the universal eschatological worship of him, the establishment of his eschatological reign, and the holy transformation of his
worshippers. It is strongly contended that these four tenets provide a theological framework for a better appreciation of the visions of worship in Isaiah,
particularly that of 45:23–24. The result is outlined as follows.

Isaiah 45:23–24 indeed envisages the universal eschatological worship
of YHWH, and it needs to be appreciated against the backdrop provided
by the larger eschatological narrative of the book of Isaiah. Together with
many similar eschatological visions across the book, this vision anticipates
the grand vision in 66:22–24. At the eschaton, all humankind will join Israel
to come to Jerusalem for the worship of YHWH.

The theme of universal worship in Isaiah responds to the realization of
YHWH's earthly dominion, which also means his coming salvation to Israel.
In the context of Isaiah 44:24–45:25, his universal kingship is grounded in
the Isaianic monotheistic conviction: YHWH is not only the God of Israel
but also the only God of the whole universe, and thus he is the only Savior
of this world. While this oracle highlights that YHWH's earthly rule will be
carried out through his gentile messiah Cyrus, the readers will notice that
various eschatological agents are also raised for the same divine mission
across the book. As his universal reign has not been fully realized by Cyrus,
they will naturally expect that another human agent will fulfill this eschatological vision.

The Old Testament teaches that YHWH promises to respond to the unho-
liness of his people, and therefore all biblical visions of eschatological worship
have a purgative element. This is notably sounded across the book of Isaiah.
All the worshippers of YHWH at the coming eschatological age will be made
holy. In the context of this Isianic oracle, the Israelites are reminded not to
reject his salvation but earnestly seek him. All other nations are also called
to renounce their idolatries, then turn to him for their salvation. All this is

certainly only a new beginning since they all are required to live up to their holy conduct as YHWH's faithful worshippers.

Finally, the vision of eschatological worship is grounded in Israel's covenant relationship with YHWH. Although the term covenant does not appear in this Isaianic oracle, its idea nonetheless runs beneath it. What needs to be appreciated is that the book of Isaiah celebrates the extension of YHWH's covenant with Israel. In fulfillment of the covenant promise to Abraham, Jacob, and the nation Israel, all other nations are invited to join this nation to receive his covenant blessing.

CHAPTER 3

Paul's Reading of Isaiah 45:23

The previous chapter has observed the vision of the universal worship of YHWH in Isaiah 45:23 within the Jewish eschatological matrix formed by the Old Testament (or the Jewish Scripture) and contoured in the book of Isaiah. Following up on its result, the present chapter will pose an important question in this study, How does the Jewish Christian Paul read and utilize this Isaianic vision in his letter? Several things are considered to answer this question.

First of all, besides in Paul's letters, the use of Isaiah 45:23 is attested in two documents of the Second Temple literature. The first is a Qumran writing labeled as 4Q215a – Time of Righteousness. The second is a Jewish Synagogue prayer known as the Aleinu prayer.[1] These documents provide us with windows to the interpretation of the vision in the Second Temple era, and thus it will flesh out insights on how Paul's contemporaries had read and utilized the vision.[2] We are obligated, therefore, to analyze the vision in these two literary contexts.

Paul's use of Isaiah 45:23 is noted not only in Philippians 2:10–11 but also in Romans 14:11. Analyzing Paul's treatment of the Isaianic vision in Romans, therefore, will help us to profile his use of the vision in Philippians.

---

1. We also note that the citation of Isaiah 45:23 also appears in another ancient Jewish prayer known as *Nishmat Kol Hai* (נשמת כל הי). The prayer is attested in Talmud (*Pesharim* 118a) as *Birkat ha-Shir*, and recited as a thanksgiving song for rainfall in *Berakot* 59b. Although the prayer has existed since the first century AD, the section that cites Isaiah 45:23 is largely regarded as a later expansion from the late first millennium AD. For this reason, this prayer will not be discussed in the present study. See the discussion of this prayer in Posner, Kaploun, and Cohen, *Jewish Liturgy*, 134.

2. Indeed, an excellent comparative study between the use of Isaiah in Qumran writings and the one in Paul's letter to the Romans has been made in Shum, *Paul's Use of Isaiah*.

In doing so, we note that Paul's use of Isaiah has been a subject of interest in current biblical studies.[3] In an engagement with them, we will briefly draw the approach in reading Paul's use of Isaiah 45:23 in Romans.

Like many other pious Jews in the Second Temple era, these three interpreters of this Isaianic vision generally shared the same eschatological conviction: in the eschaton, YHWH will reign powerfully on earth to demonstrate his covenant faithfulness to Israel, and on that day all nations will submissively worship him as their only God and Savior. This justifies the present chapter to apply the same eschatological framework developed in the previous chapter in reading those texts. With all this in mind, we shall now discuss the reception of Isaiah in these three Second Temple documents

3.1 The Use of Isaiah 45:23 in 4Q215A – Time of Righteousness

The book of Isaiah enjoys great popularity in the Qumran community. There are twenty-two manuscripts of Isaiah in its library of which two are well preserved (1QIsa[a] and 1QIsa[b]), 6 *pesharim* (commentaries) of Isaiah, and a large number of Isaianic quotations, citations, and allusion in its non-biblical writings.[4] The study on the use of Isaiah in these writings reveals that the book greatly contributes to the shaping of the theology and the self-understanding of this sectarian community.[5] From this library's collection, close attention is given to one non-biblical writing that utilizes Isaiah 45:23. The manuscript is formerly identified as part of 4Q215 (Testament of Naphtali) but now is perceived as an independent document labeled as 4Q215a (Time of Righteousness). The document is predicted to be written or copied in 30 BC – AD 20.[6]

Before analyzing the motif of the eschatological worship of YHWH in this text, several aspects relating to the condition of the document need to be

---

3. Wagner, *Heralds of the Good News*; Shum, *Paul's Use of Isaiah*; Hays, *Conversion of the Imagination*, 25–49; Stanley, *Arguing with Scripture*; Moyise, *Paul and Scripture*, 73–96; Wilk, "Isaiah in 1 and 2 Corinthians," 133–58.

4. See Flint, "Interpretation of Scriptural Isaiah," 389–406. Wise, Abegg, and Cook, *Dead Sea Scrolls*, 656–57.

5. Blenkinsopp, *Opening the Sealed Book*, 92–93; Shum, *Paul's Use of Isaiah*, 102.

6. This estimation is based on the orthographical and morphological analysis of the document. Chazon and Stone, "215a. 4QTime of Righteousness," 173.

noted. First, the scroll is estimated to be more than four meters in length, but it is now extant only in six small fragments, of which only about 180 words can be restored.[7] The second column in fragment 1ii, which contains the allusion to Isaiah 45:23, is the largest and most readable. Hence, the discussion on the reception of this Isaianic vision is subjected to this physical limitation. Second, although no conclusive decision is made on the genre of this document due to its poor preservation,[8] the surviving fragments attest to a strong poetic character[9] and eschatological overtones.[10] Finally, the origin of this document is still debated (i.e. whether it is sectarian writing in the late first century BC or pre-sectarian writing at the beginning of the second century BC).[11] The survived manuscript (frag. 1ii) notably shares many expressions that can be associated with sectarian writing,[12] but it also lacks what scholars define as sectarian ideology.[13] Despite the disagreement, the fact that the document was preserved in the *yahad*'s library indicates that the document is not only the earlier product of this community but also its theology still befits the sectarian mindset.

Taking all this into consideration, we will read this fragment of 4Q215a from the perspective of what we know of the *yahad* community. With all this in mind, we now examine the motif of the eschatological worship of YHWH in this text. For analysis, we provide the English translation of 4Q215a frg. 1ii adopted from Torleif Elgvin and Årstein Justnes:[14]

---

7. Chazon and Stone, "215a. 4QTime of Righteousness," 174–75.

8. For a poetic eschatological writing, see Chazon and Stone, "215a. 4QTime of Righteousness," 174. For a Sapiential Apocalyptic writing, see Elgvin and Schuller, "Wisdom With or Without," 18–19.

9. There are numerous synonymous parallelisms (see lines 6–7 and 7–8).

10. Fragment 1 narrates the termination of the era of wickedness and the dawn of the glorious eschatological age.

11. For a sectarian writing, see Abegg, "Time of Righteousness," 1–12. For a non-sectarian writing, see Elgvin, "Eschatological Hope," 89–102; Justnes, "4Q215A," 141–61.

12. Such as the elect of righteousness (line 3), the period of wickedness (line 5), the service/worship of righteousness (line 9). See Abegg, "Time of Righteousness," 6–7.

13. Such as exclusivism and the language of war.

14. Elgvin and Justnes, "Appendix," 166. The emphasis is added.

Line	Translation
1	…] their splendor […
2	] human heart. And also their work [
3	and dread for (the) oppressor and trial of (the) pit. And they shall be refined by them to become the elect of righteousness and he will wipe out all their sins
4	because of his loving-kindness. For the period of wickedness has been completed and all injustice will […. For]
5	the time of righteousness has come, and the land will be full of knowledge and glorification of God in [his] be[auty. For]
6	the age of peace has come and the laws of truth and the testimony of justice to instruct [every mortal]
7	in the ways of God [and] in the mighty acts of his deeds [and in his knowledge] forever. *Every ton[gue]*
8	*will bless him and every mortal will bow down to him* [and they will be] of on[e mi]nd. For he [knew][15]
9	their work before they were created, and he assigned the service of righteousness as their borders [
10	in their generations. For the dominion of good has come and he has raised up the throne of [righteousness]
11	and is highly exalted. Insight, prudence and sound wisdom are tested by [his] holy pl[a]n.

3.1.1 The Universal Eschatological Worship of the God of Israel

The motif of the universal eschatological worship of God, which echoes the Hebrew Isaiah 45:23, is found in lines 7–8. This has been strongly argued by Årstein Justnes in his presentation of 4Q215a.[16] Having said this, since it is still less appreciated, it is necessary here to establish the intertextual connection between the two texts. First of all, the expression of worship closely

---

15. Or "determined / prepared / established."
16. See Justnes, *Time of Salvation*, 288, 345–46.

resembles that in Isaiah 45:23. The expressions כול לשון and כול אנש notably parallel that in the Isaianic vision, although in reverse order:

1QIsaᵃ 45:23:	לי תכנרע כול ברד	A: to me *every knee* shall bow down
	ותשבע כול לשון	B: *every tongue* shall swear
4Q215a frg. 1ii 7–8:	כול לש[ון] תברכנו	B: *every tongue*[17] shall bless him
	וכול אנש ישתחוו לו	A: *every human* shall bow own to him

There are some, but insignificant, differences between the two passages: (1) while Isaiah 45:23 has ברך (knee), 4Q215a has אנש (human being); (2) while Isaiah has כרע (in *qal* stem), 4Q215a has הוה (in *hishtaphel* stem), both carry the same idea of "to bow down"; (3) while Isaiah has שבע (to swear), 4Q215a has ברך (to bless) that carries a stronger religious nuance (cf. ἐξομολογέω in the LXX);[18] and (4) while Isaiah has the pronominal suffixed preposition לי (to me) and 4Q215a has suffixed preposition לו (to him), both refer to YHWH, the God of Israel.

Second, the case for detecting an allusion to Isaiah 45:23 is supported by numerous allusions to the Isaianic texts in this short fragment. The clause "the land will be full of knowledge and glorification of God" (line 5) alludes to Isaiah 11:9. The clause "He has raised up the throne of […]" alludes to Isaiah 52:13.[19] The verb "has come" (בא; lines 5, 6, dan 10) recalls the advent language in Isaiah 60:1 and 62:11.[20]

Finally, there is a strong thematic link between them. Both are primarily concerned with the coming era of the righteousness of God (line 5; cf. Isa 45:8, 23–24), and his salvation (lines 5–6, 10; cf. Isaiah 45:8, 21–22) in which the universal reign of God (line 5–7, 10–11; cf. Isa 45) and the universal worship of him (lines 7–8; cf. Isa 45:23–24) are in focus. All this strongly suggests that this fragment of 4Q215a appeals to Isaiah in portraying the eschatological

---

17. The corrupted word לש[.] in line 7 is constructed as לש[ון] (tongue). See Elgvin and Justnes, "Appendix," 164, in the note of line 7.

18. Justnes, *Time of Salvation*, 322.

19. Justnes, 332.

20. Justnes, "4Q215A," 114–15; Chazon, Parry, and Ulrich, "Case of Mistaken Identity," 113–14.

age of salvation in general, and to Isaiah 45:23 to picture the universal worship of God in particular.

The homage (lines 7–8) should be construed as worship, as the use of the verb "to bless" (ברך) conveys a strong religious nuance. The word אל (line 5) must be referring to the covenant God of Israel. The phrase "every human being" (וכול אנש) and "every tongue" (כול לש[ון]) indicates the participation of all humankind in this worship. This universal thrust is also affirmed by the global acceptance of God's knowledge, laws, and ways of life in this eschatological age (lines 5–7). The theological justification of this universal worship is grounded in the monotheistic conviction expressed by a creation motif: "for he […] their work before he created them" (lines 8–9). Whether the lacuna is filled with he prepared (הכין) or "he knew" (ידע),[21] God is still depicted as the creator who controlled the whole universe.

This fragment of 4Q215a celebrates the termination of the era of wickedness and the dawn of the time of righteousness. Its eschatological scheme can be described as follows: (1) the present era of wickedness (lines 2–3) is to be followed by (2) the eradication of this wicked era (line 4), and then (3) the dawn of "the time of righteousness" (עת הצדק), which is also labeled "the age of peace" (קץ השלום) and "the dominion of good" (ממשל הצדק). It may be argued that this eschatological scheme is Isaianic. The eradication of wickedness (line 4) is parallel to the judgment in Isaiah 66:15–17 and the time of righteousness (lines 5–11) to the new creation motif in Isaiah 65:17–25 and 66:22–23.[22]

The universal eschatological worship of God will occur in the eschatological era of salvation. In this respect, the context of worship has been shifted from the events surrounding the rise of Cyrus to the conclusive eschaton. Such an eschatological reading can be justified by connecting the vision in Isaiah 45:23 with the grand eschatological vision in 66:22–24. For many Jews

---

21. The former has a stronger deterministic outlook. See Chazon, Parry, and Ulrich, "Case of Mistaken Identity," 119–20.

22. This scheme is also parallel to those in Zech 14, 1Q27, 4Q475, and 1 En. 10–11. The last needs a further clarification. 1 En. 10–11 shares many similar expressions (see Chazon, Parry, and Ulrich, 121–22) and the same eschatological scheme with 4Q215a (see Justnes, *Time of Salvation*, 369–72). However, this does not necessarily indicate the dependency of 4Q215a to the Book of Watchers. The eschatological scheme in the latter is derived from the Noachic account, as the *Urzeit* in Genesis 6–9 becomes the *Endzeit* paradigm in 1 Enoch 1–11. This *Urzeit-Endzeit* scheme is not detected in 4Q215a.

in the Second Temple era, the Isaianic visions of worship have yet to be fully realized, and thus its fulfillment is still awaited. Such a hermeneutic of Isaiah is reflected in the Qumran *Pesharim*[23] on Isaiah (4Q161–5).[24]

One difficulty with regarding this document as a product of the Qumran community is the universal notion of the worship of God in this fragment, as it seemingly stands against the *yahad*'s exclusivism. The sectaries saw themselves as the only true faithful Israel worthy to be saved at the eschaton, and all the rest of Israel and gentile nations as those to be condemned and destroyed in the eschaton (see IQS, 4QD, 1QM).[25] The fact that the document is deposited within the Qumran library indicates some variants of thoughts within their eschatological conviction.[26] The sectaries could read the universal worship of God in 4Q215a alongside with 1QM12:13–16, which is also inspired by the book of Isaiah (60:10–14):

> . . . O Zion, rejoice greatly and shine with joyful songs, O Jerusalem. Rejoice, all you cities of Judah, open your gate[s] forever. *That the wealth of the nations might be brought to you, and their kings might serve you. All those who oppressed you shall bow down to you, and the dust [of your feet they shall lick.* O daughter]s of my people, shout out with a voice of joy, adorn yourselves with ornaments of glory. Rule over the ki[ngdom of the...,] [... and I]srael to reign eternally [...][27]

The worshippers of God from the gentile nations, hence, were perceived as those serving the nation Israel with great humiliation.

3.1.2 The Eschatological Reign and Salvation of God

In 4Q215a, the universal worship will take place in the context of the establishment of God's eschatological kingship over the whole world, which is expressed through his judgment and salvation. The former is noted in lines 4: "for the period of wickedness has been completed and all injustice

---

23. See Jassen, "Survival at the End," 193–210, particularly p. 193.

24. See Flint, "Interpreting the Poetry," 161–96.

25. Vermes, *Complete Dead Sea Scrolls*, 68–69.

26. Collins, "Expectation of the End," 79–81.

27. The translation is taken from Wise, Abegg, and Cook, *Dead Sea Scrolls*, 159.

will [...]."[28] The latter, the main focus in this fragment, is conveyed by the terms "the time of righteousness" (line 5), "the age of peace" (line 6), and "the dominion of good" (line 10),[29] and the use of the advent language "has come" (בא/באה) that recalls the Isaianic language of YHWH's promise to bring salvation to his people:[30]

Isaiah 60:1	קומי אורי כי **בא** אורך
	Arise, shine, for your light *has come*
Isaiah 62:11	אמרו לבת־ציון הנה ישעך **בא**
	Say to the daughter of Zion "Behold, your salvation *has come* . . ."

The repeated use of באה/בא (lines 5, 6, 10) intensifies the eschatological nuance of the passage. In all, the text celebrates the coming of the new age, where the God of Israel will reign powerfully to eradicate all wickedness and inaugurate the age of righteousness.

This picture of salvation speaks loudly to the *yahad* community in the first century BC who strongly believed that they were living in or near the eschaton. To them, YHWH was now actively refining his faithful people, and would soon terminate all wickedness and injustice on earth through his eschatological war to usher the new era of salvation.[31] Hence, this oracle calls them, the faithful and righteous remnants of Israel, to look forward to the renewal of the earth.

The establishment of God's earthly kingship is also supported by the throne motif. Unfortunately, there is a lacuna in the phrase כסא [...]ה (line 10) that has created a debate over its precise reading. This concerns whether the phrase כסא [...]ה should be construed as "the throne of God" or "the throne of his Messiah."[32] In favor of the first, Justnes argues that כסא [...]ה

---

28. Cf. "and all injustice will come to an end" in 4Q416 frg.1. In the latter text, the judgment motif is predominant. See Justnes, *Time of Salvation*, 309–10.

29. These three names do not refer to three different eschatological periods. Rather, they point to the same eschatological reality. Justnes, *Time of Salvation*, 362.

30. Justnes, "4Q215A," 145.

31. Collins, "Expectation of the End," 79–90.

32. For the throne of God, the phrase is construed as "the throne of glory" (כסא הכבות) or "the throne of righteousness" (כסא הצדק). For the throne of the messiah, the phrase is construed

is most naturally construed as הצדק כסא.[33] This proposal is admittedly compelling, as the term צדק appears four times (three times with the article ה). However, this conjecture is not without any difficulty. First of all, the term "the throne of righteousness" (הצדק כסא) is unparalleled in Jewish writings. Furthermore, the idea that God raises his throne is very rare in ancient Jewish writings.[34] Even if the conjecture is correct, it does not necessarily eliminate its messianic overtone.

In the Jewish biblical worldview, while the heavenly throne is always associated with the throne of God, on earth he shares his throne with his human agent, as his anointed king is given the right to sit on it to rule on his behalf (cf. Ps 110:1). Accordingly, in the Jewish Scripture צדק closely correlates not only with the throne of YHWH, but also the throne of the ideal king of Israel (see Prov 16:12; 25:5). In the context of the Qumran community, several factors connect "the throne of righteousness" with "the throne of the Messiah." First, in 4Q252 – *Commentary on Genesis* 5:2, the Branch of David (cf. Isa 11:1) is referred to as the "Messiah of Righteousness" (הצדק משיח). Second, the statement "he has raised up the throne of [righteousness] and is highly exalted" (lines 10–11) may allude to the exaltation of the servant of YHWH, as this Isaianic figure is also read messianically in 1QIsaᵃ.[35] Finally, the expression "the land will be full of knowledge and praise of God" (line 5) recalls Isaiah 11:9. In the Qumran eschatological hermeneutic, this is strongly associated with the salvific realm ruled by the Messiah of Righteousness. All this shows that the messianic notion in this motif of worship should not be underrated.

3.1.3 The Motif of Holiness

The transformation process is depicted as developing in two phases in 4Q215a. The first phase occurs in the wicked period when the pious are greatly oppressed (line 3). This oppression is depicted as having a sanctifying role. We note that the word יצרופו can be read either as a *qal* imperfect or a *niphal* imperfect of צרף. Accordingly, line 3 can be read in two ways: (1) "and dread for

as "the throne of the kingship" (המלוכה כסא), "the throne of the kingdom" (הממלכה כסא), or "the throne of the Messiah" (המשיח כסא). See the discussion in Justnes, *Time of Salvation*, 332–33.

33. Justnes, *Time of Salvation*, 333–35.

34. The erection of the throne of God in Daniel 7:9 and I Enoch 90:20 is in a passive form. Justnes, *Time of Salvation*, 333.

35. See the discussion in chapter 1.

the oppressor and trial of the pit. And they shall be refined by them to become the elect of righteousness"[36]; or (2) "and dread for the oppressor and trial of the pit. And the elect of righteousness shall be refined by them."[37] In both cases, the transformation motif is apparent, as the suffering has a purifying role. The second phase occurs when the period of wickedness is terminated and the time of righteousness dawns (lines 3–7). When this happens, the full transformation of the earth will be realized (cf. 4Q416 frg.1 lines 11–14).

This Qumran text underlines the social aspect of holiness. "The period of wickedness" (קץ הרשע) is characterized by injustice and oppression. The term רשע denotes the failure to keep social commitments (i.e. transgressions).[38] As its contrast, the coming eschatological age is called "the time of righteousness" (עת הצדק), as in this era, "the laws of truth" (חוקי האמת) and "the testimony of justice" (צדק[ה] ותעודת) will guide the conduct of all humankind "in the way of God" (בדרכי אל). Two things will engender this social transformation. The first is God's eschatological judgment that will wipe out all the wickedness and injustice in the present age (lines 3–4).[39] The second is the instruction that will promote the full knowledge of God (lines 5–7). Although 4Q215a has no instructional statement, the presence of wisdom terminologies[40] indicates that the transformation in the time of righteousness is generated by an extensive instruction of God's laws.[41]

The results of this transformation are that all humankind will live under the way of God (lines 7), and they will worship him wholeheartedly (lines 7–8). The expression "they will be one mind/heart" (ד[בם אח]ויהיה לב [ל]ו) alludes to "I will give them one heart" (ונתתילהם לב אחד) in Jeremiah 32:39 and Ezekiel 11:19. In these two biblical passages, "one heart" (לב אחד) speaks of the inner transformation of Israel under the new covenant: from duplicity to the singleness of mind in worshipping YHWH. In 4Q215a, this inner transformation is applied to all humankind.

---

36. See Vermes, *Complete Dead Sea Scrolls*, 410; Elgvin and Justnes, "Appendix," 166.

37. Chazon and Stone, "215a. 4QTime of Righteousness," 180.

38. Goldingay, *Psalms Volume 2*, 698.

39. The judgment motif is briefly noted in lines 3–4. See Hempel, "Gems of DJD 36," 148–49.

40. Such as knowledge (שכל; line 7), to instruct (להשכיל; line 6), the way of God (דרכע אל; line 7), prudence (ערמה; line 11), insight (תושיה; line 11), and plan (מחשבה; line 11).

41. For the significance of Sapiential terminology in 4Q215a, see Elgvin and Schuller, "Wisdom With or Without," 31.

3.1.4 The Covenant Notion

Like many other religious groups in the Second Temple era, the idea of Israel's covenant with YHWH is foundational to the identity of the Qumran community. They saw themselves as the community of the renewed covenant. This self-understanding is reflected in numerous documents produced by the community (1QS, 1QSa, 4QD, 1QpHab, and 1QM) that frequently use the terms "covenant" and/or "(re)new(ed) covenant." Because of their faithfulness, God sent the teacher of righteousness to establish for them a "new covenant" in fulfillment of his promise in Jeremiah 31:31–33.[42]

From the perspective above, we are assured that although the term covenant does not occur in this very short fragment of 4Q215a, the idea is present. This assumption is supported by the presence of some expressions conceived with a strong covenant notion. It has been noted above that the expression "they will be one mind/heart" in line 8 has a covenant notion. In addition to this, the term "loving-kindness" (חסד) in line 4 also recalls YHWH's covenant faithfulness to Israel in the biblical writings. Finally, while the phrase "the time of righteousness" (עת הצדק) in line 5 stands in opposition to the current time of wickedness and injustice, it is also closely associated with the eschatological era where YHWH will act righteously to save Israel on account of his covenant with the nation. Such conviction is strongly voiced in Isaiah 40–55 and attested in numerous Qumran texts.[43]

What scholars have noted in the *yahad*'s ideology is the exclusive notion of YHWH's covenant with them. They claimed that they were the only true remnant of Israel, or the only group within Israel, who were faithfully keeping the covenant.[44] This certainly moves in the opposite direction from the covenant outlook in the book of Isaiah that celebrates the extension of YHWH's covenant to other nations. Although the tension is felt, and it gives a signal to us that hope for other nations does not totally disappear within the *yahad*'s eschatological matrix.

---

42. Vermes, *Complete Dead Sea Scrolls*, 68–69.

43. Such as in 1QS 11:3–15; 1QH 4:37; 7:29–31; 9:34; 11:29–31; 16:9. See the discussion in Pate, *Communities of the Last Days*, 157–60.

44. Scott, "Covenant," 493; Vermes, *Complete Dead Sea Scrolls*, 70–71.

3.1.5 Synthesis

In Qumran writings, the use of Isaiah 45:23 is noted in 4Q215a – Time of Righteousness, which was produced in the first century BC. The surviving document (frag. 1ii) contains many terminologies closely associated with the *yahad*'s writings and ambiguously reveals the sectarian ideology. The document shares with other Jewish groups in the Second Temple period a similar eschatological conviction that in the eschaton the covenant God of Israel will be worshipped by all Israel and other nations.[45] While the eschatological picture of worship in 4Q215a seemingly stands in opposition to the *yahad*'s exclusivist ideology, the hope can still be read alongside other Qumran writings that contain stronger sectarian outlooks. The universal worship of YHWH in this fragment, which is inspired by Isaiah 45:23, is seen as the focal point in the coming eschaton where the God of Israel will purify the righteous *yahad*, terminate all of the wicked of the earth through his eschatological war, and transform all humankind by his laws to bring his eschatological realm of righteousness and peace on earth. In all, the universal worship of God in 4Q215a indicates a dynamic within the Qumran community in perceiving their covenant relationship with God of Israel who is also the God of all nations. While the eschatology in Qumran writings is predominantly shaped by the *yahad*'s exclusive ideology, it has not prevailed the universal dimension of Israel's covenant identity and eschatological hope.

3.2 The Use of Isaiah 45:23 in the Aleinu Prayer

The use of Isaiah 45:23 is also found in one ancient Jewish synagogue prayer famously known as the Aleinu prayer. Its existence can be traced back to the Amidah (the Standing Prayers) of Rosh Hashanah service by Rav (Abba Arika) in the third century AD.[46] Whether he composed this prayer or utilized an existing prayer at his disposal, however, cannot be confirmed. We note that some scholars argue that the original expression of "*to perfect* [לתקן] the world under God's sovereignty" in the second part of the prayer is "*to establish*

---

45. Such a voice is noted in Tob 13:11; 14:6 *OG*ᴵᴵ; Ps. Sol. 17:29–32; Sib. Or. 3:716–723, 772–775; the Animal Apocalypse (1 En. 90:29–33), the Book of Watchers (1 En. 10:21–22), the Parables of Enoch (1 En. 48:5; 61:8–9; 62:9).

46. Di Sante, *Jewish Prayer*, 173.

[לתכן] the world under God's sovereignty," and thus it utters the yearning for rebuilding the Jerusalem Temple. This would support a post-AD 70 dating.[47] Having said this, the mention of the acts of bowing and kneeling and the absence of yearning for the restoration of the Jerusalem Temple strongly suggest a pre-AD 70 composition.[48] If this conjecture is correct, it opens a possibility to read this ancient prayer in conjunction with the Amidah. These ancient Jewish benedictions are also traced back to the Second Temple period, and thus both the Aleinu prayer and the Amidah could be uttered together by the worshippers in the temple and synagogue services at that time.[49]

The Aleinu prayer consists of two main parts. The first develops the theme of the election of Israel, which underscores several points: (1) YHWH as the only God and King of the whole universe; (2) Israel's covenantal identity as YHWH's chosen people among all nations; and (3) Israel's covenantal duty to worship God exclusively. The second section that cites Isaiah 45:23 calls YHWH to expedite the establishment of his universal dominion on earth. For our analysis the English translation of this prayer is used:[50]

Section I:

"It is our duty" (עלינו) to praise the Master of all, to exalt the Creator of the universe, who has not made us like the nations of the world and has not placed us like the families of the earth; who has not designed our destiny to be like theirs, nor our lot like that of all their multitude. [For they worship vanity and emptiness, and pray to a god who cannot save][51] We bend the knee and bow and acknowledge before the supreme King of kings, the Holy One, blessed be He, that it is he who stretched forth the heavens and founded the earth. His seat of glory is in the heavens above; his abode of majesty is in the lofty heights. He is our God, there is none else; truly, he is our King, there is

---

47. First, "Aleinu," 187–97.

48. Posner, Kaploun, and Cohen, *Jewish Liturgy*, 109.

49. Skarsaune, *In the Shadow*, 124–25.

50. Cited from Birnbaum, *Daily Prayer Book*, 136–38. Emphasis and the Hebrew words are added.

51. This part was censored since the Middle Ages because it gave a great offence to Christianity. It notably alludes to Isaiah 30:7 (vanity and emptiness) and 45:20 (pray to a god that cannot save). See Posner, Kaploun, and Cohen, *Jewish Liturgy*, 109–10.

none besides him, as it is written in his Torah: "You shall know this day, and reflect in your heart, that it is the Lord who is God in the heavens above and on the earth beneath, there is none else" (Deut 4:39).

Section II:

We hope, therefore, Lord our God, soon to behold thy majestic glory, when the abominations shall be removed from the earth, and the false gods exterminated; when the world shall be perfected (or established) under the reign of the Almighty, and all mankind will call upon thy name, and all the wicked of the earth will be turned to thee. May all the inhabitants of the world realize and know that to "thee every knee must bend, every tongue must vow allegiance" (כי לך תברע כל ברך תשבע כל לשון). May they bend the knee and prostrate themselves before thee, Lord our God, and give honor to thy glorious name; may they all accept the yoke of thy kingdom, and do thou reign over them speedily forever and ever. For the kingdom is Thine and to all eternity thou wilt reign in glory, as it is written in thy Torah: "The Lord shall be King forever and ever" (Exod 15:18). And it is said: "The Lord shall be King over all the earth; on that day the Lord shall be One, and His name One" (Zech 14:9).

3.2.1 The Universal Worship of God

The use of Isaiah 45:23 is easily detected in the second section because it appears as an almost verbatim citation:

Isaiah 45:23 MT	כי־לי תברע כל־ברך תשבע כל־לשון
The Aleinu Prayer	כי לך תברע כל ברך תשבע כל לשון

The only difference between the two is that while Isaiah 45:23 has "to me" (לי), the Aleinu has "to you" (לך) for contextual adjustment. In Isaiah 45:23, the vision is uttered by YHWH, while in the Aleinu, the vision is uttered by the worshippers as part of their devotional prayer to him.

Similar to the case in Isaiah 45, this homage is understood as both worship and submission. The former is supported by various worship expressions,[52] some monotheistic statements,[53] and the presence of the idol worship polemic in the prayer. The statement "for they worship vanity and emptiness, and pray to a god who cannot save," which alludes to Isaiah 30:7 and 45:20, certainly gives stronger its polemical tone. The latter is supported by the acknowledgment that YHWH as their king (אמת מלכנו אפס זולתו) is the supreme King of kings (לפני מלך מלכי תמלכים). This is further affirmed by the citations of Exodus 15:18 and Zechariah 14:9 that claim YHWH as the King over the whole world forever.

The worship of YHWH in the second section of the Aleinu prayer has universal thurst. As it is the case in the Isaianic vision, both "all knees" (כל ברך) and "all tongues" (כל לשון) in this prayer have universal overtones. This is strengthened by the earlier expressions, such as "all mankind" (וכל בני בשר) will call upon your name; "all the wicked of the earth" (כל רשעי ארץ) will be turned to you; and "all the inhabitants of the world" (כל יושי תבל) will realize and know.

3.2.2 The Eschatological Reign of YHWH

There are two reasons provided for this universal eschatological worship. The first reason, which is provided in the first section of the Aleinu prayer, is certainly theological. YHWH is the creator of the whole universe and the King of all kings, and therefore all nations shall worship him alone. The second reason has an eschatological dimension. The worship is a proper response to the establishment of YHWH's eschatological reign on earth. This is notably expounded in the second section of the Aleinu prayer. It starts with the eschatological expectation of the Jewish worshippers: "soon to behold thy majestic glory, when . . . the world shall be perfected [or established] under the reign of the Almighty. . . ." After this, the prayer runs with the catena of scriptural passages (Isa 45:23, Exod 15:18, and Zech 14:9) that not only brings the prayer to a climax but also utters the eschatological hope: YHWH's kingship will be

---

52. Such as "to bend," "to bow," "to prostrate," "to praise," "to exalt," "to acknowledge," and "to give honor."

53. Such as "the creator of universe," "he is our God," and "there is none else" (הוא אלהינו אין עוד; cf. Isaiah 45:22).

fully realized on earth in the age to come. The imminent force of this hope is articulated by the adverbial particle מהרה (quickly) at the beginning of the second section. In this perspective, the worship of YHWH expresses the submission to his eschatological reign. The readiness of all nations to accept the yoke of his kingdom affirms further this eschatological thrust.

The eschatological scheme in the Aleinu prayer is parallel with that in 4Q215a:

4Q215a	The Aleinu prayer (the second part)
The termination of the period of wickedness (line 4)	when the abominations shall be removed from the earth, and the false gods exterminated
Lines 5–11: the eschatological age of righteousness, peace, and good	when the world shall be perfected (or established) under the reign of the Almighty
Lines 7–8: the universal worship of YHWH (כול לש[ון] תברכנו וכול אנש ישתחוו לו) (an allusion to Isa 45:23)	all mankind will call upon thy name, and all the wicked of the earth will be turned to thee. May all the inhabitants of the world realize and know that כי לך תברע כל ברך תשבע כל לשהן (citing Isa 45:23).

As it is the case in 4Q215a, the universal worship of YHWH in this prayer is transported from the historical context of the rise of Cyrus's imperial hegemony to the age to come where a conclusive transformation of the whole earth will occur.

How this eschatological realm will be historically realized, however, is not stated, as there is no mention of any human agent to carry out the divine eschatological blueprint in the prayer. Having said this, it is worth noting that the Aleinu prayer was included in the *Rosh Hashanah Mussaf* (the Jewish New Year Liturgy) by Rav, as a prologue to "the kingship of God" portion of the Amidah. This indicates the closeness of this prayer with these eighteen Benedictions composed in the Second Temple period.[54] Although the

---

54. Posner, Kaploun, and Cohen, *Jewish Liturgy*, 81.

present forms have experienced some editorial works, the basic themes of these benedictions presumably remain unchanged. Hence, there is a thematic relationship between the two. The Aleinu calls the God of Israel to speed up the establishment of his earthly kingship so that all humankind will worship him alone. The Amidah elaborates this eschatological hope by entreating God to rebuild the city of Jerusalem, establish the Davidic kingdom, reinstate the right worship in the Jerusalem Temple, and return his presence to his holy city in the fourteenth, fifteenth, and seventeenth Blessings.

3.2.3 The Motif of Holiness

In the Aleinu prayer, the holiness motif stresses the aspects of both worship and moral conduct. Concerning the former, the duty to worship YHWH is contrasted with the idol worship of the gentile nations. This polemic is noted in the statement "for they worship vanity and emptiness, and pray to a god who cannot save" that alludes to Isaiah 30:7 and 45:20. While the devotees presently struggled with the idolatry of many nations, it is expected that when YHWH's earthly reign is fully established, the false worship (העביר) and its idols (האלילים) will be totally eradicated. This is boldly claimed in the second part of the prayer:

להעביר גלולים מן הארץ	when *the abominations* shall be removed from the earth,
והאלילים ברות יברתון	and *the false gods* exterminated

Together with the eschatological expectation that one day all humankind will realize their duty to worship the only true God, it conveys the idea of conversion.

Concerning the latter, the second part depicts "the repentance of the wicked of the earth" (להפנית אליך כל רשעי ארץ). The term רשע denotes the failure to keep the commitment to God and other people. The phrase "all the wicked of the land" (כל רשעי ארץ) occurs three times in the biblical Psalms (75:8; 101:8; 119:119) and they all refer to those failing to live according to the ethical standards set in Torah.[55] In this light, this clause speaks of the transformation of the moral conduct of YHWH's worshippers.

3.2.4 The Covenant Notion

Although the term covenant does not appear in the Aleinu prayer, the Jewish people who utter this prayer will not miss its covenant framework, as the duty to worship YHWH is grounded deeply in Israel's covenant identity as YHWH's special people. This is adumbrated at the beginning of the prayer:

> "It is our duty" (עלינו) to praise the Master of all, to exalt the Creator of the universe, who has not made us like the nations of the world and has not placed us like the families of the earth; who has not designed our destiny to be like theirs, nor our lot like that of all their multitude . . .

God the Creator has designed and established Israel to be distinct from all other nations with a purpose to worship him alone.

Having said this, like in Isaiah, the nationalism in the Aleinu prayer goes hand in hand with its universal thrust. While the first section of the prayer speaks of Israel's unique position before God set by their covenant relationship, the second section entreats their covenant God to speed up the establishment of his earthly kingship and calls the nation to participate in bringing about the messianic age where all humankind will join them to worship YHWH as the only King of the universe.[56]

3.2.5 Synthesis

The eschatological vision in Isaiah 45:23 is noted in the Aleinu prayer composed in the late Second Temple period. The prayer was likely uttered together with the Amidah by many common Jews in the temple and synagogue services to express their eschatological hope. In this spatial setting, the common pious Jews uttered their great yearning that their covenantal God would speedily establish his earthly dominion, restore the Davidic kingship, rebuild the city of Jerusalem, and perfect the worships in his holy temple. Following this, they greatly expected that all humankind would soon turn away from their idols

---

55. In Psalm 75:8, the phrase כל רשעי ארץ refers to "the proud" (vv. 5–5); in Psalm 101:8, to "all the evil doers in the city" (vv. 7–8); and in Psalm 119:119, to "those who reject God's laws."

56. Hoffman, *Gates of Understanding*, 42.

to the worship of the only true God, and from their evil deeds to the good moral conduct set by his laws. Through this prayer, the Jewish worshippers in the Second Temple era would appreciate their unique covenant identity and their mission to bring about this eschatological age of salvation.

We have discussed two receptions of Isaiah 45:23 in the Second Temple period outside the Christian circle. The one in the Aleinu prayer reflects a more general Jewish reading of the vision, as the prayer had been adopted in the Jerusalem Temple and many synagogues worship in this era. The one in the 4Q215a reveals a more sectarian thought, as the document is one of the collections in the sectarian library and befits with *yahad*'s worldview. They both demonstrate that Jewish people in the Second Temple era indeed perceived the universal worship of YHWH in Isaiah 45:23 as an eschatological vision to be fulfilled. Their reading of this Isaianic vision certainly provides some important insights for the understanding of Paul's use of the vision. With all this in mind, our discussion now moves to Paul's reading of Isaiah 45:23, particularly in his letter to the Romans.

3.3 The Use of Isaiah 45:23 in Romans 14:11

Paul's reading of the Old Testament has been a major interest in the study of Paul in the last few decades.[57] The discussion includes the way he exploits the book of Isaiah in his letter to the Romans.[58] His use of Isaiah in this letter is notably extensive,[59] and it contributes to the contour of its message and theology.[60] Since the presupposition on how Paul utilizes Isaiah will shape the reading of Roman 14:11, where Isaiah 45:23 is cited, we shall lineout our interpretative framework on Paul's in this study.

---

57. Hays, *Echoes of Scripture*; Hays, *Conversion of the Imagination*; Moyise, *Paul and Scripture*; Stanley, *Paul and the Language*; Stanley, *Arguing with Scripture*.

58. Wagner, *Heralds of the Good News*; Shum, *Paul's Use of Isaiah in Romans*.

59. In his letter to the Romans, Paul cites sixteen texts of Isaiah (Isa 1:9 in Rom 9:29; Isa 8:14 in Rom 9:33; Isa 10:22–23 in Rom 9:27–28; Isa 11:10 in Rom 15:12; Isa 27:9 in Rom 11:27; Isa 28:16 in Rom 9:33 & 10:11; Isa 29:10 in Rom 11:8; Isa 40:13 in Rom 11:34; Isa 45:23 in Rom 14:11; Isa 52:5 in Rom 2:24; Isa 52:7 in Rom 10:15; Isa 52:15 in Rom 15:21; Isa 53:1 in Rom 10:16; Isa 59:7–8 in Rom 3:15–17; Isa 59:20–21 in Rom 11:26–27; Isa 65:1–2 in Rom 10:20–21). Beside this, scholars have also noted numerous allusion to Isaiah in this letter.

60. Wagner, *Heralds of the Good News*.

The first issue is regarding the Isaianic materials Paul used in composing Romans. First of all, the New Testament writings portray Paul as a diaspora Jew committed to Judaism and trained as a Pharisee before following Christ (Acts 22:3; Gal 1:13–15; Phil 3:4–6). This profile suggests he was familiar with the Old Testament (or the Jewish Scripture) both in Hebrew and Greek language. Having said this, it is generally agreed that Paul employed the Greek Isaiah close to the LXX version in writing his letters to the churches in Rome.[61] Within this consensus, however, scholars still disagree on the matter of whether he quoted Isaiah from memory, the testimony book, or the book itself in composing this letter.[62] The reconstruction that Paul wrote Romans in Corinth and thus he had generous access to the Greek Old Testament during the composition of Romans is admittedly compelling.[63] The complex phenomena of Paul's reading of Isaiah in Romans, however, prevent us to fully commit to this reconstruction. It is more likely that he combined his memory and some Isaianic materials at his disposal in compositing this letter.[64]

The second is regarding the way Paul used Isaiah in Romans. As J. Ross Wagner's study has demonstrated, Paul has an Isaianic narrative framework in mind in exploiting the significances of various Isaianic passages in this letter.[65] This framework is notably eschatological. To Paul, Isaiah, first of all, prefigures both his end-time mission to share the gospel of Christ to the Gentiles and Israel's continuous resistance to this gospel. The tension is solved by employing the eschatological narrative of Isaiah to highlight God's faithfulness to Israel that will ensure the salvation of his people. In re-reading Isaiah's eschatological story, he is firmly convinced that both Jews and the Gentiles will one day worshipping YHWH in one voice, and enjoy his salvation.[66]

The third is regarding Paul's reading of Isaiah 45:23. As it has been thoroughly observed in the previous sections that the theme of the universal worship of YHWH is not only dominant in the book of Isaiah but also voiced out in many prophetic writings in the Old Testament. Hence, in reading this Isaianic vision, the Second Temple readers, including Paul, would have a

---

61. Wagner, 5–8.
62. Wagner, 19–28.
63. Shum, *Paul's Use of Isaiah in Romans*, 175–76.
64. Wagner, *Heralds of the Good News*.
65. Wagner, 353–54.
66. Wagner, 41.

general frame of mind regarding the universal worship of YHWH shaped by the dominant picture of the biblical prophetic writings and traditions. Kent L. Yinger, in his study on the motif of divine judgment according to deeds, correctly concludes as follows:

> This increases the probability that NT authors, when employing the motif of divine judgment (or recompense) according to deeds, are not citing or alluding to specific Scripture passages, but are drawing upon this common body of fundamental theological conviction.[67]

The same line of thought can be established in the case of Paul's reading of the vision of the universal worship of YHWH in Isaiah 45:23. Paul certainly cites this Isainic vision, and thus his way of reading the Isaianic eschatological narrative needs to be considered seriously. Having said this, the fact that this theme of worship is also spread across the Old Testament and the Second Temple writings, we also need to seriously consider that Paul is also influenced by the dominant or common perception of this eschatological theme.

The fourth is regarding Paul's rhetorical aim in using Isaiah. Romans 1:8–15 and 15:22–33 inform us that Paul's purposes to visit the churches of Rome are to proclaim the gospel among them and to establish his missionary base for reaching out to the western Roman Empire for Christ. Hence, his letter to the Romans is not merely an introductory letter. It notably serves to declare the content of his gospel of Christ, including its theological rationale, and to prepare the churches in Rome for his missionary plan. Paul must see the Isaianic materials as befitting these two rhetorical purposes so he employs them extensively in this letter.[68]

---

67. Yinger, *Paul, Judaism, and Judgment*, 283.

68. Some are doubted on the capability of the readers to appreciate his use of Isaiah in the way the modern scholars have described due to in-availability of the Greek Isaiah in the congregation and the low level of literacy of the readers. See Stanley, *Arguing with Scripture*, 38–61, 169–70. While their voices need to be considered, this study assumes that the Romans readers had enough capability to appreciate Paul's use of Isaiah. The list of the church members in Romans 16 notably includes some figures having capability to access to the Greek Isaiah scrolls, and having a high level of literacy in the Old Testament (like Priscila and Aquila). Moreover, the letter was originally intended to be read and discussed in a communal setting where those who possessed good level of literacy in the Jewish scripture could contribute to the interpretation of the letter including Paul's use of Isaiah. Finally, the scroll letter of Romans was likely delivered to the Roman churches by a carrier who was not only known to the church's leaders there, but also served as Paul's representative who had capability to clarify Paul's reading

With this framework, we now establish the context of the discourse of Roman 14:1–15:13 where the citation of Isaiah 45:23 LXX occurs. This discourse deals with the internal conflict of the Roman congregation. The conflict was generated by the existence of two different mindsets concerning discipleship exercised in the Roman churches. The Jewish Christians, whom Paul referred to as "the weak," asserted that the church should observe these Mosaic regulations. In contrast, the gentile converts, whom he labeled as "the strong," emphasized their freedom from observing Jewish dietary laws and Sabbath.[69] The conflict must be substantial that Paul who never visited Rome felt a need to intervene. Certainly, as Paul planned to establish the churches there as his missionary base for reaching out to the west of Rome (15:22–24), he was concerned with their internal disunity.

In response to the conflicting situation, he maintains that the two sets of convictions are acceptable before God, then calls the two groups to refrain from judging, but to welcome and build up each other (14:4; 15:1–2, 7). The aim of his instructions is that the readers will be able to worship God together in unity (15:6). To support this paraenesis, Paul reminds them that the Lord alone is the rightful judge in Romans 14:4, then cites Isaiah 45:23 LXX as its biblical warrant that all shall provide their account before God during the universal eschatological worship of him (14:10–12).[70] The practical implication is clear that neither the strong nor the weak has a right to judge the other (14:4, 13; 15:1).

---

of Isaiah, if it is needed. Romans 16:1–2 mentions the name Phoebe, a rich female Christian who served as deacon of the church in Cenchreae (a port city nearby Corinth) and a patron of many Christians in this city, including Paul himself. It is likely she is the bearer of this scroll letter, as Paul commended the Roman churches to welcome her. See Grieb, *Story of Romans*, 144.

69. The identification of the "weak" (and thus the "strong") in Romans 14:1–15:13 is still debated. Various interpretations are proposed: (1) the "weak" were the gentile Christians who abstained from meat under the influence of pagan religions; (2) the "weak" were some Christians who practiced an ascetic life; (3) the "weak" were Christians who observed the Mosaic law in order to gain the righteousness of God (cf. the Galatian Christians); (4) the "weak" were Jewish Christians who followed a sectarian ascetic program to express their piety; (5) the "weak" were Jewish Christians who believed that it was wrong to eat meat sold in the market, as it was tainted by idolatry; (6) the "weak" were the Jewish Christians who refrained from certain kind of food and observed certain days out of their piety and loyalty to the Mosaic law. See the discussion in Moo, *Romans*, 828–29. The present study adopts the last option (6). For the grounds, see the discussion in Moo, *Romans*, 829–33; Cranfield, *Romans*, 690–99.

70. Wagner, *Heralds of the Good News*, 337.

Within this rhetorical context, we now observe some characteristics of Paul's use of Isaiah 45:23 LXX in Romans 14:1–15:13. The biblical citation in 14:11 is notably composite, as the divine oath κατ᾽ ἐμαυτοῦ ὀμνύω in Isaiah 45:23 LXX is now substituted with a more common formula ζῶ ἐγώ λέγει κύριος in Isaiah 49:11 LXX:[71]

Romans 14:11	Isaiah 49:11 LXX
γέγραπται γάρ· ζῶ ἐγώ, λέγει κύριος,	ζῶ ἐγώ λέγει κύριος ὅτι
	Isaiah 45:23 LXX
ὅτι ἐμοὶ κάμψει πᾶν γόνυ καὶ πᾶσα γλῶσσα ἐξομολογήσεται τῷ θεῷ.	(κατ᾽ ἐμαυτοῦ ὀμνύω . . .) ὅτι ἐμοὶ κάμψει πᾶν γόνυ καὶ ἐξομολογήσεται πᾶσα γλῶσσα τῷ θεῷ

3.3.1 The Universal Eschatological Worship

The homage in Romans 14:11 is best understood as an act of worship. First, it is made explicit by the divine oath formula that the worship is offered to God. The pronoun ἐμοί certainly refers back to the divine κύριος. Second, the term ἐξομολογέω can be read in conjunction with the one in Romans 15:9. The latter is a citation from Psalm 17:50 LXX that denotes confessional praise parallel to δοξάζω (to magnify), ψάλλω (to sing), and αἰνέω (to praise) in 15:6–11.[72]

The universal scope of this worship is easily appreciated. In present discourse, Paul deals with the conflict between the Jewish and the Gentile Christians that hinders the Roman congregation to worship God in one voice (15:6). This universal outlook is affirmed by the mission thrust of Christ's redemptive work, which is conveyed by the catena of biblical citations (Pss 17:50, 116:1 LXX; Isa 11:10 LXX) in Romans 15:9–12.[73] To Paul, these biblical visions have been partly realized in the Christian community, where both Jews and Gentiles are worshipping YHWH together.

The universal worship in Romans 14:11 has a strong eschatological thrust. First of all, the worship is situated before "the judgment seat of God" (τὸ βῆμα

---

71. This formula appears twenty-two times in the LXX, and it is comparable to the formula of Israel's oath. See Hays, *Conversion of the Imagination*, 39; Seifrid, "Romans," 685.

72. See Cranfield, *Romans*, 710–11; Dunn, *Romans 9–16*, 809; Moo, *Romans*, 847.

73. In these biblical citations, the term ἔθνος (nation) appears six times.

τοῦ θεοῦ; v. 10) where all shall give their account to God. In the Roman court setting, the term βῆμα denotes "the portable official seat on which the higher Roman officials sat in their function to judge."[74] In Romans 14:10, the term must be a contextual adjustment of the biblical idea of "the throne of God" (see Dan 7:9; 1 En. 47:3), particularly with the aspect of divine judgment at the eschaton.[75] Accordingly, this eschatological worship expresses the total submission of all humankind to the final judgment of God. Second, the participants of this eschatological worship will include both the living and the dead. This is inferred by the lordship of Christ over both of them (14:9). Paul's conviction on the resurrection of the dead at the eschaton certainly contributes to such a reading. Finally, Paul's "now and not yet" eschatological scheme is at work in the depiction of universal worship in Romans 14:1–15:13. Romans 15:6 signals that the vision of the universal worship of God has been partly realized in the Christian church in Rome. Its consummation, however, will only take place when all humankind will stand before the judgment seat of God at the future eschaton (14:10–12).

Comparing the ones in 4Q215 and the Aleinu prayer Paul's treatment of the Isaianic vision of worship reveals some important insights. First of all, while he agrees with those writers in perceiving the homage Isaiah 45:23 as the universal worship of God, his eschatological scheme is somewhat different from theirs. He notably situates the worship on the judgment day itself when all shall stand before the divine court. This is not exclusively Paul's. A similar scheme appears in 1 Enoch 48:5–10 and 62:1–16. We reserve the object of worship for the discussion in the next section. It suffices here to note that in Romans 14:11 Paul implicitly includes Jesus Christ as the object of worship. This phenomenon is certainly not found in the other two writings.

3.3.2 YHWH's Eschatological Reign

The idea of YHWH's eschatological reign is noted by the term ἡ βασιλεία τοῦ θεοῦ in Romans 14:17. The kingdom has been inaugurated through the redemptive work of Jesus the Messiah and experienced by those who are in him. The extension of this kingdom takes place in tandem with the proclamation of his gospel everywhere in the world (1:16–17; 15:15–21). Hence, in this

---

74. Schaller, "Βῆμα," 215–16.

75. Kreitzer, *Jesus and God*, 102–12.

"now and not yet" eschatological framework, the messianic thrust of God's universal kingship in Romans 14:1–15:13 needs to be unpacked.

While Isaiah envisions that YHWH's universal reign would be established through the service of the gentile king Cyrus, in Romans, Paul insists that this eschatological realm can only be realized by the Root of Jesse (15:12; citing Isa 11:10 LXX), who is none other than Jesus Christ who is claimed as David's descendant and the Son of God in power (1:3–4). His use of Χριστός in his letters, including Romans, has a messianic connotation. In the LXX, this term is used to translate the Hebrew word משיח, which is closely associated with YHWH's promised king or priest who will establish his earthly reign in the Second Temple era. Accordingly, the Jewish-Christian Paul must be familiar with the messianic force of Χριστός. To him, Jesus is the long-awaited messianic king (9:5; 15:12) who has brought God's eschatological rule and salvation on earth (1:3–4; 9:4–5; 15:7–12).[76]

In Romans 14 itself, there is a close correlation between the universal worship in verse 11 and the universal lordship of Jesus Christ in verses 7–9. The Christ has died and risen again to rule all, including the living and the dead. It is in submission to Christ's universal reign that YHWH will be worshipped by all at the eschaton. Having said this, the extent to which Paul draws this correlation is debated, as there are some indications that Romans 14:11 includes Jesus Christ as the object of worship. Since this issue has great relevance for the present study, we shall discuss this phenomenon in detail.

In Romans 14:7–12, there is an interplay of the identity of κύριος in (1) the lordship of Christ, (2) the judgment seat of God, and (3) the composite citation of Isaiah 45:23 and 49:18 LXX. First of all, this composite citation makes it explicit that this universal worship is directed to κύριος who is naturally expected to sit on the judgment seat of God. However, to whom this κύριος precisely refers is ambiguous. On the one hand, the biblical divine oath formula of ζῶ ἐγώ λέγει κύριος suggests that the worship is offered to YHWH.[77] On the other hand, in the preceding passage (vv. 4 [2x], 6 [3x], 8 [3x]) the term κύριος consistently and exclusively refers to Christ. With the statement

---

76. See the discussion in Hengel, *Studies in Early Christology*, 1–7; Dunn, *Theology of Paul*, 197–99; Chester, "Christ of Paul," 109–15.

77. Cranfield, *Romans*, 710; Dunn, *Romans 9–16*, 810; Moo, *Romans*, 848.

εἰς τοῦτο γὰρ Χριστὸς ἀπέθανεν καὶ ἔζησεν, ἵνα καὶ νεκρῶν καὶ ζώντων κυριεύσῃ in verse 9, κύριος in verse 11 will logically refer to Christ.[78]

The inference above is confirmed by the fact that in Paul's letters the term τὸ βῆμα τοῦ θεοῦ (14:10) is interchanged with τὸ βῆμα τοῦ Χριστοῦ (2 Cor 5:10). In the Second Temple era, there were indeed notions that YHWH's eschatological judgments will be exercised by his agents.[79] The Christian Paul is convinced that the Messiah Jesus is the one who will carry out this divine eschatological judgment.[80] In Romans 2:16, he has underlined that God will carry out his eschatological judgment διὰ Χριστοῦ Ἰησοῦ,[81] and in 8:34 he claims that Χριστὸς . . . . ἐστιν ἐν δεξιᾷ τοῦ θεοῦ (cf. Psalm 109:1 LXX).[82] It is possible to construe accordingly that in Paul's apocalyptic imagination, the one who will sit on τὸ βῆμα τοῦ θεοῦ to carry out divine judgment in 4:10 is none other than the Messiah Jesus.

If this conjecture is correct, Romans 14:10–12 implicitly includes Jesus as the object of universal homage at the eschaton. A similar phenomenon is noted in the worship of the Son of Man in 1 Enoch 48:5, but not found in 4Q215a and the Aleinu prayer.

3.3.3 The Holiness Motif

The fact that Paul situates the universal worship on the judgment day and before the judgment seat of God certainly adds ethical thrust to this paraenetical discourse. Both "the strong" and "the weak," who were currently conflicted, need to give their account to God on the matter of whether their actions will build up or destroy the church. However, to fully appreciate the holiness thrust of this eschatological worship we need to set this worship motif within the holiness framework in this letter.

In the prescript of the letter, Paul addresses his readers as κλητοῖς ἁγίοις, which can be read as "those being called as the holy ones,"[83] or "those being

---

78. Seifrid, "Romans," 685.

79. Such as Melchizedek in 11QMelech, the Son of Man in 1 En. 48, Abel in T. Ab. 13:5 and the Davidic Messiah in Ps. Sol. 17.

80. Fitzmyer, *Romans*, 312.

81. In this verse κατὰ τὸ εὐαγγέλιόν μου underlines Paul's Christian perspective on the day of judgment. See Cranfield, *Romans*, 163; Dunn, *Romans 9–16*, 103.

82. Here, Christ's appeal (ἐντυγχάνω) before God is better understood as that Christ is able to cause his believers to stand (ἵστημι) in the divine court (cf. 14:4).

83. Oakes, "Made Holy," 175.

called to be holy ones."[84] In either case, the vision of holiness is noted, as the identity is rooted in Israel's covenantal identity as a holy nation (Exod 19:6), which conveys both ideas. Furthermore, to Paul righteousness and holiness are both God's gracious gift and a task to be accomplished.[85] While the righteous status of those in Christ is grounded not in human works but God's redemptive work through his Messiah Jesus (3:24), the recipients of this divine grace are also expected to produce good deeds for their accountability before the eschatological Judge (14:10–12), as God's grace in Christ demands a positive reciprocal response from all those having received the divine gift.[86] The role of the Holy Spirit is pivotal for the process of sanctification. As their holy identity embedded in the work of the Spirit (i.e. the circumcision of the heart [2:28–29]), they are to walk according to the Spirit, which includes the transformation of their mindset (φρονέω) that will promote a holy life (8:4–13). In the context of the communal life of the church, the demand for this transformation is set by the participle τὸ αὐτὸ φρονοῦντες in 12:16 that emphasizes not merely the agreement in opinion but also the humble attitude toward one another.[87] All this primes the readers' frame of mind for Paul's ethical exhortation in Romans 14:1–15:13.

The internal conflict in the Roman church is caused by the two opposite opinions in promoting holiness set by the Jewish and the gentile Christians concerning the Jewish dietary requirements and Sabbath observances. To deal with these two conflicting opinions, Paul provides his theological underpinning in 14:17. Holiness cannot be attained by the matter of eating and drinking, but rather through "a righteous character,"[88] "peace," and "joy" by the Spirit. The prepositional phrase ἐν πνεύματι ἁγίῳ is better attached not only to χαρά[89] but also to δικαιοσύνη and εἰρήνη[90] to underline the inward

---

84. Gorman, "'You Shall Be Cruciform,'" 150.

85. Gorman, 150.

86. Barclay, *Paul and the Gift*, 74–75, 439–46, 516–19.

87. Cf. Romans 12:3: μὴ ὑπερφρονεῖν παρ' ὃ δεῖ φρονεῖν ἀλλὰ φρονεῖν εἰς τὸ σωφρονεῖν.

88. Here δικαιοσύνη is better understood from the ethical perspective.

89. Cranfield, *Romans*, 718.

90. Moo, *Romans*, 857; Fitzmyer, *Romans*, 697.

transformation done by the Holy Spirit.[91] It is presupposed accordingly that these are the things that count before God's final judgment.

From this theological viewpoint, the dispute on the matter of the Jewish ritual purity becomes insignificant in comparison to living in harmony as God's people. Hence, in this discourse, Paul encourages them to coexist without conflict on this matter by not passing judgment on the other group nor becoming a stumbling block for them, but by welcoming and building up each other.[92] Christ's deed serves as a norm to be adopted (15:5): as he did not please himself, they all are not to do so (15:2–3); as he has welcomed them both, they are to welcome each other (15:7); and as he has become a servant for the sake of both "the weak" and "the strong," they both should not cause the ruin of those for whom Christ died (14:15; 15:8–9). By doing so, this congregation will maintain their communal holiness and worship of God in one accord (15:6). This also means that they will provide good accountability before the judgment seat of God.

3.3.4 The Covenant Framework

The term covenant (διαθήκη) only appears nine times in Paul's letters,[93] and therefore it is often assumed in the past that this theme is not dominant in Paul's theology.[94] Various recent studies, however, demonstrate that the theme significantly shapes Paul's theological thoughts and writings.[95] The letter to the Romans is a good case.[96] Although the term appears only twice (Rom 9:4; 11:27), its idea can be sensed across the letter. In the opening letter, Jesus's identity as a descendant of David (1:3) adumbrates promissory Davidic covenant (2 Sam 7:12–16), and the readers are identified as κλητοῖς ἁγίοις that echoes Israel's covenant identity (Exod 19:6). In Romans 2–3, the obligatory Sinaitic covenant runs beneath Paul's dealing with the Jewish privilege of

---

91. Rom 6:13; 8:4–8; 15:13; cf. Ezek 11:19, 36:26–28. See also Moo, *Romans*, 857; Fitzmyer, *Romans*, 697.

92. See particularly, 14:5–6, 13–16, 19, 20–21, 22–23; 15:2.

93. Rom 9:4; 11:27; 1 Cor 11:25; 2 Cor 3:6, 14; Gal 3:15, 17; 4:24; Eph 2:12.

94. This is noted in Campbell, "Covenant and New Covenant," 179.

95. Davies, *Paul and Rabbinic Judaism*; Wright, *New Testament and the People*; Ware, *Paul's Theology*.

96. Kaylor, *Paul's Covenant Community*; Tanner, "New Covenant," 95–110; Ware, "Law, Christ, and Covenant," 513–40; Shaw, "Apocalyptic and Covenant," 155–71; Leighton, "Mosaic Covenant," 161–81.

having the Mosaic laws.[97] In Romans 4, his claim that people are justified by their faith is grounded in the promissory Abrahamic covenant narrative in Genesis 15:6. In Romans 8, the elaboration of the believers' experience of the power of the Holy Spirit evokes the new covenant blessing promised by the Old Testament prophets.[98] Finally, Romans 9–11, where the term διαθήκη appears twice, accentuates the new covenant framework in dealing with the fate of his Jewish people in relationship with their eschatological hope of salvation.[99] The close relation between Israel's covenant with YHWH and her worship of him is noted in 9:4 where they appear together as Israel's privileges as the children of God.

What Paul carefully argues in Romans 1–11 is the extension of God's covenant relationship with Israel, that is in the Messiah Jesus, all other nations are included in the new covenant relationship with YHWH. On the one hand, this new covenant is deeply rooted in Abrahamic, Sinaitic, and Davidic covenants in which the Jewish people can claim their advantage in regard to God's eschatological salvation. On the other hand, the new covenant blessings, namely God's righteousness and the work of the Spirit, can be enjoyed by both Jews and the gentile nations through their faith in Christ Jesus alone.

From this point of view, Romans 14:1–15:13 deals with the internal conflict caused by two seemingly opposite views on how the Jewish and gentile Christians in Rome should build up their spiritual discipline as a new covenant community in Christ. Paul evokes the redemptive work of Jesus Christ to encourage the readers to follow his step, and the activity of the Spirit to call them to participate in this sanctifying work to produce righteousness, peace, and joy. By them, this eschatological community of Christ will enlarge the new covenant realm in Rome and beyond.

Along with 4Q215a and the Aleinu Prayer, the universal worship of God at the eschaton in Romans is grounded in the universal outlook of Israel's divine covenant. The idea of the joining of all nations into this covenant provides a

---

97. Ware, "Law, Christ, and Covenant."

98. See the discussion in Coxhead, "Cardionomographic Work," 77–95.

99. The opening section (Rom 9:1–5) claims Israel's covenant status in verse 4, in which the use διαθήκη in plural form echoes various covenants noted in the OT. In the near closing section (Rom 11:25–32), the expression αὕτη αὐτοῖς ἡ παρ' ἐμοῦ διαθήκη in verse 27 speaks of YHWH's forgiveness to this nation on account of his covenant faithfulness. Hence, the opening and the closing parts underscore YHWH's covenant faithfulness in dealing with Israel's persistent rejection.

theological ground for the universal worship of God in all these three writings. What is noted in Romans is Paul's painstaking to picture the Christian version of this eschatological realm: the inclusion of all nations is apart from the physical circumcision and the Mosaic laws. To Paul, the key interpretative element is the eschatological work of the Spirit within and among both the Jewish and the Gentile believers of Christ. This tenet apparently goes beyond the universal notion in the other two writings.

3.4 Summary

The comparative study in this chapter demonstrates that Paul's interpretation of Isaiah 45:23 in Romans 14:11 is hermeneutically complex. First of all, his interpretation shares some common features held in 4Q215a and the Aleinu prayer. It has a covenant framework, as it is grounded in Israel's covenant relationship with YHWH. It has a universal scope given that YHWH is claimed as the only God of all nations. It contains an eschatological notion responding to God's eschatological rule on earth. Finally, it calls all of his worshippers to live out their holy lives.

Within these common tenets, however, Paul's treatment of Isaiah 45:23 has its own traits that are not shared by the other two writers. His distinctive reading is grounded in the apostle's conviction on the Messiah Jesus. In 4Q215a, the messianic idea is vaguely present. In the Aleinu prayer, the messianic hope is supplied by the Amidah that utters the restoration of the Davidic kingdom. In Romans 14:11, the Messiah Jesus plays a central role in shaping the vision of eschatological worship. He is depicted as having died, risen from death, and exalted at the right hand of God to inaugurate the divine eschatological kingship in which he will rule over both the living and the dead. At the eschaton, he will sit on the judgment seat of God to receive universal worship and to judge all humankind.

Several important tenets of Paul's messianic reading of Isaiah 45:23 need to be highlighted. First, the event of the universal eschatological worship of YHWH is transported from the Isaianic historical context, the rise of Cyrus's universal hegemony, to the final eschaton. In this regard, the eschatological scheme in Romans is slightly different from those in 4Q215a and the Aleinu prayer. While in these texts the universal worship of YHWH occurs after the day of judgment, in Romans this worship will be conducted on that day, which chimes in with the conviction of the reality of Christ's parousia.

Second, it is likely in Romans 14:10–12 that the Messiah Jesus is associated with the divine χύριος. Christ becomes the object of worship because Κύριος-YHWH shares his divine authority and role to judge with Κύριος-Christ. Such a phenomenon is presented in the Son of Man in Daniel 7:13–14 who shares the divine authority to judge and receive submissive worship from all nations. This is certainly absent in 4Q215a and the Aleinu prayer.

Third, as the holiness aspect is underlined in all documents where Isaiah 45:23 is appropriated, this eschatological vision of worship has an ethical impetus. YHWH is holy, hence all the worshippers of him must be holy too. In 4Q215a the transformation is done through righteous suffering, the eradication of wickedness, and the spread of the knowledge of God and his holy ways. In the Aleinu prayer, it is generated by the termination of idol worship on earth and the repentance of the wicked. In Romans, the transformation coexists with justification in Christ and embeds in the activity of the Holy Spirit who empowers all the believers. A call is issued to all believers in Christ to actively participate in this sanctification process. The transformation is not merely individual but contains a communal dimension that the whole Roman congregation will be able to stand together in holiness on judgment day to worship God and his Christ.

Finally, while all three writings picture the universal worship of YHWH inspired by Isaiah 45:23 within Israel's covenant structure, it is in Paul's letter to the Romans we see that the extension dimension of God's new covenant with his people is voiced powerfully. Apart from the physical circumcision and the Mosaic laws but through the faith in Jesus Christ, all gentile nations are welcomed to and identified as his covenant people to experience his righteousness and the power of the Holy Spirit. Grounded in this extended covenant, all believing nations can join Israel to worship the only true God in one voice presently (15:6) and in the final eschaton (14:11).

CHAPTER 4

The Worship of Augustus
in the City of Philippi

The previous two chapters have explored the Jewish perspective on the eschatological worship of YHWH and how it shaped Paul's reading of Isaiah 45:23 in Romans 14:11. They provide us some important insights for understanding the theme of universal eschatological worship of Christ in Philippians 2:10–11. For a more full appreciation of this eschatological worship theme, however, another coordinate needs to be supplied. Philippians is a letter written by Paul to the Christian community living in Roman Philippi, and therefore, the religious-imperial context of this city needs to be considered seriously. Here, the cultic veneration of *divus* Augustus in this city deserves close attention. The cult was prominent in the religious and political landscape of the Greco-Roman society in Paul's time. Furthermore, it had an eschatological aura that is drawn upon the mythical ideology of the return of the Golden Age of Rome. We posit, therefore, that Paul, the traveling missionary in the Greco-Roman world, was fully aware of the eschatological significance of this emperor cult.

Following the train of thought above, the present chapter intends to examine both the religious-political prominence and the eschatological significance of the veneration of *divus* Augustus in Philippi. The discussions are grouped into three main sections. The first provides a general survey of Roman imperial cults, particularly the cult of Augustus, in the Greco-Roman world. The second observes the existence and the prominence of the cult of Augustus in Philippi at the time of Paul. The third investigates the eschatological significance of the cult of Augustus, particularly concerning the mythical-imperial ideology of the Golden Age of Rome. Through this inquiry, we hope to expose the connecting theme between the universal eschatological worship of Christ in Philippians 2:10–11 and the worship of Augustus in Philippi at the time of Paul.

4.1 The Worship of Augustus in the Greco-Roman World

4.1.1 The Roman Imperial Cult

The term "imperial cult" (or emperor worship or ruler cult) is a modern label, which denotes "the worship of the living emperor, his family, and ancestor and of the deceased emperor."[1] In the past, this type of cult was often regarded as a "religious vacuum" or "shells without egg," because it is perceived as lacking religious significance and functioning only to elicit political loyalty from the imperial subjects.[2] Such a perception, however, has been corrected by many "ancient Rome" specialists. Simon R. F. Price, for example, correctly argues that in defining the religiousness of the imperial cult one should not impose the modern Judeo-Christian conception of religion onto it.[3] Its strong political tenor does not make the cult less religious, since religion and politics often coalesced in antiquity.[4] In his study, Michael Lipka demonstrates that in antiquity, Roman gods were defined by their six constituent elements: (1) space (altar and temple); (2) time (festival); (3) personnel (*flamens* and *sacerdos*); (4) function (to protect, to bless, to heal, etc); (5) iconography (images and statues); and (6) ritual (encomium, prayer, sacrifice).[5] All these elements can be found in the imperial cults. This gives strong support to the view that the deified deceased emperors were truly regarded as deities by many people in antiquity.[6]

---

1. Adkins and Adkins, *Dictionary of Roman Religion*, 104.
2. This is noted in Pleket, "Aspect of the Emperor," 333–34.
3. Price, *Rituals and Power*, 11–15.
4. Price, 15–22.
5. Lipka, *Roman Gods*, 116–25.
6. Lipka, 116–125.

Scholars generally regard the Roman imperial cults as having been derived from cultic practices in the Hellenistic world.[7] The ancient Roman society did not practice the veneration of human beings,[8] while in the Pan-Hellenistic world, ideas and traditions of the cultic veneration of human figures flourished. Both Hellenistic myths and philosophies also supplied the grounds for such practices. The pantheon of the Hellenistic deities consists of the whole range of deities from the greatest Zeus to the more localized spirits. Included in this pantheon are demi-gods in human forms, such as Heracles.[9] Many Greek philosophers also supported such an idea, as they taught that human beings who displayed extraordinary power, virtue, and performed great benefactions to the community should be regarded as divine humans[10] and received ἰσόθεοι τιμαί from the societies.[11] In the Pan-Hellenistic world, therefore, offering ἰσόθεοι τιμαί to heroes, great benefactors, and kings even after their deaths became a living tradition.[12] These practices were later adopted by Romans during their interaction with, and their expansion of power in the East. By the second century BC, a sizeable number of appointed Roman governors, generals, and high ranking officers in the East were sporadically honored with ἰσόθεοι τιμαί in numerous Greek cities.[13] What is observed by Roman historians is that the practice of human veneration had been gradually restricted only to imperial figures (emperor and his family members) since the Augustan era.[14]

---

7. Klauck and McNeil, *Religious Context*, 285–88; Fear, "Ruler Worship," 1014; Price, *Rituals and Power*, 53–77.

8. Klauck and McNeil, *Religious Context*, 285.

9. Fear, "Ruler Worship," 1010.

10. Plato applies the appellation θεῖος ἀνήρ to "poets," "seers," "philosophers," and even "politicians." In *Eth. Nic.* 7.1–2 and *Pol.* 2.13 (1248a) Aristotle teaches that men can become gods by excess of their virtue. Stoic philosophers also teach that great man who is perfect in his virtue can be deified. See Fishwick, *Imperial Cult*, I.1:41–42; Fear, "Ruler Worship," 1020; Colish, *Stoic Tradition*, 30–31, 34.

11. Fishwick, *Imperial Cult*, I.1:21–31.

12. Klauck and McNeil, *Religious Context*, 252–82.

13. The repercussion of the idea of apotheosis can be traced as early as in the late third century BC. Klauck and McNeil, *Religious Context*, 283–84. One poem at that time (Quintus Ennius, *Annales*, 116–117) depicts the apotheosis of Romulus.

14. Bowersock, *Augustus and the Greek*, 118–19; Fear, "Ruler Worship," 1014.

Since its initiation during the Augustan reign,[15] the imperial cults gradually became the fastest growing and most widespread religious phenomenon in the Roman Empire. For most of the Greco-Roman societies, the venerations were not regarded as a rival or threat, but complementary to the various local cults. During religious festivals, the deified emperors were often worshipped together with traditional local deities. The political interest to impress Rome with public loyalty certainly contributed to the wide acceptance of these cults. This explains why the cults received only little resistance in the Greco-Roman world. All this ensured that the imperial cults became the most significant trans-regional or transcontinental religious practices in the first century AD.

The practices of the imperial cults are complex. In the Latin West, the cults were usually imposed by the central imperial authority of Rome, while in the Greek East, they were mostly initiated by the local authorities to impress the central government.[16] The venerations were conducted at municipal and provincial levels.[17] The non-Romans usually observed both the cults of the living and the deceased emperors, while the Romans only worshipped the deceased emperors who had gained apotheosis from the Senate of Rome.[18] This was so because Roman political tradition demanded that the *princeps* should always be equal with his fellow senators.[19] This also suggests that most of the Roman cities or colonies, including Philippi, would only officially venerate the defied deceased imperial figures.

Should the ἰσόθεοι τιμαί to deified emperors be perceived as "giving honor" or "worship"? The two could hardly be differentiated since in the Greco-Roman society the difference between giving honor and worship was not in kind but degree.[20] The highest honor that could be offered to human beings was giving them ἰσόθεοι τιμαί, the honor equal to those paid the gods. This

---

15. The first establishment of the provincial temple of the imperial cult in Pergamon in Asia was in 29 BC. This is noted in Dio Cassius, *Roman History*, 51.20.6–9.

16. Fear, "Ruler Worship," 1016.

17. Beard, North, and Price, *Religions of Rome*, 349.

18. Cassius, *Roman History*, 51.20.6–8.

19. The emperor's claim of his divinity during his reign would create a political imbalance. Thus, the unwritten code of conduct was strictly observed: the apotheosis of Roman emperors could only be granted by the vote of the Senate of Rome after their death. (Pliny the Younger, *Pan.* 2.3–4). The murder of Julius Caesar and Caligula shortly after their claim of divinity served as a strong reminder to any future emperor. See the discussion in Gradel, *Emperor Worship*, 54–69; Fear, "Ruler Worship," 1016.

20. Fishwick, *Imperial Cult*, I.1:32–33.

includes constructing temples for the deified figures, offering them sacrifices, and assigning priests for them.[21] In the Judeo-Christian perspective, which strongly adhered to monotheism, this practice is strongly prohibited, as humans should neither claim equality with God nor receive any divine-like honor. With this overview done, we now take a closer look at the cult of *divus* Augustus.

4.1.2 The Rise and Prominence of the Cult of Augustus

The most prominent emperor to be worshipped in the imperial cults in the early empire is *divus* Caesar Augustus. Although Julius Caesar is the first imperial figure to be officially deified by the Senate of Rome (42 BC),[22] it is generally perceived that Augustus is the one who laid the foundation of the Roman imperial cults.[23] This established his cult as the most prominent cult in the early empire. Since the significance of his cult is important for our thesis, the development of this cult will be traced below.

During his lifetime, Augustus received many forms of ἰσόθεοι τιμαί. During the Roman civil wars (42–30 BC) the young Octavian claimed for himself as the son of *divus* Julius to justify his involvement in the Roman civil wars and to garner public support for his military campaigns.[24] After restoring peace and confidence to the Empire, the Senate of Rome granted him the title Augustus (27 BC) that acknowledged the presence of divine power and authority in him.[25] In 12 BC, the *princeps* also held the highest religious office, Pontifex Maximus, that established him as the one who stands in between the heavenly gods and the earthly Roman Empire.[26] Later in 2 BC, the emperor was officially acclaimed as *Pater Patriae* that even acknowledged him as the highest patron of the nation.[27] It would be a natural conclusion that shortly

---

21. Fishwick, I.1:32–33.

22. Although Julius Caesar had received various divine honors since 46 BC. the formal apotheosis by the Senate of Rome took place only in 42 BC, two years after his assassination. Gradel, *Emperor Worship*, 61–69.

23. See Hardin, *Galatians*, 26–39.

24. Zanker, *Power of Images*, 33–37.

25. Zanker, 98–100; Beard, North, and Price, *Religions of Rome*, 182.

26. Beard, North, and Price, 189–92.

27. Price, *Rituals and Power*, 138, 142.

after he died in AD 14, the Senate of Rome officially honored and deified him as a Roman god.

During his reign, Augustus had received various cultic venerations that implicitly acknowledged his divine power and status. By a Senate decree, the libation was to be offered to his genius in every public and private banquet (30 BC).[28] When the traditional *Lares Compitales* was revived along with the restructuring of the city of Rome (7 BC), the image of the genius of Augustus was not only added between the dancing *Lares* statues at the shrine but it also gained a new name, *Lares Augusti*. By this, the public cult of *Lares* was merged with the private veneration of Augustus.[29] In AD 6, Tiberius dedicated the *Ara Numen Augusti* for worshipping the divine power in Augustus.[30] Divine abstractions, which received cultic veneration, also became associated with Augustus (*Pax-Augusta, Concordia-Augusta, Fortunate-Augusta, Victoria-Augusta, Felicitas-Augusta*). Whether the people of Rome actually worshipped the divine power in Augustus or Augustus himself was moot. In all, while his divine status was not officially promulgated during his reign, it still has to be stressed that Augustus had indeed received more cultic venerations than many traditional Roman gods in Rome.

Offering divine-like honors to Augustus might have been moderated in Rome. In the rest of the empire, however, the cult of him was passionately observed. This is reflected in the claim made by Nicolaus of Damascus:

> Because mankind addresses him thus [as Sebastos] in accordance with their estimation of his honor, they revere him with temples and sacrifices over islands and continents, organized in cities and provinces, matching the greatness of his virtue and repaying his benefaction toward them.[31]

---

28. Zanker, *Power of Images*, 79.

29. Beard, North, and Price, *Religions of Rome*, 184–86.

30. Beard, North, and Price, 207.

31. *FGrH* 90 F 125.1. The translation is cited from Price, *Rituals and Power*, 1. Nicolaus of Damascus is "a contemporary biographer of Augustus" and "a political adviser of Herod the Great." See Hardin, *Galatians*, 27.

Archeological discoveries of the cult of Augustus across the empire support this claim. Hitherto, it has been attested that the cult was observed at least in fifty-two ancient cities across the empire.[32]

The apotheosis of Augustus shortly after his death in AD 14 marks the beginning of the imperial tradition of deifying good emperors after their death. Archeological discoveries indicate the popularity of the cult of Augustus in the Greco-Roman world.[33] Furthermore, while the cults of other emperors were slowly dismantled after their deaths, his cult remained prominent over a few centuries. Such prominence is stated by Philo, one prominent Jewish philosopher in Alexandria in the middle of the first century AD:

> . . . But besides all these, the whole habitable world voted him no less than celestial honors. These are so well attested by temples, gateways, vestibules, porticoes, that every city which contains magnificent works new and old is surpassed in these by the beauty and magnitude of those appropriated to Caesar and particularly in our own Alexandria.[34]

4.2 The Worship of Augustus in Philippi

With all this in mind, we shall now examine the cult of Augustus in Philippi at the time of Paul. First of all, we will describe the general character of Roman Philippi, and then assess the evidence for the existence and prominence of the cult in this colony.

4.2.1 The Roman Philippi at the Time of Paul

Various studies in the last few decades have enabled us to draw quite accurately the general character of Roman Philippi at the time of Paul.[35] In this

---

32. See the list of cities in Clauss, *Kaiser Und Gott*, 503–6.

33. The cult of Augustus was at least attested in at least sixteen cities in Italy, twelve cities in Asia, and twenty six cities in the province of Achaia. See Gradel, *Emperor Worship*, 249–74; Price, *Rituals and Power*, 249–74; Alcock, *Graecia Capta*, 182.

34. Philo, *Legat.* 149–50 (Colson, LCL).

35. Portefaix, *Sisters Rejoice*; Abrahamsen, *Women and Worship*; Bormann, *Philippi*; Pilhofer, *Philippi Band 1*; Koukouli-Chrysantaki, "Colonia Iulia," 5–35; De Vos, *Church and Community*; Oakes, *Philippians*; Tellbe, *Paul between Synagogue*; Hellerman, *Reconstructing Honor*.

study, we will only highlight some important features of this city that are relevant to the present study.

4.2.1.1 A Roman Colony

Ancient Philippi was located near the border between the Macedonian and the Thracian provinces, at the midpoint of the *Via Egnatia*, close to the ancient port city of Neapolis. The size of the city was about 70ha, but the controlled territory was about 1,126 to 1,890 square kilometers. This region covered the area between the Pangaion Mountain in the north and Neapolis in the south, and between the Nestos River in the east and the Strymon River in the west.[36]

Philippi was originally a Greek city, which was simultaneously occupied by the Thasians (Greeks), the Thracians, and the Macedonians. In the beginning, it was a Greek colony of Thasos with the name Krenides (or Daton).[37] The town, then, came under the Thracians, which took place before 360 BC. It gained a short period of independence in 360–356 BC, but soon the city was annexed by the Macedonian king, Philippi II (the father of Alexander the Great), who renamed it after his own name.[38] The city was under Roman control when the whole region of Macedonia fell under its dominion in the middle of the second century BC. Philippi, however, remained a Greek city until she was re-founded as a Roman colony in the late 40's BC by Antony to settle his veterans as a reward for their military service. The city was renamed as *Colonia Victrix Philippensium* to commemorate the victory over Caesar's enemies.[39] After the conclusion of the Roman civil wars, Octavian also settled his veterans there, and he changed the name of the city to *Colonia Iulia Philippensis*. Later, the city is named after his name, *Colonia Iulia Augusta Philippensis*.[40]

It is estimated that by the middle of the first century AD, Philippi was occupied by 10,000–15,000 people: 5000–11,500 residents lived inside the

---

36. See Oakes, *Philippians*, 5–10; Portefaix, *Sisters Rejoice*, 61; De Vos, *Church and Community*, 237–38.

37. Diodorus Siculus 16.3; Strabo 7.34.42–43; Apian, *Civil Wars* 4.13.104. Siculus Diodorus, *Library of History: Books XV.20 – XVI.65*, 16.3; Strabo, *Geography: Books 6–7*, 7.34.42–43; Appianus, *Roman History: Civil Wars*, 4.13.104.

38. Koukouli-Chrysantaki, "Colonia Iulia," 6–7.

39. Oakes, *Philippians*, 13.

40. Tellbe, *Paul Between Synagogue*, 212. For the discussion of colonial coins in Philippi, see pp. 96–98.

city wall and about 5,000 residents were in the surrounding suburban areas.[41] The land surrounding the city was extensively used for agriculture.[42] How prosperous this city was cannot be determined. Probably like any ancient Mediterranean society, the wealth was only shared among a few elites (3 percent of the population). They were the powerful landlords or patrons who controlled the major business of the city. The rest were the humble residents, consisting of those owning or renting small pieces of land (20 percent), the service groups (37 percent), such as traders, artisans, and farm workers, and the slaves whose lives were dependent upon these patrons (20 percent).[43]

4.2.1.2 Roman Orientation

The fact that Philippi was a Roman colony that was re-founded upon an existing Greek city certainly shaped its demographical contours. However, whether the population was dominated by the Romans[44] or the non-Romans[45] cannot be accurately determined because the available data are not sufficient for making a firm conclusion. Hence, we cautiously regard Philippi as being a diverse society, constituting Romans, the local Thracians, Macedonians, and Greeks, plus some minor tribes from other parts of the Greco-Roman world. Several considerations support this conjecture. The colony was not only situated on Greek land but also re-founded upon a Greek city. Accordingly, the re-founding of the colony (42 BC) must have left some space for the indigenous Greeks and for those who migrated from the surrounding areas.[46] Moreover, the *Via Egnatia* and the nearby seaport city, Neapolis, provided good access to this city from the rest of the Greek east. Finally, the archeological discoveries of many cults associated them with these ethnic groups.[47] Although most of them were dated in the second century AD, these cults were not newcomers in the Macedonian land, not even in the first century AD.

---

41. See Pilhofer, *Philippi Band 1*, 74; Oakes, *Philippians*, 45; De Vos, *Church and Community*, 238–39.

42. The city was chosen as veteran settlement primarily for its fertile soil and strategic location. The *Via Egnatia* provided a good access to market its agricultural products.

43. Oakes, *Philippians*, 33–35.

44. De Vos, *Church and Community*, 241–43.

45. Oakes, *Philippians*, 40–50.

46. Oakes, 18–24; contra Bormann, *Philippi*, 20.

47. Portefaix, *Sisters Rejoice*, 67; Abrahamsen, *Women and Worship*, 11; Oakes, *Philippians*, 71–74; De Vos, *Church and Community*, 239.

Having said this, as most scholars agree, the society in Philippi had a strong Roman orientation.[48] Many Romans in this city were the descendants of Roman veterans who were proud of their Roman origins. Although Greek was popularly spoken on the street, the official language remained Latin in the first century AD.[49] The city also enjoyed the status of *Ius Italicum* that granted the local government of Philippi a right to settle its own affairs autonomously without the intervention of the provincial authority.[50] The local administrative structure followed closely that in Rome, which is indicated by the presence of the *duumvir, aediles, quaestor,* and *decurion.*[51] Its citizens also possessed Roman privileges, such as the right to enter into Roman marriage, to trade their estate, and to gain the protection of Roman laws.[52] All this maintained the distinctiveness of the Roman colony of Philippi from the surrounding Greek-Macedonian cities.

Roman Philippi was a strictly hierarchical society. The residents were divided into non-Romans and Romans. The majority of the Romans in this city were from the tribe of Voltinia.[53] The Roman citizens were further divided according to their status (i.e. free-born, freedman), ancestry (i.e. patrician, plebian), and *census* or *ordo* (i.e. Senator, Equestrians).[54] High offices were

---

48. Tellbe, *Paul Between Synagogue*, 213–19; De Vos, *Church and Community*, 245–47; for the Roman military orientation, see Hellerman, *Reconstructing Honor*, 69–80.

49. The languages of inscriptions in Philippi in the first to third century AD. are mostly in Latin. This is noted in Pilhofer, *Philippi Band 2*; see also Portefaix, *Sisters Rejoice*, 68–69.

50. Tellbe, *Paul Between Synagogue*, 214.

51. *IIvir iure dicundo Philippis* is the highest judicial magistrates in the Roman colony of Philippi. This office is attested in the inscriptions nos. 219, 253, 324, 438, 717, 719, and 743. *Aediles* are responsible for maintaining public buildings and regulating public festivals. This office is attested in the inscription nos. 120, 127, 161, 216, 217, 249, 253, 395, 438, 484, 707, 714, and 743. Inscription no. 213 has *aedilis Philippis. Quaestor* served as supervising the financial affair of the city. This office is attested in the Inscription nos. 127, 127c, 213, 214, 253, 385,438, 719, 720, and 743. Inscription no. 718 has *quaestor Coloniae Philippensium. Decurion* is a member of the senatorial order in the Italian and provincial towns under the administration of Rome. This office is attested in the inscriptions nos. 127b, 127c, 252, 707, and 718. The inscription No. 395 has *Philippis decuria*, and the inscriptions nos. 127b, 322, 433, 484, 502 have *decuria Philippis*. The number of inscriptions follows Pilhofer, *Philippi Band 2*, particularly pp. 1145–47.

52. Tellbe, *Paul Between Synagogue*, 214.

53. There are about fifty-five inscriptions attesting this *tribus*. See Pilhofer, *Philippi Band 2*, 1144.

54. Hellerman, *Reconstructing Honor*, 6–11. Since the military reformation done by Augustus, the military *ordo* of *Equestrians* gained its prestige in the Roman society. See also Raaflaub, "Political Significance," 212.

open only to free-born citizens. Practically, the top offices (i.e. *duoviri*) were exclusively shared among the patricians with a high census who were also the high patrons in the city. The lower rank offices were available to freedmen (i.e. *liberti*). At the bottom were the slaves who comprised 15–30 percent of the population.[55] Once they gained manumission from their Roman masters, they earned the status of *liberti*, and their offsprings were counted as free-born citizens. The presence of Augustales indicates that there were some wealthy *liberti* in Philippi.[56] All this shapes the Roman orientation of the Philippian society at the time of Paul.

4.2.1.3 The Religious Landscape

Roman Philippi at the time of Paul was a polytheistic society. Archeological discoveries attest to the presence of the cults of both Roman and local deities. They indicate that while each ethnic group in this city had its own deities, the imperial gods, including *divus* emperors, were worshipped by all as the official cults in the colony. Roman deities were generally venerated inside the city wall, while the local cults (Silvanus, Dionysus, Thracian riders) were observed on the acropolis and outside the city wall.[57] In addition to this, we also note that the cults of female deities (Diana and Isis) gained popularity among the local women.[58]

Within this religious landscape, the archeological evidence at the Forum of Philippi attests to the popularity of the imperial cults in this colony: (1) the remains of two imperial temples from the second century AD,[59] (2) an

---

55. Oakes, *Philippians*, 17.

56. *Augustales* is an organization consisting of some wealthy liberti to assist the imperial cult, particularly the cult of Augustus. This office might be related to the *Sodales Augustales* established by Tiberius in AD 14 to preside over the cult of Augustus and his family. See Beard, North, and Price, *Religions of Rome*, 387–88; Price, *Rituals and Power*, 114. In Philippi, this office is attested in the inscriptions nos. 037, 043, 145, 256, 276, 289, 321, 412, 455, 463, 639, and 721. See the inscriptions in Pilhofer, *Philippi Band 2*.

57. This arrangement befits religious space in Rome where all temples of Roman deities were situated within the *pomerium* of the city. See Bormann, *Philippi*, 30–67; Pilhofer, *Philippi Band 1*, 92–113.

58. Portefaix, *Sisters Rejoice*, 75–121; Abrahamsen, *Women and Worship*, 26–39, 53–66.

59. The North-East Temple was constructed in the middle of the second century AD. Its structure, however, was laid upon the foundation of the previous structure. The layout indicates that the previous structure had the same function. This suggests that the first century temple also served for the imperial cults. Sève and Weber, "Monument Honorifique," 470–72; Bormann, *Philippi*, 41.

honorific monument of the seven *sacerdotes* of the *Diva Augustae* (Livia) dated to the end of the first century AD;[60] (3) the fragments of imperial statues (probably Gaius and Lucius Caesar) associated with the imperial cults from the first century AD.[61] Besides these, there are numerous inscriptions on the stones found in Philippi that are closely associated with imperial cults, as they mention *divus* Caesars,[62] *flamines*,[63] *sacerdotes*,[64] and Augustales.[65]

4.2.2 The Existence of the Cult of Augustus

The name of the colony, *Colonia Iulia Augusta Philippensis*, indicates that Augustus was the chief patron of the colony. Therefore, we rationally expect that his cult was officially observed in this colony after his deification by the Senate of Rome in AD 14. Some epigraphic and numismatic evidence found in Philippi affirms this inference.

4.2.2.1 Epigraphic Evidence

The inscription no. 282, which is dated to AD 36/37, attests that Augustus Caesar had been addressed as a deity (*divus*) in the AD 30s in Philippi:

> A […]
> Ti(berius) C[easa]r divi Augusti f(ilius),
> divi [Iuli] n(epos), trib(unicia) potes[t(ate)] XXXIIX,
> Dru(tus) Caesar Ti(beri) Aug(usti) f(ilius),

---

60. The location is in front of the North-East Temple. Abrahamsen, *Women and Worship*, 80, dates it in the late second century AD, approximately at the same time of the construction of the Forum and the North-East Temple. Sève and Weber, "Monument Honorifique," 470–72, 477–79, however, argues that the monument might have existed before the temple, given that the construction of this temple required the re-adjustment on the base of this monument. This indicates that the structure had been probably established prior to the temple. One inscription at the base of this monument suggests that the structure was established probably in the late first century AD.

61. Koukouli-Chrysantaki, "Colonia Iulia," 16.

62. *Divus Julius* is attested in the inscriptions nos. 282, 700, 701, 702, and 703; *divus Augustus* in nos. 002, 031, 088, 241, 282, 513a, 700, 701, 702, and 703; and *divus* Claudius in no. 001. See Pilhofer, *Philippi Band 2*.

63. For *flamen divi Augusti*, see the inscriptions nos. 031, 241, 531, 700, 701, 702, and 703; *flamen divi Claudi*, no. 001; *flamen divi Iuli*, see nos. 700, 701, 702, and 703. Pilhofer, *Philippi Band 2*.

64. *Sacerdos divae Augustae*, see the inscriptions nos. 002 and 226. Pilhofer, *Philippi Band 2*.

65. See the inscriptions nos. 037, 043, 145, 256, 76, 289, 321, 412, 455, 463, 639, and 721. Pilhofer, *Philippi Band 2*.

divi [Aug(usti)] n(epos)], divi Iuli pro[n(epos)], tr(ibunicia)
    pot(estate) II
Cad[m]us, Atimetus, Marti[alis],
C(ai) Iuli [Au]gusti liberti, mo(numentum) d(e) [s(uo)]
[f(aciendum) c(uraverunt)].[66]

The builders of the monument (Cadmus, Atimetus, and Martialis) are identified as the freedmen (*liberti*) of Augustus. Due to their strong bond, we
rationally expect them to be devotees and proponents of the cult of Augustus
in this colony.[67]

4.2.2.2 Numismatic Evidence

Roman coinage can be classified into two types. The first is the Roman
Imperial Coinage (RIC), which was issued by the central imperial authority in Rome and distributed in the whole empire. The second is the Roman
Provincial Coinage (RPC), which was issued and distributed in the provincial
cities.[68] The RPC has the standard image and name of the living emperor
on the obverse, and various local images and ethnic legends on the reverse.
In the colonial type of the RPC, the images and the legends usually relate
to the status, background, and uniqueness of the colony, including various
symbols, images, and monuments of the imperial cults.[69] Accordingly, the
RPC is commonly utilized by Roman specialists in their study of the imperial
cults in the provincial areas. Since the re-founding of Philippi as a Roman
colony in 42 BC, various types of colonial coins had been minted, distributed,
and used in this city. Among them, there are some coins minted during the
Augustan–Neronian era that is relevant to the present study, as they illustrate
the development of the cult of Augustus in Philippi.[70]

---

66. Pilhofer, *Philippi Band 2*, 342.

67. Bormann, *Philippi*, 198.

68. In the Eastern region, the RPC survived until the middle of the third century AD. For
the discussion of this terminology, see Butcher, *Roman Provincial Coins*, 9–13, and Mattingly,
Roman Coins, 204.

69. Burnett, Amandry, and Alegre, *Roman Provincial Coinage Part I*, 45.

70. They are identified as the RPC nos. 1650, 1653/1, 1653/17, 1655. Burnett, Amandry,
and Alegre, *Roman Provincial Coinage Part I*, 309 for the legends; Burnett, Amandry, and
Alegre, *Roman Provincial Coinage Part II*, 80–81 for the Indexes and Plates.

The RPC no. 1650 was issued probably around 10–2 BC to commemorate the re-founding of the colony by Octavian in 30 BC.[71] The obverse has the image of the head of Augustus and is inscribed with the words *COL(onia) AVG(ustus) IVL(ius) PHIL(ippensis) IVSSV AVG* to honor Augustus as the chief patron of the colony of Philippi. The reverse has the image of the three pedestals with the twin statues of Julius Caesar on each side and Augustus standing on the middle one. The image is surrounded by the words *AVG(ustus) DIVI F(ilius) DIVO IVL(io)*[72] that recall Octavian's claim as a son of god during the Roman civil wars. This type of coin was minted and distributed to promote the ἰσόθεοι τιμαί of Augustus as the founder of the Philippian colony. As Roman Provincial Coinage often depicts unique local architecture,[73] the twin statues on the reverse reflect the existing honorific statues of Julius Caesar and Augustus at the Forum of the city.[74] This is supported by the discovery of some fragmented statues of the imperial family closely associated with the imperial cults at this place.[75] If this conjecture is correct, it can be easily imagined what kind of honor Augustus received during his reign when the people of Philippi conducted the cultic veneration of Julius Caesar before these twin statues.

The RPC nos. 1653 and 1655 are similar to no. 1650. The obverse of the RPC no. 1653 has the image of Claudius and thus was probably minted after AD 42, while the obverse of the RPC no. 1655 has the image of Nero and thus was minted in his second consulship (AD 57). On the reverse, these two coins also have the twin statues of Julius Caesar and Augustus standing on the middle pedestal. The thing that needs to be highlighted is that the middle pedestal is now inscribed with the word: *DIVUS AVG(ustus)*, which indicates

---

71. The use of the title Augustus indicates that the coin was minted after 27 BC. The laureate on the head of Augustus suggests that the coin was minted probably in his mature age. Grant, *From Imperium to Auctoritas*, 275; Burnett, Amandry, and Algre, *Roman Provincial Coinage Part I*, 39.

72. Burnett, Amandry, and Algre, *Roman Provincial Coinage Part I*, 308; Bormann, *Philippi*, 35.

73. For the arguments that the reverse of the imperial coin represents the reality of the city, see Burrell, *Neokoroi*, 7–11.

74. In the colony of Narbo an altar to worship Augustus was also set up at the *Forum* of the city. This is attested in *ILS* no. 122.

75. Koukouli-Chrysantaki, "Colonia Iulia," 16.

that by the middle of the first century AD the emperor had been regarded as a Roman deity, and thus he received cultic veneration in Philippi.

Based on the epigraphic and numismatic evidence, it can be concluded that Augustus had received the ἰσόθεοι τιμαί during his reign in Philippi, and soon after his death and apotheosis in AD 14, the emperor was officially venerated as *divus* in this colony. The RPC nos. 1653 and 1655 demonstrate that Augustus was still worshipped at the Forum in Philippi during the reign of Claudius and Nero, and thus it was witnessed by Paul during his visit to this city.

4.2.3 The Prominence of the Cult of Augustus

The next question to be posed is this, How prominent was the cult of Augustus in the religious landscape of Philippi at the time of Paul? This section contends that this cult was more prominent than the cults of other imperial figures and many traditional deities in Philippi. Concerning the former, there were only four imperial figures who received apotheosis from the Senate of Rome by the middle of the first century AD: Julius Caesar, Augustus, Livia (Augustus's wife), and Claudius. Accordingly, only these four figures should be considered as being worshipped in Philippi at the time of Paul's writing of Philippians.[76] The emperors Tiberius and Gaius are excluded from the list because they both were not deified by the Senate (the latter even received condemnation). Claudius received his apotheosis in AD 54, but his cult might not be significant due to his unpopularity among Roman nobles.[77] So far, there is only one inscription attesting to the existence of his cult in Philippi.[78] The cult of Livia, Augustus's wife, was probably introduced in AD 44, but its fame came probably only by the end of the first century AD when the honorific monument of her *sacerdotes* was erected. As noted in the RPC no. 1650, Julius Caesar was the first Roman ruler to be worshipped in Philippi. However, the cult owed its existence and popularity to Augustus. Indeed, there is a saying that it was to accommodate the greatness of Augustus that Julius Caesar had to be

---

76. Cohick, "Philippians and Empire," 170.

77. Seneca Petronius, *Satyricon. Apocolocyntosis.*

78. See the inscription no. 1. Pilhofer, *Philippi Band 2.*

deified.[79] The veneration of Julius Caesar, hence, is intended to endorse the popularity of Augustus. All this leaves us with the cult of Augustus.

The bond between the colony of Philippi and Augustus remained strong during and after his reign. Many of the early settlers were Augustan veterans.[80] There were also many of Augustus's freedmen.[81] As Augustus was their chief patron, there must be strong proponents of his cult in this colony. The popularity of *divus* Augustus is reflected in the series of colonial coins in Philippi. During his reign, the coins had acclaimed Augustus as the founder of the colony,[82] the son of *divus* Julius Caesar, and the chief patron.[83] During the Julio-Claudian era, the coins commemorated his victory in the battle at Philippi (42 BC)[84] and acknowledged him as the patron deity of the colony.[85] The inscriptions in Philippi also attest to Augustus being the most popular emperor there. The number is almost twice that of other famous later emperors (Trajan, Hadrian, and Antonius Pius).[86] All this gives a strong impression that the cult of Augustus would be the most prominent imperial cult in Philippi in the first century AD.

More significantly, the cult of Augustus would have also been more prominent than other traditional cults in Philippi. The statue, altar (later the temple), and cultic veneration of Augustus were all situated at the Forum, the noblest space in the Roman city.[87] While the traditional cults were observed only by their devotees, the cult of Augustus was observed by all residents. There is evidence that his cult was popular among the traders there. An altar

---

79. Ovid, *Metamorphoses, Volume II*, 15.758–61.

80. See the discussion in Pilhofer, *Philippi Band 2*, 90–91.

81. See the inscription No 282. Pilhofer, *Philippi Band 2*, 95.

82. The RPC no. 1645 has the image of Augustus on the obverse and the image of the priest sloughing the land on the reverse to symbolize the re-foundation of the colony.

83. Noted in the RPC no. 1650. Burnett, Amandry, and Alegre, *Roman Provincial Coinage Part II*.

84. The RPC nos. 1651–2 promote *VIC(toria) AVG(ustus)*. Burnett, Amandry, and Alegre, *Roman Provincial Coinage Part II*.

85. The RPC nos. 1653–1655. Burnett, Amandry, and Alegre, *Roman Provincial Coinage Part II*.

86. There are sixteen inscriptions attesting the name Augustus (see nos. 031, 088, 241, 249, 282, 296, 452, 531a, 539, 539a, 544, 670, 700, 701, 702, and 703), while Trajan has only nine inscriptions (see nos. 254, 283, 349, 414, 497, 522, 559, 667, and 703), Hadrian eight inscriptions (see nos. 208, 254, 283, 349, 475, 617, and 703a), and Antonius Pius eight inscriptions (see nos. 201, 240, 454, 324a, 349, 357, 386a, and 395). Pilhofer, *Philippi Band 2*.

87. Hellerman, *Reconstructing Honor*, 85–86.

dedicated to Mercurius-Augustus was placed in the *Macellum*.[88] This is attested by the inscription no. 250:[89]

> Mercurio
> Aug(usto) sacr(um)
> Sex(tus) Satrius C(ai) f(ilius)
> Vol(tinia) Pudens
> [...] Philipp(ensis).

The festivals to commemorate Augustus were usually set at some important events in his life, which were usually declared as public holidays. The festivals included not only ritual ceremonies but also public performances, games, and banquets. The rite was led by his *flamen* who was the patron of the colony.[90] The fund for the festivals was also shared among the Augustales, which comprised of some wealthy freedmen.[91] All this speaks loudly about the prestige of the veneration of Augustus in Philippi.

4.3 The Eschatological Significance of the Worship of Augustus

Proceeding from the prominence of the cult of Augustus in Philippi, this section further contends on its eschatological significance. The correlation

---

88. Mercurius is the son of Jupiter and Maia. In antiquity, he was worshipped as the god of trade (especially the grain trade), abundance, and commercial success. It is worth noting that Mercury was a popular god in Britain and Gaul. In the Celtic region, he was often equated with various native gods (Mercurius-Artaios, Mercurius-Arvernus, Mercurius-Cissonius, Mercurius-Gebrinius, Mercurius-Moccus, and Mercurius-Visucius). See Adkins and Adkins, *Dictionary of Roman Religion*, 151–52.

89. Although the date of this inscription is not certain, the use of Latin indicates that the inscription probably comes from the first two centuries AD. It is plausible to posit that the altar was built during the Julio-Claudian era, when the cult of Augustus was vigorously promoted.

90. The Roman priest is not a religious professional, but an office to be competed among the local elites. Holding the status as *flamen divi Augusti* (see Inscriptions nos. 031, 241, 531, 700, 701, 702, and 703 in Pilhofer, *Philippi Band 2*) would highly increase the social honor of the nobles in the Roman society. See Hellerman, *Reconstructing Honor*, 80–84.

91. In Philippi, there are fourteen inscriptions attesting the *Augustales*. See Inscription nos. 037, 043, 074b, 145, 256, 276, 289, 321, 412, 255, 463, 505, 639, and 721 in Pilhofer, *Philippi Band 2*.

between this cult and the Augustan imperial ideology of the return of the Golden Age is the focus of our discussion.[92]

4.3.1 The Myth of the Golden Age in Antiquity

The mythical cosmogony of the Four Metallic Races provided people in the Greco-Roman world with a narrative paradigm to understand their existence and experience in the world they lived in. The earliest account of this cosmogony is documented in Hesiod's writings, *Works and Days*, from the seventh century BC.[93] The myth was widely shared in the Mediterranean regions. In the Jewish writing of Daniel (2:32–33) it appears as "the Four Metallic Statue," and in the writing of Ovid as "the Four Metallic Ages."[94] Hesiod's cosmogony basically narrates a gradual deterioration of the world (lines 109–201): (1) the Golden Race lived in harmony with the gods in a perfect world; (2) the Silver Race was less pious, and thus their lives were shortened; (3) the Bronze Race was violent, and thus it vanished from the earth in war; (4) finally, the Iron Race was so wicked that all the gods had to leave the human sphere (lines 200).[95] The thrust of this cosmogony is that the perfect life (lines 110–27) has been a past experience, and human beings are now living in a time of hardship, sickness, crime, and violence, and where death is a common experience and destiny. Under Zeus's curse, the Iron Race will be destroyed eventually (lines 180–1). This linear progression leads inexorably to the doom of the human race on earth.[96]

A hope to escape from this cruel fate, however, is still voiced. The Race of Heroes is creatively introduced between the Bronze and Iron Races, and this race enjoys eternal bliss.[97] The narrative of this race accommodates not only the Homeric legend of the heroic war at Troy where many courageous heroes fell but also the myth of the Elysium land where eternal bliss can still

---

92. For the eschatological thrust of this mythical ideology, see Jewett, "Corruption and Redemption," 25–46; Jackson, *New Creation*, 60–80.

93. Hesiod, *Op.* 109–201 (Most, LCL).

94. Ovid, *Metamorphoses, Volume I*, 1.89–150.

95. The last deities to leave were *Adios* (Shame) and *Menesis* (Retribution). See Athanassakis, *Hesiod*, 92–93.

96. Johnston, *Vergil's Agricultural Golden Age*, 8; Clausen, *Commentary on Virgil*, 121; Cancik, "End of the World," 105.

97. See the discussion in Athanassakis, *Hesiod*, 93; Clausen, *Commentary on Virgil*, 119.

be experienced.[98] In the standard Greek belief, all heroes went down to Hades after their death.[99] Hesiod, however, creatively narrates that the survived heroes lived in this blessed land eternally (lines 168–173). This story provided a glimmer of hope for escaping the cruel fate of life,[100] and thus it was widely circulated in the Greco-Roman world.[101]

4.3.2 Virgil's Remaking of the Myth

The first century BC is known not only as the age of the expansion of Roman power (in Europe, Asia, and Africa) but also the period of the unceasing civil wars caused by the competition for power among the Roman warlords. The most devastating was the series of wars from 49–30 BC, where the Roman state was practically controlled by the triumvirs, who opposed one another. At that time, people perceived themselves as living in the darkness of the Iron generation. Horace eloquently portrays the general sentiment of this chaotic and bloody period:

> Now another generation is crushed by civil war, and Rome collapses under its own power! . . . that city will be destroyed by *us*, an unholy generation whose blood is accursed; and the ground will be taken over once again by the savage beast.[102]

In this dark and chaotic age, there was a yearning to escape from this cruel fate. Horace recalled the myth of the Elysium land to offer a glimmer of hope to the righteous ones.[103] In contrast, the Roman poet Virgil prophetically voiced another solution in his *Eclogues* (42–35 BC).[104] The *Eclogues* are bucolic poems that have the character of a simple pastoral life of the

---

98. The Proteous's prophecy to Menelaus is noted in Homer, *Odyssey*, 4.561–69.

99. Menelaus was transported to Elysium because of his relationship with the Zeus's daughter, Helen. See Athanassakis, *Hesiod*, 93.

100. Death by lightning was often regarded as a miraculous transportation to this blessed island (Elysium). Burkert, *Greek Religion*, 198.

101. This is attested in Aratus, *Phaen.* 96–113; Pindar, *frag.* 129–30; Aristophanes, *Ran.* 448–59; Euripides, *Hipp.* 732–751; Theocritus, 22.36–45; Virgil, *Aeneid*, 6.637–62; Horace, *Epodes*, 16.39–66. See Hadas, *Hellenistic Culture*, 212–22.

102. Horace, *Epodes*, 16.1, 9–10. See also the discussion in Watson, *Horace's Epodes*, 479.

103. Horace, *Epodes*, 16.39–46, 63–66; See also Watson, *Horace's Epodes*, 479–87.

104. In antiquity, poets had the prophetic roles. Here, Virgil's *Eclogues* 1–10 were written for public performance, which provided a channel to deliver various prophetic messages. Hardie, *Virgil*, 9.

country herdsmen. In the hands of Virgil, however, they become vehicles of his sophisticated thought, as the poems play between cosmic grandeur and miniature pastoral setting.[105] In his *Eclogue* 9.45–50, the star that appeared in 42 BC is claimed not only as *sidus Iulium* (the sign of the apotheosis of Julius Caesar) but also the arrival of the mythical Golden age that will lead to the fertility of the earth:

> Daphnis, why are you gazing at the old constellation rising? See! *The star of Caesar* (*Caesaris Astrum*), seed of Dione, has gone forth – the star to make the fields glad with corn, and the grape deepen its hue on the sunny hills. Graft your pears, Daphnis; your children's children shall gather the fruits you have shown.[106]

In his *Eclogue* 4, which was written in 40 BC, Virgil proclaimed the end of the Iron generation and the imminent arrival of the Golden Race:

> Now is come *the last age* of Cumaean song; the great line of the centuries begins anew. Now the Virgin (*Astrea* and *Justice*) returns, the reign of Saturn returns; now a new generation descends from heaven on high. Only do you, pure Lucina, smile on the birth of the child, under whom *the iron brood* shall at last cease and *a golden race* spring up throughout the world! Your own Apollo is king. . . . But for you, child, the earth untilled will pour forth its first pretty gifts, gadding ivy with foxglove everywhere, and the Egyptian bean blended with the laughing briar; unbidden it will pour forth for you a cradle of smiling flowers. Unbidden, the goats will bring home their udders swollen with milk, and the cattle will not fear huge lions. The serpent, too, will perish, and perish will the plant that hides its poison; Assyrian spice will spring up on every soil. . . . Earth will not suffer the harrow, nor the vine the pruning hook. . . . See how the world bows with its massive dome – earth and expanse of

---

105. Hardie, *Virgil*, 5.
106. Virgil, *Eclogues*, 9.45–50.

sea and heaven's depth! See how all things rejoice in the earth
that is at hand.[107]

As this poem has great importance for the understanding of the Roman
imperial ideology, a short assessment is made below.

First, the *Fourth Eclogue* pronounces the imminent return of the Golden
Age in the Roman world. While the myth of the Golden Race is originally
Greek, Virgil creatively reworked it by his infusion of the Cumaean Sibyls'
prophetical oracle of the *ultima aetas* (the last age) to establish his powerful
eschatological vision for Roman audiences.[108] The ancient Etruscans believed
that the rise, lifespan, and doom of kingdoms were allotted by gods and
prophesied by Cumaean sibyls. The civil *saeculum* (age or generation) begins
with the founding of a city or state and lasts as long as one member of the
founding generation lives, and then a new epoch begins. The belief that ten
saecula were given to the Etruscans was incorporated into the Roman myth
as the duration of the Roman rule on earth.[109] This *Eclogue* prophesies the
arrival of the last *saeculum*,[110] but what is striking is Virgil's confidence in it.
Instead of the doom of Rome, this last *saeculum* will usher in the glorious age
for Romans. Interestingly, the poem speaks not of the *aetas aurea* or *aurem
saeculum* (the Golden Age) as it is in Ovid's *Metamorphoses*, but the *gens
aurea* (the Golden Race) underlining the establishment of the sovereignty of
the Roman race (line 7) who is destined to rule the whole world. The motifs
of the return of gods (Saturn and Virgo) and the reign of gods (Saturn and
Apollo) establish the idea of the divine sovereignty and peace (*Pax Deorum*)
on earth, which secures the glory and eternity of the eschatological age of
Rome.[111] Unlike Hesiod's cosmogony, the *Eclogue* announces that the end of
the Iron generation will be followed by the dawn of the Golden one. While
it is possible to speculate that behind this lies the Stoic concept of an eternal

---

107. Virgil, *Eclogues*, 4.4–52. For the discussion, see Clausen, *Commentary on Virgil*, 117; Cancik, "End of the World," 117.

108. Cancik, "End of the World," 117–18.

109. Cancik, 117.

110. Vulcacius had announced that the last *saeculum* would be in 44 BC. See Nisbet, "Virgil's Fourth Eclogue," 159.

111. The reign of Apollo will precede the return of Saturn on the earth. Coleman, *Vergil*, 134.

recycling cosmogony,[112] there is no clear evidence to suggest that Virgil adopts this Stoic thought. Rather, the *Eclogue* suggests that the new Golden Race will not be displaced, but it will remain forever to sustain Rome for eternity.[113]

Second, using pastoral language the *Fourth Eclogue* describes the mythical transformation of the whole cosmos. As all threats on earth are eradicated, the divine *Pax* (Peace) will rule even among the animal and plant kingdoms (lines 23–35). The earth becomes bountiful. Soils and cattle are highly productive in all lands to fulfill human needs without any labor (lines 18–21, 40–45). As a consequence, all international trade would be terminated (lines 37–39).[114] There is also a sense of progression in Virgil's depiction of the Golden Race. With the coming of this Golden Race, the old evils have yet to lose their power totally. A new war led by the Roman heroes is still be needed to eliminate these threats to secure this blissful age (lines 31–36).[115]

Third, the *Fourth Eclogue* prophesies the birth of a child who is given by the gods as a sign of the end of the old generation and the dawn of the new one (lines 8–9). This child will usher in the transformation of the world (lines 15–17).[116] Interestingly, the natural transformation and the gift of a mysterious child are somewhat comparable with Isaiah 7:14 and 11:6–9 (cf. Sib. Or. 3:788–95), as both speak of the transformation of the cosmos through the birth of a child. Virgil might have adopted this tradition from the East, although there is no secure evidence for such a conjecture. Despite the ambiguity of the identity of this newborn child,[117] the yearning for hope remains clear. This god-sent figure will bring into realization the new Golden Age in the Roman world. By the end of the first century BC, all had acknowledged that it was Octavian, known as Augustus, who fulfilled this eschatological hope.

---

112. Brent, *Political History*, 96–108.

113. Nisbet, "Virgil's Fourth Eclogue," 160; Cancik, "End of the World," 118–19.

114. Johnston, *Vergil's Agricultural Golden Age*, 2–3.

115. Clausen, *Commentary on Virgil*, 125.

116. Nisbet, "Virgil's Fourth Eclogue," 172–76.

117. Scholars have identified him as (1) a child of Asinuis Pollio, the consul who negotiated the Brundisium Treaty to unite Antony and Octavian, (2) a child born of the marriage between Antony and Octavia, (3) a child of Octavian and Scribonia, (4) Octavian himself, and (5) a personification of the new Golden Age. See Syme, *Roman Revolution*, 218–20; Cancik, "End of the World," 117.

4.3.3 The Imperial Version of the Golden Age

Octavian's victory over Mark Antony at Actium in 31 BC practically ended the old republican era and inaugurated the imperial era. This new Roman reality was complex and had led to major discussions among Roman specialists. In the military sphere, Augustus's reformation not only established professionalism in Roman armies but also consolidated the power of the *principate* over them.[118] With his *potestas* and *auctoritas*, the political power of the senate rapidly declined.[119] Augustus, then, established a new equilibrium of the empire according to his autocratic version. The Pax Romana was born. The economic activities, such as agricultural cultivation, industries, and cross-provincial trade, grew expansively to promote the wealth of the empire. This led further to the establishment of numerous new Roman cities across the empire. Rome itself was gradually transformed from the city of wood and bricks to that of marble. A new cultic excitement had arisen in the whole empire. Everywhere, new and grand temples were built, while the old ones were impressively restored.[120] All this was part of the establishment of the Golden Age of Rome.

To support this phenomenal transformation a new ideology was needed. The imperial intention was to utilize the popular hope nurtured during the civil wars. This regime established the claim that the eschatological hope of the Return of the Golden Race had found its fulfillment under the reign of Augustus, and was further maintained by the successive emperors.[121] To appreciate this, we will briefly discuss the establishment of this mythical-eschatological ideology, particularly the series of official events during the Augustan reign that promoted this imperial ideology.

The first is that the gate of the temple of Janus was closed by the decree of the Senate of Rome. The event occurred in 29 BC, which was shortly after the conclusion of the civil war.[122] According to Roman mythology, this temple was built by king Numa as the index of peace and war: the gate needs to be

---

118. See Chapter 3 of *RGDA* in Cooley, *Res Gestae*, 62–63. See also Raaflaub, "Political Significance," 203–28.

119. See Chapter 34 of *RGDA* in Cooley, *Res Gestae*, 98–99.

120. Augustus, *Res Gestae* 34; Suet. *Aug.* 28.3. See the discussion in Zanker, *Power of Images*, 110–14, 135–56; Favro, "Making Rome," 234–63.

121. Zanker, *Power of Images*, 167–238; Galinsky, *Augustan Culture*, 99–127.

122. Augustus, *Res Gestae* 13.

opened during the war and closed in the time of peace. At that time, the gate had remained open for over two centuries due to continuous Roman involvement in wars.[123] Hence, the closing of this gate in 29 BC officially proclaimed the end of the very long bloody era caused by the Roman civil wars. This symbolic event was followed up by Augustus's decisions of reducing the number of Roman soldiers and stationing his legions only at the border territories of the empire and in some troubled provinces for maintaining the security of the regions and the interest of Rome.[124] To most people who had been living under the shadow of wars, this would be good news, as it provided a sense of peace.

The second is the celebration of the *Ludi Saeculares* (Secular Games) in 17 BC that officially proclaimed the arrival of the Golden Age of Rome. The festival aimed to celebrate the end of one *saeculum* and to prolong the lifespan of the empire for another *saeculum*. It was usually observed every 100–110 years. The last was in 146 BC, and thus it should be celebrated again in the 40's BC.[125] The festival had been long delayed, however, due to the protracted civil wars. In 17 BC, driving on the public demand of this tradition, Augustus utilized the event to proclaim the arrival of the Golden Age of Rome.[126] During the festival, the *Carmen Saeculare* composed by Horace was solemnly sung by the children's choir. Some stanzas are cited to illustrate its eschatological significance:[127]

> Destinies you uttered proved true, O Parace;   line 25
> What you so ordained, may the fixed and changeless
> End of time preserve, and let blessings past be
>   Ever continued.

---

123. The last would be after the First Punic War in 235 BC. Mellor, *Historians of Ancient Rome*, 359n1.

124. Augustus, *Res Gestae* 3.

125. The *sidus Iulum* appeared at that time (Virgil, *Eclogues*, 9. 45–50) was claimed as the sign of gods for a new *saeculum*. Beard, North, and Price, *Religions of Rome*, 205.

126. Zanker, *Power of Images*, 167–72.

127. The translation is cited from Zanker, *Power of Images*, 170–71.

May our earth, abundant in fruits and cattle,   line 29
Yield the headed grain as a crown for Ceres
May our crops be nurtured with wholesome rains and
  Jupiter's breezes.

. . .

Trust and Peace and Honor and ancient Manners   line 57
Venture back among us, and long-neglected
Upright Conduct; Plenty comes too, and brings her
  Horn of abundance

. . . .

If you find our Palatine altars pleasing,   line 65
Prosper Roman power and Latium's fortunes
Five years more extend them, and thence forever
  Down through the ages

The hymn proclaims that the Roman people were now living in the last *saeculum*, which was also the new Golden Age of Rome. The motifs of super-abundance and the return of the ancient Roman goddesses (*Fides, Pax, Honos, Pudor*, and *Virtus*; lines 57–60) recall the description of the Golden Race in Hesiod's *Works and Days* and Virgil's *Fourth Eclogue*. It underlines that prosperity comes together with the return of the *mos* (or *mores*) *maiorum*. Although in reality, the ancient moral conduct continued to decline rapidly during the Augustan era, the belief in the necessity to return to righteous conduct, guided by ancestral virtues, was still strongly voiced.[128] The prayer offered to the gods expresses the hope that this last *saeculum* will be eternal (lines 67–68).

The third event is the establishment of *Ara Pacis Augustae*, which was situated at the edge of *Campus Martius*. The monument was built in 13 BC and dedicated in 9 BC to commemorate the military victory of Augustus over Gaul and his safe return to Rome in 13 BC.[129] Close attention is given to the crafted scenes on the three sides of the altar, as they articulate the Augustan concept of peace in the Golden Age. On one side is crafted the scenery of

---

128. Augustus, *Res Gestae* 8.5. See also Zanker, *Power of Images*, 156–62; Galinsky, *Augustan Culture*, 128–40.

129. Augustus, *Res Gestae* 12.2. See also Galinsky, *Augustan Culture*, 155.

bountiful nature with the presence of *dea Pax* and her two infants, *Tellus* and *Venus*.[130] On another side is crafted the portrait of *dea Roma* sitting on a bundle of armor, which articulates the militaristic undergirding of this Golden Age.[131] The complement of these two pictures is the plate at the southern side. It depicts Augustus, as Pontifex Maximus, offered a sacrifice to secure the *Pax Deorum* and thus Pax Romana.[132] These three images virtually articulate the Augustan imperial ideology: the Golden Age of Rome will be peaceful, prosperous, glorious, and eternal, and all this is offered by Augustus through his military power and priesthood.[133] To reinforce the greatness of Augustus, the obelisk *Solarium Augusti* was placed near this altar (ca. 10 BC) to cast its shadow on this altar at the celebration of Augustus's birthday, which symbolically proclaims that at his birthday the constellation of stars had already determined his reign of peace (*natus ad pacem*).[134]

In all, during the time of his reign, the imperial power of Rome had acclaimed Augustus as the god-sent Caesar who terminated the Iron Age, the Roman civil wars, and inaugurated the new Golden Age through his military power and religious authority.

4.3.4 The Prevalence of the Mythical-Imperial Ideology

The mythical-eschatological ideology described above was not only normatively proclaimed during the official imperial events in Rome but was also enthusiastically propagated in many Roman writings. Virgil, who previously made no claim on the identity of the god-sent child in his *Fourth Eclogue* (40's BC), explicitly associated this eschatological figure with Augustus in his *Aeneid* (29–19 BC):

> Here is Caesar and all seed of *Iulius* designated to pass under heaven's spacious sphere. And in truth is he whom you so often hear promised you, Augustus Caesar, *son of a god* (*divi genus*), who will again establish *a golden age* (*aurea saecula*) in Latium amid once ruled by Saturn; he will advance his empire beyond

---

130. Zanker, *Power of Images*, 173–74, see figures 135–136.
131. Galinsky, *Augustan Culture*, 108, see figure 42.
132. Galinsky, 143, 145, see figures 58 and 62.
133. See the discussion on *Ara Pacis Augustae* in Brent, *Imperial Cult*, 50–61.
134. Zanker, *Power of Images*, 144.

the Garaments and Indians to a land which lies beyond our stars, beyond the path of year and Sun, where sky-bearing Atlas wheels on his shoulders the blazing star-studded sphere.[135]

A similar claim is found in Ovid's *Metamorphoses*:

> With him [Augustus] as ruler of the world, you have indeed, O Heavenly ones, showered rich blessings upon the human race! So then, that his son might be born of mortal seed, Caesar must need to be made a god. . . . *Jupiter controls the heights of heaven and the kingdoms of the tri-formed universe; but the earth is under Augustus' sway.* Each is both sire and ruler.[136]

The mythical ideology of Augustus is also found in some private expensive cameos. A cameo known as *Gemma Augustae* (AD 9) attests to the popularity of the Augustan ideology among the Roman aristocrats.[137] The upper scene depicts Augustus as sitting on the throne in the guise of *deus Jupiter* with *dea Roma*, and the lower scene depicts the victory of the Roman legion over their enemies in Dalmatia. While this cameo acknowledges Tiberius's contribution, Augustus's position as a divine agent to bring into realization the Golden Age of Rome is clearly in focus.

This ideology reverberated across Asia, where the cult of Augustus was popularly practiced.[138] The Priene calendar inscription records the decision of the provincial council of Asia in 9 BC to mark the birth of Augustus (23 September) as the beginning of the new calendar year in Asia:

> A decision of the Hellenes in Asia; proposed by the high priest Apollonios son of Menophilos of Aizanoi. Whereas the providence that ordains our whole life has established with zeal and distinction that which is most perfect in our life by bringing Augustus, whom she filled with virtue as a benefaction to all humanity; *sending us to those after us a savior who put an end to war brought order to all things*; and Caesar, when he appeared,

---

135. Virgil, *Aeneid*, 6.789–97.

136. Ovid, *Metamorphoses, Volume II*, 15.758–60, 858–59 .

137. For a full discussion on *Gemma Augustae*, see Galinsky, *Augustan Culture*, 120–21; Zanker, *Power of Images*, 230–32.

138. Part of the cause is the rivalry among the Greek cities in Asia. Price, *Rituals and Power*, 126–32; Zanker, *Power of Images*, 302–6.

the hope of those who preceded [. . .] placed, not only surpassing those benefactors who had come before but also leaving to
those who shall come no hope of surpassing (him); and *the birth
of the god was the beginning of good tidings to the world through
him* . . . For this reason, with good fortune and for salvation this
was decided by the Hellenes in Asia. The New Year will begin
in all the cities on the ninth day before the Calends of October,
which is the birth of Augustus.[139]

It is claimed in this inscription that Augustus is the god-sent savior who
has "put an end to war, brought order to all things." Accordingly, his birth
should be regarded as the "beginning of good news to the world." The decision was the council's response to the proposal submitted by the Roman
proconsul of the province, Paullus Fabius Maximus, which is also recorded
in the inscription:

[It is difficult to know whether?] the birth of the most divine
Caesar is a matter of greater pleasure or greater benefit. We could
justly consider that day to be equal to *the beginning of all things.
He restored the form of all things to usefulness, if not to their
natural state, since it had deteriorated and suffered misfortune* . . .
Thus a person could justly consider this to be the beginning of
life and of existence, and the end of regrets about having been
born . . . Therefore, it seems proper to me that the birthday of
the most divine Caesar be the one, uniform New Year's day for
all the polities.[140]

Some familiar motifs of the return of the Golden Age are noted: (1) the
whole cosmos has badly deteriorated and suffered misfortune (the Iron Age);
(2) the birth of Augustus has put an end to this Iron Age; and (3) Augustus
has restored the world into its original perfect condition (the Golden Age). As
the Roman colony of Philippi was situated not far from the province of Asia,
the society there would have been very familiar with this imperial ideology.

---

139. Cited from Friesen, *Imperial Cults*, 33. The Greek text is found in OGIS 4581.3ff.
Emphasis is added.

140. OGIS 4581.3ff. The translation is cited from Friesen, *Imperial Cults*, 33.

4.3.5 The Worship of Augustus and the Golden Age of Rome

With all this in mind, the relationship between the cult of Augustus and the Roman mythical ideology of power can be plausibly established. First of all, the worship of Augustus religiously acknowledges the emperor as the god-sent savior who possesses divine power to rule the world. There was a common perception in the Greco-Roman world that human beings who had great achievements, performed extraordinary deeds, and offered great services to humankind actually had divine origins. This is applied to Augustus in the Roman mythical ideology. Virgil claims Augustus as a *divi genus* who brought back the realm of gods on earth.[141] Suetonius also attests to one rumor that was widely circulated, which is about the divine involvement in the birth of Augustus.[142]

Second, in the context of ancient euergetism, the leader was expected to provide εὐργέσια to his subjects. In response, they were to give τιμαί to him, which include some forms of ἰσόθεοι and posthumous τιμαί.[143] This is notably applied to Augustus who was acclaimed as having bestowed many benefactions on his subjects. The greatest one was the realization of the eschatological Golden Age, which promoted him to be the greatest εὐργέτης in the Roman world. It would only be appropriate, therefore, for those who lived and enjoyed this eschatological realm to offer him ἰσόθεοι τιμαί or worship.

Finally, the apotheosis in AD 14 established Augustus as the patron god of the empire who protected and sustained the peace and security of the Golden Age of Rome on earth. Accordingly, the worship of Augustus would maintain the *Pax Deorum* in the whole Greco-Roman world. At the same time, this worship professed political submission to the imperial commonwealth established by Augustus. Such an ideology is notably presented in the *Grand Camée* (AD 17). The cameo has three scenes: (1) the upper scene depicts *divus* Augustus surrounded by the deceased imperial family; (2) the middle scene portrays the emperor Tiberius in the guise of Jupiter sitting together with his mother, Livia (Augustus's wife), surrounded with the imperial members; (3) the lower scene presents how Rome conquered other

---

141. Virgil, *Aeneid* 6.789–97.

142. Suetonius, *Aug.* 94.4 narrates the infant story of Augustus based on Asclepias's *Theologoumena* that how Augustus was regarded as the son of Apollo.

143. Aristotle, *Art of Rhetoric* 1.5.9. See also the discussion in Klauck and McNeil, *Religious Context*, 263–64.

nations.[144] The ideology reflected in this cameo is apparently developed from the earlier *Gemma Augustae*. Augustus, the patron god of the Roman Empire, is overseeing the empire from heaven, and on earth his successor Tiberius and his armies carry forward Augustus's legacy, to preserve and extend the glory of the Golden Age of Rome. In this imperial ideology, the worship of Augustus is politically demanded.

In all, we can say that the cult of Augustus is grounded in the perception propagated by the imperial power: Augustus is the god-sent Caesar who terminated the Iron Age and inaugurated the Golden Age in the whole empire. In this imperial veneration, Augustus's divinity is acknowledged, his greatest service and benefaction is appreciated, his posthumous role as an imperial god is believed in, and his eschatological realm is being succumbed by the imperial subjects.

4.4 Summary

Since Paul's letter to the Philippians is written to the Christians in the Roman colony of Philippi, the religious-political environment of this colony needs to be expounded for a greater appreciation of the significance of the depiction of universal eschatological worship of Jesus Christ in 2:10–11. In this regard, the cultic veneration of *divus* Augustus has great relevance. Since its initiation, the cult of Augustus flourished across the empire. Both in the Latin West and the Greek East, the emperor was fashionably worshipped by both Roman and non-Roman subjects. By the middle of the first century AD, this cult was arguably the most widespread, popular, and prominent religious phenomenon in the Greco-Roman world.

In Roman Philippi, ἰσόθεοι τιμαί had been offered to Augustus since his reign. After his death and apotheosis, the cult of him was still well preserved. In the middle of the first century AD, when Paul visited this city, the cult of Augustus was more prominent than the cults of other imperial figures and many traditional cults. The strong historical bond between this *divus* emperor and the colony certainly contributes to the popularity of this cult.

The fame of the cult of Augustus was generated by the propagation of a mythical ideology: Augustus is the god-sent savior who has ended the cruel

---

144. Kreitzer, *Striking New Images*, 78.

Iron Age and inaugurated the eschatological Golden Age in the whole empire during his reign, and now as a divine lord in heaven, he is still actively maintaining this glorious realm of Rome. In this imperial worldview, the worship of *divus* Augustus is a proper response from all imperial subjects to acknowledge his divinity, to appreciate his benefactions, and to submit to the eschatological sovereignty of Rome. As a consequence, the cultic veneration of Augustus is religiously and politically demanded by the imperial power.

CHAPTER 5

The Setting of Paul's Letter to the Philippians

Given that the present study aims to explicate the significance of the universal worship of Christ in Paul's letter to the Philippians, it is necessary to establish some important features of this letter as exegetical handles for reading the worship motif. To do so, the present chapter divides the discussion into four main sections. The first deals with the issue of the integrity of the letter, namely whether Philippians should be perceived as a single coherent letter or a composite letter consisting of several fragments of Paul's letters. The second provides a sketch of the letter writer, the letter recipients, and their relationship. The third establishes some pivotal problems addressed in the letter. The last discusses the issue of whether the letter has an anti-imperial stance.

5.1 The Integrity of the Letter

This study presupposes that the present letter of Philippians is one coherent letter. We note that scholarly opinions are still divided concerning the integrity of this letter. While the majority of the English commentaries on this letter hold this point of view,[1] some commentators contend for the view that the present letter of Philippians consists of fragments of three different letters of Paul (A = 4:10–20; B = 1:1–3:1 4:1–9 4:21–23; C = 3:2–21) compiled

---

1. Hawthorne, *Philippians*; O'Brien, *Philippians*; Fee, *Philippians*; Bockmuehl, *Philippians*; Fowl, *Philippians*; Hansen, *Philippians*; Witherington III, *Philippians*.

by the later editor(s), probably at the end of the first century AD.[2] Indeed, this is a prominent view of the continental scholarship.[3] Since the issue has great relevance for our discussion in chapter 6, this section will provide the arguments to support the position adopted in this study.

5.1.1 The External Evidence

It is often argued that Polycarp's statement ὃς καὶ ἀπὼν ὑμῖν ἔγραψεν ἐπιστολάς in his letter to the Philippians (3:2) implies his knowledge that Paul wrote more than one letter to this beloved church.[4] Moreover, the fact that Paul's pseudo-letter to the Laodiceans (second century AD) exclusively depends on the hypothetical letter B, but lacks letters A and C suggests that in the earliest stage letter B stood apart from letters A and C.[5]

In response to the first argument, it can be counterargued that Polycarp's statement can be read differently. The plural ἐπιστολάς could be an inference he drew from Paul's statement τὰ αὐτὰ γράφειν ὑμῖν in Philippians 3:1. Indeed, Polycarp's statement τοῖς [ἐπαινουμένοις] ἐν ἀρχῇ τῆς ἐπιστολῆς αὐτοῦ in his Philippians 11:3 clearly speaks of a single letter.[6] In response to the second argument, Markus Bockmuehl reminds us that the argument out of silence is not enough to secure the partitive theory.[7] Indeed, all manuscripts of Philippians, including P[46] from the late second century AD, unanimously attest that Paul's letter to the Philippians is a single coherent letter.

5.1.2 The Internal Evidence

The composite-letter theory is also supported by some internal phenomena. First, the thanksgiving section, which is usually situated at the beginning of Paul's letters, occurs near the end of the letter (4:10–20).[8] Second, the travel plan is usually followed by the farewell section and closing greeting (see Rom 15:22–16:23; 1 Cor 16:1–12), but in Philippians, this section appears in the

---

2. Beare, *Philippians*; Reumann, *Philippians*.

3. This is noted in Bormann, *Philippi*, 87–126.

4. Reumann, *Philippians*, 8–9.

5. Sellew, "Laodiceans," 17–28.

6. Although the text is rather corrupt (the verb is missing), the general drift is clear. See the note in Holmes, *Apostolic Fathers*, 292–93; Bockmuehl, *Philippians*, 22.

7. Bockmuehl, *Philippians*, 22.

8. Reumann, *Philippians*, 9; Sellew, "Laodiceans," 18.

middle of it (Phil 2:19–30).[9] Finally, the statement τὸ λοιπόν, ἀδελφοί μου, χαίρετε ἐν κυρίῳ in 3:1 seemingly marks the end of the letter, but it continues with a harsh warning: βλέπετε τοὺς κύνας, βλέπετε τοὺς κακοὺς ἐργάτας, βλέπετε τὴν κατατομήν in 3:2, which appears discontinuous.[10]

Although these arguments have some weight, in our opinion they are not convincing. With regard to the structure of Philippians, the deviation from the common structure of the other Pauline letters does not necessarily imply the composite nature of the letter. Paul's writing should not be strictly constrained by the typological structure of his letters. He certainly has the freedom to structure his letter to accommodate his rhetorical aims. In this line of thought, it can be argued that the thanksgiving section in 4:10–20 is rhetorically intended.[11] It is worth noting that in response to the Philippians' gift Paul never explicitly says, "thank you," but carefully locates their gifts in the context of their partnership in the gospel (4:15–16; cf.1:5). Here, two aspects of this partnership in 1:3–11 are revoiced in 4:10–20: the sharing of their troubles (1:7: cf. 4:14) and their fruit in Christ (1:11; cf. 4:17). As the letter opens with the theme of partnership in the gospel, it would be natural to end it with the same theme. From this perspective, Paul's response to the Philippians' gift at the end of the letter is not incomprehensible.

Concerning Paul's statement in 3:1, several points can be made in response. First of all, the phrase τὸ λοιπόν ἀδελφοί μου χαίρετε ἐν κυρίῳ can be construed either as a closing greeting "finally, my brothers, farewell in the Lord"[12] like the case of λοιπόν, ἀδελφοί, χαίρετε in 2 Corinthians 13:11, or as a transitional exhortation in the middle of the letter "well then or beyond that, my brothers, rejoice in the Lord"[13] like the case of λοιπὸν οὖν, ἀδελφοί, ἐρωτῶμεν ὑμᾶς καὶ παρακαλοῦμεν ἐν κυρίῳ Ἰησοῦ in 1 Thessalonians 4:1. In Philippians 3:1, the latter seems more plausible, considering that the remark is immediately followed by τὰ αὐτὰ γράφειν ὑμῖν ἐμοὶ μὲν οὐκ ὀκνηρόν, ὑμῖν δὲ ἀσφαλές.

---

9. Sellew, "Laodiceans," 18.

10. Reumann, *Philippians*, 9; Sellew, "Laodiceans," 17–18.

11. For example, Garland, "Composition and Unity," 152, argues that the "thank you" noted is delayed as to consider Philippians' anxiety on Paul's condition of imprisonment.

12. Reumann, *Philippians*, 456–57.

13. Witherington III, *Philippians*, 185–87.

To which exhortations τὰ αὐτά (the same things) refer is admittedly ambiguous. Three conjectures have been made and contested: (1) it is prospective, pointing to the warning in 3:2–3;[14] (2) it refers to some earlier instructions (either oral or letters), which relate to the warning in 3:2–3;[15] and (3) it is retrospective, referring to the previous exhortations in the letter.[16] The last option makes better sense, and thus it is adopted in this study. In 1:27–2:18, Paul has made various instructions (1:27; 2:2, 5, 12, 14, 18) to encourage his readers to continue living according to the gospel of Christ narrated in 2:6–11, and now in 3:2–4:4, he intends to repeat them in a different way. Some parallel expressions confirm this inference:

	1:27–2:30	3:2–4:4
1	Μόνον ἀξίως τοῦ εὐαγγελίου τοῦ Χριστοῦ πολιτεύεσθε (1:27a)	Συμμιμηταί μου γίνεσθε, ἀδελφοί, καὶ σκοπεῖτε τοὺς οὕτω περιπατοῦντας καθὼς ἔχετε τύπον ἡμᾶς . . . ἡμῶν γὰρ τὸ πολίτευμα ἐν οὐρανοῖς ὑπάρχει (3:17, 20)
2	στήκετε ἐν ἑνὶ πνεύματι, μιᾷ ψυχῇ συναθλοῦντες τῇ πίστει τοῦ εὐαγγελίου (1:27c)	οὕτως στήκετε ἐν κυρίῳ, ἀγαπητοί (4:1)
3	ἥτις ἐστὶν αὐτοῖς ἔνδειξις ἀπωλείας, ὑμῶν δὲ σωτηρίας, καὶ τοῦτο ἀπὸ θεοῦ (1:28)	τοὺς ἐχθροὺς τοῦ σταυροῦ τοῦ Χριστοῦ, ὧν τὸ τέλος ἀπώλεια, . . . , ἐξ οὗ καὶ σωτῆρα ἀπεκδεχόμεθα κύριον Ἰησοῦν Χριστόν (3:18–20)
4	ἵνα τὸ αὐτὸ φρονῆτε, ..., τὸ ἓν φρονοῦντες (2:2)	Εὐοδίαν παρακαλῶ καὶ Συντύχην παρακαλῶ τὸ αὐτὸ φρονεῖν ἐν κυρίῳ. (4:2)
5	Τοῦτο φρονεῖτε ἐν ὑμῖν ὃ καὶ ἐν Χριστῷ Ἰησοῦ (2:5)	Ὅσοι οὖν τέλειοι, τοῦτο φρονῶμεν (3:15)
6	τὸ δὲ αὐτὸ καὶ ὑμεῖς χαίρετε καὶ συγχαίρετέ μοι (2:18)	Χαίρετε ἐν κυρίῳ πάντοτε· πάλιν ἐρῶ, χαίρετε (4:4)

---

14. Fee, *Philippians*, 293.

15. Vincent, *Philippians*, 164–65; Garland, "Composition and Unity," 164–65.

16. Lightfoot, *Philippians*, 125–26; Reed, "Philippians 3:1," 63–90; Bockmuehl, *Philippians*, 180–82.

In this light, Philippians 3:1 basically claims that Paul's effort to repeat the earlier instructions in 1:27–2:18 is not troublesome to him, but a safeguard to his readers.[17] If this is correct, τὸ λοιπόν ἀδελφοί μου χαίρετε ἐν κυρίῳ is better read not as a closing greeting, but a transitional statement.

The transition from the exhortation of joy in 3:1 to Paul's warnings (βλέπετε τοὺς κύνας, βλέπετε τοὺς κακοὺς ἐργάτας, βλέπετε τὴν κατατομήν) in 3:2 is seemingly harsh. This, however, may not necessarily indicate that 3:2–4:4 belongs to a separate letter. Paul's overall tone in this discourse is still quite friendly, and thus the repeated use of βλέπετε (3x) can be rhetorically intended. As Paul draws a clear boundary between *us* (Paul and the Philippian congregation) and *them* (the Judaizing Christians) in this section,[18] some strong words are necessarily needed for warning the readers of the danger of the Judaizing teaching.[19]

The last point to be made is about Paul's prayer report section in 1:3–11. It is generally appreciated that in this section, Paul not only offers his praise and thanksgiving to God on the church's behalf but also introduces some important themes to be covered in the rest of the letter.[20] From the rhetorical point of view, this section can be regarded as the *exordium*.[21] Careful observation on this prayer report shows that the passage introduces not merely the themes elaborated in the hypothetical letter B, but also the rest of the letter.[22] The theme of the *koinonia* in Christ voiced in 1:5–8 appears not only in 1:25–27 and 2:1, but it is also noted in 3:10 and 4:15. The idea of rejoicing together in the Lord occurs across the letter.[23] The importance of the adopted frame of mind (τοῦτο φρονεῖν in 1:7) is expounded in the two major paraenetical discourses in the letter (1:27–2:18; 3:2–4:4). The theme of the suffering together

---

17. Having said this, we do not think that τὰ αὐτά refer only to the χαίρω exhortations in 2:18 and 2:28–3:1. Cf. Fee, *Philippians*, 292–93; contra Bruce, *Philippians*, 101–2; Hawthorne, *Philippians*, 124.

18. Garland, "Composition and Unity," 167.

19. Scholars are divided on whether βλέπετε should be translated as "watch out for" (O'Brien, *Philippians*, 353–54; Fee, *Philippians*, 293n36), or "consider" (Hawthorne, *Philippians*, 125; Garland, "Composition and Unity," 166–67).

20. Doty, *Letters in Primitive Christianity*, 33; Murphy-O'Connor, *Paul the Letter-Writer*, 62–64.

21. Witherington III, *Philippians*, 51–54.

22. Jewett, "Epistolary Thanksgiving," 40–53.

23. Phil 1:4, 18, 25; 2:2, 17, 18, 28, 29; 3:1; 4:1, 4, 10.

in Christ (1:7) also appears in the whole letter.[24] The eschatological orientation (1:6, 10–11) is accentuated not only in 2:10–11 and 2:16–17; but also in 3:10–11, 20–21; 4:5. All this demonstrates the whole letter of Philippians is coherently written as a single letter.

To conclude our discussion, the present study adopts the view that Philippians is one coherent letter of Paul. While the composite-letter theory might be attractive, its arguments are not convincing. In contrast, the single letter thesis is less speculative and can be well defended.

Excursus: The Epistolary Type and Rhetorical Structure

In the last few decades, scholarly attention has been given to the epistolary and rhetorical analysis of Philippians. They indeed have provided some useful insight for understanding the nature of this letter. We also note, however, that these two approaches are also used both to support and oppose the integrity of the letter to the Philippians. This section provides a brief response to these two lines of Philippians study.

With regard to the former, while Philippians exhibits many characteristics of friendship[25] and family letters,[26] it is also apparent that Philippians has a strong hortative nature. This is reflected by the liberal use of imperative and purposive statements in sections 1:27–2:18 and 4:1–19. Even the narrative accounts (1:12–26; 2:19–30) have their paraenetical goals.[27] In this respect, whether it is a friendship or family letter, Paul clearly uses this form of letter for his rhetorical purpose. If it is a friendship letter, he wrote it with the expectation that his request would be highly honored by the readers.[28] If this is a family letter, he employed it as a launching pad for his exhortation.[29]

With regard to the latter, the rhetorical nature of Paul's letter to the Philippians has been increasingly appreciated.[30] Being confident of it, some

---

24. Phil 1:29–30; 2:7–8, 17, 27–30; 3:10; 4:12–14.

25. Hansen, *Letter to the Philippians*, 6–12.

26. Alexander, "Hellenistic Letter-Forms."

27. It is worth noting that Paul's account in 1:12–26 prepares his exhortation in 1:27, his travel plan in 2:19–30 ends with the exhortation to honor Epaphroditus for his Christ-like ministry (2:29–30), and his testimony in 3:4–14 provides the ground for his exhortation in 3:17.

28. Stowers, *Letter Writing*, 59.

29. Alexander, "Hellenistic Letter-Forms," 99.

30. Bockmuehl, *Philippians*, 38–40; Reumann, *Philippians*, 19; Hansen, *Philippians*, 13–15; Witherington III, *Philippians*, 21–30.

scholars have tried to establish a formal rhetorical structure of this letter.[31] While this study appreciates the rhetorical dimension of the letter, it does not attempt to impose any formal structure on it. The reasons are as follows. It remains disputed whether Philippians has a certain formal rhetorical structure. Even if there is, the complexity and diversity of the materials in the letter becomes a major obstacle for any scholar attempting to discern it. This is reflected in the disagreement among the rhetorical specialists on the precise structure of this letter.[32] Hence, instead of imposing any rhetorical structure from outside the text, it is better to analyze and formulate Paul's various rhetorical strategies from within the text.[33]

5.2 The Writer, the Recipients, and their Relationship

5.2.1 Paul, the Slave of Christ Jesus

The prescript of the letter (1:1) discloses that the senders are Paul and Timothy. However, the first-person-singular orientation in the letter gives a strong impression that the apostle Paul is the one responsible for its whole content.[34] Attention is given to his designation as δοῦλος Χριστοῦ Ἰησοῦ.

As this identity revolves around Χριστός, the significance of this title needs to be established in the first place. The term appears about 270 times in Paul's undisputed letters, and more than half of them appear independently in reference to Jesus. In Philippians, the term appears sixteen times independently out of thirty-seven times. It was popularly presumed in the past that the titular force of Χριστός had largely receded into merely another personal name of Jesus in the Pauline churches. According to this line of thought, the gentile believers in Philippi were not able to appreciate the messianic significance of Χριστός.[35] The present study, however, views that the gentile readers in

---

31. Watson, "Rhetorical Analysis," 57–88; Bloomquist, *Function of Suffering*, 120–38; Witherington III, *Philippians*, 21–30.

32. See Hansen, *Philippians*, 14.

33. For this approach, see Synman, "Rhetorical Analysis," 783–809.

34. This is noted in Phil 1:7–8, 12–26, 27b, 30; 2:2, 16–18, 19, 23–24, 25, 27–28, 3:1, 4–14, 17–18; 4:1–4, 10–19. It is likely that the mention of Timothy relates to Paul's plan to send this young associate to the Philippian congregation (2:19–24).

35. Bousset, *Kyrios Christos*, 121–22; Hahn, *Titles of Jesus*, 189–93.

Philippi were able to appreciate its messianic thrust. At the time of Paul, Christianity was still part of Judaism, and the bond between the Hellenistic and Jewish churches remained strong.[36] Indeed, the public discourses of the gentile churches were still dominated by the Jewish Christian teachers.[37] Therefore, it is quite rational to assume that Paul and his associates explained with clarity to their gentile converts in Philippi the meaning of Χριστός in their sharing of the gospel.[38] Accordingly, this Hellenistic congregation could still appreciate the messianic significance of this term in this letter. Bearing this in mind, we now observe the significance of Paul's identity as a δοῦλος of Christ in this letter.

Paul's identity as δοῦλος Χριστοῦ is attested in many of his letters,[39] but its appearance in the prescript of the letter is only attested in his letters to the Romans and Philippians. Whereas in the former it appears together with his identity as the ἀπόστολος of Christ, in the latter it stands independently. Reading Philippians, it is easily appreciated that the identity anticipates the great story of Christ in 2:6–11 where he is presented as taking the μορφὴ δούλου.[40] In the Greco-Roman world δοῦλοι (slaves) generally connoted a humble and severe status, as this group of people was placed at the bottom of society,[41] though some slaves could gain privilege, prestige, and even power in society due to their association with a powerful κύριος.[42] It is also worth noting that in the biblical tradition the term δοῦλος κυρίου (a slave of YHWH) was an authoritative figure who led the nation of Israel.[43] In this light, Paul's

---

36. This is indicated by the ecumenical meeting in Jerusalem (Acts 15) and the gentile collection to support the Palestinian churches (Rom 15:25–27; 2 Cor 8:1–4).

37. See Hengel, *Between Jesus and Paul*, 72–73.

38. Hence, the use of Χριστός without further explanation may indicate that "the identification of Jesus as the Messiah has become so firm and routinized that the title itself is a sufficient way to designate him." Hurtado, *Lord Jesus Christ*, 99; cf. Dunn, *Theology of Paul*, 197.

39. See Rom 1:1, Gal 1:10, 1 Cor 7:22, and Phil 1:1; cf. Eph 6:6; Col 1:7; 4:7, 12; 2 Tim 2:24. There are also five occasions where the verb δουλεύω has Christ as its object. See Rom 12:11; 14:18; 16:18; Phil 2:21–22; cf. Eph 6:7.

40. Bockmuehl, *Philippians*, 50; Fowl, *Philippians*, 17; Nebreda, *Christ Identity*, 52.

41. Fee, *Philippians*, 62–64; Fowl, *Philippians*, 16–17.

42. Harris, *Slave of Christ*, 35–36.

43. Moses in Numbers 12:7–8 LXX, David in Psalm 88.21 LXX, and the prophets in Jeremiah 25:4 LXX. See Bockmuehl, *Commentary on the Epistle*, 50.

identity as δοῦλος Χριστοῦ Ἰησοῦ can signify both his authority and humble position. Having said this, the emphasis in Philippians is heavily on the latter.[44]

Paul's identity as δοῦλος Χριστοῦ Ἰησοῦ profoundly shaped his orientation and conduct of life. First of all, as a slave of Christ, Paul committed himself to magnifying Christ (1:20–22) by doing fruitful works for him, laboring strenuously for the proclamation of his gospel, even during his imprisonments (1:7, 12–13; 2:22). His life conduct was greatly shaped by the story of Christ, seeking a κοινωνία with this Lord in both his suffering death and resurrection (3:10–11). This is amplified in the context of his relationship with his readers. Despite his imprisonment, his main concern is still on the spiritual welfare of this church (1:24–26; 2:12–18). He claims that he longs for them with the affection of Christ and is ready to live and to die for their well-being (1:18, 24–26; 2:17). Finally, what matters to Paul is how he can provide a good account of his service to the Philippians before Christ at his parousia (2:16; 3:20). All this demonstrates that as a slave of Christ Jesus, Paul's life is fully oriented to Christ Jesus, and this is amplified in his service to the church.

In Philippians, Paul presents himself as a suffering slave of Christ (1:7, 17, 21, 30; 2:17; 3:10; 4:11–12, 14). Particularly significant is the image of one who is being imprisoned for the sake of Christ and his gospel (δεσμός in 1: 7, 12–14, 17). The letter was written during his imprisonment. The possibility of his imminent release suggests that Paul's custody was probably to secure his appearance at the Roman trial before the verdict (1:19, 25–26). This inference is supported by the rationale that as a free-born Roman citizen, Paul possesses a judicial right for protection and justice (Acts 16:37–39; 22:22–29; 25:10–12). The place of his custody could be in Rome, Ephesus, or Caesarea.[45] The severity of Paul's condition during the custody is not certain. Judged according to our modern standards, the treatment of prisoners in antiquity is generally very bad.[46] That said, much of a prisoner's treatment depended on the charge, the social status of the person, and the type of custody. If the letter was written in Rome, the custody was probably quite lenient. Based on

---

44. Bockmuehl, *Philippians*, 50–51.

45. For Rome, see O'Brien, *Philippians*, 19–26; Bockmuehl, *Philippians*, 30–32; Cassidy, *Paul in Chains*, 124–35. For Ephesus, see Hansen, *Philippians*, 19–25. For Caesarea, see Hawthorne, *Philippians*, xxxix–l.

46. See Wansink, *Chained in Christ*, 33–55. For the treatment with regard to the type of custody, see Rapske, *Book of Acts*, 20–35.

the account in Acts (28:30), Paul was allowed to rent a room and welcome his visitors.[47] Even so, this did not reduce the mental distress suffered during such custody due to the possibility of a death verdict (1:21–24; 2:17).

Two pivotal notions of the image of Paul's imprisonment need to be briefly discussed. First, the imprisonment is for the sake of Christ and his gospel (1:29–30), and he regards it as being like Christ in his suffering death (3:8). To Paul, his identity as the slave of Christ means that he will not be spared from what happened to his Lord Jesus Christ who had suffered as a slave of God for the sake of the salvation of humankind (2:6–8). As this way of suffering reveals God's power to save, Paul expects to have a deeper *koinonia* with Christ's suffering (3:10).

Second, the image of Paul's imprisonment in Philippians has an anti-imperial trait. Paul's claim that his imprisonment was in the defense of and for the progress of the gospel of Christ (1:7, 12)[48] suggests that his proclamation of the gospel had put him in conflict with the imperial power. We note that Seyoon Kim objects to this reading by underlining Paul's positive attitudes toward the Roman court, the praetorian guards, and Caesar's household in the letter:[49]

> Had he (Paul) intended this through preaching the gospel, how could he expect to be acquitted at his trial and released from prison? Clearly Paul was thinking that he could explain to the court that his gospel did not mean this, that it was not treasonous, in spite of some of its language . . . Thus, his expectation for his acquittal clearly suggests that in his mind his gospel was not anti-imperial . . . Paul believed that the Roman court would be intelligent and fair enough to accept his explanation and *apologia*.[50]

In response to his objection, it is important to note that Paul's conflict is not with the Roman judicial system, or any imperial persons, but rather with the evil power that drives the Roman empire to oppose the gospel of Christ.

---

47. Rapske, *Book of Acts*, 227–42. In this case, financial assistance (Phil 4:10, 18) might supply his lodging and daily expense.

48. Cf. Philemon 9 and 13.

49. Kim, *Christ and Caesar*, 44–45.

50. Kim, 44.

When the empire suppresses this gospel, Paul would resist unflinchingly. In contrast to Kim's opinion, we find no positive appraisal of the imperial authority in this letter. Paul's confidence in his imminent release is not grounded in the Roman judicial system, but in the power of the Holy Spirit (1:19).[51] It is by this divine power that the progress of the gospel across the empire could not be stopped by any human power, including localities where the imperial power is strong, such as the Roman prison (1:12–18), the *praetorium* (1:12), the household of Caesar (4:22), and the Roman colony of Philippi (1:27–28).

5.2.2 The Church at Philippi

The opening letter also indicates that this letter is addressed to the church of Christ in Philippi. Therefore, it is necessary to provide an overview of this community. The reconstruction of this community is dependent on this letter, Paul's statements in his other letters (2 Cor 8:1–4 and 1 Thess 2:2), the Lucan account in Acts 16:11–40, and our limited knowledge of Roman Philippi.

With regard to Acts 16, although the historical accuracy of Acts was frequently doubted in the past, nowadays there is a growing appreciation for it.[52] The present study adopts this positive approach to the historical credibility of this writing. The use of "we" in verse 11 implies the direct involvement of the writer in the story of Paul's mission in the city of Philippi. This is further supported by the fact that the narrative becomes more circumstantial and detailed, which demonstrates the writer's knowledge of Philippi.[53] In verse 12, the πύλη likely refers to one of the city gates found in the ruins of the ancient Philippi, and the ποταμός refers to its nearby river. The ἀγορά in verse 19 is associated with the Roman Forum. The ἄρχοντες and στρατηγοί in verses 19–20 refer to *duumvir*, the highest political body of the city (i.e. *duumvir iure dicundo Philippis*).[54] Finally, τὰ ἔθη (the customs) in verse 21 denote the Roman *mos maiorum*. All this demonstrates the writer's sensitivity to the circumstance of Roman Philippi.

---

51. This is also admitted in Kim, *Christ and Caesar*, 45.

52. See the discussion in Bockmuehl, *Philippians*, 10–12; Fowl, *Philippians*, 12–14; Bruce, *Philippians*, 4–7; Johnson, *Acts of the Apostles*, 5–7; Witherington III, *Acts of the Apostles*, 24–46.

53. Bockmuehl, *Philippians*, 12; Pilhofer, *Philippi Band 1*, 153–59; Witherington III, *Acts of the Apostles*, 586–88.

54. This is attested in the inscriptions nos. 219, 253, 324a, 438. See Pilhofer, *Philippi Band 2*.

One critical issue concerning the historical credibility of Acts 16 is the writer's statement that Philippi is a "leading city of that district of Macedonia" in verse 12. First, it is historically attested that Macedonia is not a district but a province. Second, the word πρῶτος is often associated with a capital city, whereas Philippi was never the capital of the province of Macedonia, nor the capital of one of the districts in Macedonia. The problems are complicated by various readings attested in early manuscripts:[55] (1) πρώτη τῆς μερίδος Μακεδονίας πόλις (𝔓[74], ℵ, A, C, Ψ, 33[vid], 36, 81, 323, 945, 1175, 1891, pc); (2) πρώτη τῆς μερίδος τῆς Μακεδονίας πόλις (𝔐); (3) πρώτη μερίδος τῆς Μακεδονίας πόλις (B); (4) πρώτη τῆς Μακεδονίας πόλις (614, 1241, 1505, 1739, 2495, pc, sy[h]); (5) πρώτη μερίς Μακεδονίας πόλις (E, sa[mss]); (6) κεφαλὴ τῆς Μακεδονίας (D, sy[p]).

To solve this textual problem, two possible solutions can be offered. The first is to follow the NA[26-28] that amends the text with πρώτη[ς] μερίδος τῆς Μακεδονίας πόλις, which can be translated as "a city of the first district of Macedonia." Accordingly, Philippi is described as one of the cities in the first district of Macedonia.[56] This conjecture is supported by Livius's testimony that the province of Macedonia was divided into four districts.[57] While this is a possible solution, this conjecture is not supported by any manuscript. The second solution is to adopt the first option reading, which is supported by many early manuscripts: πρώτη τῆς μερίδος Μακεδονίας πόλις. This phrase can be translated as "a first city of the portion of Macedonia." In this conjecture, the adjective πρῶτος does not denote the capital city but a title of honor, and the term μερίς is read not as a technical term for a "district" but rather "a portion" of Macedonia.[58] It can be argued that the status of Philippi as a Roman colony deserves some honor in the Greco-Roman world, given that the city is historically associated with the rise of the Macedonian hegemony and Augustus's power.[59] In all, the claim made in Acts 16:12 concerning the status of Roman Philippi should not be used to undermine the historical

---

55. See the discussion in Barrett, *Acts of the Apostles*, 778–79.
56. Bruce, *Book of the Acts*, 357; Conzelmann, *Acts of the Apostles*, 310.
57. Livius, 45.29.
58. Witherington III, *Acts of the Apostles*, 489.
59. Witherington III, 490–91.

credibility of this Acts account. With this in mind, we now proceed to establish the general outlook of Roman Philippi at the time of Paul.

5.2.2.1 The Profile

According to Acts 16:11–40, the Philippian church was established by Paul during his missionary journey in the province of Macedonia in AD 49–50 (or 50–52).[60] When this letter was composed, the congregation probably comprised 50–100 believers.[61] This estimation comes by considering a number of figures mentioned in Paul's letter to the Philippians and Acts 16.[62] The letter could have been written in AD 50 in Corinth, AD 54–57 in Ephesus, AD 60 in Caesarea, or AD 60–62 in Rome.[63] Assuming that the church continued to grow through the proclamation of the gospel (1:5, 7), the later the letter was composed, the bigger the congregation would have been. Craig Steven de Vos argues that the church was about thirty believers based on the size of a small *domus* or an *insula* workshop.[64] This figure is too low, considering that the community was led by at least two ἐπίσκόποι (overseers) and two διακόνοι (deacons) and that it was able to give financial support to Paul's ministry. The spatial limitation should not limit the growth of the church. The Christian meeting could be arranged in an open space (Acts 16:13) or several *insulae*.

The Philippian church was a Greek-speaking congregation.[65] Although Latin was the official language in Philippi, Greek was also popular as this language was both the lingua franca in the Roman East and the native language of Philippi. During his visit to this city, Paul very likely shared the gospel in Greek, just as his letter was also written in this language. As it was with other Pauline churches, this congregation consisted mainly of gentile converts. Whether the members were predominantly of Roman or Greek

---

60. For AD 49–50, see Bockmuehl, *Philippians*, 12; for AD 50–52, see Witherington III, *Philippians*, 84.

61. Cf. Portefaix, *Sisters Rejoice*, 237; Oakes, *Philippians*, 61.

62. Acts 16 mentions two figures (Lydia and the Jailer). Philippians mentions five names (Epaphroditus, Euodia, Syntyche, Syzygus, and Clement) and some overseers and deacons which are counted at least as four persons. Altogether, there are ten to eleven figures. If each person represents one household, and each household presumably consists of five to six members, then the church would have more than fifty people.

63. See the discussion in Hawthorne, *Philippians*, xxxvi–xliv.

64. De Vos, *Church and Community*, 260–61.

65. Portefaix, *Sisters Rejoice*, 137; Oakes, *Philippians*, 61.

origins, however, can hardly be determined.[66] What can be suggested from Paul's use of various colonial terminologies in the letter (πολιτεύομαι in 1:27; πολίτευμα in 3:20; συστρατιώτης in 2:25; φιλιππήσιοι in 4:15) is that this community had a strong Roman orientation.[67]

Jewish Christians might be present in this congregation, but they were probably only a few and non-influential.[68] The arguments are in order. First of all, Acts 16:11–40 gives the impression that there were only a small number of Jews in Philippi at the time of Paul. The προσευχή at the riverside (vv. 13 and 16) can be translated as "a place of prayer" or "a house of prayer," which can be associated with the Jewish synagogue.[69] However, the fact that Acts consistently employs the term συναγωγή when referring to the Jewish house of prayer,[70] and that only in this account the term προσευχή is used, gives an important hint. It is more likely that this προσευχή simply refers to a field outside the city where a few Jews and God fearers usually gathered for worship.[71] This inference is supported by the fact that in this narrative Paul meets not any Jewish male, but only some women who were gentile worshippers of YHWH (vv. 13–14). This strongly suggests that not many Jews were resident in Philippi.[72] To be sure, there is an inscription that attests to the presence of a synagogue in Philippi, but it is dated to the third to fourth century AD.[73]

Second, as many have noted, Paul's letter to the Philippians lacks biblical references. There is no biblical citation found in this letter, but a few allusions to the Old Testament.[74] This reinforces the hypothesis of a limited Jewish presence. Finally, while in Philippians 3:2–9 Paul deals with the Judaizing teaching, it does not say anything about the dominance of the Jewish Christians

---

66. For Roman ethnic, see Peterlin, *Paul's Letter*, 167; for Roman citizens, see De Vos, *Church and Community*, 251–52; for Greek origins, see Oakes, *Philippians*, 66–67.

67. Tellbe, *Paul Between Synagogue*, 223.

68. Tellbe, 220–23; De Vos, *Church and Community*, 252–54; Peterlin, *Paul's Letter*, 166.

69. This is attested in 3 Macc (7:20), Philo (*Flacc.* 45, 47, 49), and Josephus (*Ag. Ap.* 2:10; *Life* 277, 280, 293; *Ant.* 14:2580). See Johnson, *Acts of the Apostles*, 292; Fowl, *Philippians*, 13.

70. Acts 9:20; 13:5, 14; 17:1; 18:4; 19:8.

71. Bockmuehl, *Philippians*, 14.

72. According to Bruce, *Book of the Acts*, 310–11, it requires at least ten Jewish males to constitute a synagogue. Cf. Fitzmyer, *Acts of the Apostles*, 585.

73. See the Inscription no. 387a in Pilhofer, *Philippi Band 2*, 465; see also the discussion in Koukouli-Chrysantaki, "Colonia Iulia," 28–35.

74. Phil 1:19; 2:6–8; 2:9–11; 2:14–15; 4:18. See the discussion in Silva, "Philippians," 835–39.

in this community. As many have argued, these Judaizers can be some Jewish or Gentile Christians from other cities who tried to influence the gentile believers in Philippi.[75]

Paul's general description of the condition of the believers of Christ in Macedonia in 2 Corinthians 8:1–2, particularly the statement ἡ κατὰ βάθους πτωχεία αὐτῶν implies the humble situation of the Philippian congregation. De Vos argues that the community predominantly "comprised people who belonged to the artisan classes" with a number of slaves, but no ruling elite.[76] Oakes provides a more detailed profile based on his social reconstruction of the city in the middle of the first century AD: "43 percent service community, 25 percent poor, 16 percent slaves, 15 percent colonist farmer, and one percent élite landowners."[77] Despite their differences, both portray the dominance of service groups (traders and artisans). This figure is justified since these groups of people were easily connected to Paul's lifestyle (Acts 16:14; 18:3).[78] In his letter to the Philippians, Paul indeed employs various commercial images in 3:7–8 (κέρδος-ζημία; ζημιόω-κερδαίνω) and 4:15–18 (εἰς λόγον δόσεως καὶ λήψεως; τὸν πλεονάζοντα εἰς λόγον ὑμῶν; ἀπέχω δὲ πάντα καὶ περισσεύω).[79] We also expect the presence of farmers and slaves as Philippi was situated in a pastoral setting where its livelihood depended on agriculture.[80] Finally, Acts 16 attests to the conversion of a low-rank officer and his household (vv. 27–34) and probably a slave (v. 16).

As traveling in Paul's time was very expensive, the presence of some wealthy figures should be seriously considered.[81] Lydia who is mentioned in Acts 16:14 befits this category. She is described as πορφυρόπωλις πόλεως from Thyatira. Her business was probably not connected with the expensive murex-dyeing garment, but the so-called "Turkey red" garment associated with the industry in Thyatira (cf. Rev 2:18),[82] which is less expensive. However,

---

75. Fee, *Philippians*, 293–94; Bockmuehl, *Philippians*, 183–84.

76. De Vos, *Church and Community*, 244–60.

77. Oakes, *Philippians*, 60–61.

78. The spreading of the gospel after Paul's visit was mainly dependent on them. Notably, merchants and artisans might have a good access to other groups (i.e. farmers, slaves, and patrons) in Philippi. See De Vos, *Church and Community*, 258.

79. De Vos, *Church and Community*, 258.

80. De Vos, 91.

81. Oakes, *Philippians*, 61.

82. De Vos, *Church and Community*, 257–58.

the fact that she could provide a place to stay for Paul and his three colleagues in her *domus* or *insula* indicates she was more than a humble merchant.[83]

In all, the Philippian congregation was founded by Paul in AD 48–52 during his mission work in Macedonia. By the time of the writing of this letter, the community comprised probably 50–100 Christians. This was a Greek-speaking congregation where the members were mostly Gentiles, although some Jewish Christians might be present. Similar to the orientation of the society in Philippi, this community had a strong Roman orientation. The members were generally humble merchants, artisans, and slaves. Even so, there might be one or two wealthy members in this congregation.

5.2.2.2 The Corporate Identity

It is also important to observe how Paul portrays the Philippian congregation in this letter. In the prescript, he addresses the readers as οἱ ἅγιοι ἐν Χριστῷ Ἰησοῦ.[84] This designation, which is rooted in the Jewish Scripture, signifies their election as God's people (cf. Rom 1:7; 1 Cor 1:2; 3:17). In the LXX, the term ἅγιος carries the meaning of קדוש, and it is used to designate God's people being consecrated for God's service.[85] To articulate the same idea, Paul also employs a more contextual term τὸ πολίτευμα ἐν οὐρανοῖς (the heavenly commonwealth) in Philippians 3:20 that profoundly shapes a new social identity of Christians in Philippi.[86] While the outsiders regard them as an illegal *collegium* of the lower classes, Paul portrays them in this letter as the heavenly colony stationed in Philippi. This social identity has an eschatological overtone given that the term τὸ πολίτευμα ἐν οὐρανοῖς is

---

83. Witherington III, *Acts of the Apostles*, 492.

84. In his letters, Paul often addresses his readers as ἅγιοι in the prescript (Rom 1:1; 1 Cor 1:2; 2 Cor 1:1; cf. Eph 1:1; Col 1:2), and called them as ἅγιοι in the body of letters (Rom 1:1, 7; 8:27; 15:25, 26, 31; 16:2; 15:1; 1 Cor 1:2; 6:1, 2; 14:33; 16:1, 15; 2 Cor 1:1; 8:4; 9:1, 12; 13:12; 1 Thess 3:13; Phil 1:1; 4:21, 22; 5:7; cf. Eph 1:1, 4, 15, 18; 2:19; 3:8, 18; 4:12; 5:3; 6:18; Col 1:2, 4, 22, 26; 2 Thess 1:10; 1 Tim 5:10).

85. See ἔθνος ἅγιον in Exod 19:6; ἄνδρες ἅγιοι in Exod 22:30; λαὸς ἅγιος in Deut 7:6. Balz, "ἅγιος," *EDNT* 1:18; Fowl, *Philippians*, 17–18.

86. According to Nebreda, Nebreda, *Christ Identity*, 38, "Social Identity" refers to that "part of a person's self-concept that derives from his or her membership in a group." From this point of view, τὸ πολίτευμα ἐν οὐρανοῖς can be seen as part of Paul's formation a new social identity for the Philippian church (see pp. 282–83).

a Romanized version of ἡ βασιλεία τοῦ θεοῦ (the kingdom of God).[87] In this letter, Paul highlights that God's earthly dominion has been inaugurated through Christ's death and resurrection, but its full realization would be at his parousia (2:10–11; 3:20; cf. 1 Cor 15:20–28). During this interim period, this eschatological kingdom is expanding throughout the whole world, including in the city of Philippi (1:5–6; 4:3).[88] His statements that they are expectantly waiting for their σωτήρ and κύριος in the form of the Messiah Jesus (3:20) and that their names were registered in the book of life (4:3) strengthen this eschatological thrust.

The readers' identities as the holy ones in Christ, the children of God, and members of the heavenly commonwealth have an ethical impetus: they are to live out their citizenship worthily according to the gospel of Christ (1:27) and live out their holiness in a depraved world (2:15–16). All this will have bearing on our quest to understand the universal worship theme in the letter.

5.2.3 The *Koinonia* in the Gospel of Christ

There is some warm and mutual affection between Paul and the Philippian Christians expressed in the letter, such as their sharing of joy (2:2; 2:18; 4:1), struggles (1:29–30; 4:14), the ministry for the gospel (1:7; 4:3), and boasting in the Lord Jesus Christ (1:26; 2:17). To underline this kind of affection the term κοινωνία (koinonia) is employed. In antiquity, the term denotes a close relationship involving mutual interest and sharing,[89] which is widely used in Greek literature to express a close bonding within a group, such as family, friendship, business partnership, sharing ownership of property, citizenship, religious organization, etc.[90] In this letter, the idea of *koinonia* is first introduced at the beginning (1:5), and it reverberates throughout the whole letter. There are about thirty-two verses that articulate the idea of κοινωνία in this short letter,[91] which includes the use of various terms[92] and compound words

---

87. In Pauline letters, this term and its equivalent occur nine times: Rom 14:17; 1 Cor 4:20; 6:9; 15:50; Gal 5:21; cf. Eph 5:5 (ἐν τῇ βασιλείᾳ τοῦ Χριστοῦ καὶ θεοῦ); Col 4:11; and 1 Thess 2:12 (τὴν ἑαυτοῦ βασιλείαν); 2 Thess 1:5. See Kreitzer, "Kingdom of God," 524.

88. For the "already-not yet" eschatological scheme, see Dunn, *Theology of Paul*, 461–66.

89. See BDAG, 552–53.

90. Hansen, *Letter to the Philippians*, 48.

91. See the discussion in Koperski, *Knowledge of Christ*, 79–80.

92. Such as κοινωνία (2:1; 3:10), συγκοινωνός (1:7), συγκοινωνέω (4:14), κοινωνέω (4:15).

with the prefix-συν.[93] All this demonstrates that *koinonia* is one major theme in the letter.[94] The theme has an important rhetorical function, as reading Paul's exhortation across the letter the readers are continuously reminded of their unique relationship with Paul.

The nature of the *koinonia* between Paul and the Philippian congregation needs to be highlighted. First of all, it is worth noting that Philippians 1:5 informs us that this relationship is shaped by the gospel (εἰς τὸ εὐαγγέλιον). Although the name Jesus Christ does not appear, in this letter the gospel is exclusively associated with Christ (see 1:27).[95] Accordingly, this *koinonia* has a triangular relationship, involving Paul, the Philippian congregation, and their Lord Jesus Christ.[96]

Second, to Paul, the gospel of Christ is both the message of God's redemption through the Messiah Jesus (2:6–11; cf. Rom 1: 3–4; 1 Cor 15:1–4) and God's power to save (1:5–6; cf. Rom 1:16–17). With regard to the former, their relationship involves the proclamation of the gospel of Christ. Paul and the Philippian church are "partners" (συγκοινωνοί) in their defense, confirmation, and imprisonment for this gospel ministry (1:7).[97] This also includes the sharing of financial assistance (4:10–20).[98] With regard to the latter, their relationship involves a deep engagement with God's redemptive work in Christ that produces a new identity,[99] norm of conduct,[100] and orientation of life.[101]

---

93. Such as συναθλέω (1:27; 4:3), σύζυγος (4:3), συμμιμητής (3:17), συνεργός (2:25), συστρατιώτης (2:5), συγχαίρω (2:17–18), σύμψυχος (2:2), συμμορφίζω (3:10), σύμμορφος (3:21).

94. Peterman, *Paul's Gift*; Swift, "Theme and Structure," 234–54. Other major themes are joy in the midst of suffering and living worthily according to the gospel of Christ. See Bloomquist, *Function of Suffering*; Witherington III, *Acts of the Apostles*, 25.

95. In Paul's letters, the term εὐαγγέλιον always appears singular form, and it usually refers to the Messiah Jesus. Dunn, *Theology of Paul*, 168.

96. In Philippians, the term underscores the relationship within the church (1:27; 2:2; 3:17), between Paul and the Philippians (1:7; 2:1, 17–18, 25; 4:3, 10, 14–15), between Paul and Jesus Christ (3:10), and between the Philippians and Jesus Christ (3:21).

97. These three words have a strong evangelistic nuance. See Keown, *Congregational Evangelism*, 210.

98. Certainly, this financial assistance can be construed within the giving-receiving motif in the ancient friendship (cf. Paul's letter to Philemon). Having said this, the motif for κοινωνία in the proclamation of the gospel is predominant in Philippians. Hence, it is not without reason that instead of saying "thank you," Paul locates their gift in the context of the Philippians' worship of God (4:18 ὀσμὴν εὐωδίας, θυσίαν δεκτήν, εὐάρεστον τῷ θεῷ). See Peterman, *Paul's Gift*, 160.

99. Nebreda, *Christ Identity*, 283–84.

100. Wojtkowiak, *Christologie Und Ethik*, 129.

101. Martin, "Christology in the Prison Epistles," 193–218.

Third, their *koinonia* in the gospel of Christ also has an eschatological thrust. According to Philippians 1:5–6, their evangelical partnership is embedded in God's active work of his salvation, as it has started from the first day of their faith in Christ, continues in the present day, and will be consummated at the day of Christ.[102] This also raises the confidence that their partnership of suffering will end not in destruction (1:28) but the consummation of their future salvation (3:20–21). This eschatological notion, as it shall be demonstrated later, is one important coordinate in understanding the significance of the motif of the universal worship of Christ in this letter.

To sum up the discussion, it can be said that in his letter to the Philippians Paul presents himself as a slave of Christ who is entrusted with missions to proclaim the gospel of Christ and to build up his church. Because of his ministry for the gospel of Christ, he is currently imprisoned in Roman custody. The Philippian church – addressed as God's holy people in Christ and depicted as citizens of the heavenly commonwealth stationed in Philippi – are the readers. This community currently waits for the parousia of their Lord Jesus Christ. In this letter, Paul raises one principal theme: the *koinonia* in the gospel of Christ, which strongly binds Paul and his readers. Not surprisingly, this evangelical *koinonia* is also christologically centered and eschatologically oriented. With regard to the former, Christ is to be magnified through their proclamation of his gospel and their life transformation according to his gospel. With regard to the latter, their relationship is embedded in God's work within and among them, and thus will be consummated in their salvation on the day of Christ. All this has a rhetorical impact in the letter.

5.3 The Addressed Problems

The occasion that called for the letter of Philippians is Paul's reception of the financial assistance from the church of Philippi (4:18). The letter, however, is written not merely to convey his appreciation of this gift, but it also reveals Paul's intent to address some serious challenges faced by this congregation. We provide a sketch of the complex predicament of this community below.

First of all, Paul's statement of "not being frightened in anything by the opponents" in 1:28 suggests that the Philippian Christians were facing strong

---

102. Hansen, *Philippians*, 48–51.

opposition in their city. Their opponents (ἀντικείμενοι) are better associated not with the Judaizers (3:2), but the local pagans.[103] This is supported by a couple of reasons. The opposition is described as life-threatening, which might involve physical abuse and imprisonment (1:29–30),[104] whereas the threat in 3:2 is concerned more with a theological dispute. Moreover, in 1:30, Paul associates the struggle of the church with his own suffering in the past (cf. 1 Thess 2:2; Acts 16:19–24) and in the present (1:7; 4:14) where the involvement of Roman authority can be sensed.[105] All this supports the conjecture that the passage deals with the struggle of the church in the pagan imperial society of Philippi.

According to Philippians 1:27, the point of conflict between the Philippian Christians and their society is the faith of the gospel of Christ. What precisely, however, is the thing in this gospel that is strongly opposed by the imperial pagan society in Philippi? Some scholars argued that the tension is over ethics.[106] In supporting this interpretation, Wojtkowiak presents the following arguments: (1) τῇ πίστει should be construed as dative of instrument (by means of the faith of Christ) or dative of association (with the faith of Christ);[107] (2) the missionary expression is not detected in this passage; (3) the conflict should be read in connection with τέκνα θεοῦ ἄμωμα μέσον γενεᾶς σκολιᾶς καὶ διεστραμμένης in 2:15.

While part of the Christians' struggle in Philippi is to take on gospel-like behavior within the pagan environment, it is doubtful whether the qualities of being humble and concerned for others (2:3–4) has elicited social resistance. In fact, this noble ethos will be a positive point that makes Christianity attractive in a pagan society. It is quite different, however, if the claims of Christ's redemptive work (2:6–8) and his worship as the universal divine κύριος (2:9–11) are in view. The colony of Philippi is a polytheistic society, in

---

103. Oakes, *Philippians*, 84–89; Tellbe, *Paul Between Synagogue*, 232–34; De Vos, *Church and Community*, 263; Bormann, *Philippi*, 218.

104. De Vos, *Church and Community*, 264–65. Certainly, we can add family mistreatments and social-economic sanction. For the former, see Portefaix, *Sisters Rejoice*, 195–98; for the latter, see Oakes, *Philippians*, 96.

105. According to Acts 16:20–24, Paul's proclamation of the gospel in Philippi was violently opposed by the local traditionalists and imperial authority. Presently, he was imprisoned by the Roman authority due to the very same reason (Phil 1:12–18).

106. Wojtkowiak, *Christologie Und Ethik*, 128, 130–31.

107. Cf. Lightfoot, *Philippians*, 106.

which each ethnic group is worshipping its own deities. In the polytheistic worldview, the adoption of a new cult does not mean the abandonment of the old ones. Judaism, including Christianity, is an exception. The adoption of the faith of the gospel of Christ requires the renouncement of all past religious beliefs and practices. Accordingly, the christological passage claims that all beings and powers in heaven, on earth, and under the earth (thus, it includes all the deities worshipped in Philippi) will one day submissively worship the Lord Jesus Christ. Such an exclusive claim has certainly created a strong religious and political resistance in Philippi, particularly from the traditionalists and the imperial officials.

The public hatred is inflamed further by the strong commitment of the Philippian church members to proclaim the gospel of Christ. The dative τῇ πίστει in 1:27 is better construed as a dative of advantage (for the sake of) to underline that Christians' "striving together" (συναθλοῦντες) is for the faith of the gospel.[108] This includes not only their holding firmly the gospel of Christ (2:16) and their gospel-like conduct (2:3–4), but also their bold defense and confirmation of this very gospel (1:7).[109] The association of συναθλέω in this verse with the proclamation of the gospel is strong. First, the *koinonia* in the gospel of Christ is a major theme of the letter, and this exhortation is articulated in relation to this *koinonia* (1:27). Second, the only other use of συναθλέω in Paul's writings is in 4:3, and in this verse, the verb is notably associated with evangelistic work. Finally, Paul also associates their current struggles with his past and present sufferings (1:29–30) caused by his missionary activities (1:12–14; 4:14). As this gospel promotes the worship of YHWH and his Messiah Jesus and denounces other religious practices, the proclamation of this gospel must be offensive to the polytheistic society of Philippi.

Excursus: The Cult of Augustus and the Civic Opposition in Philippi

The contribution of the imperial cult, particularly the cult of Augustus, to the struggle of the Philippian congregation needs to be unpacked. The apotheosis of Augustus in AD 14 had officially incorporated this Caesar into the

---

108. O'Brien, *Philippians*, 152; Bockmuehl, *Philippians*, 99; Fowl, *Philippians*, 63; Hansen, *Philippians*, 97.

109. Keown, *Congregational Evangelism*, 107–24.

pantheon of Roman deities to be worshipped by the imperial subjects. Hence, in the time of Paul *divus* Augustus was a patron god of the Roman colony of Philippi to be worshipped along with other Roman traditional deities.[110] As the conflict in 1:27–28 was with the pagan imperial society at large, it can be further argued that the cult of Augustus contributed to the civic opposition toward Christianity in this city.

First of all, Roman people are generally conservative in observing their religious *pietas*.[111] This is reflected in Cicero's statement: "No one shall have gods to himself, either new gods or alien gods unless *recognized by the State*. Privately they shall worship those gods whose worship they have duly received from their ancestors."[112] As Augustus is one of the Roman deities, by the Roman *mos maiorum*,[113] he should be venerated as part of religious *pietas*. Withdrawing from this cultic practice means violating this pivotal tradition. Second, as it has been elaborated in the previous chapter, the cult of Augustus not only expresses the loyalty of the imperial subjects to the emperor but is also an essential pillar of the *Pax Deorum* and the Pax Romana.[114] Accordingly, the Christians' withdrawal from his cult will be regarded as a very serious offense to the imperial power.[115]

We note that Oakes strongly argues that the imperial cult is not the pressing issue for the Philippian Christians.[116] As he has made a strong and cogent case, his arguments will be presented in order. First, the active involvement in the cults (decorating the statues, providing the feasts, and leading the rituals) is limited to the households of wealthy patrons who are mostly pagans.[117] Second, the cults are non-obligatory, and so no attempt is made to monitor

---

110. Barclay, *Pauline Churches*, 352–55, notes that "the imperial cults were not an independent element of religious life, but were generally incorporated into already existing tradition."

111. Galinsky, *Augustan Culture*, 87–88, 288–312.

112. Cicero, *De legibus* 2.8.19. The translation is from Conzelmann, *Acts of the Apostles*, 131–32. Emphasis is added.

113. *Mos (mores) maiorum* is the unwritten code derived from the social norms of the ancient fathers to guide the Roman conduct in private, social, political, military, and religious life.

114. Remus, "Persecution," 436.

115. Cf. Kim, *Christ and Caesar*, 35.

116. Oakes, "Re-Mapping the Universe," 313.

117. Oakes, 311.

closely the participation. As a consequence, the Christian absence from such observances will not be problematic.[118]

While these two arguments carry some weight, they overlook the fact that since its first arrival in Philippi, Christianity has been regarded as problematic by many local traditionalists (1:30; cf. Acts 16:20–22 and 1 Thess 2:2). This means Christians are being watched, and their absences from the participation in the imperial cults will be suspiciously noted. To be sure, the non-obligatory nature of this cult means that Christian believers will not be officially charged for their absence in the cult. However, the perception of disloyalty to the empire can lead to their being ostracized. By abandoning the traditional cults these gentile converts have borne the brunt of the resentment from some religious *collegia*. This will be more glaringly so if it concerns the cult of Augustus who is regarded as the patron deity of the colony. Accordingly, Christians can be accused of being disloyal to the imperial authority and thus suffer from public hatred in Philippi. Among them, those who have no legal standing in Roman laws are most vulnerable (cf. Act 16:22–24).

Second, Philippians 2:1–4 and 4:2 disclose that there is an internal conflict in the congregation. How detrimental this friction is not clearly stated. Paul's mentioning of the names of those in dispute, Εὐοδία and Συντύχη, indicates that the conflict has been known to the whole congregation and disturbed the harmony of the church.[119] To suggest that the conflict has created a sharp division as the case of the church in Corinth, however, is too far-fetched.[120] Paul's friendly tone expresses his confidence that the unity of the church can be restored through his letter and internal mediation (4:3).[121]

The exact points of conflict between the two leading women are not stated. Philippians 2:1–4 implies that the conflict is not over doctrinal belief, but generated by the worldly ethos of "rivalry" (ἐριθεία) and "empty glory" (κενοδοξία) that has driven some members to look after "their own interest" (τὰ ἑαυτῶν

---

118. Oakes, 312–13.

119. These two women probably held a certain role or position in the church. This conjecture is supported by the social-cultural makeup of the Roman Philippi that allowed noble and wealthy women to publicly hold some religious roles. See Portefaix, *Sisters Rejoice*, 33–58; Abrahamsen, *Women and Worship*, 74–84; Witherington III, *Philippians*, 236–37. Whether they served as διάκονοι, however, is far from certain. Contra Peterlin, *Paul's Letter*, 109–11.

120. Contra Peterlin, *Paul's Letter*, 123–28.

121. O'Brien, *Philippians*, 479; Bockmuehl, *Philippians*, 239.

σκοποῦντες).[122] Such an ethos is probably percolated down from the cultural mindset of pagan imperial society in Philippi,[123] which Paul describes in 2:15 as the crooked and twisted generation (γενεᾶς σκολιᾶς καὶ διεστραμμένης). A common pursuit in the Greco-Roman society is the attainment of high social status and honor, which is notably reflected in Augustus's *Res Gestae* that claims the highest status and honor for him. As this ethos has penetrated the life of the Philippian church, it hurts the internal *koinonia* and weakens the community in facing external threats.

Third, the expectation to live blamelessly as the children of God in the midst of "the crooked and twisted generation" (γενεᾶς σκολιᾶς καὶ διεστραμμένης) in 2:15 implies the presence of an ethical struggle for many Christians in this pagan imperial society. Their faith in Christ demands both the renunciation of past worldly behavior and the adoption of gospel-like conduct, and they are alien to the pagan society of Philippi.[124] The adjective σκολιός and the participle of διαστρέφω have ethical notion too, as both underline the twisted morality of the Philippian society and stood in opposition to the standards held by Christianity.[125] Those familiar with the Jewish Scripture, however, might discern an implicit critique of idolatry. The phrase γενεᾶς σκολιᾶς καὶ διεστραμμένης apparently alludes to Deuteronomy 32:5 LXX, in which the nation of Israel is accused as τέκνα μωμητά γενεὰ σκολιὰ καὶ διεστραμμένη because of their idol worship. Accordingly, Paul's negative statement implicitly describes the practices of idol worship in the city.

Living within the pagan imperial society that is both corrupt before God's eyes and hostile to the gospel of Christ is never easy. This has engendered some insubordination among some members, the attitudes of which are expressed by γογγυσμός (grumbling) and διαλογισμός (reasoning). Furthermore, the phrase χωρὶς γογγυσμῶν καὶ διαλογισμῶν in 2:14 also evokes the failure of the Exodus community to obey YHWH and his servant Moses.[126]

---

122. Bockmuehl, *Philippians*, 239.

123. Hellerman, *Reconstructing Honor*, 157–63, emphasizes on the influence of the imperial ethos of *cursus honorum*.

124. Wojtkowiak, *Christologie Und Ethik*, 128, 144–57, rightly highlights that Christ-like ethos in 2:3–8 was simply alien or not within the coordinate of the Roman *mos maiorum*.

125. For the meaning of σκολιός, see BDAG, 930; for διαστρέφω, see BDAG, 237.

126. Exod 15:24; 16:2, 7 (2x), 8 (3x), 9, 12; 17:3; Num 11:1; 14:2, 27 (2x), 29, 36; 16:11; 17:6, 20 (2x), 25.

Fourth, Paul's strong warnings of βλέπετε τοὺς κύνας, βλέπετε τοὺς κακοὺς ἐργάτας, and βλέπετε τὴν κατατομήν presuppose that the congregation has been exposed to the Judaizing teaching.[127] This teaching is certainly attractive to the gentile believers in Philippi who currently suffered from various persecutions, as Judaism is one of the acknowledged religions (*religio licita*) in the Roman Empire. While the Jewish Christians remain as part of Judaism, the Gentile Christians are regarded as an illegal religious *collegium*. Hence, joining Judaism through circumcision provides the security these gentile converts crave.[128] Despite this attraction, there is no strong indication to support the view that this teaching has deeply penetrated the church.[129] In contrast to Paul's treatment in Galatians, the Judaizing threat is only briefly dealt with in Philippians (3:2–9) and without any strong polemical tones. Hence, the discourse is preventive prophylactic in nature. As the Judaizing teaching is problematic, precautionary steps, such as strong warnings in 3:2, should be taken.

Fifth, although it is possible to construe those walking as the enemies of the cross of Christ (περιπατοῦσιν … τοὺς ἐχθροὺς τοῦ σταυροῦ τοῦ Χριστοῦ) in Philippians 3:18 as referring to the Judaizers in 3:2,[130] the present study regards this term as referring to those who were previously attracted to the gospel of Christ but have now renounced their faith in Christ so as to embrace a hedonistic life and avoid suffering.[131] The arguments are threefold. The use of περιπατέω (to walk) indicates their problem is not on the theology they hold, but the ethics they perform, which is in contrast to Christ's suffering on the cross. Moreover, the terms κοιλία (belly) and αἰσχύνη (shame) are better treated not as references to Jewish dietary requirements or circumcision, but fleshly desires, such as gluttony and sex.[132] Finally, the phrase οἱ τὰ ἐπίγεια

---

127. The data in Paul's other letters suggest that one tenet of this teaching is that faith in Christ needs to be supplemented or perfected by adopting Judaism, with an emphasis on circumcision and the observance of Torah (Gal 5:11). This is also reflected in Paul's reference of κατατομή in 3:2 and his claims μὴ ἔχων ἐμὴν δικαιοσύνην τὴν ἐκ νόμου in 3:9.

128. Bockmuehl, *Philippians*, 190; Tellbe, *Paul Between Synagogue*, 261–67.

129. Hansen, *Philippians*, 218.

130. Hawthorne and Martin, *Philippians*, 233; Witherington III, *Philippians*, 215; Silva, *Philippians*, 179–82.

131. O'Brien, *Philippians*, 453–54; Fee, *Philippians*, 367; Bockmuehl, *Philippians*, 229; Hansen, *Philippians*, 264.

132. Hansen, *Philippians*, 264–65; Contra Silva, *Philippians*, 182–83.

φρονοῦντες indicates that their frame of mind is in opposition to the frame of mind of those claiming to belong to τὸ πολίτευμα ἐν οὐρανοῖς in 3:20, which is expressed in 2:5–11 and 3:4–15.[133] As the readers are living in a perverse pagan society, the temptation to return to a worldly life is great. With great grief, Paul reminds them not to be tempted by this indulgent lifestyle, as this will lead to destruction (ἀπώλεια).

To sum up the discussion, the predicament of the Philippian congregation is notably complex. In general, this heavenly community is struggling, as they live in a pagan imperial society that is regarded as perverse and corrupt before God and hostile to the gospel of Christ. In this situation, various challenges arise. Externally, there is strong civic opposition from the imperial pagan society that makes life difficult. As their sufferings start to increase, some members renounce their faith, while others lose their joy and live with a grumbling attitude. Furthermore, there is an internal conflict caused by a worldly mindset penetrating the church and it has weakened the church. To complicate the matter further, the arrival of Judaizing teaching attracts some church members who crave a trouble-free life. All this has weakened the *koinonia* of this church in the gospel of Christ. Paul's letter to the Philippians, therefore, intends to address this complex challenge.

5.4 The Anti-Imperial Stance

The last issue to be discussed concerns the alleged imperial trait of Paul's letter to the Philippians. So far, we have established not only the presence and the significance of the cult of Augustus in Philippi, but also its contribution to the struggle of the Philippian church. The further posed question is whether Paul's letter to the Philippians confronts the Roman imperial power. As there are a lot of disagreements on this issue, this section intends to establish the position held in the present study.

We note that whether Paul has an anti-imperial mindset remains a hotly debated issue in the current Pauline scholarship. With the risk of oversimplifying the issue, the current scholarly opinions can be grouped into four views. The first argues that Paul still maintains his confidence in the imperial

---

133. O'Brien, *Philippians*, 457–59; Fee, *Philippians*, 374.

power, and thus his letters express no opposition toward Rome.[134] The second contends that Paul strongly opposes the imperial power due to its arrogance, brutality, and oppression toward not only Christianity but also humankind.[135] The third insists that although the imperial power and cults have caused troubles to the gentile Christians, they are insignificant in Paul's theological reasoning, and thus in his letters.[136] The fourth view contends that in his letters Paul indeed polemically engages in certain ways with the Roman imperial power and cults for the sake of Christ and his gospel.[137] While their discussions are relevant, the scale of the debate is clearly beyond the scope of the present study. Bearing the complexity of this issue in mind, this study will focus the discussion primarily on Paul's letter to the Philippians. The position adopted in this study is not simply derived from the general mindset of Paul (i.e. whether or not he holds anti-imperial ideology) but is rather established from the context and content of this particular letter.

It is generally acknowledged that the letter contains various expressions that are associated with imperial power. First of all, many terms associated with the imperial propaganda of the emperors are found in the letter. The term εὐαγγέλιον in the letter[138] recalls the imperial εὐαγγέλια of the Roman Caesars,[139] the phrases ἡ εἰρήνη τοῦ θεοῦ and ὁ θεὸς τῆς εἰρήνης in 4:7–9 evoke the imperial jargon of the *Pax Deorum* (ἡ εἰρήνη τοῦ θεῶν),[140] and Jesus's titles

---

134. This position is presented in Blumenfeld, *Political Paul.*

135. Horsley, *Paul and Politics*; Horsley, *Paul and the Roman*; Elliott, *Arrogance of Nations.*

136. Kim, *Christ and Caesar*; Bryan, *Render to Caesar*; Barclay, *Pauline Churches*, 345–87, see particularly his response to N. T. Wright's position in ch. 19.

137. Wright, *Paul and the Faithfulness of God*, particularly chs. 5 and 12.

138. Phil 1:5, 7, 12, 16, 27 (2x); 2:22, 4:3, 15.

139. In the imperial discourses, the birth, recovery from illness, victory in war, and accession to the throne of the emperors are proclaimed as εὐαγγέλια. See the inscription in *Eretus* on the island of Lesbos (*IG* XII Supp. 124); Philo, *Legat.* 18, 22, 99, 231; Josephus, *J.W.* IV, 618. In the *Priene* calendar inscription (9 BC), the birth of Augustus is claimed as the beginning of εὐαγγέλια for the world.

140. The establishment of the Roman version of *Pax Deorum* was conveyed in the *Ara Pacis Augustae* in the Field of Mars in Rome. See the discussion on pp. 113–14.

of κύριος (2:11; 3:20)[141] and σωτήρ (3:20)[142] echo the honorific address given to the emperors in the Roman East to acknowledge their power to save the imperial subjects and to destroy the imperial enemies.

Second, numerous terms closely associated with the Roman colony of Philippi are also found. In 4:15, Paul addresses the Philippians not as Φίλιπποι, highlighting their ethnicity, but as Φιλιππήσιοι (Latin: *Philippensis*) to underline its colonial name and status. The use of πολίτευμα (3:20) and πολιτεύομαι (1:27) recalls the standing of the Roman colony Philippi within the Roman commonwealth and the duty of its citizens. Paul's addressing Epaphroditus as συστρατιώτης (2:25) is to be read against the background of the colony's being settled by Augustus's legions after the Roman civil wars.

Finally, the letter contains various imperial imageries. The universal acclamation of κύριος Ἰησοῦς Χριστὸς in 2:11 adumbrates the imperial ovation of κύριος Καῖσαρ during his parousia in the Greek East or the ritual oath in the imperial cults. The expression ἐν οἷς φαίνεσθε ὡς φωστῆρες ἐν κόσμῳ in 2:15 echoes the service of the colony of Philippi as "a beacon of Roman order" in Macedonia.[143] Paul's statement of σωτῆρα ἀπεκδεχόμεθα κύριον Ἰησοῦν Χριστόν in 3:20 is analogous to "waiting for the parousia of the Roman Caesars to save their colony in the diaspora from the enemies."[144]

Having said all this, many of these imperial expressions also have their parallels in the LXX. For example, the term εὐαγγέλιον is also associated with the good news of the coming of YHWH's eschatological salvation in Isaiah (40:9; 52:7; 61:1–3).[145] In Isaiah 52:7, the eschatological εἰρήνη τοῦ θεοῦ is closely connected with this Isaianic εὐαγγέλιον. The term κύριος serves as a Greek reverential substitute for the Tetragrammaton in the LXX. God is also

---

141. Augustus is addressed as κύριος in BGU, 1197.1.15, and probably in Ditt. Or. 606; Tiberius in P. Oxy. 1.37.5; Nero in Ditt Syll. 3.814.31. See Foerster, "κύριος," *TDNT* 3:1054–58. Although Augustus forbade Roman people to address him in this manner, the extent of power described in the *RGDA* 26–33 claims his lordship over the whole world.

142. Julius Caesar is addressed as σωτήρ in Ditt. Syll.3 no. 760; Augustus in *Priene Calendar Inscription* (*OGIS* II, 458, pp. 48–60, particularly lines 33–36); Gaius (Caligula) in Philo, *Legat.* 22; Claudius in *IGRR*, IV, 12 and *IGRR*, IV, 584. See also Foerster, "Σωτήρ," *TDNT* 10:1010–12.

143. This is noted in Bryan, *Render to Caesar*, 84.

144. Wright, "Paul's Gospel," 173–74.

145. Note that Paul cites Isa 52:7 in Rom 10:15. See Dunn, *Theology of Paul*, 167–68; contra Stanton, *Jesus and Gospel*, 19–20.

commonly referred to as σωτήρ in Psalms and Isaiah.[146] The description of worship in Philippians 2:10–11 is indeed Paul's reworking of Isaiah 45:23–24 LXX. The imagery of light echoes either the imagery of light in Isaiah[147] or the expression οἱ συνιέντες φανοῦσιν ὡς φωστῆρες τοῦ οὐρανοῦ in Daniel 12:3 LXX.

All this being the case, a critical issue needs to be resolved: does Paul use these imperial and colonial terms (1) analogically and accommodatingly,[148] or (2) polemically and confrontationally?[149] The present study inclines to the latter. The grounds for this stand are threefold.

First of all, Paul's imprisonment by the Roman authority (1:12–26) indicates that there has been already a conflict between the imperial power and Paul. He certainly has no ideological intention to overthrow the Roman power.[150] However, when the empire, as a whole self-contained structured power, keeps opposing and suppressing the proclamation of the gospel of Christ, there can be no compromising response from Paul, whose greatest desire is to magnify the Lord Jesus Christ and proclaim his gospel (1:18–20).[151] He boldly testifies that his imprisonment by Rome cannot hinder the progress of the gospel of Christ that he faithfully proclaims (1:12–18). Reading this letter, those in Philippi will sense the power struggle between God's kingdom and the Roman imperial power on the case of the progress of the gospel.

Second, it has been established above that the opponents in Philippians 1:27–30 are best construed not as Judaizers, but the locals in Philippi. This infers that the readers are currently facing civic opposition. Our discussion above demonstrates the involvement of imperial power.[152] In this context, the call for standing together firmly for the faith of the gospel of Christ in 1:27 and 4:1 needs to be regarded as Paul's confrontational response to the suppressing actions of the imperial power in Philippi. Amid the strong opposition from

---

146. See Pss 24:5; 26:1, 9; 61:3, 7; 64:6; 78:9 LXX and Isa 12:2; 45:15, 21; 62:11 LXX.

147. See Isa 9:2; 42:6; 49:6; 60:3.

148. Bryan, *Render to Caesar*; Kim, *Christ and Caesar*; Cohick, "Philippians and Empire," 166–82; Barclay, *Pauline Churches*, 376–79.

149. See Georgi, *Theocracy in Paul's Praxis*, 72–78; Collins, "Worship of Jesus," 234–57; Wright, "Paul's Gospel"; Heen, "Phil 2:6–11"; Oakes, "Re-Mapping the Universe"; Cassidy, *Paul in Chains*, 178–84; Beck, *Anti-Roman Cryptograms*, 47–61.

150. Kim, *Christ and Caesar*, 50–53; Bryan, *Render to Caesar*, 89–90.

151. Witherington III, *Philippians*, 101–2.

152. See "Excursus: the Cult of Augustus and the Civic Opposition in Philippi" in this chapter.

the local imperial authority and society, he reminds the readers to continue standing firmly together, giving his own imprisonments as examples, for the gospel of Christ.

Finally, as it has been argued above, the civic and imperial persecution in Philippi is primarily caused not by Christian ethical conduct, but rather the confrontation over worship (i.e. pagan worship versus Christian worship). All Christian converts have renounced their past religious practices, including those that pertain to the popular cult of Augustus, in order to commit themselves to worship YHWH and his (Messiah) Christ Jesus. This must be a great offense to the imperial society in Philippi. All this strongly suggests that Paul's use of imperial expressions was polemical (i.e. to confront certain claims of Augustus propagated by the imperial power).

We note some objections to this reading. The first argument relates to Paul's attitude toward the Roman court. It has been claimed based on Romans 13:1–7 that Paul maintains some positive attitude toward Roman authority, including the power to bring justice. Following this line of thought, Seyoon Kim argues that despite his imprisonment by the Roman authority in his letter to the Philippians Paul still maintains his confidence in the Roman court he will face. Hence, in reading Philippians 1:12–26, he makes a claim as follows:

> Since he basically viewed pagan courts as part of the unrighteous world (1 Cor 6:1) it was only realistic for him to consider this. But ultimately faith and hope rise to the top, dispelling anxiety and despair: he "knows" (Phil 1:19, 25) that if he explains Christ with all the wisdom and boldness that the Holy Spirit supplies in response to the Philippians' fervent prayers, the court will see that the gospel is quite innocent of the anti-imperial charge (1:19–20, 25–26; 2:24).

Our reading on this passage, however, is somewhat different from Kim's. We do not sense Paul's positive attitude toward the Roman court in this passage. To be sure, Paul does not oppose every dimension of the Roman rule, as he still maintains "the Jewish positive understanding of human authorities as created and intended by the one God."[153] Having said this, as Kim is also aware of, Paul does regard the Roman court as part of the unrighteous power

---

153. See Wright, *Paul and the Faithfulness*, 1308.

(1 Cor 6:1) that will be destroyed by Christ at the eschaton (1 Cor 15:24). In the case of Philippians 1:12–26, Paul's confidence to win his case comes not from his faith in the Roman judicial justice. Rather, it is grounded in his strong conviction that the Spirit of Jesus Christ will deliver him in response to the readers' prayers (v. 19) and that his work for Christ within the Philippian church has not ended yet (v. 25).

Another objection comes from Christopher Bryan who claims that there is no anti-imperial motive explicitly stated in the letter.[154] His case is constructed along these lines. First, Paul's treatment of the terminology is shaped by the *midrash qal va-chomer* (from light to heavy):

> if the Philippians know what might be due from them and to them rarely as citizens of Rome, *then by how much more* they should know what is due from them and to them as citizens of a realm whose emperor is lord of lords and king of kings![155]

Second, the primary role of the heavily imperial passages (1:27–30; 2:6–11; 3:18–21) is not to oppose the imperial power, but to tackle some internal concerns of the church (2:2–4, 12–14; 4:2–3).[156]

Our study of the letter, however, leads to a different conclusion. While Bryan correctly says that Paul's midrashic method (*qal va-chomer*) is at work in his use of these imperial expressions, the anti-imperial notion of Paul's statements is not thereby necessarily diminished. The context must determine whether or not the expressions are used polemically. An analysis of this context will demonstrate the weakness of Bryan's case. First of all, Bryan's assertion that Paul's concern in Philippians is primarily on the unity of the church is too easy a claim, as it fails to appreciate the imperial involvement in the civic opposition in 1:27–30 as a backdrop of Paul's appeal for unity in 2:2–4. In this section, Paul notably makes an appeal to the readers for the unity of the church to face the external opposition, before he deals with the internal conflict. Furthermore, reading the christological passage, the readers in Philippi will easily appreciate the tension between the cultic confession ὅτι κύριος Ἰησοῦς Χριστὸς acclaimed in 2:11 and the public confession of

---

154. See the discussion in Bryan, *Render to Caesar*, p. 89 on Phil 2:6–11, and p. 84 on Phil 20–21.

155. Bryan, *Render to Caesar*, 84.

156. Bryan, 84–90.

Augustus in the cult of him. Together, they strongly suggest that the call for standing firmly in unity for the faith of the gospel of Christ in 1:27 has an anti-imperial stance.

Second, the two exhortations in 2:12–14 not only hark back to the previous exhortation of unity in 2:2–4 but also have to be situated in the context of living in a γενεᾶς σκολιᾶς καὶ διεστραμμένης (2:15). This way of describing their social context evokes the notion of idols worship in Philippi, including the cult of Augustus, as it echoes Israel's problem of idolatry in the Old Testament (Deut 32:5). Read in this way, standing firmly in unity also implies the rejection of the present cults of any Roman emperor, in favor of the worship of Jesus Christ.

Third, Paul's exhortation of στήκετε ἐν κυρίῳ in 4:1 needs to be read against not only the exhortation in 4:2–3 but also the phrase τοὺς ἐχθροὺς τοῦ σταυροῦ τοῦ Χριστοῦ in 3:18–19. To avoid imperial and social pressure in Philippi, some converts have abandoned their faith. In response to this situation, Paul exhorts the readers to stand firm in the Lord with the eschatological encouragement that it is the Lord Jesus Christ, not Augustus or any Roman Caesar, who will save them by his power to subject all things to himself (3:20–21).

Finally, we need to make a brief response to John Barclay. Being aware of the imperial hegemony of Rome and the religiopolitical significance of its imperial cults in Paul's time, he makes a strong claim that they both are less significant in Paul's theological thought.[157] The primary reason for his view is that to Paul, the power of Rome and its emperor cults are not independent entities, but subordinate to more significant power (i.e. sin and death). They both are regarded as merely another presentation of the evil powers that are controlling the world to oppose the one and only God.[158] Hence, instead of raising up the *divus* emperors to be confronted in his letters, Paul reduces them "to bit-part players in a drama scripted by the cross and resurrection of Jesus."[159] In other words, to Paul, all *divus* emperors are incompatible with his Lord Jesus Christ, and therefore they are not dealt with heightened attention in his letters.[160]

---

157. Barclay, *Pauline Churches*, 374, 383–87.

158. Barclay, 383–85.

159. Barclay, 386–87.

160. Barclay, 374.

Barclay's view above has been countered by Wright, and they need not be repeated here.[161] Barclay is correct in pointing out Paul's theological reasoning that all *divus* emperors are insignificant to the divine lordship of Christ. However, in our opinion, he tends to undermine the dynamic of the pastoral dimension of Paul's letters. The observance of the imperial cults has been a real struggle for the church of Christ in Philippi, and thus they need to be dealt with sensitively. From this point of view, the case that the cults of emperors are not explicitly mentioned in the letter to the Philippians is not due to the insignificance of the imperial cults and powers. Rather, it is a careful rhetorical strategy to undermine their theological significance[162] and his circumstantial sensitivity. Concerning the former, as Oakes rightly argues, in Philippians Paul carefully redraws the map of the universe in his readers' mind by moving its center from the emperor to Christ.[163] Concerning the latter, on his side, Paul is currently imprisoned by the Roman authority and waiting for the final judicial verdict of his case. On the Philippians' side, the congregation is facing various threats from the local imperial power and society. This is not to say that numerous readers are Roman citizens with a strong Roman orientation. Paul who claims himself as the one not running and boxing aimlessly (1 Cor 9:26) wrote the letter to the Philippians with a deep thought to address this core issue wisely. Like in many other letters, he does not oppose the whole structural power of Rome, although he is aware of its demonic force, but focuses on the primary and relevant challenge faced by the church: the imperial power and its emperor cults have been opposing and threatening the sharing of the gospel of Christ, to which Paul and the church in Philippi are fully and faithfully committed.

In all, it can be cogently defended that Paul was indeed engaged with the imperial power polemically in various ways in this letter. Although he had no intention to overthrow the Roman Empire, his conviction in and proclamation of the gospel of Christ and the struggle of his beloved church caused by the imperial pressure have put him in opposition to the imperial power.

---

161. Wright, "Paul's Gospel," 1317–19.

162. Barclay, *Pauline Churches*, 286, claims that "Paul's gospel is subversive of Roman imperial claims precisely by not opposing them within their own terms, but by reducing Rome's agency and historical significance to just one more entity in much greater drama."

163. Oakes, "Re-Mapping the Universe," 321–22.

CHAPTER 6

The Universal Worship of Christ in Philippians 2:6–11

In Paul's letter to the Philippians, the universal eschatological worship of Jesus Christ is depicted as the conclusion part of the christological passage in 2:6–11:[1]

ὃς ἐν μορφῇ θεοῦ ὑπάρχων
οὐχ ἁρπαγμὸν ἡγήσατο
τὸ εἶναι ἴσα θεῷ,
ἀλλὰ ἑαυτὸν ἐκένωσεν
μορφὴν δούλου λαβών,
ἐν ὁμοιώματι ἀνθρώπων γενόμενος·
καὶ σχήματι εὑρεθεὶς ὡς ἄνθρωπος
ἐταπείνωσεν ἑαυτὸν
γενόμενος ὑπήκοος μέχρι θανάτου,
θανάτου δὲ σταυροῦ.
διὸ καὶ ὁ θεὸς αὐτὸν ὑπερύψωσεν
καὶ ἐχαρίσατο αὐτῷ τὸ ὄνομα
τὸ ὑπὲρ πᾶν ὄνομα,
ἵνα ἐν τῷ ὀνόματι Ἰησοῦ
πᾶν γόνυ κάμψῃ
ἐπουρανίων καὶ ἐπιγείων καὶ καταχθονίων
καὶ πᾶσα γλῶσσα ἐξομολογήσηται

---

1. The text is cited from Nestle et al., *Novum Testamentum Graece*. The emphasis is mine.

ὅτι κύριος Ἰησοῦς Χριστὸς
εἰς δόξαν θεοῦ πατρός.

Before probing the function of this eschatological worship motif in the letter, it is necessary to observe its semantic weight in this christological passage, assuming that its significance will reverberate across the letter. To investigate this, the discussion is broken down into three major sections. The first develops some presuppositions in reading this christological passage. Since the passage has been debated in almost every aspect of its interpretation, establishing a good framework will help us to circumvent unnecessary debates and to stay focused on the objective of our analysis. The second section establishes that Philippians 2:10–11 indeed depicts the universal worship of Jesus Christ at the eschaton. The third, then, draws out some important significances of this eschatological worship motif in reading this christological passage.

6.1 Working Framework for Reading Philippians 2:6–11

6.1.1 The Context of Paul's Letter to the Philippians

Since Ernst Lohmeyer's seminal work, *Kyrios Jesus*, in 1927/1928, it is the majority opinion in modern biblical scholarship that the christological passage in Philippians 2:6–11 was originally a pre-Pauline "hymn." The basic arguments of this assumption are several. First, the passage has a self-contained character that allows the passage to stand on its own.[2] The relative pronoun ὅς is used to introduce this pre-Pauline material.[3] Second, the passage has poetic and creedal characteristics.[4] Third, the passage contains some non-Pauline expressions (i.e. μορφὴ θεοῦ, ἁρπαγμός, ἴσα θεῷ, μορφὴ δούλου, ὑπερυψόω, and καταχθόνιος).[5]

Despite the popularity of this view, the arguments above are not conclusive. The self-contained character of the passage and the use of the relative pronoun ὅς only suggest a pre-Philippians composition. It can be argued back that Paul himself composed this christological passage in a separate setting,

---

2. Lohmeyer, *Kyrios Jesus*, 136; O'Brien, *Philippians*, 198–99.

3. Cf. Col 1:15 and 1 Tim 3:16.

4. O'Brien, *Philippians*, 188–93; Bockmuehl, *Philippians*, 116.

5. Noted in O'Brien, *Philippians*, 199.

and later incorporated it into his letter to the Philippians. Indeed, Paul's educational and theological training stands him in good stead for writing poetical-creedal passages. The use of uncommon Pauline terminologies also does not necessarily prove the non-Pauline composition. As Bockmuehl rightly argues, "we do not have sufficient material of the apostle's on a wide range of subjects to come to definite conclusions regarding the hymn's authorship."[6] Indeed, some Pauline favorite expressions are found in this passage, such as θάνατος,[7] σταυρός,[8] εἰς δόξαν θεοῦ πατρός.[9] Unfortunately, they are often treated as Paul's interpolations,[10] rather than evidence of his authorship. Finally, as it will be demonstrated in the following section, Paul's use of Isaiah 45:23 LXX in Philippians 2:10–11 reflects some similar treatments with the one in Romans 14:11. All this calls for the proposal of Paul's own composition to be seriously considered. Indeed, more and more scholars have come to adopt this position recently.[11]

Taking Philippians 2:6–11 as an early Christian hymn that has been appropriated by Paul in his letter, Martin argues that the original message of this christological composition is properly determined when the passage is read in its original setting and form.[12] In our opinion, even if this assumption is correct, this approach is unsustainable, as both the original setting and form of the passage cannot be precisely determined.[13] What we have now is only the final form of the passage found in Paul's letter to the Philippians. The present study, therefore, intends to read this christological passage within the context of this letter. Even if the passage was not composed by him, this approach is still well grounded, as Paul incorporates the passage into his letter precisely because he agrees with its theology, Christology, eschatology, and ethics.[14]

---

6. Bockmuehl, *Philippians*, 118.

7. See Rom 5:10; 6:3–5; 1 Cor 11:26; Col 1:22.

8. See 1 Cor 1:17–18; Gal 5:11; Eph 2:16; Phil 3:18; Col 1:20.

9. See Phil 1:11; 4:20.

10. This, however, has been challenged in Hofius, *Der Christushymnus Philipper*, 3–17.

11. Hooker, "Philippians," 88–100; Fee, "Philippians," 29–46; Bockmuehl, *Philippians*, 118–19; Fowl, *Philippians*, 113.

12. Martin, *Hymn of Christ*, 289–93.

13. Hooker, "Philippians," 89.

14. Bockmuehl, *Philippians*, 119, rightly states that "the exegete is duty-bound to accept that Paul uses all the material because in his opinion it says what he wants and that he means what he says."

Furthermore, as the writer of Philippians, he certainly can freely modify and interpolate the passage in order to make it his own.[15] In this approach, Paul's christological, eschatological, and ethical dispositions become the interpretative keys in reading this passage. The other implication of this approach is that the significance of this christological passage needs to be appreciated against the sociopolitical, religious context of the Philippian congregation and the literary context of the letter to this community.[16]

6.1.2 Philippians 2:6–11 as the Narratival Gospel of Jesus Christ

Philippians 2:6–11 can be regarded as the narratival gospel of Jesus Christ. Whether this christological passage is construed as a hymn, poem, prose, encomium, or hymnos, scholars are generally aware of its narrative quality.[17] The narrative elements of the passage are presented as follows.[18] It has characters, such as Jesus, God the Father, and all creatures. It describes some sequential events, namely Christ's incarnation, death on the cross, resurrection-ascension, and parousia.[19] The passage also has a strong sense of movement. The two verbs of γίνομαι denote the action of "becoming" rather than a "state of being."[20] The first γίνομαι refers to Christ's incarnation (cf. Rom 1:3 and Gal 4:4), while the second denotes his obedient death on the cross. The conjunctions διὸ καί and the ἵνα subjunctive construction not merely perform a logical function but draw its chronological progress. Hence, the passage has a plot, which is shaped according to a "U," or "V," (i.e. an "abasement-exaltation" pattern). All this demonstrates that Philippians 2:6–11 can be explicated as

---

15. In the past, the expression θανάτου δὲ σταυροῦ (v. 8) and εἰς δόξαν θεοῦ πατρός (v. 11) have been popularly regarded as a product of Paul's interpolation.

16. Fowl, *Philippians*, 113.

17. Fee, *Philippians*, 193–94; Hellerman, *Reconstructing Honor*, 130; Gorman, *Inhabiting the Cruciform God*, 13–17.

18. Every story generally encompasses three elements: events, characters, and setting. It also can be added the plot that interpretatively describes the action and movement in the story. See Powell, *What Is Narrative Criticism?*, 35.

19. We view that verses 9–11 consists of two separated events: (1) the resurrection-ascension of Christ (v. 9), and (2) his parousia as the universal lord (vv. 10–11). Fee, *Paul's Letter*, 220, 223; Hawthorne and Martin, *Philippians*, 125–31; Bockmuehl, *Philippians*, 140–41, 146. Contra Käsemann, "Critical Analysis of Philippians," 78–79; Nagata, "Philippians" 284–85. Both read verses 9–11 as a single event of the resurrection-ascension of Christ.

20. See BDAG, 198 (point 5c); cf. Hays, *Faith of Jesus Christ*, 96–97.

a narrative. This story of Christ notably goes beyond history, as it also incorporates the realm of the proton and the eschaton. The setting covers the whole cosmos, and the "master plot" concerns the fate of all humankind and the whole cosmos.[21] As such, the story can be regarded as a meta-narrative.

We define this meta-narrative as the gospel of Jesus Christ. The relative pronoun ὅς at the beginning of verse 6 connects this narrative with the phrase ἐν Χριστῷ Ἰησοῦ at the end of verse 5, indicating that the narrative intends to expound on who Jesus Christ is. Although the term εὐαγγέλιον (gospel) does not appear in this christological passage, it appears eight times in this letter,[22] and it has great importance. As the *koinonia* between Paul and the readers is in the gospel of Christ (1:5), Paul exhorts them to continue living worthily according to this gospel in 1:27, which anticipates the christological passage in 2:6–11. If in Romans 1:3–4 and 1 Corinthians 15:3–4 the message of the gospel consists of Christ's death and resurrection, Philippians 2:6–11 provides a fuller version of the gospel, which includes Christ's origin, incarnation, suffering, death, resurrection-ascension, and parousia.

The messianic significance of this gospel narrative needs to be highlighted. As it has been noted above, in Paul's letters Χριστός is not merely another name of Jesus, but a title with messianic force. In the christological passage, this messianic significance is adumbrated by the idea of the Son of God. Although the term υἱὸς θεοῦ does not appear in this passage, the concept is undoubtedly present. First, in the Jewish biblical tradition, the Messiah is also called the Son of God. Psalm 2 LXX describes Χριστός as the king installed by YHWH on Mount Zion (vv. 2, 6), and he is called as "my son" by YHWH himself (v. 7). Paul's use of this term in his letters indicates that he is familiar with this messianic idea.[23] Second, the participle clause ἐν ὁμοιώματι ἀνθρώπων γενόμενος echoes Paul's statements in other letters, namely ὁ θεὸς τὸν ἑαυτοῦ υἱὸν πέμψας ἐν ὁμοιώματι σαρκὸς ἁμαρτίας (Rom 8:3) and ἐξαπέστειλεν ὁ θεὸς τὸν υἱὸν αὐτοῦ, γενόμενον ἐκ γυναικός (Gal 4:4).[24] These linguistic connections suggest that this participle clause depicts the incarnation of the Son of God. Third, the universal acclamation κύριος Ἰησοῦς Χριστὸς εἰς δόξαν θεοῦ

---

21. For meta-narrative, see Resseguie, *Narrative Criticism*, 203.

22. Phil 1:5, 7, 16, 27 (2x), 2:22; 4:3, 15.

23. Rom 1:3; 8:3; Gal 4:4.

24. Wanamaker, "Philippians," 184.

πατρός presupposes Jesus as the Son of God. Paul's discourse in 1 Corinthians 15:24–28 further supports the conceptual presence of the Son of God in Philippians 2:6–11. In this passage, God is referred to as the Father and Christ as the Son.[25] In all, this christological passage is better regarded as the narratival gospel of the Messiah Jesus, the Son of God.

6.1.3 The Reading of the Eschatological Narrative in Isaiah

The present study construes this narratival gospel of Christ as a creative reading of the eschatological narrative of Deutero-Isaiah, particularly the vision of worship in 45:23–24 and the role of the servant of YHWH in 52:13–53:12. This conjecture is supported not only by the idea of bringing the gospel (εὐαγγελίζω), which is sounded loudly in this portion of Isaiah,[26] but also by numerous terminological links between the narratival gospel and these two Isaianic passages:[27]

Philippians 2:6–11	Deutero-Isaiah LXX
Verse 7: ἀλλὰ ἑαυτὸν ἐκένωσεν μορφὴν δούλου λαβών	**MT 53:12:** הערה למות נפשו **LXX Isaiah 52:13:** ἰδοὺ συνήσει ὁ παῖς μου (or ὁ δοῦλος μου in Aquila)
Verse 8: γενόμενος ὑπήκοος μέχρι θανάτου,	**LXX Isaiah 53:8:** ἀπὸ τῶν ἀνομιῶν τοῦ λαοῦ μου ἤχθη εἰς θάνατον **LXX Isaiah 53:12:** ἀνθ' ὧν παρεδόθη **εἰς** θάνατον ἡ ψυχὴ αὐτοῦ
Verse 9: διὸ καὶ ὁ θεὸς αὐτὸν ὑπερύψωσεν	**LXX Isaiah 52:13:** . . . καὶ ὑψωθήσεται καὶ δοξασθήσεται σφόδρα
Verse 10–11: ἵνα ἐν τῷ ὀνόματι Ἰησοῦ πᾶν γόνυ κάμψῃ ἐπουρανίων καὶ ἐπιγείων καὶ καταχθονίων καὶ πᾶσα γλῶσσα ἐξομολογήσηται ὅτι κύριος Ἰησοῦς Χριστὸς εἰς δόξαν θεοῦ	**LXX Isaiah 45:23–24a:** ὅτι ἐμοὶ κάμψει πᾶν γόνυ καὶ ἐξομολογήσεται πᾶσα γλῶσσα τῷ θεῷ λέγων δικαιοσύνη καὶ δόξα πρὸς αὐτὸν

---

25. Wanamaker, 184–85.

26. Isa 40:9; 52:7; 60:6; 61:1.

27. This is noted in Bauckham, *Jesus and the God of Israel*, 43.

It is contended that Philippians 2:10–11 not merely alludes to Isaiah 45:23–24 LXX but is a careful reworking (midrash)[28]of this Isaianic vision. To see this exegetical activity at a glance, a comparative table is provided below:

Parallel	Chiastic	Philippians 2:10–11	Isaiah 45:23b–24a LXX
A	X	ἵνα ἐν τῷ ὀνόματι Ἰησοῦ	ἐμοὶ
	Y	πᾶν γόνυ κάμψῃ ἐπουρανίων καὶ ἐπιγείων καὶ καταχθονίων	κάμψει πᾶν γόνυ
B	Y'	καὶ πᾶσα γλῶσσα ἐξομολογήσηται[29]	καὶ ἐξομολογήσεται πᾶσα γλῶσσα
	X'	-------- ὅτι κύριος Ἰησοῦς Χριστὸς εἰς δόξαν θεοῦ πατρός	τῷ θεῷ λέγων δικαιοσύνη καὶ δόξα

As it is noted above, both passages can be construed as being parallel and having a chiastic structure. The reworking of the Isaianic vision in Philippians is described as follows. First, the letter preserves the unique expressions of homage in the LXX version of Isaiah (κάμψει πᾶν γόνυ and ἐξομολογήσεται πᾶσα γλῶσσα) with some contextual adjustments. The verb position is shifted, and the form is changed from the future indicative to the aorist subjunctive. Second, the divine pronoun ἐμοί is substituted by ἐν τῷ ὀνόματι Ἰησοῦ. Third, there is an addition of the phrase ἐπουρανίων καὶ ἐπιγείων καὶ καταχθονίων in between πᾶν γόνυ κάμψῃ and καὶ πᾶσα γλῶσσα ἐξομολογήσηται. Finally, τῷ θεῷ λέγων δικαιοσύνη καὶ δόξα is substituted by ὅτι κύριος Ἰησοῦς Χριστὸς εἰς δόξαν θεοῦ πατρός. As the last observation has not been fully appreciated, we will elaborate on it below.

---

28. Nagata, "Philippians," 283; Hurtado, "Case Study," 91–92; Bockmuehl, *Philippians*, 114–15.

29. There are two variants: (1) ἐξομολογήσηται (aorist subjunctive form) is attested in 𝔓[46], ℵ, B, F; (2) ἐξομολογήσεται (future indicative form) is attested in A, C, D, F*, G, K, L, Ψ[vid], 075, 0278. The latter has stronger futuristic tone, but difference between two is insignificant, since the telic ἵνα subjunctive construction can have this notion too. The subjunctive form is preferred as the original reading. It is more natural to expect that Paul purposely changed the form of both κάμπτω and ἐξομολογέω from future indicative in the LXX to aorist subjunctive in Philippians than that he only changed one of them.

The phrase εἰς δόξαν θεοῦ πατρός can be regarded as a doxological conclusion of the whole narrative of Christ (cf. 1:11 and 4:20).[30] Some regard this final phrase as not being part of the original composition or as part of a Pauline interpolation.[31] Hofius rightly demonstrates, however, that the doxological ending is an essential part of this christological narrative, and thus should be regarded as its original element.[32] In this line of thought, it is argued further that ὅτι κύριος Ἰησοῦς Χριστὸς εἰς δόξαν θεοῦ πατρός is the reworking of τῷ θεῷ λέγων δικαιοσύνη καὶ δόξα in Isaiah 45:23–24 LXX. The arguments are in order: (1) the conjunction ὅτι carries the function of λέγων, introducing a direct statement of the confessional praise; (2) the saying δικαιοσύνη καὶ δόξα is substituted with the confessional praise ὅτι κύριος Ἰησοῦς Χριστὸς εἰς δόξαν θεοῦ πατρός; and (3) the final phrase εἰς δόξαν θεοῦ πατρός elaborates the δόξα and accommodates τῷ θεῷ. If this is correct, the phrase εἰς δόξαν θεοῦ πατρός is grammatically antecedent to κύριος Ἰησοῦς Χριστὸς, rather than to ἐξομολογήσηται or the whole ἵνα-clause.[33] The exegetical implications of this conjecture will be utilized in the discussion in the following section.

While the allusion to Isaiah 45:23 LXX is generally appreciated, the echo of the servant of YHWH in Isaiah 52–53 LXX in this Christ-narrative is rather disputed.[34] Thus, it is necessary to present arguments to support this point of view. First, in Isaiah 40–55, the servant figure has a prominent role in the establishment of YHWH's earthly reign and salvation. Indeed, the Servant account in 52:13–53:12 is narrated immediately after the oracle of salvation in 52:7–10. As the motif of "Your God reigns" and "the return of the Lord to Zion" (52:7–10) befits the vision in Isaiah 45:22–24, to read these two eschatological passages in conjunction would be quite tenable.

Second, the often cited reason for objecting to the echo of Isaiah 52–53 is that the Isaianic figure of the servant of YHWH is not understood as messianic in the Second Temple Judaism.[35] This objection has been responded

---

30. Bockmuehl, *Philippians*, 148.

31. Martin, *Hymn of Christ*, 36–38, 273; Jeremias, "Zu Phil 2:7," 187.

32. Hofius, *Der Christushymnus Philipper*, 8–9, 54–55, 65–66.

33. O'Brien, *Philippians*, 250–51.

34. The motif of the servant of YHWH has been strongly contended in Cerfaux, *Christ in the Theology*, 377–80; Jeremias, "Zu Phil 2:7," 182–88; Bauckham, *Jesus and the God of Israel*, 42–44; Silva, *Philippians*, 125; Hansen, *Philippians*, 149–50. The refutation comes from Hooker, *Jesus and the Servant*, 120–23; O'Brien, *Philippians*, 268–71.

35. See Hooker, *Jesus and the Servant*, 120–23.

to in chapter 2 by demonstrating that the Isaianic servant motif is not totally absent in the Second Temple writings, as it is popularly presumed. Particularly significant is the evidence that the servant figure is read messianically in 1QIsaᵃ. Furthermore, as this servant motif is detected in Romans 4:25 and 1 Corinthians 15:3, Paul certainly can employ it in Philippians 2:6–11 too.

Finally, there is a conceptual parallel between Isaiah 52:13–53:12 and Philippians 2:6–11, namely the humiliation of the servant is followed by the exaltation of him.

The humiliation of the servant	
Isa 53:12b:	ἀνθ᾽ ὧν παρεδόθη εἰς θάνατον ἡ ψυχὴ αὐτοῦ
Phil 2:8:	γενόμενος ὑπήκοος μέχρι θανάτου
God's exaltation of the servant	
Isa 53:12a:	διὰ τοῦτο αὐτὸς κληρονομήσει πολλοὺς καὶ τῶν ἰσχυρῶν μεριεῖ σκῦλα
Isa 52:12:	καὶ ὑψωθήσεται καὶ δοξασθήσεται σφόδρα
Phil 2:9:	ὁ θεὸς αὐτὸν ὑπερύψωσεν

Objections to this parallel have been raised, but in our opinion they are not convincing. It is noted that while Isaiah 52:13 LXX employs παῖς, Philippians 2:7 uses the term δοῦλος. It can be counterargued, however, that the LXX uses παῖς and δοῦλος interchangeably to translate the Hebrew עבד in Isaiah.[36] It is also criticized that if ἑαυτὸν ἐκένωσεν in this verse corresponds strictly with ὧν παρεδόθη εἰς θάνατον ἡ ψυχὴ αὐτοῦ in Isaiah 53:12 LXX, it creates an inappropriate chronological order in the narrative of Christ, namely his death on the cross comes before his incarnation.[37] It can be argued, however, that the servant motif appears in the form of an allusion, which does not require a strict chronological correspondence between the two passages.[38] Indeed, ἑαυτὸν ἐκένωσεν rightly captures the spirit of the servant's obedience to the point of death. In all, the motif of the Isaianic servant of YHWH in the christological passage can be justifiably defended.

---

36. The use of παῖς is noted in Isa 42:1, 19; 49:6; 50:10; 52:13 LXX, while δοῦλος in 42:19; 48:20; 49:3, 5 LXX.

37. O'Brien, *Philippians*, 270.

38. Hansen, *Philippians*, 150.

6.1.4 Philippians 2:6–11 as a Polemic Against the Imperial Narrative of Augustus

Paul's letter to the Philippians has an anti-imperial stance. In this vein of thought, it is further argued that this narratival gospel presents Jesus as being in opposition to the Roman Caesars. The narrative notably uses some imperial expressions associated with Roman emperors and applies them to Christ Jesus. The phrase τὸ εἶναι ἴσα θεῷ evokes the popular practice of offering ἰσόθεοι τιμαί to Roman emperors and imperial family members.[39] The term μορφή θεοῦ notably parallels Philo's criticism of Caligula's pretense to be god (Apollo) by dressing himself and his statue in a divine-like manner.[40] The acclamation κύριος Ἰησοῦς Χριστός also resembles the imperial ovations κύριος Καῖσαρ. Taking into account the imperial pressures on the Philippian church and Paul's present imprisonment, this narratival gospel of Christ implicitly subverts public imperial discourses that propagate the greatness, lordship, and worship of the Roman Caesars.

To be more precise, this study contends that this gospel of Christ is narrated to counter the imperial narrative of Augustus. There are several grounds for thinking so. First, as a Roman colony with a strong Roman orientation, the observation of the imperial cults in Philippi follows closely the practices in its mother city Rome. Up to the time of the composition of Philippians, there were only four imperial figures officially deified and thus worshipped: Julius Caesar, Augustus, Livia (Augustus's wife), and Claudius.[41] From all these candidates, Augustus stands out, as in Paul's time, he was the greatest Roman emperor and regarded as an ideal ruler to be imitated.[42] Second, the Roman colony of Philippi has a strong bond with this *divus* Caesar. As the colony owes its existence to Augustus, he is regarded as the patron god, and his cult

---

39. See Heen, "Phil 2:6–11," 125–36.

40. Philo, *Legat.* 110.

41. Cohick, "Philippians and Empire," 170.

42. Caligula cannot be the object of worship, as he was officially condemned after his death. The worship of Nero might be popular among the Hellenists during his reign. However, since he had not officially gained his apotheosis, it is unlikely that he was officially worshipped in this Roman colony. Claudius was divinized, but due to his unpopularity among the Romans, his cult would not be significant. Augustus's wife, Livia, was also deified and her cult was popular in Philippi. However, she should be also excluded because of her gender. This leaves us only with Julius Caesar and Augustus. Between the two, Augustus would be a better candidate, given that he was the one who established the realm of peace in the Greco-Roman world. See also the discussion on p. 103–5, 114–18.

is popularly observed there. It is worth noting that in this city *divus* Augustus is also closely associated with *deus* Mercurius, the son of *deus* Jupiter.[43] Hence, the claim of the lordship of Christ as the Son of God the Father evokes in the readers' mind the imperial claim of the lordship of Augustus as the son of Jupiter.[44] Third, the cult of Augustus was the most widespread emperor cult in the empire in the first century AD. Significant numbers of archeological and inscriptional evidence demonstrate the popularity of the cult of Augustus in Greece and Asia Minor.[45] Paul, the traveling missionary in this region, must be aware of the significance of the imperial propaganda of Augustus and the worship of him.[46]

Two popular public discourses on Augustus prevalent in the Roman province of Asia need to be seriously considered as forming the imperial backdrop of the Christ-narrative in Philippians. The first is the new calendar inscriptions in the province of Asia in 9 BC. The Greek copy is attested in the cities of Priene, Apamea Kobotos, Maionia, and Eurmenia, and its Latin copy in Apamea Kobotos and Dorylaion. Paul must have encountered this inscription during his lengthy stay in Ephesus (Acts 19:10), as Priene was situated near to this city. This public inscription acclaims Augustus as the divinely sent savior and the greatest benefactor of the world, whose birth is pre-ordained by gods, and therefore, it becomes the beginning of all good news.

The second is the *Res Gestae Divi Augusti*. The account was originally written by Augustus and read before the Senate of Rome shortly after his death in AD 14, then was later inscribed in bronze at his Mausoleum in the *Campus Martius*. It has various functions,[47] and one of them is to portray Augustus as an ideal model of the Roman ruler.[48] As an authoritative official account, it

---

43. Mercurius-Augustus is noted in the inscription no. 250 in Pilhofer, *Philippi Band 2*, 100.

44. The close relationship between Augustus and Jupiter is noted in Ovid, *Metamorphoses, Volume II*, 15.858–9.

45. See Porter, "Paul Confronts Caesar," 172–73.

46. Porter, 173–74.

47. Such as: (1) epitaph, (2) a political testament, (3) a rendering of accounts for his reign, (4) a description of his new political system, and (5) a bid for his deification. See Cooley, *Res Gestae*, 30.

48. Cooley, *Res Gestae*, 34, states that "these decrees were intended not only to reward a benefactor, but also to encourage others to emulate him." The use of material of bronze also signifies that his account was morally authoritative as a role model of society (see p. 3).

was well known among the Roman writers (Seneca, Suetonius, and Tacitus),[49] and widely circulated in the province of Galatia during the first century AD. Its three surviving copies have been discovered in this region: (1) *Ancyra* (Latin and Greek text), (2) *Pisidian Antioch* (Latin text), and (3) *Apollonia* (Greek text).[50] As Paul had visited *Pisidian Antioch* (Acts 13:14–52), he had likely seen Augustus's *Res Gestae* inscribed at the two pillars at the entrance of the imperial temple in the city.

Although these two imperial inscriptions were situated not in Macedonia, these commendations of Augustus represented the public appraisal of Augustus in the Greek East in the first century AD. Given that the province of Asia was not far from this colony and that the Roman Philippi was situated at *via Egnatia*, the praise of Augustus in Asia could easily reach this city and spread among its residents. It is justified, therefore, to assume that these two public discourses of Augustus are familiar to both Paul and the Philippian congregation.

Considering this imperial backdrop, the present study proposes that this narratival gospel of Christ should be read against the public discourse of Augustus endorsed in the imperial society at that time. An objection has been raised to this conjecture as there is no mention of Augustus at all in Paul's letter to the Philippians. An explanation can be offered in defense of this proposal. In Paul's theological frame of mind (φρονεῖν),[51] Christ Jesus is the universal Lord, and thus he must be the center of the whole universe. Hence, throughout this letter, Paul takes great efforts to reshape the readers' worldview by moving the center of the universe from *divus* Augustus to Jesus Christ.[52] He does it, however, sensibly considering his current imprisonment, the readers' struggle under the imperial pressure, and the Roman orientation of the Philippian society (including some of the readers) into his consideration. While there is no mention of this greatest Roman emperor who is also

---

49. The reception of Augustus's *Res Gestae* is attested in Seneca (*Apol.* 10.1), Suetonius (*Aug.*), Tacitus, (*Ann.* 1.10.1–4). See Cooley, *Res Gestae*, 50–51.

50. Cooley, *Res Gestae*, 6–18.

51. For the significance of φρονεῖν in Paul's letter to the Philippians, see the discussion in chapter 7.

52. Oakes, "Re-Mapping the Universe," 319–22.

the most admirable patron of the Philippian colony, Paul's call to exercise φρονεῖν in 2:5 and 3:15 will lead the readers to appreciate it.[53]

6.2 Philippians 2:10–11 as the Universal Worship of the Messiah Jesus

Although it is generally appreciated that Philippians 2:10–11 depicts the universal worship of Christ at the eschaton, the precise reading of these two verses is still debated among biblical scholars. This section, therefore, intends to establish our interpretation of them.

6.2.1 Worship or Submission?

Should the homage be understood as worship or submission? Admittedly, the clause πᾶν γόνυ κάμψῃ . . . καὶ πᾶσα γλῶσσα ἐξομολογήσηται can be construed as an expression of both worship and submission.[54] The present study regards it as primarily depicting the act of worship, although the notion of submission should not be discounted. The grounds for this are as follows.

First, this expression of homage is appropriated from the Isaianic vision where it is directed to the God of Israel[55] and set against the idol worship of the gentile nations. Second, as it has been exposed in the previous chapter, both 4Q215a and the Aleinu prayer consistently read the homage as an act of worship. The former even replaces the verb שבע (to swear) with ברך (to bless or praise) that strengthens the idea of worship. Third, the use of ἐξομολογέω in Isaiah 45:23 LXX in translating שבע also strengthens the notion of worship,[56] and this is adopted in both Romans 14:11 and Philippians 2:11. All this affirms that πᾶν γόνυ κάμψῃ . . . καὶ πᾶσα γλῶσσα ἐξομολογήσηται should be understood as an act of worship. In the Isaianic context, the worship demands submission to YHWH's plan of salvation carried out by his gentile messiah, Cyrus. Similarly, in Philippians context, worship and submission are merged,

---

53. See the discussion of "think this" statement in Philippians 1:7, 2:5, and 3:15 in chapter 7.

54. Hawthorne and Martin, *Philippians*, 127; Hansen, *Philippians*, 163; Bockmuehl, *Philippians*, 145.

55. Here, the pronoun ἐμοί (to me) in verse 23 refers back to God of Israel in verses 21 (ἐγὼ ὁ θεός καὶ οὐκ ἔστιν ἄλλος) and 22 (ἐγώ εἰμι ὁ θεός καὶ οὐκ ἔστιν ἄλλος).

56. In Pss 6:6; 29:10; 48:19; 75:11 LXX, the term ἐξομολογέω is often used to translate the *hiphil* ידה (to praise).

and they offered to both God and his Messiah Jesus. The notion of submission is conveyed by the acknowledgment of Jesus Christ as κύριος in 2:11 and various "obedience" expressions (i.e. ὑπακούω, μετὰ φόβου καὶ τρόμου and χωρὶς γογγυσμῶν καὶ διαλογισμῶν) in 2:12–14, while the worship overtone is articulated by various cultic expressions (i.e. ἄμωμος, σπένδω, θυσία and λειτουργία) in 2:15–18.

Some scholars diminish the notion of worship in preference to submission.[57] Käsemann contends that Philippians 2:10–11 has no concern for cultic matter but focuses on the issue of domination.[58] Construing that verse 9 depicts the enthronement of Christ to be the new *Pantocrator*,[59] he regards the statement κύριος Ἰησοῦς Χριστὸς as public acclamation of the submission to the new universal Lord.[60] While Käsemann is correct in identifying the imperial imagery in verses 9–11, he fails to appreciate that the submission to the *Pantocrator* Jesus is expressed precisely through the Isaianic language of worship. One of his arguments for denying the notion of worship is that the phrase ἐπουρανίων καὶ ἐπιγείων καὶ καταχθονίων denotes the rebellious spiritual powers occupying the triadic universe. This reading, however, has been mostly rejected nowadays.

Following Käsemann is Oakes who argues that while the homage in Isaiah 45:23 contains both worship and submission,[61] the emphasis in Philippians 2:10–11 is on the latter.[62] His main argument is that the problem faced by the church at Philippi is not a cultic matter (i.e. the observance of imperial cults) but the issue of submission to the imperial ideology of power that claims the universal lordship of the Roman emperors. It has been defended in the previous chapter, however, that in Philippi Christians' withdrawal from the public worship of Augustus indeed had caused civic oppositions toward them. Accordingly, the notion of worship is not easily circumvented in this gospel narrative, as it gains support not only from its literary context (2:12–18) but also from the religious context of Philippi.

---

57. Käsemann, "Critical Analysis of Philippians," 78–81; Oakes, *Philippians*, 169–90.

58. Käsemann, 80–81.

59. Käsemann, 80–81.

60. Käsemann, 79–80.

61. Oakes, *Philippians*, 169–70.

62. Oakes, 169–70.

We also note that P. M. Casey admits that Philippians 2:10–11 depicts the veneration of Jesus Christ:[63]

> Philippians 2:6–11 is one of a handful of New Testament passages generally treated as a hymn. . . . At the same time, the hymn does raise Jesus to an extraordinarily high position. He is pre-existent at the beginning, and after his exaltation he is given the name of God. . . . The words "every knee shall bow" and "every tongue shall confess" are from Isaiah 45:23, where "swear" has been interpreted in terms of early Christian confession of Jesus. . . . This piece is accordingly very important for our understanding of fully developed Pauline Christology. It is, however, a piece of text written in an epistle; *it cannot be shown to have been part of normal worship.*[64]

To him, however, this veneration should not be regarded as worship, but a traditional sign of respect to a superior figure.[65] The reason is that the passage depicts Christ's position as being "on the verge of deity," but not being a deity.[66] Whether one agrees or disagrees with him, this view is closer to worship rather than submission. In the Greco-Roman society, the difference between giving honor and worship was not in kind but degree. Certainly, this is not the case in the Jewish perspective that marks clearly the boundary between God and his creation.

6.2.2 The Object of Worship

Another crucial issue is the object of this eschatological worship. Presupposing that Paul did not breach traditional Jewish monotheism, some scholars view that the worship is directed to God in or through the name of Jesus.[67] James D. G. Dunn, for example, maintains that the worship is "not addressed to Christ, but give praise to God for Christ."[68] In his point of view, giving the confessional praise κύριος Ἰησοῦς Χριστὸς is part of worshipping God:

---

63. Casey, *From Jewish Prophet*, 113–14; Casey, "Monotheism," 214–33.

64. Casey, "Monotheism," 226–27. The emphasis is mine.

65. Casey, *From Jewish Prophet*, 113.

66. Casey, 114.

67. Vincent, *Philippians*, 62; Beare, *Philippians*, 86–87; Dunn, *Theology of Paul*, 252–60.

68. Dunn, *Theology of Paul*, 259.

At the very least we have to recognize that the Philippian hymn (2:6–11) envisaged acclamation of and reverence before Christ which, according to Isaiah, God claimed for himself alone. . . . Yet, at the same time, we have to note that the final line of the hymn: "every tongue confess that Jesus Christ is Lord, to the glory of God the Father" (2:11). This means that the acclamation of Jesus Christ as Lord involved no heavenly coup or takeover, no replacement of God by Christ. On the contrary, it *was* God who would be glorified in the confession of Jesus. And not because the one was identified with the other (Jesus is Lord, God is Father). But, most obviously, because the one God (of Isaiah 45) has chosen to share his sovereignty with the exalted Christ.[69]

Against this conjecture, the present study argues that the main object of the worship in this christological passage is Jesus Christ, although God is also in view. First, to be sure, in the history of interpretation, the prepositional phrase ἐν τῷ ὀνόματι ʾΙησοῦ in verse 10 has been construed in three different ways: (1) the preposition ἐν is regarded as temporal that underlines the occasion of worship (when the name of Jesus is invoked);[70] (2) the preposition ἐν is understood as instrumental that explains the means of worship (through the name of Jesus the worship is offered to God);[71] and (3) the preposition ἐν highlights the reference that the worship is in honor of the name of Jesus.[72] Following the majority opinion, this study sees that it is more cogent to construe the preposition ἐν as indicating that the name of Jesus is the reverential object of worship (i.e. "*at* the name of Jesus" or "*in honor of* the name of Jesus"). The justification for this is as follows.

We note that besides in Philippians 2:10, Paul also uses the phrase ἐν τῷ ὀνόματι ʾΙησοῦ in several other passages where the preposition ἐν has spatial and instrumental meanings.[73] These two meanings, however, do not fit the

---

69. Dunn, 251–52. He basically argues that God has shared his sovereignty but not his divine identity with Christ.

70. BDAG, 713; Moule, "Further Reflection," 270; Martin, *Hymn of Christ*, 251.

71. Vincent, *Philippians*, 62; Barth, *Philippians*, 68; Beare, *Philippians*, 86–87.

72. This conjecture is adopted by the majority of commentators nowadays. See O'Brien, *Philippians*, 239–40; Hawthorne and Martin, *Philippians*, 92; Fee, *Philippians*, 223; Bockmuehl, *Philippians*, 145; Hansen, *Philippians*, 163–64.

73. 1 Cor 5:4; 6:11; cf. Eph 5:20; Col 3:17; 2 Thess 3:6.

current context because the acclamation of every tongue that κύριος Ἰησοῦς Χριστός strongly suggests that the act of bowing down is directed to Jesus.[74] This is confirmed by the fact that the phrase ἐν τῷ ὀνόματι Ἰησοῦ is the substitution of the divine pronoun ἐμοί (to me) in Isaiah 45:23 LXX, which marks the object of bowing knees. Hence, in substituting ἐμοί with ἐν τῷ ὀνόματι Ἰησοῦ Paul very likely maintains the same sense. As Bockmuhel has rightly noted, in the setting of the Jewish worship the acts of "praising" (ἐξομολογέω and ἐπαινέω) and "praying" (προσεύχομαι) "in the name of the Lord" (ἐν ὀνόματι κυρίου) are understood as offering worship to God.[75] Admittedly, to depict the object of worship κάμπτω and γόνυ are usually followed by the preposition πρός and the accusative (cf. Eph 3:14) or the dative alone (cf. Rom 11:4).[76] It can be argued, however, that the case in Philippians 2:10–11 is unique, as the idea of worship is articulated by both κάμπτω and ἐξομολογέω. Thus, the use of ἐν dative construction (instead of πρός accusative) might intend to accommodate the verb ἐξομολογέω.[77]

Second, the correlation between the phrase τῷ ὀνόματι Ἰησοῦ and the phrase τὸ ὄνομα τὸ ὑπὲρ πᾶν ὄνομα needs to be unpacked. According to Moule, τὸ ὄνομα τὸ ὑπὲρ πᾶν ὄνομα is Jesus, and thus Ἰησοῦ should be an appositional dative (the name is Jesus) highlighting that the worship is offered to Jesus.[78] Many other scholars, however, correctly maintain that τὸ ὄνομα τὸ ὑπὲρ πᾶν ὄνομα refers to יהוה, the name of the God of Israel because in the Jewish worldview there is no other name greater than this Tetragrammaton.[79] Out of reverence, the name was no longer uttered in the Second Temple era. The term κύριος is employed in the LXX as the conventional reference to the Name.[80] Accordingly, Ἰησοῦ can be construed as a possessive genitive (the Name [κύριος] which belongs to Jesus).[81] Having said this, the difference between "the name Jesus" and "the name that belongs to Jesus" is insignificant, as the investiture of the name of God had associated the name Jesus

---

74. Hansen, *Philippians*, 163–64.

75. See Pss 43:9; 104:3; 3 Kgdms 8:44 LXX. Bockmuehl, *Philippians*, 145.

76. This is noted in Hawthorne, *Philippians*, 92.

77. Cf. ἐν τῷ ὀνόματί σου ἐξομολογησόμεθα εἰς τὸν αἰῶνα διάψαλμα in Ps 43:9 LXX.

78. Moule, "Further Reflection," 270; MacLeod, "Exaltation of Christ," 441–42.

79. See Pss 8:1, 9; 138:2; 148:13. Bockmuehl, *Philippians*, 142.

80. Bauckham, "Worship of Jesus in Philippians," 131.

81. O'Brien, *Philippians*, 240; Hawthorne, *Philippians*, 92; Hansen, *Philippians*, 164.

with the Tetragrammaton. Indeed, some also construe τῷ ὀνόματι Ἰησοῦ as an explicative genitive (the name that is Jesus).[82] Because the Name has been endowed to Jesus, now the name Jesus (or the name that is Jesus) becomes far above every name that is named (Eph 1:20–21), including the names of angels (Heb 1:4). In this respect, it is not justifiable to say that the worship is offered to the Name that belongs to Jesus, but not to the name Jesus.[83]

To be sure, the bestowal of the Tetragrammaton on Jesus can be understood in two ways. First, YHWH has shared his divine sovereignty with the Messiah Jesus.[84] In Jewish writings, the investiture of the divine name upon the exalted figures signifies their possession of divine authority to rule on YHWH's behalf.[85] Second, YHWH shares his unique divine identity with Jesus that confirms him as the divine Lord.[86] In the Old Testament, the proper name of God is also understood as a divine hypostasis, because it signifies his divine nature and identity (Isa 30:27). Accordingly, the investiture of the Name in Exodus 23:20–22 signifies that this angelic figure is an extension of the divine identity of the God of Israel.[87] In this light, the investiture of the Name above all name underlines not only YHWH's grant of his divine authority but also the extension of his unique identity to Jesus Christ. This is an essential part of the reworking of the Isaianic vision. As the name Jesus now bears the name of God, the phrase ἐν τῷ ὀνόματι Ἰησοῦ is now fully comparable with the divine pronoun ἐμοί in Isaiah 45:23 LXX.[88] The scope of homage, which covers the whole triadic universe, further affirms that the name of Jesus, which now bears the Tetragrammaton, is to be construed as a divine hypostasis. In all, the endowment of "the name above all names" has portrayed Jesus Christ as partaking of the identity of the God of Israel, and thus he is worthy to be worshipped by the whole creation.

---

82. Nagata, "Philippians," 279.

83. Contra Hawthorne, *Philippians*, 92; Fee, *Philippians*, 223n31.

84. Dunn, *Theology of Paul*, 252.

85. This is noted in the case of the heavenly *Melchizedek* in 11QMelch, the angel *Iaoel* in Apoc. Ab. (10:3; 17:33), *Metatron* in 3 En. (12:5) and Sanh. (38b).

86. Bauckham, "Worship of Jesus in Philippians," 131.

87. See the discussion in Fossum, *Name of God*, 84–87.

88. It is worth noting that in Romans 14:11 to introduce the citation of Isaiah 45:23 Paul starts with the formula ζῶ ἐγώ, λέγει κύριος (cf. Isa 49:18 LXX), in which κύριος is associated with YHWH.

Finally, the ending phrase εἰς δόξαν θεοῦ πατρός indicates that the envisaged worship also has God the Father in view. As it has been argued above, this phrase is antecedent to ὅτι κύριος Ἰησοῦς Χριστὸς, and thus is an integral part of this confessional praise. This shows us that the confessional praise to Jesus will never subvert the position of the Father as the God of all creation, but only redound further to his glory. Although Philippians 2:10–11 is independent of the depiction of the worship of the Son of Man in 1 Enoch 48, the parallel between the two is worth noting. This passage depicts that the Messiah Son of Man existed before creation (vv. 2–3; cf. Phil 2:6), shares divine authority to judge at the eschaton (vv. 8–10; cf. Phil 1:10–11), and thus will be worshipped together with the name of the Lord of the Spirits (v. 5; cf. Phil 2:10–11). Their parallels are notable:

1 Enoch 48:5	Philippians 2:10–11
All those who dwell upon the earth shall fall and worship before him (the Son of Man)	At the **name** of Jesus every knee should bow...
They shall glorify, bless, *and* sing the name of the Lord of the Spirits.	And every tongue confess that Jesus Christ is Lord, to the glory of God the Father

There is a slight difference between these two pictures of worship. In 1 Enoch, while the bowing is directed at the Son of Man, the praise is exclusively offered to the name of the Lord of the Spirits. In Philippians, both bowing and praise are directed to the Messiah Jesus who is endowed with the name of God, and this worship will redound to the glory of the Father. The comparison above demonstrates that the worship of Christ is made more explicit than the worship of the Son of Man. In all, the worship in Philippians 2:10–11 has both Christ and God as its object. Since this gospel focuses on the story of Christ, the emphasis should be on the worship of Christ.

6.2.3 The Worshippers

In the Isaianic context, the phrases of κάμψει πᾶν γόνυ and πᾶσα γλῶσσα refer to all nations, and this is also the case in 4Q215a and the Aleinu prayer. In Philippians 2:10, however, this universal scope is extended cosmologically.

This is conveyed by the three genitive substantive adjectives ἐπουρανίων καὶ ἐπιγείων καὶ καταχθονίων. These participles have been interpreted differently as referring to (1) the whole creation,[89] (2) all animate creatures in the universe,[90] and (3) all demonic powers occupying the whole universe.[91] The present study adopts the second option with the following consideration.

The ancient Jewish cosmology portrays the universe as being divided into various segments, such as heaven, earth, sea, and Sheol/Hades. The last is the underworld associated with the realm of death.[92] As it was noted in the previous chapter, while the worship of YHWH at the eschaton is generally depicted as being offered by all humankind, some texts in the Old Testament and the Second Temple writings describe the involvement of the dead and the angelic creatures in this worship. This metaphysical thought is presented in Romans 14:8–12 where Paul depicts that the universal worship before the judgment seat of God will involve the dead. Accordingly, the addition of ἐπουρανίων καὶ ἐπιγείων καὶ καταχθονίων greatly expands the realm of worship from being offered by all humankind to being offered by all creatures in the whole universe.

One popular opinion in the past argues that the three substantive adjectives represent the demonic spiritual powers in the triadic universe.[93] Supporting this reading is the common ancient belief that the whole universe was occupied by various spiritual powers that had great influence over human affairs.[94] However, since these three adjectives are part of the reworking of the vision in Isaiah 45:23, it is easier to regard them as indicating the broadening of the

---

89. The substantive adjectives are read as genitive neutral plural, representing the whole creation. Lightfoot, *Philippians*, 115.

90. The substantive adjectives are read as genitive masculine plural. Here, ἐπουρανίων connotes the angels in heaven, ἐπιγείων the living humans on earth, and καταχθονίων the dead in Sheol. See Hofius, *Der Christushymnus Philipper*, 52–53, 123–31; Fee, *Philippians*, 224–25; Bockmuehl, *Philippians*, 146.

91. The substantive adjectives are read as genitive masculine plural. See Käsemann, "Critical Analysis of Philippians," 78–79; Gnilka, *Philippians*, 39.

92. The heaven and earth is attested in Gen 1:1; the heaven, earth and sea in Exod 20:11; Sheol (or Hades) in Pss 6:5; 9:17; the heaven, earth, and Hades in Matt 16:18–19. See the discussion of the ancient cosmology in Janzen, "Earth," *ABD* 2:245–48.

93. Käsemann, "Critical Analysis of Philippians," 78–79.

94. The pagans recognized them as gods or demons (P. Lond. 46.167; P. Oxy. 9.1380; Livy 1.32.10). Both Jewish and Christian apologetics, however, regarded them as part of creation, either as YHWH's loyal servants (Ps 103:20; Dan 7:10; 1 En. 10:9; Gal 1:8; Heb 1:7) or the rebellious spirits (1 En. 6:1–8:4; Matt 12:24–28).

domain of worshippers (i.e. from all humankind to all creatures [including all evil powers]), rather than the substitution of worshippers (i.e. all humankind is replaced by all evil spirits). The parallel thought in the New Testament is found in the eschatological worship of the Lamb in Revelation 5:13.[95]

Ralph. P. Martin entertains the idea that some creatures "with their freedom of choice may choose never in any circumstance to submit to God or his Christ" even at the eschaton.[96] To support this reading, he affirms that the ἵνα subjunctive clause has a *telic* sense, but argues further that not all divine goals are attained.[97] In our opinion, however, the worship is construed as definitely being offered by both the righteous and the wicked creatures. The grounds are as follows. First, in the Isaianic vision, the presence of the wicked in the eschatological worship of YHWH is noted in 45:24.[98] Second, to Paul, the eschatological worship of Christ will occur at the day of Christ (Phil 1:6; 1:10–11; 2:16) and be situated before the judgment seat of God (Rom 14:10–12). Accordingly, the worship will be offered by both the righteous and wicked creatures.[99] Finally, in the Jewish worldview, YHWH's eschatological reign is theologically "an unstoppable certainty."[100] Hence, the universal eschatological worship of YHWH and his Messiah will be inevitable for all.

6.2.4 The Event of Worship

The vision of the universal worship of YHWH in Isaiah is expressed as part of the divine oath, which underlines the divine commitment to accomplish it. In Paul's appropriation of this Isaianic oracle, Jesus is depicted as the one who fulfills this eschatological vision. The issue is whether the vision has been fully realized, or is still to be awaited. Käsemann construes Philippians 2:10–11 as depicting the present event, arguing that the composer deliberately replaces the future indicative κάμψει and ἐξομολογήσεται with the aorist subjunctive κάμψῃ and ἐξομολογήσηται to terminate the futuristic force of Isaiah 45:23

---

95. Bauckham, "Worship of Jesus in Philippians," 131.

96. Hawthorne and Martin, *Philippians*, 129–30.

97. Hawthorne and Martin, 129–30.

98. The MT reads "shall come to him [YHWH] and be ashamed all those rage against him." The LXX reads "to him [YHWH] shall come and be ashamed all those who separate themselves."

99. This picture of worship is different from those in Isa 66:22–4; Zech 14:16; cf. 1 En. 10:21–22; 90:29–33; 4Q215a, where the eschatological worship of God is situated after the day of judgment and where the worshippers are all survivors of YHWH's judgments.

100. Bockmuehl, *Philippians*, 146.

LXX.[101] Along with him is Nagata who argues that Philippians 2:9–11 depicts a single event, as it follows strictly the Jewish imagery of enthronement. In his view, the subordinate ἵνα subjunctive has no concern with any historical frame but simply provides the theological ground for the universal lordship of Jesus.[102]

In general, however, scholars situate the event of worship at the parousia of Jesus Christ.[103] This is also the view adopted in this study. The supporting arguments are in order. First, in Isaiah the verbs κάμπτω and ἐξομολογέω appear in the future indicative form (κάμψει and ἐξομολογήσεται). Therefore, we expect that Paul must be familiar with their future nuances. In Romans 14:10–12, he indeed locates this universal worship at the day of judgment and before the judgment seat of God. Following this line of thought, the universal worship in Philippians 2:10–11 should be read in connection with the day of Christ where everyone will give an account before God (1:10–11, 2:16; 3:9). Given that the construction ἵνα aorist subjunctive expresses the purpose,[104] it is quite natural to expect that this subordinate clause retains this futuristic notion[105] (i.e. the vision of the universal worship of Christ will be fulfilled only at the eschaton).[106]

Second, the eschatological worship of Christ will be offered by not merely the demonic powers, but rather all creatures in the whole universe.[107] Even if – for the sake of argument – one is persuaded that Philippians 2:10–11 depicts the subjugation of the rebellious spirits, in the Pauline eschatological framework the depicted event will be still in the future. The inauguration and the extension of God's reign in Christ involve the subjugation of

---

101. Käsemann, "Critical Analysis of Philippians," 78–79. This conjecture is to support his interpretation that Phil 2:10–11 depicts the present subjugation of all rebellious spiritual powers.

102. Nagata, "Philippians," 278–79, 285–86.

103. Kreitzer, *Jesus and God*, 117; O'Brien, *Philippians*, 243; Fee, *Philippians*, 223; Hansen, *Philippians*, 167.

104. Bockmuehl, *Philippians*, 144, 146.

105. For the futuristic aorist, see BDF, no. 333 and 369.

106. In the context of the divine will, both the notions of purpose and result tend to be overlapped due to the Jewish conviction of God's sovereignty. See Wallace, *Greek Grammar*, 474; Martin, *Hymn of Christ*, 249; O'Brien, *Philippians*, 239.

107. Contra Käsemann, "Critical Analysis of Philippians," 78–79.

all hostile powers,[108] and their final subjugation will only occur at the final/future eschaton.

Third, in the eschatological realm established by Christ, all believers of him have been participating in the heavenly adoration of Christ. The full actualization of their universal worship, however, will only occur at the climax of Christ's lordship at the eschaton. The reason is that many people on earth are still worshipping idols and opposing the gospel of Christ Jesus, as it is voiced in 1:28.

In all, Philippians 2:10–11 depicts the universal worship of God and Christ at the eschaton. This homage is an expression of not merely submission but also worship. Indeed, worship is the predominant idea. The object of worship is both God the Father and his Messiah Jesus Christ, and in the context of this narratival gospel, the latter is the focal point. The scope of worship is universal, which is extended from all humankind to all creatures in the triadic universe. The worship will occur on the day of Christ or his parousia, where all shall stand before the judgment seat of God to give their account.

6.3 The Significances of the Motif of Eschatological Worship of Christ

With the reading established above, this study now investigates the significance of the universal eschatological worship of Christ in the christological passage itself. It is acknowledged that this christological passage has christological, soteriological, anti-imperial, and ethical thrusts. The discussion below will demonstrate how the worship motif contributes to them.

6.3.1 Christology

It is no doubt that Philippians 2:6–11 conveys the christological conviction of the earliest Christianity.[109] The motif of eschatological worship in verses 10–11 entails the public acknowledgment of Jesus as the divine κύριος, and the use of Isaiah 45:23–24 LXX is pivotal for this inferential claim. This vision expresses the cultic-eschatological monotheism of Jewish people that

---

108. See 1 Cor 15:20–28; cf. Eph 1:20–21; Col 2:15; cf. Ign. *Trall.* 9:1; Pol. *Phil.* 2:1; Justin, *Apol.* 1:42; Irenaeus, *Haer.* 10:1.

109. Hurtado, "Case Study," 86–87; Bauckham, "Worship of Jesus in Philippians," 128.

claims: when YHWH reveals his universal kingship on earth, all nations will worshipfully acknowledge YHWH as the only true God.[110] In the Philippians' christological passage, this vision of worshipping YHWH is applied to the Messiah Jesus, as the confessional praise of God's δικαιοσύνη and δόξα is substituted with the confessional praise: κύριος Ἰησοῦς Χριστὸς εἰς δόξαν θεοῦ πατρός. This makes Philippians 2:10–11 the christological version of this Isaianic cultic and eschatological monotheism.[111]

In the Greco-Roman world κύριος was a language of power, denoting a figure that has power at his disposal to control someone or something. The term had wide-ranging applications, such as the owner of slaves, the patron of the society, the king, and even the deity.[112] Hence, it is employed in the LXX as a conventional reference to יהוה – the unique name of the God of Israel.[113] When κύριος is acclaimed in the context of worshipping Jesus, it affirms his divine status.[114] It is worth noting that θεός and κύριος are used simultaneously in Isaiah 45:20–25 to refer to YHWH. In Romans 14:11, however, while τῷ θεῷ refers to YHWH, the divine ἐμοί implicitly refers to κύριος-Christ. In Philippians 2:11, the idea of the divine Christ becomes more apparent, as κύριος is explicitly associated with Jesus Christ and θεός with the Father (πατήρ).[115] The acclamation of Jesus Christ as the divine κύριος does not infringe upon the divine status of YHWH, as this praise will only redound to the glory of the Father (εἰς δόξαν θεοῦ πατρός). This is another way of saying that both Christ and the Father have become part of the divine identity of YHWH. Therefore, Hurtado rightly states that "the exalted claims made about Jesus here represent a distinctive 'mutation' in traditional Jewish monotheism, but certainly not an outright rejection of it."[116]

The picture of the eschatological worship of Christ leads to some significant ramifications for our understanding of the christological passage. First,

110. Bauckham, "Worship of Jesus in Philippians," 132.

111. Bauckham, 133.

112. Fitzmyer, "Κύριος," EDNT 2:329.

113. Fitzmyer, "Κύριος," EDNT 2:330; Bauckham, Jesus and the God of Israel, 199.

114. Bauckham, "Worship of Jesus in Philippians," 133.

115. Bauckham, Jesus and the God of Israel, 209–10; cf. Hurtado, "Case Study," 91–93; Hawthorne and Martin, Philippians, 126.

116. Hurtado, "Case Study," 95.

verse 6a depicts the divine status of the Messiah Jesus. With a few exceptions,[117] scholars generally hold the view that this Christ-narrative starts with the depiction of Christ's pre-incarnate condition.[118] In this interpretation, the participle ὑπάρχων has a temporal notion ("when"),[119] and the participle ἐν ὁμοιώματι ἀνθρώπων γενόμενος should be read as "being born in the likeness of men."[120] The critical issue is whether this verse also depicts Christ as a divine being. To solve it, much scholarly effort has been given to defining the precise meaning of the phrase ἐν μορφῇ θεοῦ ὑπάρχων. Unfortunately, this phrase is ambiguous, as this phrase μορφὴ θεοῦ is an *hapax legomenon* not only in Paul's letters but also in the entire New Testament. Various interpretations of this phrase have been contested in modern biblical scholarship: (1) the essential and unchangeable attribute of God;[121] (2) the mode of being of God;[122] (3) Christ's equal status with God;[123] (4) as an equivalent to the image-glory of God;[124] and (5) the external glorious appearance of God.[125]

To solve this exegetical enigma, this study proposes as follows. In the Jewish worldview, divinity is always eternal,[126] which can neither be gained nor lost. Accordingly, if Jesus is depicted as the divine κύριος at the eschaton, he must be also divine at the proton. From this rationale, whatever μορφὴ θεοῦ may mean, the understanding of verse 6 must start with the recognition of the divine status of Christ. In this line of thought, the precise meaning of μορφὴ θεοῦ will be defined in this study.

---

117. Such as Talbert, "Problem of Pre-Existence," 141–53; Howard, "Phil 2:6–11," 368–87; Dunn, *Christology in the Making*, 114–21; Dunn, "Christ, Adam, and Preexistence," 74–83.

118. See the discussion in Martin and Nash, "Philippians 2:6–11," 114–16.

119. Bockmuehl, *Philippians*, 114; Fee, *Pauline Christology*, 376–77. For its consessive notion, see Lightfoot, *Philippians*, 110; for its causal nation, see O'Brien, *Philippians*, 211, 214.

120. As it is the case of τοῦ γενομένου ἐκ σπέρματος Δαυὶδ κατὰ σάρκα in Rom 1:3 and γενόμενον ἐκ γυναικός in Gal 4:4.

121. Lightfoot, *Philippians*, 110; Hawthorne, "Form of God," 96–110; Jowers, "Meaning of Μορφή," 739–66; Fee, *Pauline Christology*, 378.

122. Käsemann, "Critical Analysis of Philippians," 45–88.

123. Schweizer, *Lordship and Discipleship*, 62; Wright, "Ἁρπαγμός," 321–52.

124. For the glory of God, see O'Brien, *Philippians*, 209; for the image of God, see Dunn, *Theology of Paul*, 281–88; Hooker, "Philippians," 88–100; for the glory and image of God Martin, *Hymn of Christ*, 102–20.

125. Bockmuehl, "Form of God," 11–19; Hellerman, "Μορφη Θεου," 779–97; Fowl, *Philippians*, 91–94.

126. Pss 90:2; 93:2; Isa 40:28.

In ancient Greek literature, the term μορφή generally denotes the idea of "something visible in appearance," and only rarely does it refer to "the essence of something" and "the concept of an idea."[127] In this Christ-narrative, the last meaning can be excluded, as it does not contextually fit the term μορφὴ θεοῦ. The meaning of μορφή as essence should also be avoided. The divine essence is eternally unchangeable, whereas the passage narrates the change from the μορφὴ θεοῦ to the μορφὴ δούλου. This leaves us with the more common meaning of μορφή. The term μορφὴ θεοῦ denotes "the glorious visual appearance of God." This meaning, as Bockmuehl demonstrates, is grounded in Jewish religious thought.[128] The surprising thing in this verse is that the μορφὴ θεοῦ is applied to the existence of Jesus. Wright's grammatical study provides a good insight: the articular infinitive τὸ εἶναι ἴσα θεῷ has an epexegetic relation with ἐν μορφῇ θεοῦ.[129] In this light, it is argued that although "the form of God" is not equivalent to the status of "being equal with God," it nevertheless expresses the divine status of Christ.

Second, in the light of what has been established above the nature of Christ's acts of "emptying" and "humbling himself" (κενόω[130] and ταπεινόω) in verses 7–8 should be construed from the recognition of Christ's divine status. Grammatically, the nature of the act of κενόω is shaped by (1) the construction of οὐ . . . ἀλλά, (2) the adverbial participles μορφὴν δούλου λαβών, and (3) ἐν ὁμοιώματι ἀνθρώπων γενόμενος. The last denotes Christ's act of incarnation. The use of ὁμοίωμα (likeness) in verse 7, which shares the semantic value with μορφή, serves to harmonize the tension between Christ who was fully human during his incarnation but at the same time eternally

---

127. See the discussion in Fabricatore, *Form of God*, 82–84.

128. See Bockmuehl, "Form of God," 1–23. In this article, he underlines that although the Jewish Scripture generally prohibits any visual presentation of YHWH (Deut 4:12, 15), some biblical passages describe the glorious appearance of YHWH, which signifies his presence among his people (Exod 16:10; 24:17; 33:17–23; 40:34–38; 1 Kgs 8:11; Isa 6:3; Ezek 1:26–28; 10:4; 43:3; 44:4). In some Second Temple writings, God is even perceived as having a μορφή. Josephus, *Ag. Ap.* 2.190, describes God as having a μορφή, although it is hidden from humans. Philo, *Mos.* 1.66, describes the burning bush encountered by Moses as the most beautiful μορφή, and then associates it with the image of God.

129. Wright, "Jesus Christ Is Lord," 83; Burk, "Articular Infinitive," 253–74.

130. The verb κενόω literally means "to make empty," and metaphorically denotes "to be deprived of" or "to make no effect." See BDAG, 539.

equal with God.[131] Following this line of thought, we now observe the other two aspects of Christ's kenosis.

The construction οὐ . . . ἀλλά places emphasis on the positive affirmation after ἀλλά.[132] Accordingly, the clause οὐχ ἁρπαγμὸν ἡγήσατο τὸ εἶναι ἴσα θεῷ is supplied to define and to strengthen Christ's self-emptying action (ἑαυτὸν ἐκένωσεν). Unfortunately, the meaning of ἁρπαγμός is also highly contentious, as it is not only a *hapax legomenon* in the New Testament and the LXX but also a rarely used word in Greek literature.[133] To overcome this linguistic challenge, scholars generally define the meaning through its cognate ἁρπάγμα, but this has generated various meanings, such as *res retinenda, res rapta, res rapienda, raptus,* and the idiomatic sense.[134] The critical issue is whether ἁρπαγμός should be construed as the attitude toward something that *has* or *has not* been possessed. If the eschaton-proton rationale adopted in our discussion of μορφῇ θεοῦ is applied, the right understanding of οὐχ ἁρπαγμὸν ἡγήσατο should start with the appreciation of Jesus's equality with God. From this vantage point, ἁρπαγμὸν ἡγήσατο speaks not about a desire for divine status, but rather a proper attitude toward it.[135] Such a meaning indeed has been proposed in Hoover's study, which is: "to regard something to be taken advantage of or to regard something to be used for one's own advantage."[136] Therefore, reading in conjunction with οὐχ ἁρπαγμὸν ἡγήσατο τὸ εἶναι ἴσα θεῷ, Christ's attitude toward his divine status is about using it not for his own interest and advantage, but the sake of others. This logically leads to the process of kenosis.

Christ's kenosis is further defined by the participle μορφὴν δούλου λαβών. The background of slaves helps us grasp the thrust of this phrase. In the Greco-Roman society, slaves were located at the bottom of the society's hierarchy, their role was mainly to serve their lord.[137] Against this backdrop,

---

131. See Bockmuehl, *Philippians,* 137; Hansen, *Philippians,* 152.

132. Thekkekara, "Neglected Idiom," 306–14.

133. Its appearances are mostly as patristic citations of or allusion to this verse. See Wright, "Jesus Christ Is Lord," 62.

134. Wright, "Jesus Christ Is Lord," 81.

135. Contra Dunn, "Christ, Adam, and Preexistence," 74–83; Vollenweider, "Der 'Raub' Der Gottgleichheit," 413–33, particularly 429; Heen, "Phil 2:6–11," 148.

136. Hoover, "Harpagmos Enigma," 95–119, particularly 118; Wright, "Jesus Christ Is Lord," 56–98.

137. See Moule, "Further Reflection," 268.

verses 6–8 presents Jesus as the one who is eternally equal with God, but in his incarnation, he voluntarily relinquished his divine glory to embrace the lowest position of humankind (μορφὴ δούλου) for serving others. Christ's abnegation, however, expresses neither the idea of giving up his divine status, as this status is not something that can be given up,[138] nor the idea that Christ's μορφὴ θεοῦ is concealed by his μορφὴ δούλου, as this will undermine the force of κενόω that requires something of the pre-existent Christ to be relinquished.[139] Since μορφὴ θεοῦ refers to Christ's glorious visual appearance, the renunciation of μορφὴ θεοῦ does not affect inherently his divine status.

Finally, God's exaltation of Christ in verse 9 is read as the divine confirmation of who the Messiah Jesus really and always is. It is indisputable that the exaltation refers to the event surrounding the resurrection and ascension of Jesus Christ.[140] The exaltation consists of two parallel divine actions, ὑπερυψόω (to exceedingly exalt) and χαρίζομαι (to graciously give). Concerning the former, while in the LXX, ὑπερυψόω is used almost exclusively to express adoration to YHWH,[141] in Philippians 2:9 this super exaltation is applied to Jesus and performed by God himself. Concerning the latter, God has graciously granted Jesus with his own unique name (יהוה). In connection with the universal worship of Christ, these two actions of God (ὑπερυψόω and χαρίζομαι) virtually confirm the divine status and identity of Christ.

In all, the universal eschatological worship of Christ radically shapes the understanding of Jesus in this narratival gospel. As he will be acclaimed and worshipped as the divine Lord in the eschaton, he must be the one having equality with God since the proton. This also means that "the form of God" describes Christ's pre-existent divine glory, his kenosis, and humble obedience portrays his relinquishing of all his past glory (without disturbing his divine status). His glorious exaltation needs to be understood as God's affirmation of his eternal divine status. Together with the worship of Christ, they become

138. Bauckham, *Jesus and the God of Israel*, 41.

139. Contra O'Brien, *Philippians*, 220–221, 224.

140. Hurtado, "Case Study," 93.

141. See Ps 97:9 LXX and Dan 3:52–88 LXX. In the Jewish biblical worldview, only YHWH is worthy of the highest praise, as the highest exalted position is strictly associated with his throne in heaven that symbolizes his sole sovereignty over the universe (Ps 103:19). See Nagata, "Philippians," 266; Bauckham, *Jesus and the God of Israel*, 161.

a part of the unique identity of the one and only God. This has been rightly stated by Bauckham:

> The exaltation of Christ to participation in the unique divine sovereignty shows him to be included in the unique divine identity. But since the exalted Christ is first the humiliated Christ, since indeed it is *because* of his self-abnegation that he is exalted, his humiliation belongs to the identity of God as truly as his exaltation does.[142]

6.3.2 Soteriology

The soteriological thrust of Philippians 2:10–11 can be apprehended by reading this worship motif in conjunction with the vision of eschatological worship in the Jewish writings, particularly the one in Isaiah 45:23–24. In the Jewish perspective, the eschatological worship of YHWH is associated with not only the concept of eschatological monotheism (i.e. the acknowledgment of YHWH as the only true God) but also eschatological salvation (i.e. the realization of his eschatological earthly reign).[143] To the faithful and righteous believers, this will be the time of salvation, but to those who reject him, it will lead to divine judgment. This salvific thrust is strongly conveyed in Isaiah 45:21–23:

> Was it not I, the LORD?
>   And there is no other god besides me,
> a righteous God and *a* Savior;
>   there is none besides me
> "Turn to me and *be saved*,
>   all the ends of the earth!
>   For I am God, and there is no other.
> By myself I have sworn;
>   from my mouth has gone out righteousness
>   a word that shall not return:
> "To me, every knee shall bow,
>   every tongue shall swear allegiance."

---

142. Bauckham, *Jesus and the God of Israel*, 45.
143. Hofius, *Der Christushymnus*, 46; Bauckham, "Worship of Jesus in Philippians," 132–33.

This thrust is consistently found in 4Q215a and the Aleinu prayer where the vision is employed. Even in Romans 14:10–12, where the judgment motif is predominant, this salvific notion is not moderated. Before the judgment-seat of God, all shall give their account, but the Lord Jesus Christ, the one executing the divine judgment (2:16), will enable all the faithful to be saved on the judgment day (14:4). On this ground, all those in Christ will praise God for his eschatological salvation.

In this line of thought, the confessional praise ὅτι κύριος ᾿Ιησοῦς Χριστὸς εἰς δόξαν θεοῦ πατρός will also contain salvific thrust. This praise notably substitutes λέγων δικαιοσύνη καὶ δόξα in Isaiah 45:24 LXX. In this Isaianic context, both the term δικαιοσύνη and δόξα are closely associated with God's work of salvation. These two terms are notably used in Philippians 1:11 to signify the consummation of salvation in Christ. This is also affirmed by that in early Christianity the confession κύριος ᾿Ιησοῦς was a standard profession of faith that lead to salvation.[144] Romans 10:9–13 indeed associates such a confession with "calling upon the name of the Lord" (citing Joel 3:5 LXX) that leads to salvation.[145] All this affirms that the universal eschatological worship of Jesus Christ in this narratival gospel has a strong salvific thrust.[146]

The covenant framework of the salvific notion of the universal eschatological worship of Christ needs to be appreciated. As it is noted in Romans 14:11, to Paul the universal eschatological worship motif is undergirded by the new covenant between YHWH and the nation Israel, the realm of which has been expanded to all nations. In Romans 15:5–6, therefore, he calls both the Jewish and the Gentile Christians in Rome to worship God as one people of him. In Philippians, this new covenant framework is noted by the Spirit motif in 3:3: ἡμεῖς γάρ ἐσμεν ἡ περιτομή, οἱ πνεύματι θεοῦ λατρεύοντες.[147] Under the blessing of the new covenant (2 Cor 3:6), all believers of Christ have

---

144. O'Brien, *Philippians*, 249; Hawthorne and Martin, *Philippians*, 129.

145. In the OT, salvation exclusively belongs to YHWH, and it is graciously offered to Israel and all nations. Hence, those calling on the name of YHWH will experience salvation (Joel 3:10). This conviction was appropriated by the early Christians in the calling on the name of Jesus (1 Cor 1:2). See Seifrid, "Romans," 652–60.

146. It is not without ground, therefore, that the readers are exhorted to continue working out their σωτηρίαν (salvation) immediately after the confession in Phil 2:11.

147. For a more comprehensive interpretation of this clause, see the discussion in chapter 7.

experienced inner circumcision by the spirit of God (ἡμεῖς γάρ ἐσμεν ἡ περιτομή) that enables them to worship God properly (οἱ πνεύματι θεοῦ λατρεύοντες).[148]

The recognition of the salvific thrust of this worship motif affirms the soteriological notion of both Christ's abnegation and his exaltation in verses 7–9. These verses allude to the servant of YHWH in Isaiah 52–53. According to this portion of Isaiah, God's eschatological reign and salvation (52:7–10) will be established through the sacrificial act of the faithful servant and the vindication of him (52:13–53:12). Reading in conjunction with this servant passage, we argue that Christ's kenotic deed and the exaltation of him by God have a redemptive dimension, as they fulfill the picture of the servant of YHWH.

First, verse 8 depicts Jesus as obediently serving God[149] even to the point of death.[150] The phrase γενόμενος ὑπήκοος μέχρι θανάτου alludes to ἀνθ' ὧν παρεδόθη εἰς θάνατον ἡ ψυχὴ αὐτοῦ in Isaiah 53:12 LXX,[151] and thus his death is in fulfillment of the sacrificial role of the servant. This means that Christ's noble deed is part of God's redemptive plan to save all humankind. This soteriological thrust is further highlighted by the phrase θανάτου δὲ σταυροῦ, which is located at the nadir of Christ's story. In the Greco-Roman world crucifixion was the most horrific punishment.[152] So horrific was this capital execution that it was reserved only for non-Roman criminals and slaves who committed horrific crimes.[153] In the Jewish point of view, this punishment is also associated with the practice of hanging criminals on the tree

---

148. cf. Rom 8:15, 26–27, 1 Cor 6:19; 12:3; Gal 4:6. For the new covenant framework of the Spirit motif, see Fee, *Philippians*, 298.

149. As the servant of YHWH, Christ's obedience is directed to God. Käsemann, "Critical Analysis of Philippians," 74–75, argues that the submission is to θάνατος in order to destroy this evil power that controlled human destiny. However, the use of μέχρι θανάτου, instead of θανάτῳ or εἰς θάνατον, repudiates this conjecture. See Fowl, *Story of Christ*, 63. This is confirmed by the fact that it is God himself who exalted Christ (v. 9) and will receive all the glories (εἰς δόξαν θεοῦ πατρός) in the worship of Christ (vv. 10–11).

150. The preposition μέχρι θανάτου describes the extent of his servitude. See Hansen, *Letter to the Philippians*, 156. Although μέχρι can denote the extent of space (as far as), or length of time (until), in the present context this preposition better describes the degree. See BDAG, 644.

151. Bauckham, *Jesus and the God of Israel*, 205.

152. Cicero, *Verr.* 2.5.165, regards crucifixion as "the most cruel and disgusting penalty." O'Collins, "Crucifixion," *ABD* 1:1207–8.

153. Cicero, *Verr.* 2.5.166–169. See Hengel, *Crucifixion*, 99.

(Deut 21:22–23), which signifies God's curse upon the convicts.[154] In Paul's *Christologoumenon*, however, the crucifixion of Christ becomes the focal point of his gospel (1 Cor 1:23) because it underlines the sacrificial act of the Messiah Jesus to bear the sins of humankind (cf. Rom 3:24–25; 1 Cor 15:3). The phrase θανάτου δὲ σταυροῦ, therefore, reminds the readers of the salvific benefit of Christ's death on the cross.

Second, the exaltation of Christ is also the enthronement of the Messiah Jesus that inaugurates God's eschatological reign and salvation. Although Philippians 2:9 does not employ the enthronement language of Psalm 109:1 LXX (κάθου ἐκ δεξιῶν μου)[155] but that of Isaiah 52:13 LXX (ἰδοὺ συνήσει ὁ παῖς μου καὶ ὑψωθήσεται καὶ δοξασθήσεται σφόδρα),[156] it can still be argued that ὑπερυψόω conveys the idea of enthronement. In this Isaianic passage, the term ὑψόω translates the Hebrew verb רום. This word has a strong correlation with the throne of God, as it is noted in Isaiah 6:1 (את־אדני ישב על־כסא רם ונשא). This notion is affirmed by the allusion to Isaiah 52:23 in 4Q215a ii.10: "for the dominion of righteousness has come, *he raised the throne of* […] ([..] וירם כסם ה)." The use of ὑψόω in describing the vindication of Jesus in Acts 2:33 (τῇ δεξιᾷ οὖν τοῦ θεοῦ ὑψωθείς) and 5:31 (τοῦτον ὁ θεὸς ἀρχηγὸν καὶ σωτῆρα ὕψωσεν τῇ δεξιᾷ αὐτοῦ) further confirms the association of ὑψόω with the enthronement imagery in Psalm 109:1 LXX.

The idea of enthronement is also adumbrated in the statement χαρίζομαι τὸ ὄνομα τὸ ὑπὲρ πᾶν ὄνομα. The phrase "the Name above all names" refers to the Tetragrammaton (יהוה or κύριος). In Jewish literature, the investiture of the divine name upon exalted figures signifies the possession of divine glory and authority to rule on YHWH's behalf. Against this background, the clause describes the enthronement of Christ by which God imparted him with his divine glory and authority so that he will rule on his behalf. Moreover, alluding to Isaiah 52:13, this exaltation is also the fulfillment of God's eschatological dominion and salvation.[157] Isaiah 52–53 pronounces that

---

154. Philo, *Spec. Leg.* 3.153; *Poster C.* 61; *Som.* 2.212; 4QpNah 3–4.1.7–8; 11QT 64:6–13. See the discussion in Green, "Crucifixion," 199; Bockmuehl, *Philippians*, 135.

155. Notably, Paul employed this enthronement motif to underscore the unique status of the exalted Christ (Rom 8:34 and 1 Cor 15:25 9; cf. Eph 1:20; Col 3:1). Bauckham, *Jesus and the God of Israel*, 173; Hurtado, "Case Study," 93.

156. Bauckham, *Jesus and the God of Israel*, 198.

157. In the Jewish *theologoumenon*, the enthronement of YHWH signifies his reign over Israel (Pss 9:7; 22:3), all nations (Ps 29:10), and the whole universe (Ps 99:1; Isa 37:16).

YHWH will return, be enthroned on, and reign from Mount Zion, and the vindication of his suffering servant will establish this realm of salvation. This is appropriated in the christological passage to underline that God's vindication of the Messiah Jesus, who died on the cross, marks the inauguration of God's eschatological reign and salvation.[158]

Finally, the semantic relationship between the conjunction διὸ καί and the ἵνα–subjunctive clause needs to be carefully construed. The combination of the conjunction διό and the adverb καί establishes a strong inferential force.[159] Scholars have noted the element of reciprocity in ἐταπείνωσεν ἑαυτὸν . . . διὸ καὶ ὁ θεὸς αὐτὸν ὑπερύψωσεν,[160] but it is debated whether διὸ καί has the notion of reward.[161] The use of the verb χαρίζομαι underscores God's grace, and thus it prevents any thought of God's exaltation as a reward. Hence, διὸ-καί is better construed in the context of the divine approval of Christ's redemptive deed in verses 6–8. This is supported by the fact that the exaltation of Christ is followed by ἵνα–subjunctive, which indicates that God's vindication of Christ itself is not the end result but a means to achieve a greater purpose, the worship of Jesus Christ by the whole creation at the eschaton, as it is noted in verses 10–11. In this light, this christological passage presents how God and his Messiah are working together to bring into realization the eschatological realm of salvation culminated in the universal eschatological worship of him.

To sum up the discussion, the universal eschatological worship of Jesus Christ in Philippians 2:10–11 marks the consummation of God's eschatological reign and salvation. In this vein, Christ's kenotic deed in verses 6–8 describes how the Messiah Jesus has fulfilled God's redemptive plan to save all humankind, and Christ's exaltation in verse 9 underlines his enthronement by God to establish the divine eschatological reign that saves all humankind.

---

158. A similar idea is noted in Acts 2:34–36; 5:31. In Acts 2:34–36 God enthroned Jesus (citing Ps 109:1 LXX) to be the Lord (κύριος) and the Messiah (Χριστός). Similarly, in Acts 5:31 God enthroned Jesus (ὕψωσεν τῇ δεξιᾷ αὐτοῦ) to be ruler (ἀρχηγός) and savior (σωτήρ).

159. For διὸ, see BDAG, 198; for καί, see BDAG, 393.

160. See Lightfoot, *Philippians*, 113; Martin, *Hymn of Christ*, 233; Hansen, *Philippians*, 159.

161. For reward reading, see Schweizer, *Lordship and Discipleship*, 63; Silva, *Philippians*, 127; Hansen, *Philippians*, 161. O'Brien, *Philippians*, 234; Fee, *Philippians*, 220.

6.3.3 Anti-Imperial Stance

At the time of the writing of Philippians, the deified emperor Augustus had been widely worshipped in the Greco-Roman world, including in Philippi – worshipping in acknowledging him as the divine lord and savior, showing gratitude for his benefaction, and professing submission to the imperial power. It is further contended in this section that the depiction of the universal worship, which professes Jesus Christ as κύριος in Philippians 2:10–11, has a strong anti-imperial stance, as it challenges all these imperial appraisals. However great Augustus's power and his benefaction, he can never be divine κύριος, as only Jesus befits this position. Despite the fame and scale of the worship of Augustus at that time, it will be the worship of Jesus to be universally observed at the eschaton. The extension of worshippers, which includes ἐπουρανίων καὶ ἐπιγείων καὶ καταχθονίων, demands that this greatest deified Caesar, who was worshipped as *deus* Mercurius-Augustus in Philippi, be numbered among his worshippers. The appreciation of this anti-imperial thrust will shape our reading of this christological passage.

To firmly establish the line of thought above the exact expressions where the Christ-story is compared with the Augustus-story need to be demonstrated. Two outlines are noted, using the contributions of Dieter Georgi and Peter Oakes:

Phil 2:6–11	Dieter Georgi[162]	Peter Oakes[163]
Verses 6–8	the deeds of the emperor	the deeds of the emperor candidate
Verse 9	the apotheosis of the emperor	the enthronement of the emperor
Verses 10–11	the worship of the emperor	the submission to the emperor

According to Oakes, the enthronement of the new emperor serves as the narrative backbone of this christological passage. The arguments are twofold: (1) the critical issue in verses 10–11 is not about worship but (political) authority, as the civic opposition in Philippi was not generated by Christians'

---

162. Georgi, *Theocracy in Paul's Praxis*, 76–77.
163. Oakes, "Re-Mapping the Universe," 319; *Philippians*, 133.

withdrawal from the imperial cult;[164] and (2) verse 9 depicts the installment into power while the apotheosis marks the withdrawal from it.[165]

While his conjecture is appealing, we find that Dieter Georgi's scheme has greater accuracy. Our arguments are as follows. First, the cult of Augustus has heavily contributed to the persecution of Christianity in Philippi. Second, the Roman constitution does not recognize the practice of the enthronement of the emperor. The office and power to reign as *imperator* is endowed by the Senate of Rome on a yearly basis. Third, in the Greco-Roman worldview, the apotheosis of Caesar is not understood as a creation of a new god, but rather the Senate's ratification of what has been ordained by the council of gods.[166] One essential ingredient in this ratification is the testimony of some trustworthy eyewitnesses before the Senate that confirms that the deceased Caesar has been accepted into the realm of gods. The testimony is usually based on some divine omens, such as the appearance of stars or eagles in the sky. This would be a parallel with the testimony of the earliest Christians who claimed to witness the resurrection-ascension of the Messiah Jesus (Acts 2:32–33), among them was Paul himself (1 Cor 15:4–8; Gal 1:15–16). This opens up the same hermeneutical possibility for the original readers, the Philippian Christians. Finally, in the ancient worldview to be divine means not only to gain divine status but also to have power and office to rule. Such a cosmogony is noted in Virgil's praise of Augustus:

> And you above all, Caesar (Augustus), whom we know not what company of the gods shall claim ere long: whether you choose to watch over the cities and care for our lands, that so the great globe may receive you as the givers of increase and lord of seasons . . . whether you add yourself as a new star to the lingering month, where, between the Virgin and the grasping Claws, a space is opening . . . whatever you are to be, grant me a calm voyage, give assent to my bold empire, and pitying with me the rustics who know not their ways, enter upon your kingdom, and learn even to hearken to our prayers![167]

---

164. Oakes, "Re-Mapping the Universe," 319–20.

165. Oakes, 318–19; *Philippians*, 133.

166. Contra Gradel, *Emperor Worship*, 298.

167. Virgil, *Georgics*, 1.25–42.

The Latin poem composed by a chief centurion for the dedication of the temple of Augustus's sons (Caius and Lucius) in Campania also presents a similar idea:

> For when time shall demand you as a god, Caesar
> And you shall return to your seat in heaven, whence
> You will rule the world, may it be these who in your stead
> Hold sway here on earth and rule us by your felicitous vow[168]

The apotheosis of Augustus, therefore, should not be understood as his withdrawal from the power to rule, but rather another phase in his effective rule: to be a divine guardian of the Golden Age of Rome. This mindset is presented in the *Grande Camée de France* where the *divus* Augustus is depicted as the divine κύριος who guards the peace of the empire. All this demonstrates that it is more plausible that the heavenly enthronement of the Messiah Jesus in Philippians 2:9 evokes the memory of the apotheosis of Augustus rather than a supposed enthronement of him into power.

First of all, Christ's glorious existence and his divine status in verse 6 challenge the imperial claim of the divine origin and status of Augustus. In regard to the former, the Roman poet Virgil acclaims Augustus as *divi genus*,[169] and the historian Suetonius records the rumor surrounding the birth of Augustus attested in Asclepias's *theologoumena* that the emperor has a human mother but a divine father (Apollo).[170] With regard to the latter, during his reign, Augustus received various honorific titles (*divi filius*, *Princeps*, *Augustus*, *Pontifex Maximus*, and *Pater Patriae*) that extolled him as the divine vicegerent on earth. He was also honored with many ἰσόθεοι τιμαί (temples, altars, festivals, games, cults, and ritual sacrifices). The images of his being μορφὴ θεοῦ were promoted in his honorific statues, mass production portraits,[171] and the coins across the empire. In Philippi, he received ἰσόθεοι τιμαί during his reign and was worshiped as *divus* after his death (AD 14). Against all this imperial backdrop, the divine pre-existence of the Christ Jesus

---

168. The inscription is found in *CIL* 10.3757; *ILS* 137. The translation is cited from Gradel, *Emperor Worship*, 269.

169. Virgil, *Aeneid*, 6. 793.

170. Suetonius, *Aug.* 94.4.

171. There were about 20,000–25,000 portraits of Augustus across the empire. See Crossan and Reed, *In Search of Paul*, 143–44.

in verse 6 greatly challenges the popular perception of Augustus's divine origin and status in Philippi. In the Jewish-Christian monotheistic framework, the challenge is not so much who is superior, as who the real equal with God is. The gospel in Philippians 2:6–11 strongly asserts that it cannot be Augustus, but the Lord Jesus. The reason is that the following acts in verses 6–8 could only be performed by the one who is truly equal with God.

Second, Philippians 2:7–8 polemically contrasts Christ's deeds with those of Augustus. A critical question to be posed is how this contrast is precisely depicted. Favoring the *res rapienda* reading, Erik M. Heen argues that verse 6 echoes Caesar's craving after divine status.[172] However, as it has been established above, the term ἁρπαγμός is best understood in relation to a selfish attitude in exploiting the divine status. Hence, the critique focuses more on the way Augustus exploited his divine-like status.

The public imperial discourses across the empire acclaimed Augustus as a great leader who had provided many great services to the State and humankind. His greatest service is the establishment of the realm of peace on earth, the Pax Romana, which is associated with the eschatological Golden Age. Through Augustus's reign, gods had returned and ruled the world, and the earth had also responded by producing bountiful harvests. All this created a strong impression that Augustus exploited his divine-like status in a way that provided the greatest service to his subjects, both Romans and non-Romans. As Philippi had strong historical bonds with the military victories of Augustus, and indeed the colony was planted in Macedonia to represent the imperial power over this conquered region, we cogently expect that the public space in this city was filled with many kinds of eulogy celebrating the divine conquering power of Augustus.

What has also been noted by many Roman historians is that this divine-like status also provided the imperial justification for eliminating any potential rival and subjugating other nations to establish the new divine order on earth, the Golden Age of Rome. Indeed, these were the normal associations of having a divine status at that time.[173] For example, in *Ara Pacis Augustae*, *Dea Roma* is portrayed as wearing her military costume and surrounded by

---

172. Heen, "Phil 2:6–11," 125–54.

173. Crossan and Reed, *In Search of Paul*, 288.

the spoils of the conquered nation.[174] In the *Gema Augustae*, this goddess also accompanies Augustus who sits on his throne in the guise of *Deus* Jupiter receiving *corona civica*. Below this scene is the subjugation of many nations by the imperial military force. Some less flattering accounts of Augustus, which underline his cruelty, indeed were circulated among those who experienced imperial oppressions. Tacitus notices those critics in his writing in his *Annales*:

> On the other side it was argued that "filial duty and the critical position of the state had been used merely as a cloak: come to facts, and it was from the lust of dominion that he excited the veterans by his bounties, levied an army while yet a stripling and a subject, seduced the legions of a consul, and affected a leaning to the Pompeian side. Then, following his usurpation by senatorial decree of the symbols and powers of the praetorship, had come the death of Hirtius and Pansa . . . *After that, there had been undoubtedly peace, but peace with bloodshed* – the disasters of Lollius and Varus, the execution at Rome of a Varro, and Egnatius, an Iullus."[175]

So does Suetonius in his writing of *Divus Augustus*:

> *He did not use his victory with moderation*, but after sending Brutus' head to Rome, to be cast at the feet of Caesar's statue, he vented his spleen upon the most distinguished of his captives, not even sparing them insulting language. For instance, to one man who begged humbly for burial, he is said to have replied: "the birds will soon settle that question." When two others, father and son, beg for their lives, he is said to have bidden them cast lots or play *mora*, to decide which should be spared, and then to have looked on while both died, since the father was executed because he offered to die for his own son, and the latter thereupon took his own life. Because of this the rest, including Marcus Favonius, the well-known imitator of Cato, saluted

---

174. See Figure 42 in Galinsky, *Augustan Culture*, after p. 107.
175. Tacitus, *Ann.* 1.10 (Moore, LCL). The emphasis is mine.

Antony respectfully as Imperator, when they were led out in chains, but slashed Augustus to his face with the foulest abuse.[176]

Against the cruelty of this imperial backdrop, Philippians 2:6–8 highlights that the true God-sent κύριος has used his equality with God in a manner which is opposite to Augustus's. If the latter exploited his divine status violently to obtain his lordship over the world, the former demonstrated it by relinquishing his divine glory and power to serve others. This christological passage, thus, powerfully shapes the understanding of what divinity is all about: the real equal with God would never exploit his divine status for selfish aims, but is always ready to forsake his own glory to serve and save. This would be a powerful critique of imperial realities relating to *divus* Augustus.

Finally, as the universal worship of Jesus Christ has a salvific notion, it also questions the imperial claims of salvation centered on Augustus. To Paul, the imperial version of peace and salvation is only an illusion, as the whole of nature was still subjected to futility and corruption (Rom 8:19–23).[177] The phrase θανάτου δὲ σταυροῦ indeed evokes the memory of Augustus's bloody execution of some thirty thousand runaway slaves in 36 BC, which was done to deter any future insurrection of slaves.[178] The imperial version of salvation, hence, has no place for humble and ordinary people, but oppression. In contrast, the gospel of Christ proclaims that the real salvation has been established by the one truly equal with God who willingly took the form of a slave to humbly serve others by dying on the Roman cross. In him, the real εἰρήνη τοῦ θεοῦ can be experienced (4:7). This true σωτήρ, whom they are awaiting expectantly, will come as the victorious Lord (3:20–21).

In all, the depiction of universal worship of Jesus Christ at the eschaton in this christological passage challenges the popular worship of Augustus everywhere across the empire, and thus the greatness of this emperor, and the salvation provided by him. To Paul and the Philippian Christians, the true God-sent Savior is Jesus Christ who is eternally equal with God but who

---

176. Suetonius, *Aug.* 13 (Rolfe, LCL). The emphasis is mine.

177. See the discussion in Jewett, "Corruption and Redemption," 31–46.

178. The event relates to the joining of a massive number of runaway slaves with Sextus Pompey's military campaign in 36 BC. In *Res Gestae* Augustus claims that he had handed over some thirty thousand slaves to their masters. But other ancient accounts (Appian, *Bell. Civ.* 5.13.131; Dio Cassius, *Romans History,* 49.12.4–5; Oros 6.18.33) report that he also crucified some six thousand slaves whose masters could not be identified.

has renounced his own glory, becoming a human, then dying on the cross to save all humankind. Therefore, it is also this Christ who has been exalted into heaven as the universal divine Lord, and before whom all shall submissively worship at the eschaton. This powerful message would surely assure the Philippian Christians, who were oppressed by the imperial power at that time, of their decision to believe in Christ.

6.3.4 Ethics

In the context of Philippians, there is no doubt that the christological passage has an ethical impetus. In this line of thought, it is further argued that the motif of universal worship of Jesus Christ also has ethical significance. It has been established that the vision in Isaiah 45:23 has a transformative coordinate. Accordingly, Paul's appropriation of this vision of worship in Philippians includes this dimension.

In the prescript, Paul addresses the readers as "the holy ones in Christ Jesus" (οἱ ἅγιοι ἐν Χριστῷ Ἰησοῦ), and in the prayer report section, he expresses his hope that they all will be blameless on the day of Christ (1:10–11). The grand event to be awaited on that day is not only the resurrection of the dead that will include the transformation of their body (3:10–11, 21) but also the universal worship of Christ (2:10–11) and his final judgment (3:9). Together, they build the expectation that all believers of Christ will join this universal worship of Christ at the eschaton "in holiness." The ethical entailment of this worship motif becomes apparent when we supply the picture of universal eschatological worship in Romans 14:10–12 where worship is situated before the judgment seat of God.

In biblical teaching, the holiness of God's people has both cultic and moral dimensions. Concerning the former, various rituals are observed by Jews to maintain their cultic holiness, but to Paul, they have only little value for those who are now in Christ (3:4–6; cf. Rom 14:1–6). The issue of the object of worship, however, is greatly relevant to the gentile believers in Philippi. Accordingly, the depiction of the universal eschatological worship of Christ entails that their cultic holiness must include the reorientation of their cultic behavior, namely from worshipping idols, including the participation in imperial cults, to worshipping God and his Christ.

Concerning the latter, in agreement with Hurtado,[179] the eschatological worship that acclaims Jesus as universal κύριος authoritatively demands that Christ's deed in verses 6–8 be treated as a norm for the lives of his believers. Some scholars emphasize the idea of the imitation of Christ (συμμιμητής),[180] while others prefer to employ the idea of *conformitas*[181] or *examplar*[182] to avoid the sense of strict imitation of Christ's deed, as it has a redemptive dimension. Whatever the case, the universal eschatological worship of Christ establishes Christ's deed as the standard ethical benchmark of moral/ethical holiness for those who are in Christ.

In Philippians, the transformation into holiness is described in two stages. At the present moment, God is actively and powerfully working within and among believers of Christ to perfect their holiness and salvation (1:6; 2:13). At his parousia, Christ will perform a final transformation by which the body of believers will be changed into his perfection (3:21). While these two stages of transformation are dependent on and secured by God, the active participation of God's people is required at the present stage (1:27; 2:12; 3:12–15; 4:5–9). This participation includes the two aspects of holiness mentioned above, the exclusive worship of God and his Christ and the adoption of a Christ-like ethos.

One crucial issue to be discussed is the nature of God's exaltation of Christ in verse 9. Generally, scholars acknowledge the element of reciprocity in the statement ἐταπείνωσεν ἑαυτὸν . . . διὸ καὶ ὁ θεὸς αὐτὸν ὑπερύψωσεν,[183] and the inferential force of the conjunction διό-καί (therefore).[184] However, disagreement occurs concerning whether this conjunction expresses the notion of approval, vindication, or reward.[185] In defining the nature of this exaltation, we contend that the following ἵνα–subjunctive indicates that God's vindication of Christ is not the end objective but to attain a final purpose in verses

---

179. Hurtado, "Jesus as Lordly Example," 125.

180. Hawthorne, "Imitation of Christ," 163–80; Kurz, "Kenotic Imitation of Paul," 103–26.

181. Hurtado, "Jesus as Lordly Example," 125; Hooker, "Philippians," 90–91.

182. Fowl, *Story of Christ*, 92–95.

183. Lightfoot, *Philippians*, 113; Martin, *Hymn of Christ*, 233; Hansen, *Philippians*, 159.

184. For διό, see BDAG, 198; for καί, see BDAG, 393.

185. For reason-approval, see Wright, "Jesus Christ Is Lord," 86; Oakes, *Philippians*, 152–54. For vindication, see Bockmuehl, *Philippians*, 140; Fowl, *Story of Christ*, 66. For reward, see Schweizer, *Lordship and Discipleship*, 63; Hellerman, *Reconstructing Honor*, 154–55; Silva, *Philippians*, 127; Hansen, *Philippians*, 160–61.

10–11: the universal worship of Jesus Christ at the eschaton. Accordingly, the ethical thrust of this end-time worship considerably shapes the notion of Christ's exaltation.

In this line of thought, we argue that the exaltation of Christ has the notion of both divine approval and vindication. The exaltation clearly demonstrates that God approved Christ's deed and publicly ordain him to be the universal Lord who can demand both worship and obedience. The enthronement imagery and the Isaianic allusion in this exaltation give support to this inference. Christ's deeds not only demonstrate the noble character of the Messiah Jesus but also fulfill God's redemptive plan. In conformity with the role of the servant of YHWH, God has approved and enthroned him to be the Lord of all who has the power to save. Furthermore, Christ is depicted as the one eternally equal with God, and who in obedience to the divine plan had renounced all his glory and experienced a shameful death on the cross for the sake of all humankind. Hence, it is theologically required that his exaltation would also carry the notion of vindication, in the sense of restoring his rightful position to the world. The sense of reward in this vindication, however, should be avoided, given that the one eternally equal with God does not need any reward of his acts.

The notions of approval and vindication in God's exaltation of Christ have an important role in the early Christian discipleship. The former establishes Christ as the Lord of all who demands worship, submission, and obedience. The latter provides eschatological encouragement, particularly when the gospel is read in conjunction with the teaching of self-humiliation – God's exaltation in earliest Christianity.[186] The implication of this reading will be elaborated in the next chapter where the function of the eschatological worship motif in Paul's paraenesis in Philippians is in focus.

6.4 Summary

Philippians 2:10–11 depicts the universal worship of Jesus Christ at the eschaton in fulfillment of the biblical vision in Isaiah 45:20–25. In depicting

---

186. See Matt 11:23; 23:12; Luke 1:52; 10:15; 14:11; 18:14; 2 Cor 11:7; Jas 4:10; 1 Pet 5:6. The use of compound word ὑπερ-υψόω in Phil 2:9 can be perceived as God's reciprocal response to Christ's extreme self-abasement. Nagata, "Philippians," 266.

this worship the passage does not merely allude to this Isaianic vision, but carefully reworks it: (1) the context of worship is transported from the rise of Cyrus to the day of Christ; (2) the worship of YHWH is now applied to his Messiah Jesus; and (3) worship is cosmologically extended, so as to include all creatures in the whole universe. In the context of Paul's letter to the Philippians, this creative reworking of the Isaianic vision of worship engenders the christological, soteriological, anti-imperial, and ethical significances, which are noted in reading the narratival gospel of Christ.

Christologically speaking, the universal worship of Christ at the eschaton establishes Jesus as the divine κύριος who shares the unique divine identity with YHWH, who is the God of both Israel and the whole creation. From the Jewish monotheistic perspective, this claim is very striking, nonetheless, it is developed within Isaianic monotheistic coordinates. This picture of worship at the eschaton demands him to be regarded as being equal with God in his protological state. From this perspective, his kenotic deed reveals, rather than negates, the nature of divinity, and his exaltation is the divine confirmation of who Jesus really and always is. Together, they become part of the unique divine identity of the one and only God.

Soteriologically, the universal worship of Christ at the eschaton also sets the salvific tone of this christological passage. Depicted as a climactic end of this Christ-narrative, this worship celebrates the consummation of God's eschatological reign through his Messiah Jesus under the new covenant blessing. As the self-abnegation and the exaltation of Christ allude to Isaiah 52:13–53:12, both need to be understood in the context of the fulfillment of the role of the Isaianic servant of YHWH. Accordingly, Christ's acts of κενόω and ταπεινόω are to fulfill the divine mission of salvation, and God's vindication of him is the public enthronement of Christ as the universal Lord who has all power to reign and to save.

The glorious depiction of Jesus Christ at the eschaton notably polemically opposes the imperial narratival gospel of Augustus. The claim that it will be the Messiah Jesus, not Augustus, who will be worshipped by all creatures at the eschaton denounces the greatness of this Roman emperor who is widely acclaimed and propagated in the imperial discourses. Accordingly, Christ's deeds in verses 6–8 also profess that it is the Messiah Jesus, and not Augustus, who has a divine origin and is the real equal with God. This is reflected by his noble attitudes and deeds, which are in the totally opposite direction of those of Augustus. While the latter has exploited his divine-like status violently and for his own greatness, the former has expressed his divine status by renouncing his own glory and dying shamefully on the cross for the salvation of all humankind. Thus, it is the Messiah Jesus, not Augustus, who has been enthroned by God as the universal Lord, and who will be worshipped by all creatures in the whole universe.

Finally, as the biblical visions of worship have a transformative dimension, the universal worship of Christ has also an ethical impetus. Reading Philippians 2:10–11 in conjunction with 1:10–11 and 2:12–16, all believers of Christ in Philippi will be called to join this universal eschatological worship of Christ in holiness. Two aspects of holiness are underlined. First of all, the picture of the eschatological worship of Christ authoritatively demands all Christians to worship him (and God) exclusively and wholeheartedly. Moreover, it demands them to pattern their lives according to the example set by Christ in this gospel. The exaltation of him in 2:9 both supplies this divine authority and ensures the salvation of all those in Christ who are faithfully working out their holiness.

CHAPTER 7

The Function of Philippians 2:10–11

This chapter is the heart of the present study, which deals with the function of Paul's depiction of the universal eschatological worship of Christ in his letter to the Philippians. It is generally appreciated that the christological passage in 2:6–11 provides a principal ground for Paul's exhortations in this letter.[1] Particularly significant is its function in the two major paraenetical discourses, 1:27–2:18 and 3:2–4:4.[2] It is justifiable, therefore, to assume that this eschatological worship motif also has a significant role in these two major sections of Philippians.

The chapter contends that the christological, soteriological, ethical, and anti-imperial thrusts of the universal eschatological worship of Christ in Philippians 2:10–11, which have been established in the previous chapter, provide the theoretical framework for these two discourses. To expound them properly, the passages will be read against Paul's "think this" (τοῦτο φρονεῖτε) instruction in 2:5. While this is a common approach for understanding the significance of this narratival gospel in Philippians,[3] the correlation between this instruction and the other two "think this" statements in the letter (τοῦτο φρονεῖν in 1:7; τοῦτο φρονῶμεν in 3:15) is often overlooked. Hence, to properly highlight the eschatological significance of the worship motif in the christological passage, the present study will situate the instruction in 2:5 within the larger "think this" framework in the letter.

---

1. Hansen, *Philippians*, 31, regards Phil 2:6–11 as "the heart of the letter." Gorman, *Apostle of the Crucified*, 419, claims this christological passage as the centerpiece of the letter.

2. See Fowl, "Christology and Ethics," 140–53; Kurz, "Kenotic Imitation of Paul," 103–26; Dodd, "Story of Christ," 154–61.

3. This is noted in most of the current contemporary commentaries.

To do so, the discussions are arranged into three major parts. The first establishes Paul's eschatological framework in the letter based on his three "think this" statements. The subsequent two sections, then, examine the role of the worship motif in the two major paraenetical discourses noted above. By doing this, we hope to bring into light the significance of the universal eschatological worship of Christ in this letter.

7.1 Paul's Eschatological Frame of Mind

Paul's letter to the Philippians reveals his intent to shape his readers' mindset. This aim is detected by his use of the verb φρονέω in the letter.[4] In this short letter, the term appears ten times out of twenty-three times in Paul's letters.[5] Its significance is reflected not only in the frequency of its occurrence but also in the way Paul exploits its meaning. In antiquity, this term has a wide spectrum of meanings associated with the various activities of the mind. This is reflected by the various ways this term is used in the letter: (1) to think of something or someone as τὸ ὑπὲρ ἐμοῦ φρονεῖν in 4:10; (2) to be in possession of one's mind as οἱ τὰ ἐπίγεια φρονοῦντες in 3:19; and (3) to think in a certain way or to have a certain disposition as τοῦτο φρονεῖν ὑπὲρ πάντων ὑμῶν in 1:7, τοῦτο φρονεῖτε ἐν ὑμῖν in 2:5, and Ὅσοι οὖν τέλειοι, τοῦτο φρονῶμεν in 3:15.[6] The last notably reveals his intention to shape the frame of mind of the readers that will affect their behaviors.[7]

Meeks and Fowl correctly observe that the verb φρονέω, together with its cognate noun φρόνησις, evokes the idea of practical reasoning in the Greco-Roman moral philosophy, and it is creatively used by Paul in his letter to the Philippians to shape the reader's way of thinking.[8] A careful observation on the contents of Paul's "think this" statements reveals further that they are strongly

---

4. The significance of Paul's use of φρονέω in Philippians has been increasingly appreciated in the study of this letter. See Cousar, *Philippians and Philemon*, 17–18; Fowl, *Philippians*, 28–28; Fowl, "Christology and Ethics," 145; Meeks, "Man from Heaven"; Doble, "Vile Bodies," 5–6.

5. The use of this term is noted in 1:7; 2:2 (2x), 5; 3:15 (2x), 19; 4:2, 10 (2x).

6. LSJ, 1955–56; BDAG, 1065–66.

7. Martin, *Philippians*, 90–91, defines φρονέω as "the combination of intellectual and affective activity which touches both head and heart and lead to a positive course of action"; Meeks, "Man from Heaven," 333, labels it as "practical reasoning" or "practical wisdom."

8. Fowl, *Philippians*, 28–29; Meeks, "Man from Heaven," 329–36.

eschatological. As they are crucial for understanding the role of Philippians 2:10–11, their eschatological thrusts need to be unpacked properly.

7.1.1 Paul's Τοῦτο Φρονεῖν in 1:5–7

In Paul's letters, the prayer report section usually introduces various pivotal issues and themes to be developed in the rest of the letter.[9] In Philippians, it can be further added that the prayer report section in 1:3–11 is used intentionally to shape the eschatological mindset of the readers. Our analysis of Paul's "think this" statement and his petition prayer demonstrates this.

The statement is first sounded in 1:7: as it is right for me "to think this" (τοῦτο φρονεῖν) about you all. The demonstrative pronoun τοῦτο is notably retrospective,[10] referring back to verses 5–6. Hence, Paul's τοῦτο φρονεῖν relates to his ongoing *koinonia* with the Philippian congregation εἰς τὸ εὐαγγέλιον.[11] The thing to be underlined in their unique relationship is expressed in the clause ὁ ἐναρξάμενος ἐν ὑμῖν ἔργον ἀγαθὸν ἐπιτελέσει ἄχρι ἡμέρας Χριστοῦ Ἰησοῦ. Their partnership is deeply embedded in God's salvific activity within and among[12] them from the very beginning until the day of Christ.[13]

"This way of reasoning" (φρονεῖν) is not only theological and soteriological, but also eschatological. The "good work" (ἔργον ἀγαθόν) is associated with the divine work of salvation (cf. 2:12–13),[14] which includes their partnership in the gospel of Christ.[15] The term ἐπιτελέω is an intensified meaning of τελέω that carries the idea of "to bring to an end."[16] The preposition ἄχρι underlines the sustainability of the divine activity *until* the day of Christ Jesus.[17] Together,

---

9. Murphy-O'Connor, *Paul the Letter-Writer*, 62–65.

10. Fee, *Philippians*, 199n25.

11. In Paul's letters the term εὐαγγέλιον always appears in singular form, referring to that of Christ. See Dunn, *Theology of Paul*, 168. In Philippians, the κοινωνία in the gospel of Christ includes both the partnership in proclaiming the gospel (cf. 1:7; 4:15) and the participation in the salvific realm of Christ (cf. 2:1; 3:10–11). The emphasis in 1:5 is more on the former. O'Brien, *Philippians*, 61–61; Fee, *Philippians*, 82–83; Bockmuehl, *Philippians*, 60; Hansen, *Philippians*, 48–49.

12. The preposition ἐν has both personal (in) and communal (among) senses (cf. 12:13).

13. Scholars generally appreciate a close correlation between their evangelical *koinonia* in v. 5 and the divine completing activity in v. 6. See Hansen, *Philippians*, 50.

14. Bockmuehl, *Philippians*, 61.

15. Hansen, *Philippians*, 50.

16. BDAG, 383; Mahoney, "Ἐπιτελέω," *EDNT* 1:42.

17. The preposition ἄχρι denotes the continuous extension of time. BDAGD 160.

they powerfully impart the idea that God will fully accomplish his salvific work among them until the eschaton. The peculiar phrase "the day of Christ Jesus" (ἡμέρα Χριστοῦ Ἰησοῦ) is not only associated with his parousia but also appropriated from the biblical idea of "the day of the Lord" (ἡμέρα κυρίου)[18] that denotes the time when God will reveal his earthly dominion through his eschatological judgment and salvation. In the present context, the phrase stresses this salvific notion. In all, the "think this" statement reveals Paul's confidence in his partnership with the readers in the gospel of Christ, which is fully grounded in God's completing his salvific activity until the eschaton.

We note that O'Brien suggests that God's ἐνάρχομαι-ἐπιτελέω framework in this theological reasoning is derived from the statements of "the first and the last" in Deutero-Isaiah.[19] While this is plausible, there is no linguistic evidence to confirm this allusion. A better conjecture is that this eschatological framework is derived from the narratival gospel of Christ in Philippians itself. Paul's partnership with the Philippian church is notably in the gospel, and in this letter, the gospel is virtually narrated in 2:6–11. The "think this" statements in both 1:7 and 2:5 provide a linguistic key for this connection. This Christ-narrative underlines that as God has started his redemptive work through Christ, he will surely complete it until all creatures submit and worship his Christ for his glory at the eschaton. This proton-eschaton scheme certainly frames Paul's theological reasoning on God's active works in his *koinonia* with the Philippians church. In this respect, we can say that Paul's eschatological frame of mind on their *koinonia* in the gospel of Christ is inspired and shaped by the gospel narrative itself.

Integral to this eschatological frame of mind is the expectation of holiness in Paul's prayer for the readers in 1:9–11:

> ἵνα ἡ ἀγάπη ὑμῶν ἔτι μᾶλλον καὶ μᾶλλον περισσεύῃ
> ἐν ἐπιγνώσει καὶ πάσῃ αἰσθήσει
> εἰς τὸ δοκιμάζειν ὑμᾶς τὰ διαφέροντα,
> ἵνα ἦτε εἰλικρινεῖς καὶ ἀπρόσκοποι εἰς ἡμέραν Χριστοῦ,
> πεπλη ρωμένοι καρπὸν δικαιοσύνης τὸν διὰ Ἰησοῦ Χριστοῦ
> εἰς δόξαν καὶ ἔπαινον θεοῦ.

---

18. Kreitzer, *Jesus and God*, 112–13.
19. See Isa 41:4; 44:6; 48:12. O'Brien, *Philippians*, 64–65.

This petitionary prayer needs to be appreciated within their gospel partner-ship, as it arises from this very context. Although the church in Philippi is currently in trouble and Paul is imprisoned elsewhere, their gospel partner-ship persists, as both have been faithfully fighting for the gospel (1:7).

The prayer is generated from Paul's eschatological reasoning of God's com-pleting activity of his salvation and anticipates the universal eschatological worship of Christ depicted in the narratival gospel of Christ. This is affirmed by the phrase εἰς ἡμέραν Χριστοῦ in verse 10, which the preposition εἰς un-derlines the idea of "in preparation for."[20] In this letter, the day of Christ not only marks (1) the consummation of salvation in Christ (1:6; 3:20–21) but also (2) the day where all shall give their account to God (2:16; 3:9) and (3) the day where the universal worship of Christ shall be conducted (2:10–11). Accordingly, the day of Christ in this prayer, while it emphasizes the judgment motif, also harks back to the consummation of God's salvation in 1:6 and anticipates the eschatological worship of Christ in 2:10–11. This appreciation of the day of Christ will shape our reading of this prayer.

First of all, the prayer expresses Paul's eschatological expectation that his readers will be found holy at the eschaton. In the prescript, they are already addressed as "the holy ones in Christ Jesus" (οἱ ἅγιοι ἐν Χριστῷ Ἰησοῦ), which brings to mind Israel's covenant identity as the holy nation (ἔθνος ἅγιος) in Exodus 19:6 LXX.[21] Foundational to this covenant identity is this train of thought. In Christ, the readers are in a relationship with the Holy One of Israel, and being in this relationship, they are reflecting his holy character.[22] Therefore, it is natural for Paul to expect his readers to be found holy at Christ's parousia. This is articulated notably in two purpose statements: (1) ἵνα ἦτε εἰλικρινεῖς καὶ ἀπρόσκοποι εἰς ἡμέραν Χριστοῦ and (2) πεπληρωμένοι καρπὸν δικαιοσύνης τὸν διὰ Ἰησοῦ Χριστοῦ.[23]

The thrusts of holiness in these two clauses needs to be briefly elabo-rated. Concerning the first statement, the term εἰλικρινής denotes "purity" or "sincerity," having the image of judging the quality of an object under the

---

20. O'Brien, 79.

21. Porter, "Holiness, Sanctification," 397–98.

22. Brower and Johnson, "Introduction," xix.

23. Both the ἵνα subjunctive and the participle clause have a *telic* force. These purposive statements are parallel with those in 1 Cor 1:8 and 1 Thess 3:13; 5:23.

sunlight.[24] The term ἀπρόσκοπος denotes the idea of either "being without fault" or "not causing any offense."[25] In the context of divine judgment, the former notion is predominant. Hence, ἵνα ἦτε εἰλικρινεῖς καὶ ἀπρόσκοποι underlines the absence of sin (or evil deed) in their lives. Concerning the second, holiness is articulated through the metaphor of a bountiful harvest.[26] The use of δικαιοσύνη introduces the theme of righteousness. In this prayer, however, Paul does not speak about the imputation of Christ's righteousness upon the believers. Instead, their ethical conduct and their sanctification process are in view.[27] The participle πεπληρωμένοι is in perfect-passive form, indicating that the readers have been filled with καρπὸν δικαιοσύνης and will be filled more and more until the day of Christ. The phrase καρπὸν δικαιοσύνης can be read as either "a fruit characterized by righteousness"[28] or "a fruit generated by righteousness,"[29] since both fit well with the context. It is worth noting, however, that in Pauline ethics, righteous conduct is generated by a righteous status before God.[30] The fruit of righteousness is filled by God through (διά) Jesus Christ.[31] This sanctification process is facilitated by the Holy Spirit,[32] which is also identified as the Spirit of Christ in this letter (1:19). In all, Paul's eschatological expectation underlines that on the day of Christ the readers will be found holy before God, in the sense of both the absence of sin and the abundance of righteous deeds generated by their righteous status in Christ.

In conjunction with the narratival gospel of Christ, the holiness expectation in this prayer anticipates the universal worship of Christ at the eschaton. As it has been established in the earlier discussion, Paul's eschatological thought that combines the judgment and the worship motifs is attested in Romans 14:10–12. In this prayer, the eschatological worship of God and

---

24. Goldstein, "Εἰλικρινής," *EDNT* 1:391. Cf. 2 Cor 2:17 where Paul claims that his pure motive in the ministry of the gospel can be defended before God (κατέναντι θεοῦ).

25. BDAG, 125–26.

26. For "a tree with bountiful fruits" at the harvest time, see Marshall, *Philippians*, 17.

27. Bockmuehl, *Philippians*, 69; Witherington III, *Philippians*, 66.

28. Here, δικαιοσύνης is either a genitive of apposition, a genitive attribution, or genitive of definition. See Fee, *Philippians*, 103–4; Hawthorne, *Philippians*, 29; Hansen, *Philippians*, 63.

29. Here, δικαιοσύνης is a genitive of "origin," as it is the case of καρπὸς ἔργου in Phil 1:22 and Gal 5:22.

30. Bockmuehl, *Philippians*, 69.

31. The participle of πεπληρωμένοι expresses an idea of "divine passive."

32. See Rom 8:1–17; Gal 5:16–26.

Christ is situated before the judgment seat of God where all the worshippers shall give their full account to him. As both passages employ the same Isaianic vision, it is plausible that the holiness expectation in this prayer relates to this eschatological event of the universal worship of Christ in 2:10–11. This reading gains support from the doxological εἰς δόξαν καὶ ἔπαινον θεοῦ. While it was common in Jewish practices to end prayers with a doxology,[33] the doxology in this prayer is conceptually and rhetorically connected with the doxological εἰς δόξαν θεοῦ πατρός in the christological passage,[34] as both are eschatologically oriented.

In connection with the τοῦτο φρονεῖν statement in 1:5–7, it can be perceived that the eschatological holiness in this prayer is a result of God's completing his salvific activity within the readers. The idea is adumbrated in the first part of the prayer that emphasizes God's gracious work to nurture the Philippians' love[35] with "foreknowledge" (ἐπίγνωσις) and "discernment" (αἴσθησις). In the Jewish wisdom tradition, particularly in the Proverbs (LXX), these two terms are closely related and associated with the divine "wisdom" (σοφία) that guides God's people to live a holy life.[36] As this wisdom has been revealed in Jesus Christ (1 Cor 1:24),[37] the foreknowledge in this letter should be associated with the knowledge of him (3:8), which is virtually presented by the gospel narrative in 2:6–11. In this light, the growth of love in the divine foreknowledge and discernment underlines the transformation of the mind based on the knowledge of the gospel of Christ. This knowledge inspires the way the readers make decisions, enabling them to prove (δοκιμάζω)[38] what the best things in life are.[39] By this, they will be able to live in holiness. Hence,

---

33. Hawthorne, *Philippians*, 29–30; O'Brien, *Philippians*, 82.

34. O'Brien, *Philippians*, 82.

35. The use of ἀγάπη indicates that their love is grounded itself in God's love to all humankind in Christ (Rom 5:5; 2 Cor 5:14; Gal 2:20). This kind of love has emotive nature, but certainly goes beyond that (Rom 13:8–9; 1 Thess 4:9–10). In the NT, ἀγάπη has become a core virtue in Christian conduct (1 Cor 13). See Schneider, "Ἀγάπη," *EDNT* 1:10–11.

36. Prov 1:20; 2:10; 3:5, 19; 5:1; 8:11, 12; 9:1; 10:23; 14:8, 33; 15:33; 17:28; 20:29; 21:30; 24:7; 28:26. (ἐπίγνωσις in 2:5; 14:8; 27:23; αἴσθησις in 2:10; 11:9; 14:6). See Delling, "Αἴσθησις," *TDNT* 1:187–88; Fowl, *Philippians*, 32; Fee, *Philippians*, 64.

37. In Paul's letters, the term ἐπίγνωσις denotes both the true knowledge of God (Rom 1:28; 10:2; Col 1:9–10) and God's revelation in Christ (Col 2:2; 3:10–11). See Bockmuehl, *Philippians*, 67.

38. BDAG, 255.

39. The participle τὰ διαφέροντα literary means "the things that really matter." BDAG, 239.

the demand to participate in God's completing activity can be drawn in this way: while God is actively growing their foreknowledge and discernment, the readers are called to decide wisely based on their knowledge of Christ (2:6–11) to establish themselves as holy.

In all, Paul's petition prayer is eschatologically oriented, directing the readers to anticipate the day of Christ where they all will join the universal worship of Christ that marks the consummation of God's salvation in them. The holiness expectation in this prayer is certainly a great challenge to the readers, as their *koinonia* in the gospel of Christ is currently challenged externally and internally. To encourage them, Paul spells out his eschatological confidence in 1:5–7 that their *koinonia* will surely end in their salvation because God himself will complete his salvific work in and among them until the day of Christ. The basis of this confidence is found in the narratival gospel in 2:6–11.

7.1.2 Paul's Τοῦτο Φρονεῖτε Exhortation in 2:5–11

Paul summons the readers with τοῦτο[40] φρονεῖτε[41] ἐν ὑμῖν ὃ καὶ ἐν Χριστῷ Ἰησοῦ in 2:5 that calls them to exercise their christological reasoning (φρονέω) on the gospel narrative in 2:6–11. We note that hitherto there is still disagreement regarding which aspect of the passage is being exploited to support Paul's exhortations due to the ambiguity in reading ὃ καὶ ἐν Χριστῷ Ἰησοῦ. Therefore, before highlighting the eschatological notion of this instruction, the precise reading of this subordinate clause needs to be established.

Some scholars maintain that the instruction calls upon the readers to adopt Christ's attitude and deed in verses 6–8. In this interpretation, the subordinate clause ὃ καὶ ἐν Χριστῷ Ἰησοῦ is translated as follows: "which was also in (the mind of) Christ Jesus."[42] Some linguistic links between Christ's redemptive actions and the ethical appeals in 1:27–2:18 give support to this

---

40. This is attested in ℵ*, A, B, C, Ψ. Although the conjunction γάρ (after τοῦτο) is attested in the earliest (𝔓[46]) and many other early manuscripts, such as ℵ[2], D, F, G, K, L, P, it is better regarded as secondary, as it reflects an effort to smoothen the reading. See Fee, *Philippians*, 197.

41. This is attested in the more ancient manuscripts, such as 𝔓[46], ℵ, A, B, C*, D, F, G, while φρονείσθω is attested in C[2], K, L, P, Ψ, and 𝔐.

42. O'Brien, *Philippians*, 205, 253–62; Fee, *Paul's Letter*, 199–201; Bockmuehl, *Philippians*, 122–23; Witherington III, *Philippians*, 137–38. The conjecture is established in this way: (1) the relative pronoun ὅ is neutral nominative, (2) the ellipsis is completed with ἦν, and (3) the phrase ἐν Χριστῷ Ἰησοῦ is understood as what took place inside the mind of Jesus Christ.

paradigmatic relation.[43] Other scholars, however, assert that the instruction calls the readers to live in the realm of salvation where Christ now reigns as their Lord. In this reading, the clause is translated in this way: "which you also (think) in Christ Jesus."[44] This interpretation is supported by the perception that the universal lordship of Jesus Christ calls all those in Christ to live in obedience (ὑπακούω) as God's children (2:12, 15) or the heavenly citizens (1:27).

In our opinion, such a dichotomy is not necessary because the two aspects find their relevance in the discourse.[45] The present study adopts the kerygmatic translation without eliminating the paradigmatic nature of this christological passage. This reading fits well "within the structure of Paul's ethics, where the ethical imperative is grounded in the theological indicative."[46] Exegetically, such a reading can be established by arguing that ἐν Χριστῷ Ἰησοῦ not only denotes the realm of Christ Jesus participated by all Christians but also establishes his narratival gospel as a referential object of the readers' deep reasoning.[47] The double notion of ἐν Χριστῷ is exegetically possible particularly when the context is elusive (cf. 1:13).[48] This idea is notably reflected in Hooker's statement:

> In Käsemann's words, Christ "ist Urbild, nicht Vorbild." But
> what is the character of his new humanity – this life in Christ?
> It seems to me nonsense to suggest that it is not the character

---

43. The word ἐκένωσεν in 2:7 with κενοδοξίαν in 2:3; ἐταπείνωσεν in 2:8 with ταπεινοφροσύνη in 2:3; ὑπήκοος in 2:8 with ὑπηκούσατε in 2:12.

44. Hawthorne and Martin, *Philippians*, 107–9; Silva, *Philippians*, 95–97; Reumann, *Philippians*, 339–40; Hansen, *Philippians*, 119–21. The conjecture is established in this way: (1) the relative pronoun ὅ is in a neutral accusative form, (2) the ellipsis is completed by adding either φρονεῖν δεῖ or φρονεῖτε (indicative), and (3) the phrase ἐν Χριστῷ Ἰησοῦ is understood as Paul's characteristic "in Christ" idiom, which speaks about the realm or the dominion of Christ.

45. Indeed, there is a growing opinion that both are exploited by Paul in his exhortations. See Hansen, *Philippians*, 121; Cousar, *Philippians and Philemon*, 51–52.

46. Hansen, *Philippians*, 121.

47. The latter is supported by the fact that the preposition ἐν can function as a marker to denote the object by which the mindset shows itself and is thus recognizable by the readers. See BDAG, 329.

48. Paul's statement ὥστε τοὺς δεσμούς μου φανεροὺς ἐν Χριστῷ γενέσθαι ἐν ὅλῳ τῷ in Phil 1:13 is a good case. The context is elusive, and thus it may render the meaning of ἐν Χριστῷ ambiguous. On the one hand, this statement can be read to mean that Paul's imprisonment is a manifestation of "his existence in the realm of Christ" or "his union with Christ." On the other hand, it can be understood as stating that his imprisonment is "because of" or "for the sake of" Christ (1:30). See Fowl, *Philippians*, 38–39.

of Jesus himself. It is only the dogma that the Jesus of History and Christ of Faith belong in separate compartments that leads to the belief that the appeal to Christian character appropriate to *those who are in Christ* is not linked to *the pattern as seen in Jesus himself.*[49]

In this perspective, the whole narrative of Christ serves as a referential object of the τοῦτο φρονεῖτε instruction from which a certain frame of mind emerges within the readers to direct and shape their behavior.[50] Accordingly, it can be further argued that the universal worship depicted at the end of this Christ-narrative provides an eschatological orientation of the paraenetical discourse. The readers' mindset has been oriented to the day of Christ in the prayer report section, and now it is further expounded that the pivotal event on that day is the worship of Christ by the whole creation. They all, therefore, need to anticipate this great eschatological event of worship. As it has been established before, the universal eschatological worship of Christ in the narratival gospel of Christ has christological, salvific, ethical, and anti-imperial significance. Now, we going to see how they will befit Paul's eschatological reasoning expressed in 1:5–7 and 1:9–11.

First of all, while the christological passage states that God's salvation in Christ will be consummated in the universal worship of him at the eschaton, the theological reasoning in 1:6 emphasizes that God is actively working within and among the readers to complete their salvation until that very day. In this respect, the story of the Philippian church in the gospel of Christ, which is embedded in God's completing activity, will also end with the worshipful communion with Christ's redemptive story on the day of Christ. This certainly provides a firm assurance for their salvation in Christ.

Second, salvation and ethics are not exclusive to each other. The ethical impetus of the christological passage is expressed not only by Christ's

---

49. Hooker, "Philippians," 91. The emphasis is added.

50. We also note that some scholars who adopt the ethical reading insert the verb εἴδετε instead of ἦν. See Meeks, "Man from Heaven," 322; Fowl, *Philippians*, 88. As a result, the instruction is read as follows: "this you think among you, which also you saw [εἴδετε] in [ἐν] Christ!" This use of ἐν is attested in Phil 1:30 (οἷον εἴδετε ἐν ἐμοί), and 4:9 (ἃ καὶ ἐμάθετε καὶ παρελάβετε καὶ ἠκούσατε καὶ εἴδετε ἐν ἐμοί). In the first case, Paul provides the readers with his own life as the example of suffering for Christ. In the second case, he uses his own life as the pattern to be followed by the readers. All this fits well with the function of the christological passage in 2:6–11, which provides a pattern to be conformed to in the Christian life.

redemptive deed but also by the universal eschatological worship of Christ. This ethical impetus is noted in Romans 14:10–12, where Paul situates the universal worship at the eschaton before the judgment seat of God, and thus where all worshippers are required to provide their account before him. This helps us to see the conceptual link between the eschatological worship of Christ in 2:10–11 and the eschatological expectation of holiness in 1:10–11. What is being further underlined in this prayer is God's completing activity in the sanctification process of the readers, as this will encourage them to work out their salvation ethically through their active participation in this divine activity.

Third, as the christological passage presents Christ as the divine Lord to be worshipped by the whole creation, the worship of him, the conviction on his redemptive work, and the obedience to him are all parts of the holy code to be observed and defended by all the followers of Christ until the day of Christ. This gospel-like holiness has great relevance to the struggle of the readers who lived in the imperial pagan society of Philippi, as it stood against the worship of Augustus, his gospel, and his life ethos propagated by the imperial power.

7.1.3 Paul's Τοῦτο Φρονῶμεν Exhortation in 3:4–15

Paul summons his readers again with τοῦτο φρονῶμεν in 3:15. As it is in the previous cases, this demonstrative article τοῦτο is retrospective, referring back not merely to 3:12–14[51] but rather to Paul's whole account in 3:4–14.[52] In observing Paul's way of thinking in this account, we draw its correlation with the previous two "think this" statements, then highlight Paul's eschatological aim in 2:8–11.

7.1.3.1 The Correlation between the Reasoning in 3:4–15 and the Earlier Ones

Paul's account demonstrates to the readers how the theological reasoning in 1:5–7 and the christological reasoning in 2:5–11 can be brought together and applied in the life of the believers of Christ. The discussion below establishes their connection.

---

51. Doble, "Vile Bodies," 7.

52. O'Brien, *Philippians*, 443–44; Fowl, *Philippians*, 165.

First of all, this passage describes the repositioning of Paul's mindset from the one grounded in Judaism to the one centered on Jesus Christ. The ultimate reason for the shift is "the knowledge of Christ Jesus" (γνῶσις Χριστοῦ Ἰησοῦ), which is noted in verse 8. To Paul, this knowledge is surpassing all things. As the shift is organic to this knowledge, its significance needs to be unpacked. First of all, Paul's knowledge of Christ Jesus is rooted in the Jewish biblical teaching,[53] which is comparable to "the knowledge of God" (ἡ γνῶσις θεοῦ).[54] Drawing from this background, this knowledge underlines his personal relationship with Christ and the ethical implication arising from it. The former is noted by Paul calling Jesus his Lord (κύριος μου) in this verse,[55] and the latter by the elaboration of τοῦ γνῶναι αὐτὸν in verses 10–11.

To highlight the experiential notion of this relationship, the phrase γνῶσις Χριστοῦ Ἰησοῦ is often translated as "knowing Christ Jesus."[56] While this way of reading might be justified, the knowledge of Christ cannot be purely about a subjective experience,[57] because this knowledge also arises from God's objective revelation. In 1 Corinthians 15:3–4, Paul confesses that knowing Christ was also grounded in the gospel of Christ, which was handed on to him by other Christians. Accordingly, in Philippians, the knowledge of Christ Jesus contextually harks back to the gospel narrative that supplies "the objective reality" of Christ.[58] This is supported by numerous terminological parallels between the two passages:

Philippians 2:5–11	Philippians 3:8–15
τοῦτο φρονεῖτε (v. 5)	τοῦτο φρονῶμεν (v. 15)
ἡγέομαι (v. 6)	ἡγέομαι (v. 8) 2x

---

53. Koperski, *Knowledge of Christ*, 65; Bockmuehl, *Philippians*, 205; contra Beare, *Philippians*, 114; Bultman, "Γινώσκω," *TDNT* 1:710.

54. Prov 30:3 LXX (γνῶσιν ἁγίων ἔγνωκα); cf. Rom 11:33; 2 Cor 2:14; 4:6; 10:5.

55. Witherington III, *Philippians*, 203.

56. Here, Χριστοῦ Ἰησοῦ is construed as objective genitive. See O'Brien, *Philippians*, 487. The surpassing-ness (ὑπερέχον) of knowing Christ reflects Paul's personal encounter with the resurrected Jesus (Acts 9:3–5; Gal 1:11–17; 1 Cor 15:8). This reading is also supported by Paul's aim τοῦ γνῶναι αὐτὸν in 3:10.

57. Park, *Submission within the Godhead*, 70, rightly states that "the knowledge of God is organic to God's revelation of himself in character and deeds."

58. Cf. Bockmuehl, *Philippians*, 206; Park, *Submission within the Godhead*, 70.

μορφή (vv. 6 and 7)	συμμορφίζω (v. 10)
εὑρίσκω (v. 9)	εὑρίσκω (v. 9)
θάνατος (v. 8)	θάνατος (v. 10)
κύριος Ἰησοῦς Χριστός (v. 11)	Χριστοῦ Ἰησοῦ τοῦ κυρίου μου (v. 8)

More importantly, Paul's eschatological aim in 3:8–11 reflects his engagement with both the redemptive and the ethical impetus of the Christ narrative. Before discussing this aim in detail, we need to explicate Paul's eschatological frame of mind imparted in his διώκω statement in 3:12–14.

In this passage, Paul makes a further claim about the eschatological orientation of life. The imagery of a running competition highlights his full commitment to pursue "the prize" (βραβεῖον).[59] This prize is best construed as the full realization of the promise of God's calling in Christ,[60] which refers back to the eschatological aim in verses 8–11.[61] Paul certainly had partly gained, been found in, and known Christ, but its full realization is set by God at the parousia. For the very reason above, Paul persistently pursues it.

The eschatological nature of Paul's use of διώκω needs to be unpacked. In Greek literature, this term is sometimes used together with καταλαμβάνω to underline the *telos* of one's laborious effort.[62] To Paul, while the relationship with Christ is grounded in God's grace, it needs to be seriously worked out in life, and this requires painstaking efforts. To illustrate this, a pair of words, διώκω – καταλαμβάνω, are employed as part of the race metaphor – "continue running until the finishing line" (διώκω δὲ εἰ καὶ καταλάβω).

Having said this, Paul pursuing activity also needs to be understood as his participation in God's completing activity (ἐπιτελέω) noted earlier in 1:6, as this is accentuated by his statement οὐχ . . . τετελείωμαι in verse 12. Whether the statement is set ironically against ὅσοι οὖν τέλειοι in verse 15 is debated.[63]

---

59. This imagery has been used in 2:16 (ὅτι οὐκ εἰς κενὸν ἔδραμον). Hence, his statement "forgetting what is behind and straining toward what is ahead" could be easily connected with it.

60. The experience of God's calling is implied in Paul's statement ἐφ' ᾧ καὶ κατελήμφθην ὑπὸ Χριστοῦ (*for which* I have been apprehended by Christ). Although ἐφ' ᾧ can be causal (NRSV "because"), reading in conjunction with the eschatological βραβεῖον, the consecutive meaning (NIV "for which") is probably the case.

61. O'Brien, *Philippians*, 421–22; Fee, *Philippians*, 342–43.

62. Herodotus, *His.* 9.58; Diodorus Siculus, *Bibl. Hist.* 17.73.3; Lucian, *Hermot.* 77.

63. For polemical reading, see O'Brien, *Philippians*, 423; Silva, *Philippians*, 177; Witherington III, *Philippians*. For non-polemical reading, see Fee, *Philippians*, 253; Bockmuehl,

Whatever the case, this τελειόω recalls God's ἐπιτελέω in his earlier eschatological reasoning. The case for this is made as follows. First, both 1:5–7 and 3:8–15 express Paul's eschatological reasoning. Second, as the paraenetical discourse in 1:27–2:18 is grounded in the eschatological reasoning in 1:5–7 and 2:5–11, we naturally expect that the discourse in 3:2–4:4 is established on the same ground. Finally, the use of τελειόω and its cognate ἐπιτελέω in these two reasonings linguistically establishes this connection. In this light, Paul's pursuing and persistent effort to attain the eschatological prize is his response to God's active work in him to complete his salvation.[64]

In all, the "think this" instruction in 3:15 summons the readers to adopt the eschatological frame of mind reflected in Paul's life account. This mindset is generated from the theological and christological reasoning noted in the earlier discourses. With this perspective, we now examine the core focus of Paul's frame of mind that states his ultimate aim of life.

7.1.3.2 Paul's Eschatological Aim in 3:8–11

Paul's knowledge of Christ has notably inspired his aim of life in 3:8–11. The aim can be construed as two parallel purpose clauses: (1) ἵνα Χριστὸν κερδήσω καὶ εὑρεθῶ ἐν αὐτῷ; and (2) τοῦ γνῶναι αὐτόν.[65] The grounds are as follows. First, in 1:29, πιστεύω (to believe) and πάσχω (to suffer) are put in parallel. Hence, it is plausible to think that in this passage these two themes are also recalled. Second, the genitive of the articular infinitive τοῦ γνῶναι αὐτὸν is telic rather than epexegetic.[66] As Koperski rightly argues, if the infinitive τοῦ γνῶναι αὐτὸν serves to explain τῇ πίστει, it construes πίστις in terms of experience, such as suffering and resurrection, which lacks cogency.[67] Third, as it will be established below, both "to gain Christ and be found in him" and "to know

---

Philippians, 224–25.

64. Paul's claim of his imperfection in 3:12 is not merely an expression of humility, but underlining that God has not yet completed his work within him.

65. To be sure, three conjectures have been proposed. For the infinitive τοῦ γνῶναι αὐτὸν is telic and parallel with the preceding ἵνα subjunctive clause, see Bockmuehl, Philippians, 213. For the infinitive is telic and expresses the purpose of the preceding ἵνα subjunctive clause, see Fee, Philippians, 313. For the infinitive is explanatory, which elaborates the preceding τῇ πίστει in 3:9, see Martin, Philippians, 133.

66. BDF, 400.5.

67. Koperski, Knowledge of Christ, 145n34, underlines that in Paul's letters πίστις is defined in term of "a conscious choice" in response to the gospel (Rom 10:14; 1 Cor 2:1–5; Gal 4:8); contra Park, Submission within the Godhead, 71.

Christ" will be realized only on the day of Christ.[68] With these preliminary points made, we now proceed to examine the two elements of Paul's aim.

First of all, the pair of subjunctive clauses ἵνα Χριστὸν κερδήσω and εὑρεθῶ ἐν αὐτῷ express the same reality of salvation in Christ to be achieved. At the same time, they highlight two different aspects of it. On the one hand, the former employs a commercial image (ζημία-κέρδος or ζημιόω-κερδαίνω) that underlines Paul's commitment to fully acquire this salvific relationship with a consequence of losing his past glorious status and achievements.[69] On the other hand, the latter highlights that God is the one who actually found Paul in Christ.[70] This embeds Paul's gaining Christ in the divine gracious action.

What Paul means by "to gain Christ and be found in him" is elaborated further with a justification metaphor in verse 9: μὴ ἔχων ἐμὴν δικαιοσύνην τὴν ἐκ νόμου ἀλλὰ τὴν διὰ πίστεως Χριστοῦ, τὴν ἐκ θεοῦ δικαιοσύνην ἐπὶ τῇ πίστει. The debate whether πίστις Χριστοῦ in the Pauline letters should be read as an objective genitive or a subjective genitive has bearings on its interpretation.[71] The present study adopts the latter. Although the supporting arguments for the two solid positions are equally persuasive,[72] the latter seemingly fits better the present context.[73] In this conjecture, verse 9 states that the righteousness on account of Christ's faithfulness stands in opposition to the one based on the work of the Mosaic laws. This righteous status is granted by God based on their faith in the faithful one. This reading fits well with the balance of divine grace and human effort in the phrase "to gain Christ and be found in him."

---

68. Fee, *Philippians*, 313, proposes that the infinitive expresses the purpose of the preceding ἵνα clause, in our opinion, creates an ambiguity on the eschatological orientation of "to gain Christ and be found in him."

69. Witherington III, *Philippians*, 203.

70. Here, εὑρεθῶ is a divine passive. Fowl, *Philippians*, 153–54.

71. This phrase appears in Rom 3:22, 26; Gal 2:16, 20; 3:22; Phil 3:9. For an objective genitive, see Fee, *Philippians*, 324–25; Hansen, *Philippians*, 239–340. For a subjective genitive, Bockmuehl, *Philippians*, 211; Fowl, *Philippians*, 154.

72. The debate is presented in Hays, *Faith of Jesus Christ*. The position of "objective genitive" is presented by Dunn, in appendix 1 of *Faith of Jesus Christ*, while the position of "subjective genitive" is defended by Hays in appendix 2.

73. Two factors are considered in this exegetical decision. First, this purpose responds to the knowledge of Christ, which is expressed in the christological passage in 2:6–11 where the notion of Christ's faithfulness is paramount. Second, as the prepositional phrase ἐπὶ τῇ πίστει articulates the importance of having faith in Christ, it will establish a nice balance between divine grace of salvation and human participation in it. See Bockmuehl, *Philippians*, 211.

With this reading established, we now explicate the eschatological orientation of this aim. Paul's calling of Jesus as his Lord in verse 8 and his claim of having been comprehended by him in verse 12 indicate that he has gained Christ and been found in him. Having said this, this (*telic*) ἵνα subjunctive construction has a future notion, as it looks forward to a full realization of his salvific status on the day of Christ.[74] Reading in conjunction with 1:10–11, 2:10–11 and 2:16, it is very likely that this verse describes Paul's expectation to be declared as a righteous worshipper on the day of Christ.

Another facet of Paul's aim is expressed by the infinitive τοῦ γνῶναι αὐτὸν. As the experience of knowing Christ surpasses all things, Paul now desires to know Christ even more. This aim is elaborated by the "participation in Christ" metaphor in verses 10–11:[75]

> τοῦ γνῶναι αὐτὸν
> A   καὶ τὴν δύναμιν τῆς ἀναστάσεως αὐτοῦ
> B   καὶ κοινωνίαν παθημάτων αὐτοῦ,
> B'   συμμορφιζόμενος τῷ θανάτῳ αὐτοῦ,
> A'   εἴ πως καταντήσω εἰς τὴν ἐξανάστασιν τὴν ἐκ νεκρῶν

The elaboration is structurally arranged in a chiasmus,[76] which affects its interpretation. The power of Christ's resurrection (A) has a strong association with the experience of the resurrection from the dead (A'), and the participation in Christ's suffering (B) with being conformed to Christ's death (B'). Syntactically, line A and line B are dependent on the object αὐτὸν in the construction τοῦ γνῶναι αὐτὸν. Accordingly, the power of Christ's resurrection and the fellowship with his suffering are the two things that give content to the goal to know Christ. The participle συμμορφιζόμενος (line B') is attached to the verb γνῶναι in the construction τοῦ γνῶναι αὐτὸν. Hence, it describes how the aim to know Christ will be accomplished. Finally, the subjunctive καταντήσω connects to συμμορφιζόμενος, underlining that being conformed

---

74. O'Brien, *Philippians*, 392; Hawthorne, *Philippians*, 140; Bockmuehl, *Philippians*, 208–9.

75. The conjunction καί after τοῦ γνῶναι αὐτὸν is not coordinate, but epexegetical, that is to elaborate the meaning of "to know Christ." Hawthorne, *Philippians*, 143; O'Brien, *Philippians*, 401.

76. Hawthorne, *Philippians*, 145; Fee, *Philippians*, 329; Hansen, *Philippians*, 243; contra Perriman, "Pattern of Christ's Sufferings," 69.

to Christ's death is driven by the hope to participate in the resurrection of the dead.

The emphasis of "knowing Christ" is on the consummating experience of the *koinonia* with Christ's power and suffering, which (as it is the case in 3:9) looks forward to the day of Christ. To participate in the resurrection from the dead means to fully experience the power of Christ's resurrection.[77] To Paul, this experience of divine power complements the fellowship with Christ's suffering. This is affirmed by the use of one definite article which unites both the power and participation to form a single entity.[78] Accordingly, the way to attain the resurrection (A') is by conforming his life to Christ's death (B'). This way of knowing Christ must be inspired by the gospel narrative of Christ, particularly his death and resurrection.[79] To Paul, this narrative not only reveals Christ's redemptive work but also provides an overarching pattern of holiness to be conformed to in life.[80]

Although they are not identical, Paul's eschatological aim in this passage is considerably parallel to the expectation of holiness in 1:10–11. This can be easily appreciated, as in the prayer report section, where the holiness expectation is a part of it, Paul introduces some prominent themes to be developed in the letter. The connection between these two passages is notably strong. First, both are primarily concerned with the standing before God on the day of Christ. Second, the term δικαιοσύνη appears in both passages. Third, both are concerned with the holiness of believers generated from the righteous status in Christ. The last needs further elaboration.

Philippians 1:10–11 emphasizes the holiness of the readers on the day of Christ. Their holiness is generated from their righteous status and produced by God "through Christ Jesus." This christological thrust is amplified in Paul's eschatological aim. Verse 9 clarifies that this righteous status is not based on the work of the laws but Christ's faithfulness and their faith in him. Verses 10–11 emphasize that righteous status and holiness on the day of Christ are

---

77. Fee, *Philippians*, 335.

78. The use of one definite article unites the power of Christ's resurrection and the participation in his suffering to form a single entity. See Granville Sharp Rule in Wallace, *Greek Grammar*, 271–72.

79. Bockmuehl, *Philippians*, 214, rightly states: "Paul's personal knowledge of him (Christ) should include the desire to share his 'mind' and the pattern of his life, both in his self-humbling obedience to death and in his glorious vindication (2:5–11)."

80. Gorman, "You Shall Be Cruciform," 160–61.

complementary to each other. Given that the holy fruit comes through Christ Jesus, Paul's life now actively engages with Christ's suffering death, by which the gospel-like holiness is produced[81] and is perfected in the resurrection from the dead.

In all, Paul's eschatological aim and his persistent labor to achieve it are inspired and shaped by the christological passage in 2:6–11 and God's completing activity in 1:6. In response to its salvific notion, Paul expects to be fully declared as a righteous worshipper on the day of Christ on the ground of Christ's faithfulness and his faith in him. In response to its ethical impetus, he expects that on that day too he will be found holy before God by patterning after Christ's death and resurrection. This aim parallels the holiness expectation in 1:10–11, as both are concerned with the righteous-holy standing before God at the day of Christ. Considering that, this eschatological reasoning is in continuation with the previous ones, the motif of the universal eschatological worship of Christ in 2:10–11 most likely also hovers in the background of this eschatological aim and Paul's pursuing it.

7.1.4 Synthesis

The observation on the contents of Paul's "think this" statements in Philippians demonstrates that Paul's reasoning is not only theological and christological, but also eschatological in nature. Three pivotal eschatological coordinates profoundly shape his way of thinking, namely the universal eschatological worship of Christ (2:10–11), God's completing activity of his salvation until the day of Christ (1:6), and the expectation to be found holy at the day of Christ (1:10–11). Their correlation can be described in the diagram below.

---

81. Gorman, 163, correctly underlines that "Paul's experience of Christ as the faithful, obedient, loving crucified Son of God leads him to reconstruct his understanding of both God's holiness and human holiness as embodied in the story of Christ's kenosis in incarnation and death."

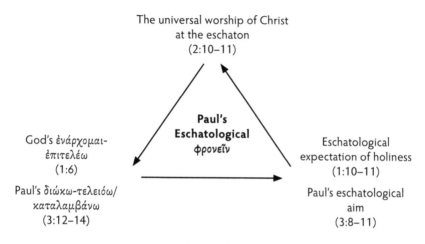

Figure 1

The gospel of Christ sets a basic eschatological narrative. God's redemptive work in Christ will surely end in the universal worship of Christ on the day of Christ. Derived from this gospel narrative is Paul's theological-eschatological frame of mind: God's active work to complete his salvific work within and among the believers until the day of Christ in 1:6. As the life and the ministry of the Philippian congregation are deeply embedded in this divine activity, Paul expects that all of his readers will be found holy (1:10–11) when they join the universal worship of Christ at the eschaton (2:10–11).

This eschatological frame of mind is also reflected in Paul's account in 3:4–15. His eschatological goal in verses 8–11 is inspired by Christ's redemptive death and resurrection in the gospel narrative and the eschatological expectation of holiness. His pursuing activity in verses 12–14 responds to God's completing activity of his salvation. As his eschatological goal and his pursuing activity look forward to the day of Christ, the motif of eschatological worship is undoubtedly present in this practical reasoning. The attentive readers, whose mind had been shaped by the earlier eschatological reasoning, would appreciate Paul's aim and pursuing statements as to his anticipation of the universal worship of Christ at the eschaton.

In all, the depiction of the universal eschatological worship of Christ is integral to Paul's triangular eschatological frame of mind in the letter. Once this framework is appreciated, the function of this eschatological worship motif can be established properly by connecting Paul's various instructions with it. The following two sections demonstrate how this eschatological frame of mind works in the two major discourses in this letter.

7.2 Reading Philippians 1:27–2:18

To define the function of the motif of the eschatological worship of Jesus Christ in this paraenetical discourse, first of all, Paul's rhetorical strategy needs to be drawn out including his rhetorical objective and the way he achieves it.[82] Following this, a close examination in this discourse is made on the three pivotal elements of Paul's eschatological reasoning (φρονεῖν), which the universal eschatological worship of Christ is a part of. Finally, we will discuss how they befit Paul's rhetorical strategy in this discourse.

7.2.1 Paul's Rhetorical Strategy

The discourse is situated between Paul's current situation report and his future travel plans report, and it is considered as the heart of the letter. The presence of six imperative[83] and four purposive[84] statements in this section demonstrate Paul's intention to direct the lives of his readers. To define the objective of this paraenetical discourse, we recall some pressing problems faced by the Philippian congregation.

The readers lived in a pagan imperial society, which was perceived as being perverse and corrupt before God and hostile to the gospel of Christ. In this ungodly environment, the community faced severe civic opposition due to their commitment to the faith of Christ. As this external threat generated great suffering, some believers had renounced their faith, while others lost their joy and lived with a grumbling attitude. Furthermore, the unity of the church was also weakened, as some prominent members conflicted. All this was detrimental to the *koinonia* of this church in the gospel of Christ. Accordingly, Paul's rhetorical objective in this discourse is to exhort the church to continue standing firmly in unity for the faith of the gospel of

---

82. Synman, "Rhetorical Analysis," 784.

83. Phil 1:27; 2:2, 5, 12, 14, 18.

84. Phil 1:27; 2:2, 15, 16.

Christ and living out their holiness according to the gospel in facing both the external and internal challenges.

This rhetorical aim is virtually expressed in the principal exhortation at the beginning of the discourse, μόνον ἀξίως τοῦ εὐαγγελίου τοῦ Χριστοῦ πολιτεύεσθε, which sets the direction for all subsequent exhortations in this discourse.[85] The readers who lived in the Roman colony of Philippi would be able to appreciate the significance of the word πολιτεύομαι, as it has a strong correlation with their social-eschatological identity as the heavenly commonwealth noted in 3:20. The term denotes the meaning of "being a free citizen" or "living as a free citizen,"[86] particularly in exercising their rights and duties.[87] Accordingly, this exhortation calls the readers to carry out their civic duty as heavenly citizens, and this needs to be done according to the gospel of Christ (τοῦ εὐαγγελίου τοῦ Χριστοῦ).[88] With this in mind, we now observe the way Paul achieves this objective in this discourse.

Based on its content, the discourse can be structured as proceeding in four phases:[89]

(1) 1:27–30 responds to the civic opposition.

(2) 2:1–4 deals with internal conflict.

(3) 2:5–11 provides the christological frame of mind for dealing with the problems.

(4) 2:12–18 is the climax that sums up this discourse.

This internal structure indicates that Paul starts with dealing with the external problem, moves to handle the internal conflict, then ends with summing up with his exhortations. Before this climactic phase, he lays down the christological frame of mind to support all the exhortations in this discourse. The discussion below will examine in more detail these four smaller rhetorical units.

How the principal ἀξίως-πολιτεύομαι exhortation should be practiced by the readers in their social context is made clear in 1:27–30. In response to

---

85. O'Brien, *Philippians*, 143; Bockmuehl, *Philippians*, 96.

86. BDAG, 846.

87. Hawthorne, *Philippians*, 55; Bockmuehl, *Philippians*, 97.

88. This reading is suggested by most of the commentators. See Cousar, *Philippians and Philemon*, 44.

89. Bockmuehl, *Philippians*, 96; Cousar, *Philippians and Philemon*, 42.

the civic oppositions, Paul exhorts them to continue standing firmly for the gospel of Christ,[90] which includes striving together for the faith of the gospel and not being frightened by their opponents (i.e. the traditionalist and the imperial officers in Philippi). To support this demand, Paul supplies some encouraging words: (1) their present struggle for the faith of the gospel of Christ is God's proof of their future salvation; (2) their suffering for Christ's sake is God's gracious gift to them along with their faith in Christ; and (3) they are also in the *koinonia* of suffering with Paul. By all this, the readers are encouraged to continue standing firmly for the gospel.

After this, in 2:1–4, Paul deals with the internal conflict in the Philippian church that has weakened its unity. This concern has briefly raised by the phrases ἐν ἑνὶ πνεύματι and μιᾷ ψυχῇ in 1:27–28, and now it becomes a pivotal issue to be dealt with thoroughly. Verses 3–4 indicate that the conflict was generated by the ethos of "rivalry" (ἐριθεία) and "empty glory" (κενοδοξία) that had driven some members to look after their own interests only. As a response, Paul summons them to have "the one-and-same way of thinking" (ἵνα τὸ αὐτὸ φρονῆτε . . . τὸ ἓν φρονοῦντες), which notably anticipates his "think this" instruction in 2:5. Accordingly, they were called to rid themselves of this selfish attitude and to adopt Christ's attitude of κενόω-ταπεινόω reflected in the gospel-narrative. This is done by regarding the interests of others as being greater than their own (ἡγούμενοι ὑπερέχοντας ἑαυτῶν).[91]

To support his exhortations in the preceding and subsequent sections, Paul calls the readers to adopt the frame of mind (τοῦτο φρονεῖτε) generated from a deep reflection of the narratival gospel of Christ. The connection with the preceding sections is established by the demonstrative pronoun τοῦτο at the beginning of the instruction that refers back not merely to 2:1–4[92] but as far as the principal exhortation in 1:27.[93] Several factors support this interpretation. The phrase τοῦ εὐαγγελίου τοῦ Χριστοῦ in this verse anticipates this christological passage, as the narrative virtually expresses the content of the

---

90. Cousar, 45.

91. The correlation between 2:1–4 and 2:6–8 is noted by their terminological parallels: (1) the use of φρονέω (2x) in 2:2 anticipates the φρονέω exhortation in 2:5; (2) κενοδοξία and ταπεινοφροσύνη in 2:3 anticipates Christ's κενόω-ταπεινόω in 2:7–8.

92. Cf. Hellerman, *Reconstructing Honor*, 154; Synman, "Rhetorical Analysis," 787–803; Doble, "Vile Bodies," 7.

93. Fowl, *Philippians*, 89–90.

gospel of Christ. The appearance of χαρίζομαι in 1:29 and 2:9 provides the terminological link between this section and the narratival gospel.[94] Finally, the statement τὸ ὑπὲρ αὐτοῦ πάσχειν in 1:29 also anticipates the depiction of Christ's suffering death in this narrative.

The connection with the subsequent section is established by the inferential conjunction ὥστε (therefore) at the beginning of verse 12.[95] Although this conjunction may connect this section with the whole preceding parts (1:27–30; 2:1–4; 2:5–11),[96] the christological reasoning in 2:5–11 is the focus.[97] This is noted by a strong correlation between the obedience of believers (ὑπακούω) in 2:12–14 and both Christ's obedience (ὑπήκοος) in 2:8 and his lordship in 2:10–11. All this suggests that the τοῦτο φρονεῖτε instruction together with its ὥστε conjunction is intended to make the christological passage relevant to the whole discourse.

In this last phase, Paul sums up his exhortations by bringing the discourse to a climax. This is indicated by the accumulation of three imperative and two purpose statements in this final section.[98] As the conjunction ὥστε also connects the present section with 1:27–2:4,[99] the problems of both civic resistance and internal conflict should be still in view. Having said this, some new elements of their predicament are also added. The civic opposition is raised precisely because the pagan imperial society there is judged to be perverse and corrupt (γενεᾶς σκολιᾶς καὶ διεστραμμένης). Living in such an environment is never easy. The gospel-like norm is not often in agreement with the general mindset of the imperial society in Philippi. Their exclusive commitment, to worship God and his Christ, also runs against its religious mind. These two struggles might cultivate insubordination among some members, as it is noted by their "grumbling" (γογγυσμός) and "reasoning" (διαλογισμός) attitudes.

---

94. Wojtkowiak, *Christologie Und Ethik*, 132.

95. BDAG, 1107.

96. Bockmuehl, *Philippians*, 149; Cousar, *Philippians and Philemon*, 59.

97. O'Brien, *Philippians*, 274; Hansen, *Philippians*, 170.

98. The imperative statements: (1) the ὑπακούω instruction (v. 12); (2) the ποιέω instruction (v. 14); (3) the χαίρω instruction (v. 18). The purpose statements: (1) ἵνα γένησθε (v. 15); (2) the prepositional phrase εἰς καύχημα (v. 16).

99. The topical links are noted as follows: (1) the unity of the church (2:2–4; cf. 2:14); (2) salvation in the midst of adversity (1:28; cf. 2:12, 16); (3) living in hostile environment (1:27–30; cf. 2:15). See Bockmuehl, *Philippians*, 149.

In response to this challenge, Paul summons the readers with μετὰ φόβου καὶ τρόμου τὴν ἑαυτῶν σωτηρίαν κατεργάζεσθε (v. 12). This instruction corresponds to the principal exhortation in 1:27a, since living worthily (as heavenly citizens) demands the readers "to work out" (κατεργάζομαι) their salvation seriously. The summon is further amplified by the πάντα ποιεῖτε exhortation that demands the readers do all things that are necessary for the sake of their salvation (v. 14). Due to the internal unrest, notes of obedience are also given: (1) καθὼς πάντοτε ὑπηκούσατε; (2) μετὰ φόβου καὶ τρόμου; (3) χωρὶς γογγυσμῶν καὶ διαλογισμῶν. The purpose of the instructions is to maintain their holiness as God's children, and this has a missional vocation, which is to shine God's light in the darkness of this world. In solving the present predicament of the church, Paul's exhortations do not lose their eschatological force, as the πάντα ποιέω instruction ends with a strong eschatological note, εἰς ἡμέραν Χριστοῦ.

Finally, Paul closes the discourse with some *koinonical* encouragements (2:17–18). As the readers' holiness is his source of boasting on the day of Christ, he states his willingness to suffer together with them till the end. Paul's being poured out as "a drink offering" (σπένδομαι) does not necessarily imply his imminent death.[100] Having said this, the notion of suffering together with his readers can be easily sensed.[101] This co-suffering is regarded as their *koinonia* of worship. For this very reason, they are to rejoice together (χαίρω and συγχαίρω) in the midst of their struggle in Christ and for his gospel.

In all, the paraenetical discourse in 1:27–2:18 intends to deal with the complex predicament of the Philippian church. The readers are summoned to continue living worthily and working out their salvation in accordance with the gospel of Christ. In response to the external opposition, they are called to stand firm for the faith of the gospel. In response to the internal conflict, they are instructed to adopt Christ's selfless and humble attitude so that they are able to live in harmony and unity. All the more, as they lived in a perverse pagan imperial society, they are reminded to maintain their holiness by working out together their salvation so that outsiders will be attracted to their sharing of the gospel of Christ. To support all this, he summons them to

---

100. Witherington III, *Philippians*, 164, rightly stresses that "Paul says 'even if,' talking about something that might happen but is not yet in process."

101. Hansen, *Philippians*, 187.

develop the mindset reflected in the christological passage, and live it out in the context of their present struggle. In this rhetorical framework, we are to understand the role of the universal eschatological worship of Christ depicted in 2:10–11. This is the task of the following section.

7.2.2. The Pivotal Element of Paul's Eschatological Frame of Mind

It has been noted in section 7.1 (Paul's Eschatological Frame of Mind) that Paul's frame of mind (φρονεῖν) is shaped by three pivotal eschatological coordinates articulated in 1:6, 1:9–11, and 2:10–11. In this section, we will examine the presence of these eschatological thoughts in this discourse.

7.2.2.1 The Expectation of Holiness

The demand for holiness is notably raised in the principal exhortation: μόνον ἀξίως τοῦ εὐαγγελίου τοῦ Χριστοῦ πολιτεύεσθε. In the Greco-Roman society, the term ἄξιος was frequently used as an honorific civic expression for the citizens who performed well in their civic duties.[102] The term is employed to mark the demand for holiness. This demand has been presented in 1:27–30 and 2:1–4, but it becomes very explicit in the final phase of the discourse, 2:12–18. As the children of God, they are to work out their salvation by laboriously doing all things for their holiness – ἵνα γένησθε ἄμεμπτοι καὶ ἀκέραιοι, τέκνα θεοῦ ἄμωμα. The use of the prefix-α in the words ἄμεμπτος, ἀκέραιος, and ἄμωμος that negates the meanings of the root words (no-blame, no-flaw, no-fault) rhetorically emphasizes the absence of sin in God's children.

According to 1:27, the standard of holiness of the heavenly πολίτευμα in Philippi was no longer defined by the predominant social and moral values of the city, such as the Roman *mos maiorum* and the gospel of Caesar Augustus, but by the gospel of Christ narrated in 2:6–11. To Paul, "holiness is essentially Christ-likeness,"[103] and some of its characteristics are elaborated in response to the struggle of the church. We will briefly unpack them in the discussion below.

---

102. This is attested in the inscription at Gazoros (about 50 km from Philippi): no. 543/ G480, lines 9–10 (cf. *IG* VII: 387, line 6). See Pilhofer, *Philippi Band 1*, 137.

103. Gorman, "You Shall Be Cruciform," 153.

First, in response to the civic imperial opposition in Philippi, in 1:27–30, Paul calls that the gospel-like holiness should be exercised "by standing firm in unity" (ὅτι στήκετε ἐν ἑνὶ πνεύματι) for the gospel of Christ. The phrase ἐνὶ πνεύματι can be construed as a human soul or the Holy Spirit.[104] In either case, the notion of unity is highlighted. The demand to stand firm is elaborated further by the two subsequent participles: (1) in one soul "striving together" (συναθλοῦντες) for the faith of the gospel;[105] (2) "not being intimidated" (μὴ πτυρόμενοι) by the opponents. The use of συναθλέω and πτύρω may evoke the memory of both the athletic competition and the military battle.[106] Due to the Philippian Christians' conflict situation, the latter is predominant. Their strife, however, does not aim to overthrow the Roman Empire, but it is done for the sake of the faith of the gospel.

There are two pivotal claims proclaimed and defended in the narratival gospel of Christ:[107] (1) the salvation of all humankind through the faith in Christ who has faithfully carried out God's redemptive work on the cross, and (2) the universal lordship and worship of Christ in the eschaton. In the Roman colony of Philippi, these claims stand against both the gospel of Augustus and the worship of him. The latter is implied by the phrase γενεᾶς σκολιᾶς καὶ διεστραμμένης in 2:15, which alludes to Deuteronomy 32:5 LXX in accentuating the problem of the worship of idols in Philippi. The most significant one is the cult of Augustus. His cult is not only popular but also very important to the Philippian society, as this deified emperor is the founder of the colony. Withdrawing from this cultic observance, gentile converts have offended the imperial society in this colony, and thus they currently suffer from various civic oppositions in this city. Accordingly, they will be now encouraged by this letter to continue standing firmly for the gospel of Christ, as this is part of their gospel-like holiness.

---

104. For a human soul, see O'Brien, *Philippians*, 62; Hawthorne and Martin, *Philippians*, 56–57; for the Holy Spirit, see Bockmuehl, *Philippians*, 99.

105. In this conjecture, τῇ πίστει is construed as dative of advantage. Bockmuehl, *Philippians*, 99; Fowl, *Philippians*, 63; Hansen, *Philippians*, 97.

106. Bockmuehl, *Philippians*, 99.

107. There is undoubtedly an evangelical thrust in μιᾷ ψυχῇ συναθλοῦντες τῇ πίστει τοῦ εὐαγγελίου. Keown, *Congregational Evangelism*, 130–31. Fowl, *Philippians*, 69, however, underlines the notion of living out the gospel-like ethos in this struggle. Although it is possible, this reading is unlikely as this gospel-like ethos will not generate any civic resistance.

Second, gospel-like holiness has a communal notion. As the gospel of Christ becomes the norm and pattern of their communal holiness, to restore the unity of the church Paul calls for exercising the frame of mind (2:5) reflected in the gospel narrative. Christ-like holiness is notably presented as counter-intuitive, counter-cultural, and counter-imperial to the society there.[108] While the imperial pagan society seeks self-glory and self-greatness, the heavenly colony in Philippi is instructed to apply Christ's κενόω-ταπεινόω attitude in their communal life. This is implied by the terminological parallel between 2:2-4 and 2:6-8. The use of φρονέω in verse 2 certainly anticipates the τοῦτο φρονεῖτε instruction in verse 5, and the attitudes of κενοδοξία and ταπεινοφροσύνη in verse 3 and Christ's κενόω-ταπεινόω in verses 7-8. To have the same and one frame of mind, therefore, is not only an exhortation to concord but also a call to live out Christ-like holiness by which their unity will be restored.[109]

Third, in response to the mutiny of some members, the gospel-like holiness includes an obedient attitude. This is noted in 2:12-14 by some statements, such as (1) καθὼς πάντοτε ὑπηκούσατε, (2) μετὰ φόβου καὶ τρόμου in the κατεργάζομαι exhortation,[110] and (3) χωρὶς γογγυσμῶν καὶ διαλογισμῶν in the ποιέω exhortation.[111] The linguistic connection between ὑπακούω (v. 12) and ὑπήκοος (v. 8) strongly signals that the believers' obedience is akin to Christ's obedience. Their obedience, first of all, is directed to God and Christ,[112] as the clause καθὼς πάντοτε ὑπηκούσατε comes immediately after the acclamation of the lordship of Christ for the glory of God. This is further affirmed by the phrase μετὰ φόβου καὶ τρόμου that echoes the exodus tradition that expresses human submission in the face of divine epiphanies (Exod 15:16 LXX). Having said this, their obedience should also be extended to Paul and the local leadership, as they carried out Christ's authority and adopted a Christ-like behavior (cf. Phil. 3:17; 4:9).[113] This is adumbrated in the phrase

---

108. Gorman, "You Shall Be Cruciform," 161.

109. Wagner, "Working Out Salvation," 265-66.

110. See Fowl, *Story of Christ*, 96-97.

111. The phrase reflects the struggle of many Philippian Christians to obey God and the appointed leaders due to their suffering or difficult condition. Hansen, *Philippians*, 179-80.

112. Bockmuehl, *Philippians*, 150; Park, *Submission within the Godhead*, 142-43. As God has enthroned Christ to be the universal κύριος in 2:9-11, the obedience should also be directed to him.

113. Fowl, *Philippians*, 118-19.

χωρὶς γογγυσμῶν καὶ διαλογισμῶν that evokes the failure of the exodus community to obey YHWH and his servant Moses.[114]

Fourth, the gospel-like holiness has a mission coordinate. This is expressed in the πάντα ποιεῖτε instruction (2:14), as the holiness expectation is immediately followed by the clause ἐν οἷς φαίνεσθε ὡς φωστῆρες ἐν κόσμῳ. This clause may allude to Daniel 12:3 LXX,[115] but it reads better in conjunction with the metaphor of "light of the nations" in Deutero-Isaiah LXX (εἰς φῶς ἐθνῶν in 42:6 and 49:6),[116] as this verse calls the readers to bring God's light of salvation to the pagan society where they lived in. The contextual meaning of the verb ἐπέχω (to hold) in the participle λόγον ζωῆς ἐπέχοντες is still being debated among scholars concerning whether it should be understood as holding fast, holding forth, or holding upon.[117] This study inclines to the first and the last options. Accordingly, the participle ἐπέχοντες serves as an instrumental modifier of the subjunctive clause ἵνα γένησθε to underline that their holiness is generated by holding firmly the word of life. However, this does not terminate its mission thrust, as the participle λόγον ζωῆς ἐπέχοντες has a metaphor of "holding a torch that gives light to the world,"[118] and λόγον ζωῆς denotes the gospel (cf. 1:14) that gives light to the world.

Finally, while this discourse focuses on the current affairs of the church, the gospel-like holiness never loses its eschatological orientation. Indeed, this orientation has been adumbrated since the principal exhortation. As the heavenly colony in Philippi was expectantly waiting for the parousia of Christ, a form of heavenly conduct should also be present, and they are reminded in 1:28 that their holy standing for the gospel of Christ is proof of their eschatological salvation. The eschatological thrust of holiness becomes explicit in the πάντα ποιεῖτε instruction (2:14–16). The demand for holiness as God's children conceptually harks back to the expectation of holiness on the day of Christ in 1:10–11. This is supported by Paul's statement that the readers' holiness corresponds to his boasting (καύχημα) on the day of Christ.

---

114. Exod 15:24; 16:2, 7 (2x), 8 (3x), 9, 12; 17:3; Num 11:1; 14:2, 27 (2x), 29, 36; 16:11; 17:6, 20 (2x), 25.

115. Fee, *Philippians*, 242.

116. Bockmuehl, *Philippians*, 158.

117. For "holding fast," see Hawthorne, *Philippians*, 103; for "holding forth," see Ware, *Paul and the Mission*, 256–70; for "holding upon," see Poythress, "Hold Fast," 45–53.

118. See LSJ, 617.

The motif of eschatological judgment undoubtedly underlies this καύχημα statement. As a slave of Christ, Paul needs to provide his ministry account before Christ at his parousia. Accordingly, it is his great expectation to provide a good report of his labor (τρέχω and κοπιάω) for the Philippian congregation. In this respect, the present holiness of the readers anticipates both Paul's and theirs standing before God and Christ on judgment day.[119] It is only on this basis that Paul's eschatological boasting will make good sense.

7.2.2.2 The Worship Notion

Numerous cultic expressions are detected in the last phase of the rhetorical strategy in Philippians 2:12–18. First of all, the phrase μετὰ φόβου καὶ τρόμου in the κατεργάζομαι instruction alludes to the exodus narrative (Exod 15:16; Deut 2:23; 11:25 LXX), which describes a proper response of all nations in witnessing the epiphany of YHWH.[120] In Isaiah 19:16 LXX, this phrase is also used to mark the conversion of the Egyptians as worshippers of YHWH. It is argued, therefore, that in this verse the use of the phrase shares a similar idea. The gentile converts in Philippi are now part of YHWH's covenant people who are worthy of his salvation, and now they are exhorted to continue working out their salvation with a worshipful attitude to God.

The cultic notion becomes more apparent in the context of the πάντα ποιεῖτε instruction, where the demand for holiness is articulated with a cultic term ἄμωμος (without blemish). In the LXX, the term is often used to describe a high quality of sacrificial victims (spotlessness).[121] As its contrast, the pagan society is described as γενεᾶς σκολιᾶς καὶ διεστραμμένης. Echoing Deuteronomy 32:5 LXX, this phrase accentuates the problem of idolatry. In this respect, in this instruction "right living" and "right worship" are conjoined.

Paul's willingness to suffer together with his readers is also expressed in cultic imagery. In 2:17, he says, "but even if I am to be poured out as a drink offering [σπένδομαι] upon the sacrificial offering [θυσία] and priestly service

---

119. For the conceptual link between the instruction in 2:14–16 and the prayer in 1:9–11, see Silva, *Philippians*, 125–26.

120. Bockmuehl, *Philippians*, 153.

121. Hauck, "ἄμωμος," *EDNT* 1:73.

[λειτουργία] of your faith."[122] In both the Jewish and the Greco-Roman antiquity, the drink offering was usually poured out upon the offering by the priests to complete the ritual service.[123] This practice is employed by Paul to emphasize their *koinonia* of suffering. As the Philippians' priestly companion, Paul is willing to pour out his own life like a drink offering to perfect their sacrificial worship.[124]

To his gentile readers, this cultic imagery was meaningful. Embracing Christianity, many of them had withdrawn from all kinds of idol worship including the emperor worship in Philippi, but could not participate in the temple worship at Jerusalem. To encourage them, Paul describes their struggle for the faith of the gospel, their gospel-like conduct, their working out the salvation in Christ, and later their ministry for the sake of the gospel (4:18) as a sacrificial offering and priestly service to God. He, as their fellow priest, will do his part to perfect their sacrificial worship. This certainly gives a strong affirmation that they all, the gentile Christians, are part of the people of YHWH who have received the new covenant blessing.

Finally, all cultic expressions notably appear only in the final phase, which is after the depiction of the universal worship of Christ, and the phrase εἰς ἡμέραν Χριστοῦ in verse 16 affirms their eschatological overtone. This says that their present worship in holiness as the new covenant people of YHWH in Philippi looks forward to the day of Christ, where the universal worship of YHWH and Christ will be consummated.

7.2.2.3 Participating in God's Active Work of Salvation

The idea of participation in God's completing activity of the salvation in Christ can be detected in 1:28 and 2:12–13. In the former, to support the demand for

---

122. Author's own translation. The precise reading of the phrase ἐπὶ τῇ θυσίᾳ καὶ λειτουργίᾳ τῆς πίστεως ὑμῶν is uncertain. The conjunction καὶ can be "coordinate" or "epexegetical." Moreover, the genitive τῆς πίστεως can be "subjective," "objective," or epexegetical. See the discussion in Hawthorne, *Philippians*, 105; Silva, *Philippians*, 129; Vincent, *Philippians*, 71; Bockmuehl, *Philippians*, 162. In this study, we perceive καὶ as "coordinate," and τῆς πίστεως as "subjective genitive."

123. This creates a difficulty in determining whether this cultic imagery is derived from the Jewish sacrificial worship or the Hellenistic one. See the discussion in Bockmuehl, *Philippians*, 160.

124. While there might be a note of suffering in this sacrificial language (σπένδομαι and θυσία), Bockmuehl, *Philippians*, 161–62, rightly underlines that this metaphor does not necessarily imply Paul's imminent death.

standing firmly for the faith of the gospel of Christ, Paul supplies his eschatological underpinning: ἥτις ἐστὶν αὐτοῖς ἔνδειξις ἀπωλείας, ὑμῶν δὲ σωτηρίας,
καὶ τοῦτο ἀπὸ θεοῦ. It is generally appreciated that "the sign/proof" (ἔνδειξις)
points to their future "salvation" (σωτηρία), which may occur imminently (cf.
1:19) or at the end-time (cf. 3:20–21). The temporal and eternal nature of
salvation in this verse should not be sharply distinguished.[125] Nevertheless,
the eschatological nature of the salvation in this verse remains strong due
to the parallel ideas between 1:27–28 (πολιτεύομαι, ἀπώλεια, σωτηρία) and
3:18–21 (πολίτευμα, ἀπώλεια, σωτήρ).

In reading the ἔνδειξις of salvation, Fowl underlines the humiliation-
vindication motif in the context of Paul's "think this" instruction in 2:5. His
view is presented as follows:

> If the Philippians will unite in a steadfast adherence to the gospel
> (will entail the practice of the virtue in 2:2–4), even in the face
> of opposition, then God will save them in the same way God
> saved the obedient, humiliated, and suffering in 2:6–11. Paul's
> admonition in v. 5 is a call to recognize this, a call to apply to
> their common life the precedent that is theirs by virtue of the
> fact that they are in Christ.[126]

In response to his reading, the possibility that the beleaguered Philippians
readers could analogically link God's past vindication of the suffering Christ
with their future salvation should certainly not be overlooked. Having said
this, it is rather doubtful that this suffering-vindication motif is the main
focus of the christological reasoning exhortation in 2:5 in dealing with the
civic opposition in 1:27–30. While the eschatological assurance is given, this
theological underpinning lacks the divine intervention motif, which is only
articulated explicitly later in 3:10–11 and 3:20–21 where the themes of resurrection and bodily transformation are in focus. Hence, we can say that
although the humiliation-vindication motif may be noted in this verse, it does
not receive extended treatment. In contrast, the ἔνδειξις can be easily read in
connection with Paul's eschatological frame of mind in 1:5–7 that highlights

---

125. See Fowl, *Philippians*, 68.
126. Fowl, "Christology and Ethics," 147.

God's completing activity of their salvation in Christ. Several arguments support this interpretation.

First, the ἔνδειξις is not a miraculous sign (omen) to be interpreted, but rather a firm conclusion from the assessment of their current struggle based on his eschatological frame of mind. Grammatically, the relative pronoun ἥτις does not only anticipate ἔνδειξις, but also harks back to τῇ πίστει τοῦ εὐαγγελίου.[127] Having said this, Paul probably has the whole of 1:27c–28a in mind,[128] given that firmly standing in one spirit is done for the faith of the gospel.

Second, the demonstrative pronoun τοῦτο at the end of verse 28 refers back to the whole preceding passage (vv. 27c–28a), as this demonstrative appears is neuter.[129] Hence, the clause καὶ τοῦτο ἀπὸ θεοῦ basically claims that the believers' firm-standing in unity for the gospel is embedded in God's completing activity within and among them. This notion is strengthened if the phrase ἐνὶ πνεύματι is understood as the Holy Spirit.[130] The act of standing firmly in unity would be part of the believers' participation in the Spirit. This is congruent with other πνεῦμα statements in the letter, which underlines the Spirit's involvement in Paul's deliverance (1:19), their *koinonia* in Christ (2:1), and their worship (3:3).

Third, this reading also fits well with Paul's subsequent statement, "for *it has been graciously given* [ἐχαρίσθη] on behalf of Christ, not only *to believe* [πιστεύειν] in him but also *to suffer* [πάσχειν] for his sake"[131] (1:29). The verb πιστεύω harks back to the striving for the "faith" (πίστις) of the gospel, and therefore πάσχω should be understood in the context of this struggle. In this light, the suffering and faith are perceived as God's gracious gift. This is congruent with Paul's earlier statement in 1:7, where their sharing in the chain, defense, and confirmation of the gospel is perceived as the divine grace to them. It is noteworthy that χαρίζομαι also appears in 2:9 to underline not only God's response to Christ's death but also his active involvement in Christ's

127. Hawthorne, *Philippians*, 58–59.

128. Bockmuehl, *Philippians*, 101.

129. O'Brien, *Philippians*, 157.

130. Fee, *Philippians*, 163–66; Bockmuehl, *Philippians*, 99.

131. Author's own translation.

redemptive work. In this light, the use of this term in 1:29 signifies God's active involvement in the present struggle of the believers.

All the arguments above demonstrate that Paul's provision of the eschatological underpinning in 1:28 is derived from his earlier frame of thinking about God's completing activity. The aim is to help the readers to appreciate their current struggle for the faith of the gospel as their active participation in the divine completing activity until the day of Christ where their salvation will be fully revealed.

With regard to Philippians 2:12–16, the conjunction ὥστε indicates that Paul's summons to his readers with "continue working out (κατεργάζεσθε) your salvation" is a direct application of the τοῦτο φρονεῖτε instruction that call the readers to observe and meditate on the christological passage. The lordship-obedience scheme is present in this instruction for two reasons. First, the universal acclamation that κύριος Ἰησοῦς Χριστὸς εἰς δόξαν θεοῦ πατρός demands full submission and obedience to God and his Christ from all those in Christ.[132] Second, immediately after the claim of Christ's lordship comes various obedience notes in verses 12–14. What needs to be unveiled is that the lordship-obedience motif should be appreciated within the context of the participation in God's completing activity of his salvation. The following discussion will establish this reading.

The instruction to work out their salvation is grounded not only in a deep reflection of the narratival gospel of Christ but also in the theological underpinning in verse 13: θεὸς γάρ ἐστιν ὁ ἐνεργῶν ἐν ὑμῖν καὶ τὸ θέλειν καὶ τὸ ἐνεργεῖν ὑπὲρ τῆς εὐδοκίας. The causal conjunction γάρ establishes the connection.[133] The participle ὁ ἐνεργῶν highlights the divine activity within the readers.[134] The verb ἐνεργέω is better construed as transitive (to produce) because it highlights God's activity to produce within the readers both the will (τὸ θέλειν) and the power (τὸ ἐνεργεῖν) to achieve it.[135] The former notably recalls the divine transformation of the mind, and the latter ensures its achievement. Conceptually, therefore, the claim of God's power within

---

132. Hurtado, "Jesus as Lordly Example," 15.

133. O'Brien, *Philippians*, 284.

134. Fee, *Philippians*, 237; Bockmuehl, *Philippians*, 153.

135. Wagner, "Working Out Salvation," 259.

and among the readers is derived from the eschatological thought of God's completing activity in 1:6.[136]

As God is at work to complete their salvation, he is now actively producing both the will to work it out and the capability to accomplish it. The latter provides a firm assurance of salvation, but this does not necessarily connote God's gracious intervention, as Fowl has argued: "In the same way as God worked to exalt the humiliated and obedient Christ and vindicated his suffering, God will also work to bring the salvation 'worked out' by the Philippians in obedience to Paul's commands."[137] Although the readers could think in this way, there is no other statement in 2:12–18 to confirm this line of thought, except the one in the christological passage. In contrast, the idea of the collaboration between God's completing activity and the believers' labor for the salvation in Christ can be easily noted by the interplay between κατ-εργ-άζομαι in the instruction and ἐν-εργ-έω in its theological underpinning.[138]

7.2.3 Synthesis

In Philippians 1:27–2:18, Paul addresses a complex predicament of the Philippian church, which was generated from the combination of external and internal threats. Principally, he summons his readers to live worthily and to work out their salvation according to the gospel of Christ. These exhortations are further amplified in various instructions, such as to stand firmly in unity, to adopt Christ's attitude, and to live in obedience to God. To support them, Paul lays down his "think this" instruction (2:5–11) by which the christological narrative becomes relevant to their struggle. In this rhetorical framework, the role of the universal worship of Christ should be defined.

Paul's frame of mind is profoundly shaped by three eschatological coordinates articulated in 1:6, 1:10–11, and 2:10–11. These eschatological aspects are not only present but also profoundly shape this paraenetical discourse. First of all, the main concern of Paul's exhortations is the holiness of his readers. This demand is applied in the context of the present struggles of the Philippian church, and it has anti-imperial (1:27–30), communal (2:1–4), and missional (2:12–15) dimensions. At the same time, it does not lose their eschatological

---

136. Fowl, *Philippians*, 121.

137. Fowl, *Story of Christ*, 97.

138. Fee, *Philippians*, 237.

orientation (2:16), as this holiness demand greatly anticipates the eschatological worship of Christ and God (2:10–11). This reading is strengthened by the
use of various cultic imageries in 2:12–18, which infer that their present holiness has a worship motive and even anticipates the climactic worship event
at the day of Christ in which both Paul and the readers hope to participate.
Finally, it is strongly underlined that these holiness instructions are embedded in God's completing activity of his salvation (1:6) that will establish their
perfect holiness on the day of Christ (1:28; 2:13). When all this is considered,
the connection between the universal worship of Christ in 2:10–11 and the
exhortations in 1:27–2:18 can be discerned in the relation to Paul's triangular
frame of mind.

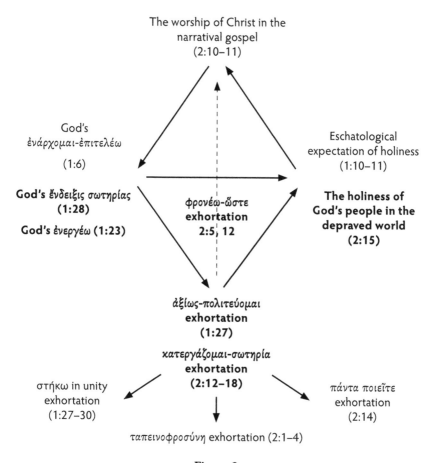

Figure 2

The way Paul discloses the eschatological elements of his way of thought, particularly in the final phase (2:12–18), helps the readers to discern the role of the universal worship of Christ. Already in the prayer report section, he has shaped his readers' minds with the idea of God's completing activity until the day of Christ (1:6) and the expectation of holiness on that very day (1:10–11). Now, at the heart of the present discourse (2:5–11), he unveils that the pivotal event on that day is the universal eschatological worship of Christ (2:10–11) in which all the believers of Christ hope to participate. After this, comes the final phase where all eschatological elements of his reasoning are articulated explicitly. Notably important are the cultic expressions that appear only in this section, and his expectation of boasting on the day of Christ (2:16), which harks back to the eschatological worship motif in 2:10–11. These are important clues to correlate the instructions with this eschatological worship motif. Accordingly, the attentive readers, whose minds have been strongly shaped by this eschatological frame of mind, will be able to discern how the instructions connect to the eschatological worship of Christ in this narratival gospel.

It can be concluded that the universal worship of Christ at the eschaton provides a fundamental eschatological orientation of Paul's instructions in this paraenetical discourse. These instructions, by which they are called to laboriously live out or work out their holiness according to the gospel of Christ, and by which they are encouraged to participate in God's activity to complete the salvation in them, intend to prepare the readers for the grand worship of Christ at the eschaton that marks the consummation of their salvation in Christ.

7.3 Reading Philippians 3:2–4:4

There are several grounds to treat Philippians 3:2–4:4 as one coherent discourse. It has been established in chapter 5, the discourse in 3:2–21 is better perceived as integral to Paul's letter to the Philippians. Following this line of thought, the material in this discourse can be easily distinguished from Paul's travel plans in 2:19–30 and the catena of exhortations in 4:5–9.[139] As

---

139. The exhortation χαίρετε ἐν κυρίῳ πάντοτε· πάλιν ἐρῶ, χαίρετε in 4:4 serves as a transition. It can be construed as either the beginning of the catena of exhortations in 4:4–9

it is the case of the discourse in 1:27–2:18, the present discourse deals with some specific issues faced by the Philippian congregation. Finally, the conjunction ὥστε in 4:1 establishes a strong inferential connection between the exhortations in 4:1–4 and the material in 3:2–21. With this framework, now we discuss this paraenetical discourse. The structure of the discussion follows closely from the previous section.

7.3.1 Paul's Rhetorical Strategy

Paul's transitional statement in 3:1 provides a clue to Paul's intent in writing the present discourse, "to write the same things [τὰ αὐτὰ] to you is not burdensome to me, but it is a safeguard to you." The phrase τὰ αὐτὰ refers back to the material in 1:27–2:18. This is supported by the parallel of four instructions in these two discourses (i.e. to stand-firm, to think the same, to think this, and to rejoice)[140] and by three thematic parallels between the two discourses (i.e. destruction-salvation,[141] faith-suffering,[142] and πολίτευμα-πολιτεύομαι).[143] All this demonstrates that Paul's primary objective in this discourse is still the same as what he wants to achieve in the previous paraenetical discourse, namely to encourage his readers to continue standing firmly in unity in Christ. With all this in mind, we now observe the rhetorical strategy of Paul.

The discourse can be divided into two major sections. The second section (4:1–4) is short and recalls some pivotal exhortations in 1:27–2:18: (1) στήκετε ἐν κυρίῳ summarizes the instruction elaborated in 1:27–30; (2) τὸ αὐτὸ φρονεῖν ἐν κυρίῳ is a practical application of the direction expounded earlier in 2:1–4; and (3) χαίρετε ἐν κυρίῳ πάντοτε. πάλιν ἐρῶ, χαίρετε recalls Paul's *koinonical* encouragement in 2:18 that ends the discourse. The first section (3:2–21) is extensive. The inferential conjunction ὥστε (therefore) indicates that the first section provides the ground for the exhortations in the second section. We note that some scholars construe this conjunction as serving to connect the exhortations in 4:1–4 with only the material in 3:20–21.[144] While

---

or the end of the discourse in 3:2–4:4 (cf. the case in 1:27–2:18). The present study adopts the latter.

140. Phil 4:1 cf. 1:27; 4:2 cf. 2:2; 3:15 cf. 2:5; 4:4 cf. 2:18.
141. Phil 3:19–21 cf. 1:28.
142. Phil 3:9–11 cf. 1:29.
143. Phil 3:20 cf. 1:27.
144. O'Brien, *Philippians*, 474–75.

this conjecture is plausible, it narrows down the basis of the exhortation, and thus makes the supporting ground less persuasive.

How the material in 3:2–21 is rhetorically structured is worthy of attention. In this section, Paul's objective is to persuade the readers to adopt his way of thought in 3:4–15. The grounds are in order. First of all, the leading exhortations are two: (1) Ὅσοι οὖν τέλειοι, τοῦτο φρονῶμεν in 3:15; (2) συμμιμηταί μου γίνεσθε, ἀδελφοί, καὶ σκοπεῖτε τοὺς οὕτω περιπατοῦντας καθὼς ἔχετε τύπον ἡμᾶς in 3:17. Concerning the latter, Paul, taking the role of an authoritative teacher,[145] and he summons the readers to join others "in imitating" (συμμιμητής) his way of thinking and pattern of life. Although τύπος can refer to Paul's life examples witnessed by the readers or some examples in this letter,[146] it rhetorically points back to his account in 3:4–14,[147] which reveals the frame of mind he calls for adoption: ὅσοι οὖν τέλειοι, τοῦτο φρονῶμεν (3:15). In this regard, the φρονέω-ὥστε framework, which is attested in 2:5–12, is basically at work in the present discourse. The adoption of Paul's frame of mind – which includes the transformation of his mindset (vv. 4–8), his eschatological aim (vv. 8–11), and his labor to attain it (vv. 12–14) – provides a solid ground (ὥστε) for the practical exhortations in 4:1–4.

Paul's frame of mind is notably set against two other types of mindset noted in the same discourse. The first mindset is shaped by the teaching (3:4–6) that emphasizes the Jewishness of God's people (ἐκ γένους Ἰσραήλ, φυλῆς Βενιαμίν, Ἑβραῖος ἐξ Ἑβραίων) on the ground of circumcision (πεποίθησιν καὶ ἐν σαρκί) and the observance of Torah (κατὰ νόμον Φαρισαῖος). Despite the debate on whether 3:2–9 deals with the Judaizing teaching as a real threat in the Philippian congregation,[148] it is generally acknowledged that in this discourse, Paul draws a contrast between *us* – who are Paul (3:4–14), his associates (2:19–30), and his readers (3:15, 17) – and *them* – who are the Judaizing Christians (3:2).[149]

---

145. The imitation of the teacher's example is widely attested in both Greco-Roman and Jewish didactic traditions. Hawthorne, "Imitation of Christ," 176–77; Bockmuehl, *Philippians*, 229.

146. Phil 1:20–22, 30; 4:9, 12–13.

147. Fee, *Philippians*, 365–66; Holloway, Περιπατεω *as a Thematic*, 167–68.

148. See Hansen, *Philippians*, 217; contra Garland, "Composition and Unity," 164–66.

149. Garland, "Composition and Unity," 167; Fee, *Philippians*, 294; Hansen, *Philippians*, 216.

The second mindset is reflected in the life of "those walking as the en-emies of the cross of Christ" (τοὺς ἐχθροὺς τοῦ σταυροῦ τοῦ Χριστου) in verse 18. Paul also refers to them as οἱ τὰ ἐπίγεια φρονοῦντες (v. 19) to contrast them with τὸ πολίτευμα ἐν οὐρανοῖς whose minds are set on Christ and his parousia (3:7–11, 20–21).[150] The relevance of these two negative mindsets to the Philippians' struggle can be construed as follows. In facing the civic op-position in Philippi, this heavenly community has greatly suffered for Christ's sake. In such a condition, the temptation to fall away from the faith in Christ is great, particularly among those who set their mind on fleshly and earthly things, and those who try to escape suffering by adopting Judaism, which is regarded as a *religio licita*.[151]

Taking this into consideration, in 3:2–21 Paul intends to persuade the readers to adopt his way of thinking and to dissuade them from taking the mindsets promoted by the Judaizers and adopted by the enemies of the cross of Christ. This is done in several ways. First, while the existence of some other mindsets is acknowledged (εἴ τι ἑτέρως φρονεῖτε in v. 15), Paul's calling the readers τέλειοι rhetorically encourages them to adopt his way of thought, as the term denotes those who have matured in thinking.[152] Second, in response to the Judaizers' pride in their circumcision and Mosaic law, Paul claims that all his previous greatness achieved in Judaism becomes insignificant in comparison to his present knowledge of Christ (vv. 7–8). They all are indeed now regarded as "losses" (ζημία) and "rubbish" (σκύβαλα). This certainly has a great rhetorical effect. Finally, in response to τὰ ἐπίγεια φρονοῦντες (v. 19), περιπατέω is intentionally used (v. 17–18) to contrast those adopting Paul's mindset with those adopting the earthly one. While the latter will end in destruction, the former will experience salvation.[153] This also certainly has both persuasion and dissuasion effects.

---

150. Whether "the enemies of the cross of Christ" refers to the Judaizing Christians in 3:2 or to those gentile Christians who abandoned the way of the cross, it is generally appreciated that οἱ τὰ ἐπίγεια φρονοῦντες stands in opposition to Paul's *phronesis* in 3:4–14. Silva, *Philippians*, 182; Bockmuehl, *Philippians*, 232; Wagner, "Working Out Salvation," 268–69.

151. Bockmuehl, *Philippians*, 190.

152. Cf. ταῖς δὲ φρεσὶν τέλειοι γίνεσθε in 1 Cor 14:20.

153. Doble, "Vile Bodies," 21–22.

In all, Philippians 3:2–21 intends to persuade the readers to adopt Paul's frame of mind in 3:4–14. When this rhetorical objective is attained, it provides solid support to the principal exhortation in 4:1–4.

7.3.2 The Pivotal Elements of Paul's Frame of Mind

7.3.2.1 The Expectation of Holiness

It has been established that Paul's eschatological aim in 3:8–11 parallels his expectation of holiness in 1:9–11. In its rhetorical context, it is further argued that the goal stands in opposition to the work of Torah promoted by the Judaizers, and to the earthly mindset of those walking as the enemies of the cross of Christ. The following discussion will elaborate on all this.

Paul's statement ἡμεῖς γάρ ἐσμεν ἡ περιτομή in 3:3 is significant, as it polemically opposes the Judaizing Christians' confidence in the flesh by boldly claiming the identity and status of him and his uncircumcised gentile readers (ἡμεῖς) as God's holy people.[154] To appreciate this, it is important to note that "circumcision" (περιτομή) is a pivotal coordinate in the traditional Jewish understanding of holiness and justification.[155] This physical sign not merely marks the Israelites as God's covenantal people,[156] it is also their obligation to Torah, by which they will be sanctified and justified. Hence, ἐν σαρκὶ πεποιθότες in the same verse is associated with having pride in this fleshly circumcision (cf. Rom 2:28).[157] The line of reasoning for such confidence is eloquently described by Nijay K. Gupta:

> those who knew (Ex 29.45–46) and followed the true God in worship identified themselves as such through a commitment to Torah and were marked by circumcision. As God's people, they were given certain privileges so that they could live life wisely and discern God's will in a way not available to others. Knowing the true God also meant knowing truth and wisdom

---

154. The phrase ἡ περιτομή (as a collective noun) points to the covenant people who stand under God's promises, the one true people of God. O'Brien, *Philippians*, 358.

155. Gorman, "You Shall Be Cruciform," 163.

156. Martin, "Circumcision in Galatia," 220–25.

157. The term σάρξ in this verse may simply denote all human worth and work. Having said this, reading in conjunction with the earlier περιτομή, the association "having confidence in flesh" (σάρξ) with "the work of the Torah" (νόμος) emerges.

more generally (Ps 111.10; Prov 1.7; 9.10), especially through
the Torah (Ps 19).[158]

According to this rationale, the uncircumcised people would be regarded as
being unholy and excluded from God's justification.

In Paul's frame of mind, the Jewish confidence in the flesh has been abandoned on the ground of his knowledge of Christ, as in this relationship both
the physical circumcision and the observance of the Mosaic laws have no
more value (σκύβαλον). The purpose of the laws cannot be attained, because "human flesh" (σάρξ) has been deeply corrupted, weakened, and controlled by sin (see Rom 8:3–8). Indeed, the mindset generated by the flesh
(τὸ φρόνημα τῆς σαρκός) is only hostile to God, as it does not submit to his
laws. Accordingly, the problem of sin can be solved only through Christ's
redemptive work on the cross (Rom 8:3). This salvific thought is virtually
expressed in verse 9, where Paul claims that God's righteousness is declared
on the grounds of Christ's faithfulness accentuated in the narratival gospel
and the faith in him.

Derived from this conviction is the appreciation that holiness (καρπὸν
δικαιοσύνης) can be produced only through Jesus Christ (Phil 1:11). In this
letter, as the spirit of God is also referred to as the spirit of Jesus Christ
(1:19), οἱ πνεύματι θεοῦ λατρεύοντες in 3:3 should also shape the notion of
Paul's concept of περιτομή. This circumcision must connote a circumcision
of the heart done by God through his Holy Spirit (cf. Rom 2:29),[159] which is
available to both the circumcised and the uncircumcised people in Christ.
As their holy status is originated by the Spirit's activity, the mindsets of those
in Christ need to be set (φρονοῦσιν) by the Spirit for their sanctification (cf.
Rom 8:4–6). Accordingly, sanctification comes apart from the work of the
Mosaic laws but through a gracious provision of the Spirit.

In the context of their struggle for the faith of the gospel of Christ, Paul
has underlined that suffering (πάσχω) for Christ's sake is God's grace to them
in 1:29. This theme of suffering is recalled in 3:10–11 and set as part of his
eschatological aim. Inspired by the gospel story of Christ, suffering with
Christ becomes part of the holy codes of God's people complimentary to his

---

158. Gupta, *Worship That Makes Sense*, 144–45.

159. Cf. Deut 10:16; 30:6; Lev 26:41; Jer 4:4; 9:25–26; Ezek 44:7. See Witherington III,
Philippians, 195.

future resurrection. This motivates him to suffer not only for Christ's sake but also in the manner of Christ's suffering (2:6–8).[160]

This Christ-like holiness stands in opposition to the ethos of those walking as the enemies of the cross of Christ. The use of περιπατέω (to walk) in verses 17–18 sets a contrast between those walking according to Paul's τύπος (adopting the Christ-like suffering) and this group of people.[161] This Christ-like holiness is rejected by them, not because of their opposition to the salvific message of the gospel of Christ, but that the orientation and norm of life expressed in the gospel contradicts their cultural ethos noted in verse 19: their god is their stomach (κοιλία), their glory is their shame (αἰσχύνη), and their mind is set (φρονέω) on the earthly things (τὰ ἐπίγεια).[162] Driven by this popular ethos some have renounced their faith in Christ to avoid suffering and pursued an indulgent and hedonistic lifestyle. As this way of life will result in destruction (ἀπώλεια), the readers are encouraged not to adopt it, but to pattern after Christ for their sanctification.

7.3.2.2 The Worship Notion

In Philippians 3:3, Paul claims that they are "the worshippers by the Spirit" (οἱ πνεύματι θεοῦ λατρεύοντες). Together with ἡμεῖς γάρ ἐσμεν ἡ περιτομή, this identity underlines their covenant relationship with God of Israel (cf. Rom 9:4–5). The significance of this identity for understanding the nature of ἡμεῖς γάρ ἐσμεν ἡ περιτομή has been expounded in the earlier discussion. Now, it is further argued that this identity has an eschatological overtone and provides a cultic notion of Paul's mindset in Christ. The arguments are in order.

First of all, the term λατρεύω denotes "to work" or "to serve." In the LXX, it appears almost exclusively in the religious or cultic sense connected to Israel's worship of YHWH.[163] Accordingly, οἱ πνεύματι θεοῦ λατρεύοντες has a strong association with worshipping God.[164] We note that this participle can be read in several ways based on the early manuscripts: (1) "worshipping God in/by the spirit" (οἱ πνεύματι θεῷ λατρεύοντες is attested in ℵ², D*, P, Ψ);

---

160. Fowl, *Philippians*, 155–56; Hansen, *Philippians*, 247.

161. Fowl, *Philippians*, 170–71; Hansen, *Philippians*, 264–65.

162. Bockmuehl, *Philippians*, 230–32; Hansen, *Philippians*, 264–65.

163. Balz, "Λατρεύω," *EDNT* 2:344–45.

164. This is reflected in many translations (NIV, NRSV, and ESV).

(2) "worshipping in/by the Spirit of God" (οἱ πνεύματι θεοῦ λατρεύοντες is attested in א*, A, B, C, D², F, G); (3) "worshipping in/by the spirit" (οἱ πνεύματι λατρεύοντες is attested in 𝔓⁴⁶). Following the majority of commentators, we adopt the second option, as this is supported by many early manuscripts. In P⁴⁶, the word θεοῦ is probably dropped by accident.[165] The word θεω in some early manuscripts was probably a later correction based on ᾧ λατρεύω ἐν τῷ πνεύματί μου in Romans 1:9 to establish the reading of "the one worshipping God through the [human] spirit." In our conjecture, the dative πνεύματι is instrumental (worshipping *by* the Spirit of God),[166] underlining that it is the Holy Spirit who enables both Paul and his readers to worship God properly (cf. Rom 8:15).[167]

Second, Paul's claim, οἱ πνεύματι θεοῦ λατρεύοντες, is best read against the claim made by the Judaizers about the true worshippers of God. According to Romans 9:4–5, ἡ λατρεία (worship) is an exclusive benefit enjoyed by Israel as YHWH's covenant people. At the time of Paul, Christianity was still part of Judaism and the majority of its followers were still Jews. Arising from this condition were the struggles within the Pauline churches concerning the status of the gentile converts. Some still insisted that to fully enjoy the covenant benefits of worshipping God, the gentile converts had to be circumcised (περιτομή), as only the circumcised people could worship in the Jerusalem Temple. To Paul, however, in Christ, all gentile converts have become the children of God (2:15) through the circumcision done by the Spirit (see Rom 2:29). Accordingly, despite being excluded from the worship in the Jerusalem Temple, they are all part of the true worshippers of God together with the circumcised believers.[168]

Third, based on the discussion above, the phrase πνεύματι θεοῦ must have great significance. As they all have been circumcised by the Spirit to be God's holy children, their worship must be also empowered by him.[169] What needs to

---

165. Bockmuehl, *Philippians*, 193.

166. Bockmuehl, 192.

167. Bockmuehl, 192; contra Cousar, *Philippians and Philemon*, 69 that construes πνεύματι as a dative of manner (in the Spirit of God).

168. This does not suggest, however, that by οἱ πνεύματι θεοῦ λατρεύοντες, Paul contrasts Christian worship with Jewish worship. Fowl, *Philippians*, 148.

169. In the other letters, Paul teaches the role of the Spirit in worship, such as: (1) Christ's community is God's temple because of the presence of his Spirit in it (1 Cor 3:16); (2) the Spirit

be further noted is that the Spirit's activity signals God's eschatological work of salvation, which has begun and is now powerfully working, within and among those in Christ.[170] In 2 Corinthians 1:22 and 5:5 (cf. Eph 1:13–14; 4:30), the Spirit is regarded as the "down payment" for the eschatological salvation. In this letter, the Spirit secures not merely Paul's imminent deliverance (1:19) but also the eschatological salvation of the congregation (1:27–28).[171] As the Spirit actively works to realize the divine eschatological reign and salvation, worshipping by the Spirit should anticipate the worship of God and Christ at the eschaton depicted earlier in the gospel narrative.

7.3.2.3 Participating in God's Active Work of Salvation

As it has been argued above, Paul's commitment to attaining the eschatological aim in Christ is best comprehended as his participation in God's completing activity of his salvation until the day of Christ. To fully appreciate its rhetorical force, the nature of this participation needs to be unpacked.

First of all, Paul's participation in God's completing activity involves his *mimesis* of Christ. Paul's twin instructions in 3:17, namely συμμιμηταί μου γίνεσθε and (2) σκοπεῖτε τοὺς οὕτω περιπατοῦντας καθὼς ἔχετε τύπον ἡμᾶς, basically call the readers to imitate him in one accord by "observing" (σκοπέω) those who put into practice the τύπος set by Paul in verses 12–14, which is generated by his new frame of mind in Christ (vv. 7–11). Although some object to it,[172] the majority of scholars regard the outlook in these verses as reflecting Paul's *mimesis* of Christ described in 2:6–11.[173] This view is adopted in the present study based on the following considerations. First, the imitation of the leaders' noble attitude and deed, including teachers, was a common convention in both the Greco-Roman world and the Jewish world.[174] This

---

distributes his gifts to empower the community to worship (1 Cor 12 and 14); (3) the Spirit intercedes to God on behalf the believers (Rom 8:26–27).

170. See the discussion in Piage, "Holy Spirit," 411.

171. The believers' firm standing "in one spirit" (ἐν ἑνὶ πνεύματι) is perceived as "a proof" (ἔνδειξις) of their eschatological salvation (1:28; cf. 3:20–21).

172. Martin, *Hymn of Christ*, 290; Dodd, "Story of Christ," 154–61.

173. Bockmuehl, *Philippians*, 229; Fowl, *Philippians*, 166; Witherington III, *Philippians*, 213–15; Kurz, "Kenotic Imitation of Paul," 115; Hawthorne, "Imitation of Christ," 173–74.

174. Kurz, "Kenotic Imitation of Paul," 115; Hawthorne, "Imitation of Christ," 173–74.

tradition is strongly attested in Paul's letters.[175] Second, several Pauline passages contain the idea of the imitation of Christ.[176] The instruction μιμηταί μου γίνεσθε, καθὼς κἀγὼ χριστοῦ in 1 Corinthians 11:1 can be translated as "become the imitator of me, as I am the imitator of Christ"[177] or "become the imitator of me, as I am of Christ."[178] Paul's statement καὶ ὑμεῖς μιμηταὶ ἡμῶν ἐγενήθητε καὶ τοῦ κυρίου in 1 Thessalonians 1:6 indicates that Paul encourages his readers to imitate not only him but also Christ.[179] Finally, in the context of Philippians, although Paul's instruction summons the readers to imitate his τύπος in 3:4–14,[180] his pattern of life in 3:10–11 notably follows after or is inspired by Christ's suffering death and resurrection in the Christ-narrative (2:8–9).

Having said this, some remarks need to be made with the characteristics of Paul's imitation. First, the imitation should not be understood in a strict or rigid sense, like a model to be virtually copied.[181] While Christ's death and resurrection are performed for the sake of all mankind, Paul's *mimesis* of his suffering, death, and resurrection is better understood in the context of his active participation (διώκω) in God's active work to complete the salvation in him.[182] Second, we do not think that Paul's repudiation of his past privileges and achievements in 3:7–8 is part of his *mimesis* of Christ's kenotic deeds in 2:6–8, as the two are in opposition to each other. The latter is done for the sake of all humankind, while the former is done because they are now regarded as having no value (σκύβαλα).[183] Accordingly, Paul's imitation of Christ focuses primarily on his *koinonia* with Christ's suffering and his resurrection.

---

175. The idea of *mimesis* is noted in Phil 3:14; 1 Cor 4:6; 11:1; 1 Thess 1:6; cf. Eph 5:1; 2 Thess 2:14.

176. See Rom 15:1–3; 1 Cor 11:1; 2 Cor 8:9; 1 Thess 1:6. This is acknowledged in Dodd, "Story of Christ," 158.

177. Kurz, "Kenotic Imitation of Paul," 106. This emphasizes Paul's identity in Christ.

178. This will emphasize Paul's identity in Christ. Dodd, "Story of Christ," 157–58.

179. Hooker, "Partner in the Gospel," 94.

180. Contra Hooker, "Partner in the Gospel," 93–94, that reads in the sense of "to be fellow-imitators of Christ with Paul."

181. Fowl, *Philippians*, 168–69, rightly argues that the imitation of Christ "cannot really operate without practical reasoning." See also Park, *Submission within the Godhead*, 94–101; contra Castelli, *Imitating Paul*, 21.

182. This idea has been proposed and defended by Hooker. See her "Philippians" and "Partner in the Gospel."

183. Dodd, "Story of Christ," 157.

Second, in Paul's participation in God's completing activity of his salvation, the lordship-obedience motif can be detected. The motif is noted in Paul's addressing Jesus Christ as his κύριος, which implies that his communion with Christ's suffering and his resurrection are done in obedience to this Lord. Given that the lordship-obedience motif has been emphasized in 2:12–14, the readers can easily connect Paul's suffering with Christ in 3:10 as part of their devotional obedience to God and Christ. At the end of the day, they will all stand in the divine court on the day of judgment to give an account before God. While this motif is present, we do not think that it receives great emphasis for two reasons. The phrase "my Lord" (τοῦ κυρίου μου) in this verse emphasizes more the personal relationship with Christ. Furthermore, the obedience expression is absent in this discourse.

We note that to emphasize the lordship-obedience motif, Sydney Park proposes the reading of 3:10 as follows. The infinitive τοῦ γνῶναι αὐτὸν is epexegetical, speaking not of experiential knowledge, but the "knowledge from the objective fact of Christ event."[184] Accordingly, the phrase καὶ τὴν δύναμιν τῆς ἀναστάσεως αὐτοῦ does not denote the power enjoyed by the believers of Christ, but "the recognition of God's sovereign power and his exceeding approval of Christ."[185] Furthermore, the phrase [τὴν] κοινωνίαν [τῶν] παθημάτων αὐτοῦ is understood not as his participation in Christ's suffering, but a salvific fellowship generated from Christ's suffering death.[186] As a result, the lordship of Christ and its salvific benefit are underlined. This manner of knowing Christ "leads to Paul's intentional conformity to Christ's death."[187]

While Park's proposal is exegetically possible, several factors make this interpretation weak. First, the use of δύναμις in this verse and its cognates (δύναμαι in 3:21, ἐνδυναμόω in 4:13) in Philippians consistently describes the believer's experience of God's power. Similarly, the term κοινωνία and its cognates (συγκοινωνός and κοινωνέω) in this letter also consistently denote the idea of the believers' participation in something. Second, the idea of participation in Christ's death and resurrection is well attested in Paul's

---

184. Park, *Submission within the Godhead*, 72.

185. Park, 73.

186. Park, 74. Here, παθημάτων is construed as a subjective genitive, instead of an objective genitive.

187. Park, 74.

letters elsewhere.[188] Accordingly, it is more likely that Paul lays a similar ethical principle in Philippians 3:10–11,[189] and that his readers read in this way. Third, in appreciation of the chiastic nature of Paul's elaboration of τοῦ γνῶναι αὐτὸν, it is argued that although the participle συμμορφιζόμενος τῷ θανάτῳ αὐτοῦ (B') is syntactically dependent on the verb γινώσκω, it is also epexegetic of κοινωνίαν παθημάτων αὐτοῦ (B). All this supports the inference that verse 10 should not be read in the way Park does.

Third, the motif of suffering-vindication is dominant, particularly in 3:10–11 and 3:20–21. The idea of *koinonia* always involves at least two parties. In the context of 3:8–14, the consummation of salvation is engendered by the mutual efforts of both God and his people. God's righteousness is declared based on Christ's faithfulness and human faith in him, and Paul's pursuing activity (διώκω) also responds to God's active work within him. Accordingly, Paul's *koinonia* with Christ's suffering will be complementary to his experience of the power of Christ's resurrection, and his becoming like Christ in his death will be reciprocated by the divine final vindication in the form of the resurrection from the dead.

The association of the resurrection from the dead in 3:11 with God's vindication is strong. This resurrection will not come from human efforts, but it will be fully dependent on God's sovereign power (3:21). In our opinion, there is no need to decide whether the δύναμις in verse 10 belongs to Christ (cf. 3:21) or God (cf. 4:13).[190] In this letter, the divine power is also assisted by the Holy Spirit, who is called both the Spirit of Christ and the Spirit of God. Notably, the gospel narrative depicts that God has exalted Christ into power as the victorious Lord. His divine power will be exercised in the resurrection of the believers, as it is noted in the description of the transformation of their bodies. In all, the resurrection from the dead is perceived as God's final and decisive completing activity at the day of Christ by which the salvation of his people will be consummated.

The humiliation-vindication motif is further adumbrated in the description of the bodily transformation that highlights further the nature of the

---

188. Rom 6:5–12; 2 Cor 4:7–11; 12:9; Gal 2:20.

189. Hawthorne, *Philippians*, 144–45; Bockmuehl, *Philippians*, 214–15.

190. For the power of God, Bockmuehl, *Philippians*, 214; Hansen, *Philippians*, 244. For the power of Christ, Fee, *Philippians*, 330.

resurrection from the dead. In 1 Corinthians 15:39–42, Paul teaches that the resurrected body will not only be imperishable but also characterized by δόξα in the sense of bearing Christ's image.[191] In this connection, the phrase τὸ σῶμα τῆς ταπεινώσεως ἡμῶν refers to the natural body of the believers which will be gloriously transformed at the resurrection day. Having said this, there are also numerous terminological connections between the passage in 2:5–11 and the one in 3:20–21 should be noted:[192]

Philippians 2:5–11	Philippians 3:20–21
μορφή (v. 6 and 7)	σύμμορφος (v. 20)
ὑπάρχω (v. 6)	ὑπάρχω (v. 20)
σχῆμα (v. 7)	μετασχηματίζω (v. 21)
ταπεινόω (v. 8)	τὸ σῶμα τῆς ταπεινώσεως (v. 21)
κύριος Ἰησοῦς Χριστὸς (v. 11)	κύριον Ἰησοῦν Χριστόν (v. 20),
δόξα (v. 11)	δόξα (v. 21)

This suggests that Paul is inspired by the christological passage in picturing the parousia event. The way Paul describes this eschatological experience recalls the experience of Christ's death and exaltation.[193] Accordingly, τὸ σῶμα τῆς ταπεινώσεως ἡμῶν is closely associated with the bodies of the believers who faithfully embraced Christ's ταπεινόω in life.[194] In this way, the message of hope in God's vindication emerges. Those embracing Christ-like suffering will be transformed into the likeness of Christ's glory at his parousia. The readers who were currently experiencing persecution for Christ and his gospel would easily appreciate their resurrection, by which their body is transformed into Christ's glory as God's vindication.

7.3.3 Synthesis

The discourse in 3:2–4:4 intends to reemphasize what has been done in 1:27–2:18, particularly the necessity to stand firmly in unity in Christ, which

191. Fee, *Philippians*, 381; Bockmuehl, *Philippians*, 236; Hansen, *Philippians*, 273.
192. Bloomquist, *Function of Suffering*, 102–3; Hansen, *Philippians*, 277.
193. Fee, *Philippians*, 382; Bockmuehl, *Philippians*, 236; Hansen, *Philippians*, 275.
194. Doble, "Vile Bodies," 25–26.

requires their readiness to live for Christ's sake and in his manner. To encourage them in this way of life, Paul lays down his frame of mind in 3:4–15, which is shaped by the narratival gospel of Christ in 2:6–11 and the theological reasoning in 1:6. The purpose is to give a *koinonical* encouragement to this suffering community by demonstrating that he also practiced what he has instructed them to do. By doing this, he hopes to persuade the readers to adopt his way of thinking and living. It is in this frame of mind that the significance of the universal worship of Christ should be defined.

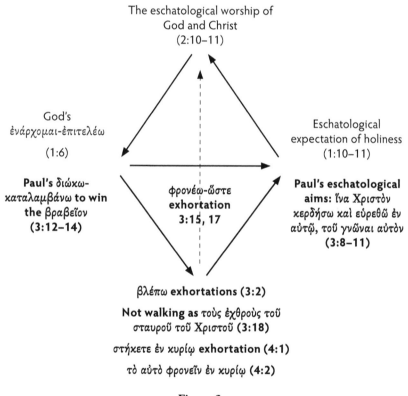

The eschatological worship of
God and Christ
(2:10–11)

God's
ἐνάρχομαι-ἐπιτελέω
(1:6)

Eschatological
expectation of holiness
(1:10–11)

**Paul's διώκω-
καταλαμβάνω to win
the βραβεῖον
(3:12–14)**

φρονέω-ὥστε
**exhortation
3:15, 17**

**Paul's eschatological
aims: ἵνα Χριστὸν
κερδήσω καὶ εὑρεθῶ ἐν
αὐτῷ, τοῦ γνῶναι αὐτὸν
(3:8–11)**

βλέπω **exhortations (3:2)**

Not walking as τοὺς ἐχθροὺς τοῦ
σταυροῦ τοῦ Χριστοῦ **(3:18)**

στήκετε ἐν κυρίῳ **exhortation (4:1)**

τὸ αὐτὸ φρονεῖν ἐν κυρίῳ **(4:2)**

Figure 3

As the case in Philippians 1:27–2:18, we detect three pivotal eschatological elements of Paul's frame of mind in this discourse. Paul sets his eschatological aim as follows: (1) to be found as righteous based on Christ's faithfulness and faith in him and (2) to be fully transformed through the participation in Christ-like suffering and resurrection. These two facets of holiness are relevant to the church in Philippi. Amid their suffering, they are strongly reminded not to adopt both the mindset of the Judaizing Christians and those walking as the enemies of the cross of Christ. Instead, they are to live out the gospel-like holiness that looks forward to its full realization at the day of Christ. Their identity as οἱ πνεύματι θεοῦ λατρεύοντες supplies a cultic nuance of Paul's eschatological aim: to be found as righteous and holy worshippers on the day of Christ. This righteousness and holiness arise from persistent toils, which are embedded in God's gracious activity to perfect his salvation, and which will be perfected by his final vindication, the resurrection of the dead.

When all the components above are considered, it can be comprehended that the significance of the universal worship of Christ is set within Paul's triangular frame of mind that provides the eschatological orientation of the discourse.

Putting Paul's thought within his rhetorical strategy in this discourse, it can be said that the first section (3:2–21) intends to persuade the readers to adopt Paul's eschatological frame of mind that greatly anticipates the grand worship of Christ at his parousia. The note of God's vindication with his resurrection will encourage them to faithfully live out this midset (i.e. to suffer for Christ's sake and in his manner). When this way of thinking is accepted, it will motivate them to stand firmly in unity in Christ in facing all the challenges from the inside and outside, which is the main course of the second section (4:1–4).

CHAPTER 8

Summary and Conclusion

In defining the rhetorical function of the exaltation part of the christological passage in Paul's letter to the Philippians, this study highlights the significance of the motif of the universal eschatological worship of Christ depicted as a conclusion of this narratival gospel (2:10–11). To support this proposal four sets of considerations have been made in reading this eschatological worship motif.

The first relates to its Jewish background. The picture of this universal worship is derived from the biblical visions of the universal worship of YHWH, particularly the one in Isaiah 45:23–24 LXX. Like many other similar biblical visions of worship, this Isaianic vision of worship has a covenantal framework, universal scope, salvific thrust, and holiness expectation. The presence of these four tenets is affirmed by our observation of the vision within its literary context, the book of Isaiah. Furthermore, our analysis on the reception of Isaiah 45:23 in Second Temple writings (4Q215a, the Aleinu prayer, and Paul's letter to the Romans) also confirms such findings. Paul's reading of this Isaianic vision in Romans is crucial for the present study. While it shares these same four common thoughts with the other two writers, nevertheless his reading is also quite distinct from theirs, as it is strongly shaped by his eschatological conviction centered on the Messiah Jesus. Romans 14:10–11 implicitly depicts Christ as the divine Lord, and thus he is included in the eschatological worship of God, which will be situated at the divine court at the eschaton. Taking this into consideration, this study contends that the depiction of the universal eschatological worship of Christ in Philippians 2:10–11 is also pregnant with these four tenets. Christ is depicted as the divine Lord to be worshipped along with God by the whole creation. The worship of him at the eschaton demonstrates God's mighty reign over the whole of creation, which also marks both the conclusion of God's redemptive work and the consummation of his salvation in Christ. All this is generated by God's new covenant with Israel, which is extended to all humankind. In response, all those in Christ are called to anticipate eagerly this grand eschatological worship that entails them providing their account before God and his Christ.

The second relates to the sociopolitical-religious context of the readers. The letter to the Philippians is written by Paul to his fellow gentile Christians living in the Roman colony of Philippi where the figure of the deified emperor Augustus predominantly shapes its religious-political landscape. To the imperial society in this city, this *divus* Caesar is not only the founder, but also the greatest savior, lord (patron), and benefactor. His cult is popularly observed. His greatest benefaction, namely the re-establishment of the mythical Golden Age under his empire, is continuously acclaimed by the imperial power and its proponents. In this imperial-religious context, our christological passage makes a robust claim that Jesus is the real divine Lord to be worshipped by all creatures in the whole universe. This certainly has an anti-imperial stance, as it subversively criticizes the imperial propaganda surrounding this greatest Roman emperor, such as his divinity, salvation, ethos, and cult.

The third relates to Paul's rhetorical purpose and strategies in Philippians. This letter is written not merely as a thanksgiving note, but rather to address a complex predicament of the church of Christ in Philippi. This heavenly community is currently living in the pagan imperial society, which is not only perverse and corrupt before God but also hostile to the gospel of Christ. Hence, the congregation deeply suffers from various civic oppositions (1:27–30). Due to this harsh condition, many believers are losing their joy in following Christ (1:26; 2:18) and living with grumbling and disobedient attitudes (2:14). In addition to this, some prominent members are in conflict (4:2–3), which weakens this troubled church. To complicate the matters further, the congregation is also confused by the Judaizing teaching (3:2) and discouraged by those walking as the enemies of the cross of Christ (3:18–19). It is to address this complex situation that Paul writes this letter, particularly the sections in 1:27–2:18 and 3:2–4:4. The main purpose of these two major discourses is to encourage the readers to continue living worthily as the heavenly citizens according to the gospel of Christ (1:27), which basically calls them to live out their holiness as God's people until the day of the Lord Jesus Christ (1:10–11;

2:14–16; 3:10–11). As its practical application, the letter summons them to continue standing firmly in unity for the gospel of Christ and in the manner reflected in this gospel until his parousia.

The fourth relates to Paul's frame of mind. The significance of the universal eschatological worship of Christ in 2:10–11 is best set within Paul's "think this" statements noted in 1:7, 2:5, and 3:15, which all are apparently eschatological. It is argued that this worship motif is integral to Paul's theological reasoning of God's completing activity of his salvation until the day of Christ (1:6; 2:13) and his expectation that both he and the Philippian church will have a good standing before God on that very day (1:10–11; 3:9–11). In this triangular eschatological frame of thought, God's completing activity aims to establish believers of Christ as righteous and holy worshippers on the day of Christ, so that they all will be worthy to join the universal worship of Christ that marks God's consummation of his salvation.

In the wake of the considerations sketched above, this study proposes that Paul's various exhortations in this letter need to be appreciated within this triangular eschatological frame of mind, even if they are intended to address the present predicament of the Philippian congregation. This way of thinking calls and encourages the readers to actively participate in God's completing activity in and among them in anticipation of the grand worship of Christ at the eschaton. To be sure, this proposal needs to be exegetically demonstrated. This is done by detecting the three elements of Paul's eschatological frame of mind in the letter and then integrating them into his rhetorical strategy. Here, the exegetical analysis of 1:3–11, 1:27–2:18, and 3:2–4:4 plays an important role.

In the prayer report section, Paul not merely introduces some important themes to be developed in the letter, but also carefully shapes the readers' mindset in an eschatological direction. His theological reasoning directs the readers to appreciate that all their toils in their *koinonia* in the gospel of Christ are deeply embedded in God's activity to perfect his salvation in them until the day of Christ (1:5–6). Grounded in this divine faithful work is their eschatological assurance that God will establish them as holy worshippers on the day of Christ (1:10–11) to anticipate the grand worship of him (2:10–11). What is implicitly demanded from the readers is their active cooperation and participation in this divine activity. In all, Paul's eschatological frame of mind in this prayer report section functions to prepare the readers for the two major discourses in the letter.

In Philippians 1:27–2:18, Paul deals with the complex predicament of the Philippian congregation. The expectation of holiness can be justifiably broken down into four instructions (1:27–30; 2:2–4; 2:12–12; 2:14–16). As this holiness is shaped by the gospel of Christ (1:27), he calls the readers in 2:5 to adopt the frame of mind that arises from a deep reflection on the christological passage (2:6–11) in dealing with their predicaments. Having said this, Paul also strongly emphasizes that their toil in working out this Christ-like holiness is deeply embedded in God's powerful activity within them (2:13). This theological underpinning is derived from the earlier theological reasoning of God's completing activity of his salvation. The eschatological orientation of the instructions is supplied by the appearance of the term the day of Christ at the near end of the discourse (2:16). This phrase not only recalls the eschatological mindset and expectation in 1:6 and 1:10–11 but also establishes a strong correlation with the eschatological worship of Christ in 2:10–11. This connection is affirmed by the worship notion of Paul's exhortations in 2:12–18. All this demonstrates that Paul's instructions in this discourse call the readers to participate in God's activity in and among them, which will establish them as holy worshippers in anticipation of the universal worship of Christ at the eschaton. In this respect, we can say that the eschatological worship motif provides the ultimate goal of Paul's instructions.

Philippians 3:2–4:4 reiterates the necessity to stand firmly in unity in Christ, which requires the readers to suffer not only for Christ's sake but also in the manner of Christ's suffering for others. Here, Paul finds it necessary to provide greater encouragement for their persistence in this Christ-like holiness. This is done by calling them to imitate him (3:17) through the adoption of his way of thinking and living in 3:7–15, which is totally in opposition to the mindsets and conducts of the Judaizing Christians (3:2–6) and those living as the enemies of the cross of Christ (3:18–19). This eschatological reasoning is undoubtedly an application of the earlier "think this" activity (1:5–7 and 2:5–11), and this is a great encouragement to his readers, as it informs them that Paul, their συγκοινωνός, also applies to himself what he instructs them to do.

The presence of the elements of Paul's triangular eschatological frame of mind can be detected in this discourse. With regard to the holiness expectation, Paul's claim in 3:3 strongly underlines that their righteousness and holiness are based not on physical circumcision and the work of the Mosaic laws. Instead, it is fully grounded in Christ's faithfulness and their faith in him (3:9). This holiness is expressed as Christ-likeness (3:10–11), and it is also contrasted with the hedonistic life of those walking as the enemies of the cross of Christ (3:18–19). The claim "we are those worshipping by the Spirit" has an eschatological notion, as the Spirit is the agent of the realization of the eschatological realm in Christ. Hence, it anticipates their standing as the worshippers of Christ on judgment day. As it is the case in Philippians 1:27–2:18, the toils to fulfill this eschatological aim in the present discourse are deeply embedded in God's completing activity of his salvation (3:10–11; 3:21). In this light, although the motif of the universal eschatological worship of Christ is not explicitly depicted, this motif certainly lies beneath Philippians 3:2–4:4. The readers, whose mindsets have been greatly shaped by their reading of Philippians 1:3–11 and 1:27–2:18, should be able to discern this nexus at work.

In all, our proposal that the depiction of the universal eschatological worship of Christ provides an eschatological orientation for Paul's instructions in his letter to the Philippians can be well defended. The significance of this motif is grounded in the biblical vision of the universal eschatological worship of YHWH and is polemically set against the imperial claims surrounding the emperor Augustus. Conceptually, this motif is integral to Paul's eschatological frame of mind conveyed by his "think this" statements. Rhetorically, it befits Paul's purposes and strategies in the two major discourses of the letter, where it is generally recognized by scholars that the christological passage in 2:6–11 provides the fundamental ground for Paul's ethical instructions. Accordingly, the universal worship of Christ majestically pictured at the end of this christological passage (2:10–11) is foundational for the development of Paul's arguments and exhortations in the letter, as it serves to motivate the readers to prepare themselves for the worship of God and Christ at the eschaton in holiness.

As a final remark, the present study recognizes both the presence of the lordship-obedience and the humility/suffering-vindication motifs in understanding the rhetorical significance of the exaltation part of the christological passage. What is proposed in this study is that these two schemes are better situated within the context of the participation of the believers of Christ in

God's activity to complete/perfect his salvation in and among them. The lordship-obedience scheme works well in 1:27–2:18, as the life of obedience to God and Christ is highlighted. In Philippians 3:2–4:4, however, the humility/suffering-vindication scheme fits better, as both the demand to suffer as the believers of Christ and the expectation of God's final intervention to complete his salvation in Christ are highlighted.

Bibliography

Abegg, Martin G. "Time of Righteousness (4Q215a): Time of War or Time of Peace?" In *Prayer and Poetry in the Dead Sea Scrolls and Related Literature: Essays on Prayer and Poetry in the Dead Sea Scrolls and Related Literature in Honor of Eileen Schuller on the Occasion of Her 65th Birthday*, edited by Jeremy Penner, Ken M. Penner, and Cecilia Wassen, 1–12. STDJ 92. Leiden: Brill, 2012.

Abernethy, Andrew T. *The Book of Isaiah and God's Kingdom: A Thematic Theological Approach*. New Studies in Biblical Theology 40. Downers Grove: IVP, 2016.

Abrahamsen, Valerie A. *Women and Worship at Philippi: Diana/Artemis and Other Cults in the Early Christian Era*. Portland, OR: Astarte Shell Press, 1995.

Adkins, Lesley, and Roy Adkins. *Dictionary of Roman Religion*. Oxford: Oxford University Press, 1996.

Alcock, Susan E. *Graecia Capta: The Landscapes of Roman Greece*. Cambridge, UK: Cambridge University Press, 1996.

Alexander, Loveday. "Hellenistic Letter-Forms and the Structure of Philippians." *Journal for the Study of the New Testament* 12, no. 37 (1989): 87–101.

Appian. *Roman History, Volume V: Civil Wars, Books 3–4*. Edited and translated by Brian McGing. Loeb Classical Library 543. Cambridge, MA: Harvard University Press, 2020.

Aristotle. *Art of Rhetoric*. Translated by John Henry Freese and Gisela Striker. Loeb Classical Library 193. Cambridge, MA: Harvard University Press, 2020.

Athanassakis, Apostolos N. *Hesiod: Theogony, Works and Days, Shield*. Baltimore: Johns Hopkins University Press, 1983.

Aune, D. E. "Early Christian Worship." In *Anchor Bible Dictionary*, vol. 6, edited by David Noel Freedman, 973–89. New Haven: Yale University Press, 2008.

Baer, David A. *When We All Go Home: Translation and Theology in LXX Isaiah 56–66*. JSOTSup 318. Sheffield: Sheffield Academic Press, 2001.

Balentine, Samuel E. *The Torah's Vision of Worship*. Minneapolis: Fortress, 1999.

Baltzer, Klaus. *Deutero-Isaiah: A Commentary on Isaiah 40–55*. Hermeneia. Minneapolis: Fortress, 2001.

Balz, Horst. "Λατρεύω." *Exegetical Dictionary of the New Testament, vol. 2*, edited by Horst Balz and Gerhard Schneider, 344–45. Grand Rapids: Eerdmans, 1991.

Balz, Horst, and Gerhard Schneider, eds. *Exegetical Dictionary of the New Testament*. 3 vols. Grand Rapids: Eerdmans, 1990–1993.

Barclay, John M. G. *Paul and the Gift*. Grand Rapids: Eerdmans, 2015.

———. *Pauline Churches and Diaspora Jews*. Tubingen: Mohr Siebeck, 2011.

Barrett, Charles K. *The Acts of the Apostles: A Critical and Exegetical Commentary*. Vol. 2: *Acts XV–XXVIII*. ICC. London: T & T Clark, 1998.

Barth, Karl. *The Epistle to the Philippians*. 40th anniversary ed. Louisville: Westminster John Knox, 2002.

Bauckham, Richard. *Jesus and the God of Israel: God Crucified and Other Studies on the New Testament's Christology of Divine Identity*. Grand Rapids: Eerdmans, 2008.

———. "The Worship of Jesus in Philippians 2:9–11." In *Where Christology Began: Essays on Philippians 2*, edited by Ralph P. Martin and Brian J. Dodd, 128–39. Louisville: Westminster John Knox, 1998.

Bauer, Walter, Frederick W. Danker, William F. Arndt, and F. Wilbur Gingrich. *Greek-English Lexicon of the New Testament and Other Early Christian Literature*. 3rd ed. Chicago: University of Chicago Press, 2000.

Beale, G. K. *We Become What We Worship: A Biblical Theology of Idolatry*. Downers Grove: InterVarsity Press, 2008.

Beard, Mary, John A. North, and S. R. F. Price. *Religions of Rome: Volume 1, A History*. Cambridge, UK: Cambridge University Press, 1998.

Beare, Francis Wright. *A Commentary on the Epistle to the Philippians*. London: Black, 1959.

Beck, Norman A. *Anti-Roman Cryptograms in the New Testament: Hidden Transcripts of Hope and Liberation*. Rev. ed. New York: Lang, 2010.

Begg, Christopher T. "The Peoples and the Worship of Yahweh in the Book of Isaiah." In *Worship and the Hebrew Bible: Essays in Honour of John T. Willis*, edited by M. Patrick Graham, Rick R. Marrs, and Steven L. McKenzie, 35–55. Sheffield: Sheffield Academic Press, 1999.

Berges, Ulrich. "Kingship and Servanthood in the Book of Isaiah." In *The Book of Isaiah: Enduring Questions Answered Anew: Essays Honoring Joseph Blenkinsopp and His Contribution to the Study of Isaiah*, edited by Richard J. Bautch and J. Todd Hibbard, 159–78. Grand Rapids: Eerdmans, 2014.

Birnbaum, Philip, trans. *Daily Prayer Book – Ha-Siddur Ha-Shalem*. New York: Hebrew Publishing Company, 1995.

Blass, Friedrich, Albert Debrunner, and Robert Walter Funk. *A Greek Grammar of the New Testament and Other Christian Literature*. Chicago: University of Chicago Press, 1961.

Blenkinsopp, Joseph. *Isaiah 56–66: A New Translation with Introduction and Commentary*. AYBRL. New York: Doubleday, 2003.

———. *Opening the Sealed Book: Interpretations of the Book of Isaiah in Late Antiquity*. Grand Rapids: Eerdmans, 2006.

Block, Daniel I. "My Servant David: Ancient Israel's Vision of Messiah." In *Israel's Messiah in the Bible and the Dead Sea Scrolls*, edited by Richard S. Hess and M. Daniel Carrol R., 17–56. Grand Rapids: Baker, 2003.

Bloomquist, L. G. *The Function of Suffering in Philippians*. JSNTSup 78. Sheffield: Sheffield Academic Press, 1993.

Blumenfeld, Bruno. *The Political Paul: Justice, Democracy and Kingship in a Hellenistic Framework*. JSNTSup 210. Sheffield: Sheffield Academic Press, 2001.

Bockmuehl, Markus. *A Commentary on the Epistle to the Philippians*. London: Black, 1997.

———. "'The Form of God' (Phil. 2:6) Variations on a Theme of Jewish Mysticism." *Journal of Theological Studies* 48, no. 1 (1997): 1–23.

Boda, Mark J. "Figuring the Future: The Prophets and Messiah." In *The Messiah in the Old and New Testaments*, edited by Stanley E. Porter, 35–74. Grand Rapids: Eerdmans, 2007.

Bormann, Lukas. *Philippi: Stadt Und Christengemeinde Zur Zeit Des Paulus*. NovTSup v. 78. Leiden: Brill, 1995.

Bousset, Wilhelm. *Kyrios Christos: A History of the Belief in Christ from the Beginnings of Christianity to Irenaeus*. Translated by John E. Steely. 5th ed. Nashville: Abingdon, 1970.

Bowersock, G. W. *Augustus and the Greek World*. Oxford: Clarendon Press, 1965.

Brent, Allen. *A Political History of Early Christianity*. London: T & T Clark, 2009.

———. *The Imperial Cult and the Development of Church Order: Concepts and Images of Authority in Paganism and Early Christianity before the Age of Cyprian*. Boston: Brill, 1999.

Brower, K. E., and Andy Johnson. "Introduction: Holiness and Ekklesia of God." In *Holiness and Ecclesiology in the New Testament*, edited by Kent E. Brower and Andy Johnson, xvi–xxiv. Grand Rapids: Eerdmans, 2007.

Bruce, F. F. *Philippians*. NIBCNT 11. Peabody, MA: Hendrickson, 1989.

———. *The Book of the Acts*. Rev. ed. NICNT. Grand Rapids: Eerdmans, 1988.

Brueggemann, Walter. *Isaiah 1–39*. Louisville: Westminster John Knox, 1998.

———. *Isaiah 40–66*. Louisville: Westminster John Knox, 1998.

Bryan, Christopher. *Render to Caesar: Jesus, the Early Church, and the Roman Superpower*. Oxford: Oxford University Press, 2005.

Bultman. "Γινώσκω." In *Theological Dictionary of the New Testament*, vol. 1, edited by Gerhard Kittel and Gerhard Friedrich, translated by Geofrey W. Bromiley, 710. Grand Rapids: Eerdmans, 1964.

Burk, Denny. "On the Articular Infinitive in Philippians 2:6: A Grammatical Note with Christological Implications." *Tyndale Bulletin* 55, no. 2 (2004): 253–74.

Burkert, Walter. *Greek Religion*. Cambridge, MA: Harvard University Press, 1985.

Burnett, A. M., Michel Amandry, and P. P. Ripollés Alegre. *Roman Provincial Coinage Volume I, Part II: Indexes and Plates*. London: British Museum Press, 1998.

———. *Roman Provincial Coinage Volume I: From the Death of Caesar to the Death of Vitellius (44BC–AD69), Part I: Introduction and Catalogue*. London: British Museum Press, 1998.

Burrell, Barbara. *Neokoroi: Greek Cities and Roman Emperors*. Cincinnati Classical Studies. Leiden: Brill, 2004.

Butcher, Kevin. *Roman Provincial Coins: An Introduction to the "Greek Imperials."* London: Seaby, 1988.

Campbell, W. S. "Covenant and New Covenant." In *Dictionary of Paul and His Letters*, edited by Gerald F. Hawthorne, 179–83. Downers Grove: InterVarsity Press, 1999.

Cancik, Hubert. "The End of the World of History and of the Individual in Greek and Roman Antiquity." In *The Encyclopedia of Apocalypticism Volume I: The Origins of Apocalypticism in Judasim and Christianity*, edited by John J. Collins, 84–125. New York: Continuum, 1998.

Casey, P. M. *From Jewish Prophet to Gentile God: The Origins and Development of New Testament Christology*. Cambridge, UK: James Clarke & Co, 1992.

———. "Monotheism, Worship and Christological Development in the Pauline Churches." In *The Jewish Roots of Christological Monotheism: Papers from the St. Andrews Conference on the Historical Origins of the Worship of Jesus*, edited by Carey C. Newman, James R. Davila, and Gladys S. Lewis, 214–33. JSJSup v. 63. Leiden: Brill, 1999.

Cassidy, Richard J. *Paul in Chains: Roman Imprisonment and the Letters of St. Paul*. New York: Crossroad, 2001.

Castelli, Elizabeth A. *Imitating Paul: A Discourse of Power*. Louisville: Westminster John Knox, 1991.

Cathcart, K. J. "Day of Yahweh." *Anchor Bible Dictionary*, vol. 2, edited by David Noel Freedman, 84–85. New Haven: Yale University Press, 2008

Cerfaux, Lucien. *Christ in the Theology of St. Paul*. Translated by Geoffrey Webb. New York: Herder and Herder, 1959.

Chazon, Esther G., Donald W. Parry, and Eugene Charles Ulrich. "A Case of Mistaken Identity: Testament of Naphtali (4Q215) and Time of Righteousness (4Q215a)." In *The Provo International Conference on the Dead Sea Scrolls:*

Technological Innovations, New Texts, and Reformulated Issues, edited by Donald W. Parry and Eugene Ulrich, 111–23. Leiden: Brill, 1999.

Chazon, Esther G., and Michael E. Stone. "215a. 4QTime of Righteousness (Plate VIII)." In *Qumran Cave 4: Volume Xxvi: Cryptic Texts and Miscellanea, Part 1: Miscellaneus Text from Qumran*, edited by Stephen J. Pfann and Philip Alexander, 172–86. DJD 36. Oxford: Clarendon Press, 2000.

Chester, Andrew. "The Christ of Paul." In *Redemption and Resistance: The Messianic Hopes of Jews and Christians in Antiquity*, edited by Markus Bockmuehl and James Carleton Paget, 109–21. London: T & T Clark, 2007.

Chiala, Sabino, and Gabriele Boccaccini. "The Son of Man: The Evolution of an Expression." In *Enoch and the Messiah Son of Man: Revisiting the Book of Parables*, edited by Gabriele Boccaccini, 153–78. Grand Rapids: Eerdmans, 2007.

Chilton, Bruce, ed. *The Isaiah Targum: Introduction, Translation, Apparatus and Notes*. Wilmington: M. Glazier, 1987.

Cicero. *The Verrine Orations, Volume I: Against Caecilius. Against Verres, Part 1; Part 2, Books 1–2*. Translated by L. H. G. Greenwood. Loeb Classical Library 221. Cambridge, MA: Harvard University Press, 1928.

Clausen, Wendell Vernon. *A Commentary on Virgil, Eclogues*. Oxford: Oxford University Press, 1994.

Clauss, Manfred. *Kaiser Und Gott: Herrscherkult Im Römischen Reich*. Stuttgart: Teubner, 1999.

Cohick, Lynn H. *Philippians*. Story of God Bible Commentary. Grand Rapids: Zondervan, 2013.

———. "Philippians and Empire: Paul's Engagement with Imperialism and the Imperial Cult." In *Jesus Is Lord, Caesar Is Not: Evaluating Empire in New Testament Studies*, edited by Scot McKnight and Joseph B. Modica, 166–82. Downers Grove: InterVarsity Press, 2013.

Coleman, Robert. *Vergil: Eclogues*. Cambridge Greek and Latin Classics. Cambridge, UK: Cambridge University Press, 1994.

Colish, Marcia L. *The Stoic Tradition from Antiquity to the Early Middle Ages*. Vol. 1. Leiden: Brill, 1990.

Collins, Adela Yarbro. "Psalms, Philippians, and the Origins of Christology." *Biblical Interpretation* 11, no. 3 (2003): 361–72.

———. "The Worship of Jesus and the Imperial Cult." In *The Jewish Roots of Christological Monotheism: Papers from the St. Andrews Conference on the Historical Origins of the Worship of Jesus*, edited by Carey C. Newman, James R. Davila, and Gladys S. Lewis, 234–57. JSJSup 63. Leiden: Brill, 1999.

Collins, John J. *The Apocalyptic Imagination: An Introduction to Jewish Apocalyptic Literature*. 3rd ed. Grand Rapids: Eerdmans, 2016.

———. *Daniel: A Commentary on the Book of Daniel*. Hermeneia. Minneapolis: Fortress, 1993.

———. "The Expectation of the End in the Dead Sea Scrolls." In *Eschatology, Messianism, and the Dead Sea Scrolls*, edited by Craig A. Evans and Peter W. Flint, 74–90. Grand Rapids: Eerdmans, 1997.

———. *The Scepter and the Star: Messianism in Light of the Dead Sea Scrolls*. 2nd ed. Grand Rapids: Eerdmans, 2010.

Conzelmann, Hans. *Acts of the Apostles*. Hermeneia 58. Philadelphia: Fortress, 1987.

Cooley, Alison. *Res Gestae Divi Augusti: Text, Translation, and Commentary*. Cambridge, UK: Cambridge University Press, 2009.

Cousar, Charles B. *Philippians and Philemon*. Louisville: Westminster John Knox, 2009.

Coxhead, Steven R. "The Cardionomographic Work of the Spirit in the Old Testament." *Westminster Theological Journal* 79, no. 1 (2017): 77–95.

Cranfield, Charles E. B. *The Epistle to the Romans: A Critical and Exegetical Commentary*. Vol. 2, *Romans 9–16*. Edinburgh: T & T Clark, 1998.

Crossan, John Dominic, and Jonathan L. Reed. *In Search of Paul: How Jesus's Apostle Opposed Rome's Empire with God's Kingdom: A New Vision of Paul's Words and World*. New York: HarperCollins, 2005.

Danker, Frederick W., Walter Bauer, and William Arndt. "Κάμπτω." In *Greek-English Lexicon of the New Testament and Other Early Christian Literature*, 3rd ed., edited by Walter Bauer, William F. Arndt, F. Wilbur Gingrich, and Frederick W. Danker. Chicago: University of Chicago Press, 2000.

Davenport, Gener L. "The 'Anointed of the Lord' in Psalm of Solomon 17." In *Ideal Figures in Ancient Judaism: Profiles and Paradigms*, edited by John J. Collins and George W. E. Nickelsburg, 67–92. Chico: Scholars Press, 1980.

Davies, Philip R. *Daniel*. Old Testament Guides. Sheffield: JSOT Press, 1993.

Davies, W. D. *Paul and Rabbinic Judaism: Some Rabbinic Elements in Pauline Theology*. 4th ed. Philadelphia: Fortress, 1980.

De Vos, Craig Steven. *Church and Community Conflicts: The Relationships of the Thessalonian, Corinthian, and Philippian Churches with Their Wider Civic Communities*. Society of Biblical Literature Dissertation Series no. 168. Atlanta: Scholars Press, 1999.

Delling, Gerhard. "Αἴσθησις." In *Theological Dictionary of the New Testament*. Vol. 1, edited by Gerhard Kittel and Gerhard Friedrich, translated by Geoffrey W. Bromiley, 187–88. Grand Rapids: Eerdmans, 1964.

Di Sante, Carmine. *Jewish Prayer: The Origins of the Christian Liturgy*. New York: Paulist Press, 1991.

Dio, Cassius. *Roman History.* Translated by Earnerst Cary and Herbert Baldwin Foster. Loeb Classical Library 83. Cambridge, MA: Harvard University Press, 2000.

Diodorus, Siculus. *Library of History: Books XV.12–XVI.65.* Translated by Charles L. Sherman. Loeb Classical Library 389. Cambridge, MA: Harvard University Press, 1980.

Doble, Peter. "'Vile Bodies' or Transformed Person? Philippians 3:21 in Context." *Journal for the Study of the New Testament* 24, no. 4 (2002): 3–27.

Dodd, Brian J. "The Story of Christ and the Imitation of Paul in Philippians 2–3." In *Where Christology Began: Essays on Philippians 2*, edited by Ralph P. Martin and Brian J. Dodd, 154–61. Louisville: Westminster John Knox, 1998.

Doty, William G. *Letters in Primitive Christianity.* Philadelphia: Fortress, 1973.

Dunn, James D. G. "Christ, Adam, and Preexistence." In *Where Christology Began: Essays on Philippians 2*, edited by Ralph P. Martin and Brian J. Dodd, 74–83. Louisville: Westminster John Knox, 1998.

———. *Christology in the Making: A New Testament Inquiry into the Origins of the Doctrine of the Incarnation.* 2nd ed. Grand Rapids: Eerdmans, 1996.

———. *Romans 9–16.* Word Biblical Commentary 38b. Waco, TX: Word Books, 1988.

———. *The Theology of Paul the Apostle.* Grand Rapids: Eerdmans, 1998.

Elgvin, Torleif. "The Eschatological Hope of 4QTime of Righteousness." In *Wisdom and Apocalypticism in the Dead Sea Scrolls and in the Biblical Tradition*, edited by F. García Martínez, 89–102. BETL 168. Leuven: Leuven University Press, 2003.

Elgvin, Torleif, and Årstein Justnes. "Appendix: 4Q215a, FRGS: 1, 2, 3, and 4 – Text and Notes." In *Sapiential Perspectives: Wisdom Literature in Light of the Dead Sea Scrolls: Proceedings of the Sixth International Symposium of the Orion Center for the Study of the Dead Sea Scrolls and Associated Literature, 20–22 May, 2001*, edited by John J. Collins, Gregory E. Sterling, and Ruth Clements, 162–70. STDJ 51. Leiden: Brill, 2004.

Elgvin, Torleif, and Eileen M. Schuller. "Wisdom With or Without Apocalyptic." In *Sapiential, Liturgical, and Poetical Texts from Qumran: Proceedings of the Third Meeting of the International Organization for Qumran Studies, Oslo, 1998: Published in Memory of Maurice Baillet*, edited by Daniel K. Falk and Florentino García Martínez, 15–38. Leiden: Brill, 2000.

Elliott, Neil. *The Arrogance of Nations: Reading Romans in the Shadow of Empire.* Minneapolis: Fortress, 2010.

Evans, Craig A. "The Messiah in the Dead Sea Scrolls." In *Israel's Messiah in the Bible and the Dead Sea Scrolls*, edited by Richard S. Hess and M. Daniel Carroll R., 85–102. Grand Rapids: Baker Academic, 2003.

Fabricatore, Daniel J. *Form of God, Form of a Servant: An Examination of the Greek Noun Μορφη in Philippians 2:6–7*. Lanham, MD: University Press of America, 2010.

Favro, Diane. "Making Rome a Word City." In *The Cambridge Companion to the Age of Augustus*, edited by Karl Galinsky, 234–63. Cambridge Companion to the Classics. Cambridge, UK: Cambridge University Press, 2005.

Fear, J. Rufus. "Ruler Worship." In *Civilization of the Ancient Mediterranean: Greece and Rome*, edited by Michael Grant and Rachel Kitzinger, 1009–25. New York: Scribner's Sons, 1988.

Fee, Gordon D. *Pauline Christology: An Exegetical-Theological Study*. Grand Rapids: Baker, 2013.

———. *Paul's Letter to the Philippians*. NICNT. Grand Rapids: Eerdmans, 1995.

———. "Philippians 2:5–11: Hymn or Exalted Pauline Prose?" *Bulletin for Biblical Research* 2 (1992): 29–46.

First, Mitchell. "Aleinu: Obligation to Fix the World or the Text." *Hakirah* 11 (2011): 187–97.

Fishwick, Duncan. *The Imperial Cult in the Latin West: Studies in the Ruler Cult of the Western Provinces of the Roman Empire*. Vol. I.1. Leiden: Brill, 1987.

Fitzmyer, Joseph A. *The Acts of the Apostles*. AYBRL. New York: Doubleday, 1998.

———. *Romans: A New Translation with Introduction and Commentary*. AYBRL. New Haven: Yale University Press, 2008.

———. "Κύριος." In *Exegetical Dictionary of the New Testament*. Vol. 2, edited by Horst Balz and Gerhard Schneider, 328–31. Grand Rapids: Eerdmans, 1991.

Flesher, Paul Virgil McCracken, and Bruce Chilton. *The Targums: A Critical Introduction*. Leiden: Brill, 2011.

Flint, Peter W. "Interpreting the Poetry of Isaiah at Qumran: The Theme and Function in the Sectarian Scrolls." In *Prayer and Poetry in the Dead Sea Scrolls and Related Literature: Essays on Prayer and Poetry in the Dead Sea Scrolls and Related Literature in Honor of Eileen Schuller on the Occasion of Her 65th Birthday*, edited by Eileen M. Schuller, Jeremy Penner, Ken M. Penner, and Cecilia Wassen, 161–96. STDJ 98. Leiden: Brill, 2012.

———. "The Interpretation of Scriptural Isaiah in the Qumran Scrolls: Quotation, Citation, Allusions, and the Form of the Scriptural Source Text." In *A Teacher for All Generations: Essays in Honor of James C. Vanderkam*, edited by Eric Farrel Mason, 389–406. JSJSup 153. Leiden: Brill, 2012.

Fossum, Jarl E. *The Name of God and the Angel of the Lord: Samaritan and Jewish Concept of Intermediation and the Origin of Gnosticism*. WUNT 36. Tübingen: Mohr, 1985.

Fowl, Stephen E. "Christology and Ethics in Philippians 2:5–11." In *Where Christology Began: Essays on Philippians 2*, edited by Ralph P. Martin and Brian J. Dodd, 140–153. Louisville: Westminster John Knox, 1998.

———. *Philippians*. THNTC. Grand Rapids: Eerdmans, 2005.

———. *The Story of Christ in the Ethics of Paul: An Analysis of the Function of the Hymnic Material in the Pauline Corpus*. JSNTSup 36. Sheffield: JSOT Press, 1990.

Friesen, Steven J. *Imperial Cults and the Apocalypse of John: Reading Revelation in the Ruins*. Oxford: Oxford University Press, 2001.

Galinsky, Karl. *Augustan Culture: An Interpretive Introduction*. Princeton: Princeton University Press, 1996.

Gammie, John G. *Holiness in Israel*. Minneapolis: Fortress, 1989.

Garland, David E. "The Composition and Unity of Philippians: Some Neglected Literary Factors." *Novum Testamentum* 27, no. 2 (1985): 141–73.

Georgi, Dieter. *Theocracy in Paul's Praxis and Theology*. Minneapolis: Fortress, 2009.

Gnilka, Joachim. *The Epistle to the Philippians*. London: Sheed & Ward, 1971.

Goldingay, John. *Psalms Volume 1: Psalms 1–41*. BCOTWP. Grand Rapids: Baker Academic, 2006.

———. *Psalms Volume 2: Psalms 42–89*. BCOTWP. Grand Rapids: Baker Academic, 2007.

———. *The Message of Isaiah 40–55: A Literary-Theological Commentary*. London : T & T Clark, 2005.

———. "The Theology of Isaiah." In *Interpreting Isaiah: Issues and Approaches*, edited by David G. Firth and H. G. M., 168–190. Williamson. Nottingham: Apollos, 2009.

Goldingay, John, and David F. Payne. *Isaiah 40–55: A Critical and Exegetical Commentary*. Vol. 2. Edinburgh: T & T Clark, 2014.

Goldstein, H. "Εἰλικρινής." *Exegetical Dictionary of the New Testament*. Vol. 1, edited by Horst Balz and Gerhard Schneider, 391. Grand Rapids: Eerdmans, 1990.

Gorman, Michael J. *Apostle of the Crucified Lord: A Theological Introduction to Paul & His Letters*. 2nd ed. Grand Rapids: Eerdmans, 2017.

———. *Inhabiting the Cruciform God: Kenosis, Justification, and Theosis in Paul's Narrative Soteriology*. Grand Rapids: Eerdmans, 2009.

———. "'You Shall Be Cruciform for I Am Cruciform': Paul's Trinitarian Reconstruction of Holiness." In *Holiness and Ecclesiology in the New Testament*, edited by K. E. Brower and Andy Johnson, 148–83. Grand Rapids: Eerdmans, 2007.

Gowan, Donald E. *Eschatology in the Old Testament*. 2nd ed. Edinburgh: T & T Clack, 2000.

———. *Theology in Exodus: Biblical Theology in the Form of a Commentary*. Louisville: Westminster John Knox, 1994.

Gradel, Ittai. *Emperor Worship and Roman Religion*. Oxford: Oxford University Press, 2002.

Grant, Michael. *From Imperium to Auctoritas: A Historical Study of Aes Coinage in the Roman Empire (49 BC – AD 14)*. Cambridge, UK: Cambridge University Press, 1946.

Green, J. B. "Crucifixion." *Dictionary of Paul and his Letters*, edited by Daniel G. Reid, Gerald F. Hawthorne, and Ralph P. Martin, 178–85. Downers Grove: InterVarsity Press, 1993.

Grieb, A. Katherine. *The Story of Romans: A Narrative Defense of God's Righteousness*. Louisville: Westminster John Knox, 2002.

Grisanti, Michael A. "שׁע." In *New International Dictionary of Old Testament Theology and Exegesis*. Vol. 4, edited by Willem A. VanGemeren, 97. Grand Rapids: Zondervan, 1997.

Gupta, Nijay K. *Worship That Makes Sense to Paul: A New Approach to the Theology and Ethics of Paul's Cultic Metaphors*. Berlin: De Gruyter, 2010.

Haber, Susan. *"They Shall Purify Themselves": Essays on Purity in Early Judaism*. Edited by Adele Reinhartz. Early Judaism and Its Literature 24. Atlanta: SBL Press, 2008.

Hadas, Moses. *Hellenistic Culture: Fusion and Diffusion*. New York: Columbia University Press, 1959.

Hahn, Ferdinand. *The Titles of Jesus in Christology*. London: Lutterworth, 1969.

Hamborg, Graham R. "Reasons for Judgement in the Oracles against the Nations of the Prophet Isaiah." *Vetus Testamentum* 31, no. 2 (1981): 145–59.

Hansen, G. Walter. *The Letter to the Philippians*. The Pillar New Testament Commentary. Grand Rapids: Eerdmans, 2009.

Hardie, Philip R. *Virgil*. Greece & Rome 28. Oxford: Oxford University Press, 1998.

Hardin, Justin K. *Galatians and the Imperial Cult: A Critical Analysis of the First-Century Social Context of Paul's Letter*. WUNT 237. Tübingen: Mohr Siebeck, 2008.

Harris, Murray J. *Slave of Christ: A New Testament Metaphor for Total Devotion to Christ*. New Studies in Biblical Theology 8. Downers Grove: InterVarsity Press, 2001.

Hartley, J. E. "Holy and Holiness, Clean and Unclean." In *Dictionary of the Old Testament: Pentateuch*, edited by T. Desmond Alexander and David W. Baker, 420–31. Downers Grove: InterVarsity Press, 2003.

Hawthorne, Gerald F. "In the Form of God and Equal with God (Philippians 2:6)." In *Where Christology Began: Essays on Philippians 2*, edited by Ralph M. Martin and Brian J. Dodd, 96–110. Louisville: Westminster John Knox, 1998.

———. "The Imitation of Christ: Discipleship in Philippians." In *Patterns of Discipleship in the New Testament*, edited by Richard N. Longenecker, 163–80. Grand Rapids: Eerdmans, 1996.

———. *Philippians.* Word Biblical Commentary 43. Waco: Word Books, 1983.

Hawthorne, Gerald F., and Ralph P. Martin. *Philippians.* 2nd ed. Word Biblical Commentary 43. Nashville: Nelson, 1999.

Hays, Richard B. *The Conversion of the Imagination: Paul as Interpreter of Israel's Scripture.* Grand Rapids: Eerdmans, 2005.

———. *Echoes of Scripture in the Letters of Paul.* New Haven: Yale University Press, 1989.

———. *The Faith of Jesus Christ: The Narrative Substructure of Galatians 3:1–4:11.* 2nd ed. Grand Rapids: Eerdmans, 1997.

Heen, Erik M. "Phil 2:6–11 and Resistance to Local Timocratic Rule: *Isa Theo* and the Cult of the Emperor in the East." In *Paul and the Roman Imperial Order,* edited by Richard A. Horsley, 125–54. Harrisburg: Trinity Press International, 2004.

Hellerman, Joseph H. *Reconstructing Honor in Roman Philippi: Carmen Christi as Cursus Pudorum.* SNTSMS 132. Cambridge, UK: Cambridge University Press, 2005.

———. "Μορφη Θεου as a Signifier of Social Status in Philippians 2:6." *Journal of the Evangelical Theological Society* 52, no. 4 (2009): 779–97.

Hempel, Charlotte. "The Gems of DJD 36: Reflection on Some Recently Published Texts." *Journal of Jewish Studies* 54, no. 1 (2003): 146–52.

Hengel, Martin. *Between Jesus and Paul: Studies in the Earliest History of Christianity.* London: SCM Press, 1983.

———. *Crucifixion.* London: SCM Press, 1977.

———. *Studies in Early Christology.* London: T & T Clark, 2004.

Hengel, Martin, and Daniel P. Bailey. "The Effective History of Isaiah 53 in the Pre-Christian Period." In *The Suffering Servant: Isaiah 53 in Jewish and Christian Sources,* edited by Bernd Janowski and Peter Stuhlmacher, 75–146. Grand Rapids: Eerdmans, 2004.

Hesiod. *Theogony. Works and Days. Testimonia.* Edited and translated by Glenn W. Most. Loeb Classical Library 57. Cambridge, MA: Harvard University Press, 2018.

Hoffman, Lawrence A. *Gates of Understanding 2: Appreciating the Days of Awe.* New York: Published for the Central Conference of American Rabbis by the Union of American Hebrew Congregations, 1984.

Hofius, Otfried. *Der Christushymnus Philipper 2,6 – 11: Untersuchungen zu Gestalt und Aussage eines urchristlichen Psalms.* Wissenschaftliche Untersuchungen zum Neuen Testament 17. Tübingen: Mohr, 1991.

———. "Ἐξομολογέω." *Exegetical Dictionary of the New Testament.* Vol. 2, edited by Horst Balz and Gerhard Schneider, 8–9. Grand Rapids: Eerdmans, 1991.

Holloway, Joseph O. Περιπατεω *as a Thematic Marker for Pauline Ethics.* San Francisco: Mellen Research University Press, 1992.

Holmes, Michael W., ed. *The Apostolic Fathers: Greek Texts and English Translations*. 3rd ed. Grand Rapids: Baker Academic, 2007.

Homer. *The Odyssey*. Translated by A. T. Murray and George E. Dimock. 2 vols. Loeb Classical Library 104–105. Cambridge, MA: Harvard University Press, 1995.

Hooker, Morna Dorothy. "Interchange in Christ." In *From Adam to Christ*, 13–25. Cambridge, UK: Cambridge University Press, 1990.

———. *Jesus and the Servant: The Influence of the Servant Concept of Deutero-Isaiah in the New Testament*. London: SPCK, 1959.

———. "A Partner in the Gospel: Paul's Understanding of His Ministry." In *Theology and Ethics in Paul and His Interpreters: Essays in Honor of Victor Paul Furnish*, edited by E. H. Lovering, Jr. and J. L. Sumney, 83–100. Nashville: Abingdon, 1996.

———. "Philippians 2.6–11." In *From Adam to Christ*, 88–100. Cambridge, UK: Cambridge University Press, 1990.

Hoover, Roy W. "The Harpagmos Enigma: A Philological Solution." *Harvard Theological Review* 64, no. 1 (1971): 95–119.

Horace. *Odes and Epodes*. Edited and translated by Niall Rudd. Loeb Classical Library 33. Cambridge, MA: Harvard University Press, 2004.

Horbury, William. *Jewish Messianism and the Cult of Christ*. London: SCM Press, 1998.

Horsley, Richard A., ed. *Paul and Politics: Ekklesia, Israel, Imperium, Interpretation: Essays in Honor of Krister Stendahl*. Harrisburg: Trinity Press International, 2000.

———, ed. *Paul and the Roman Imperial Order*. Harrisburg: Trinity Press International, 2004.

Howard, George. "Phil 2:6–11 and the Human Christ." *Catholic Biblical Quarterly* 40, no. 3 (1978): 368–87.

Hurtado, Larry W. "A 'Case Study' in Early Christian Devotion to Jesus: Philippians 2:6–11." In *How on Earth Did Jesus Become a God? Historical Questions About Earliest Devotion to Jesus*, 83–107. Grand Rapids: Eerdmans, 2005.

———. "Jesus as Lordly Example in Philippians 2:5–11." In *From Jesus to Paul: Studies in Honour of Francis Wright Beare*, edited by Peter Richardson and John Coolidge Hurd, 113–26. Waterloo: Wilfrid Laurier University Press, 1984.

———. *Lord Jesus Christ: Devotion to Jesus in Earliest Christianity*. Grand Rapids: Eerdmans, 2005.

Hwang, Jerry. "Turning the Tables on Idol Feasts: Paul's Use of Exodus 32:6 in 1 Corinthians 10:7." *Journal of the Evangelical Theological Society* 54, no. 3 (2011): 573–87.

Isaac, E. "1 (Ethiopic Apocalypse of) Enoch: A New Translation and Introduction." In *The Old Testament Pseudepigrapha: Apocalyptic Literature & Testaments*, vol. 1, edited by James H. Charlesworth, 5–90. Garden City: Doubleday, 1983.

Jackson, T. Ryan. *New Creation in Paul's Letters: A Study of the Historical and Social Setting of a Pauline Concept*. WUNT 2 272. Tübingen: Mohr Siebeck, 2010.

Janzen, W. "Earth." In *Anchor Bible Dictionary*, vol. 2, edited by David Noel Freedman, 245–48. New Haven: Yale University Press, 2008

Jassen, Alex P. "Survival at the End of Days: Aspects of Soteriology in the Dead Sea Scrolls Pesharim." In *This World and the World to Come: Soteriology in Early Judaism*, edited by Daniel M. Gurtner, 193–210. LSTS 74. London: T & T Clark, 2011.

Jeremias, Joachim. "Zu Phil 2:7: EAYTON EKENΩΣEN." *Novum Testamentum* 6, nos. 2–3 (1963): 182–88.

Jewett, Robert. "The Corruption and Redemption of Creation: Reading Rom 8:18–23 within the Imperial Context." In *Paul and the Roman Imperial Order*, edited by Richard A. Horsley, 25–46. Harrisburg: Trinity Press International, 2004.

———. "The Epistolary Thanksgiving and the Integrity of Philippians." *Novum Testamentum* 12, no. 1 (1970): 40–53.

Johnson, Luke Timothy. *The Acts of the Apostles*. Collegeville: Liturgical Press, 1992.

Johnston, Patricia A. *Vergil's Agricultural Golden Age: A Study of the Georgics*. Leiden: Brill, 1980.

Johnston, Philip. *Shades of Sheol: Death and Afterlife in the Old Testament*. Leicester: Apollos, 2002.

Jonge, Martinus De. "Messiah." In *Anchor Bible Dictionary*, vol. 4, edited by David Noel Freedman, 777–78. New Haven: Yale University Press, 2008.

Jowers, Dennis W. "The Meaning of Mορφή in Philippians 2:6–7." *Journal of the Evangelical Theological Society* 49, no. 4 (2006): 739–66.

Justnes, Årstein. "4Q215A (Time of Righteousness) in Context." In *Sapiential Perspectives: Wisdom Literature in Light of the Dead Sea Scrolls: Proceedings of the Sixth International Symposium of the Orion Center for the Study of the Dead Sea Scrolls and Associated Literature, 20–22 May, 2001*, edited by Orion Center for the Study of the Dead Sea Scrolls and Associated Literature, John J. Collins, Gregory E. Sterling, and Ruth Clements, 141–61. STDJ 51. Leiden: Brill, 2004.

———. *The Time of Salvation: An Analysis of 4QApocryphon of Daniel Ar (4Q246), 4QMessianic Apocalypse (4Q521 2), and 4QTime of Righteousness (4Q215a)*. New York: Lang, 2009.

Kaminsky, Joel S., and Anne Stewart. "God of All the World: Universalism and Developing Monotheism in Isaiah 40–66." *Harvard Theological Review* 99, no. 2 (2006): 139–63.

Käsemann, Ernst. "A Critical Analysis of Philippians 2:5–11." Translated by Alice F. Carse. In *God and Christ: Existence and Province*, edited by R. W. Funk, *Journal for Theology and Church* 5, 45–88. New York: Harper & Row, 1968.

Kaylor, R. D. *Paul's Covenant Community: Jew and Gentile in Romans*. Atlanta: John Knox, 1988.

Keown, Mark J. *Congregational Evangelism in Philippians: The Centrality of an Appeal for Gospel Proclamation to the Fabric of Philippians*. Milton Keynes: Paternoster, 2008.

Kim, Seyoon. *Christ and Caesar: The Gospel and the Roman Empire in the Writings of Paul and Luke*. Grand Rapids: Eerdmans, 2008.

Kittle, Gerhard, and Gerhard Friedrich, eds. *Theological Dictionary of the New Testament*. Translated by Geofrey W. Bromiley. 10 vols. Grand Rapids: Eerdmans, 1964–1976.

Klauck, Hans-Josef, and Brian McNeil. *The Religious Context of Early Christianity: A Guide to Graeco-Roman Religions*. London: T & T Clark, 2003.

Klawans, Jonathan. *Impurity and Sin in Ancient Judaism*. New York: Oxford University Press, 2000.

Klein, Ralph W. *Israel in Exile: A Theological Interpretation*. Philadelphia: Fortress, 1979.

Knox, Wilfred Lawrence. "The 'Divine Hero' Christology in the New Testament." *Harvard Theological Review* 41, no. 4 (1948): 229–49.

Koole, Jan L. *Isaiah III: Volume 3 / Isaiah 56–66*. HCOT. Kampen: Kok Pharos, 1997.

Koperski, Veronica. *The Knowledge of Christ Jesus My Lord: The High Christology of Philippians 3:7–11*. CBET 16. Kampen: Kok Pharos, 1996.

Koukouli-Chrysantaki, Chaido. "Colonia Iulia Augusta Philippensis." In *Philippi at the Time of Paul and After His Death*, edited by Charalampos Bakirtzēs and Helmut Koester, 5–35. Harrisburg: Trinity Press International, 1998.

Kratz, Reinhard Gregor. "Israel in the Book of Isaiah." *Journal for the Study of the Old Testament* 31, no. 1 (2006): 103–28.

Kraus, Hans-Joachim. *Psalms 1–59*. Continental Commentary. Minneapolis: Fortress, 1993.

Kreitzer, Larry Joseph. *Jesus and God in Paul's Eschatology*. JSNTSup 19. Sheffield: JSOT Press, 1987.

———. "The Kingdom of God." In *Dictionary of Paul and His Letters*, edited by Daniel G. Reid, Gerald F. Hawthorne, and Ralph P. Martin, 524–26. Downers Grove: InterVarsity Press, 1993.

———. *Striking New Images: Roman Imperial Coinage and the New Testament World*. Sheffield: Sheffield Academic Press, 1996.

———. "'When He at Last Is First!': Philippians 2:9–11 and the Exaltation of the Lord." In *Where Christology Began: Essays on Philippians 2*, edited by Ralph P. Martin and Brian J. Dodd, 111–28. Louisville: Westminster John Knox, 1998.

Kugel, James L. "Early Jewish Biblical Interpretation." In *The Eerdmans Dictionary of Early Judaism*, edited by John J. Collins and Daniel C. Harlow, 121–41. Grand Rapids: Eerdmans, 2010.

Kurz, William S. "Kenotic Imitation of Paul and of Christ in Philippians 2 and 3." In *Patterns of Discipleship in the New Testament*, edited by Richard N. Longenecker, 103–26. Grand Rapids: Eerdmans, 1996.

Leclerc, Thomas L. *Yahweh Is Exalted in Justice: Solidarity and Conflict in Isaiah*. Minneapolis: Fortress, 2001.

Leighton, Matthew B. "'Mosaic Covenant' as a Possible Referent for NOMOΣ In Paul." *Tyndale Bulletin* 69, no. 2 (2018): 161–81.

Levenson, Jon D. *Sinai & Zion: An Entry into the Jewish Bible*. San Francisco: Harper & Row, 1987.

Liddell, Henry George, Robert Scott, and Hendry Stuart Jones. *A Greek-English Lexicon*. 9th ed. Oxford: Clarendon, 1996.

Lightfoot, J. B. *Saint Paul's Epistle to the Philippians*. Grand Rapids: Zondervan, 1953.

Lindsey, F. Duane. *The Servant Songs: A Study in Isaiah*. Chicago: Moody Press, 1985.

Lipka, Michael. *Roman Gods: A Conceptual Approach*. Leiden: Brill, 2009.

Lohmeyer, Ernst. *Kyrios Jesus: Eine Untersuchung Zu Phil. 2,5–11*. Sitzungsberichte Der Heidelberger Akademie Der Wissenchaften, Philosophisch-Historische Klasse. Heidelberg: Carl Winter, 1961.

MacDonald, Nathan. "Monotheism and Isaiah." In *Interpreting Isaiah: Issues and Approaches*, edited by David G. Firth and H. G. M. Williamson, 43–61. Nottingham: Apollos, 2009.

MacLeod, David J. "The Exaltation of Christ: An Exposition of Philippians 2:9–11." *Bibliotheca Sacra* 158, no. 632 (2001): 437–50.

Mahoney, R. "Ἐπιτελέω." In *Exegetical Dictionary of the New Testament*, vol. 1, edited by Horst Balz and Gerhard Schneider, 42. Grand Rapids: Eerdmans, 1990.

Marshall, Howard. *The Epistle to the Philippians*. London: Epworth Press, 1992.

Martens, E. A. "Eschatology." In *Dictionary of the Old Testament Prophets*, edited by Mark J. Boda and J. Gordon McConville, 178. Downers Grove: InterVarsity Press, 2012.

Martin, Michael W., and Bryan A. Nash. "Philippians 2:6–11 as Subversive 'Hymnos': A Study in the Light of Ancient Rhetorical Theory." *Journal of Theological Studies* 66, no. 1 (2015): 90–138.

Martin, Ralph P. "The Christology in the Prison Epistles." In *Contours of Christology in the New Testament*, edited by Richard N. Longenecker, 183–218. Grand Rapids: Eerdmans, 2005.

———. *A Hymn of Christ: Philippians 2:5–11 in Recent Interpretation & in the Setting of Early Christian Worship*. Downers Grove: InterVarsity Press, 1997.

———. *Philippians*. NCBC. Grand Rapids: Eerdmans, 1980.

Martin, Troy W. "Circumcision in Galatia and the Holiness of God's Ecclesiae." In *Holiness and Ecclesiology in the New Testament*, edited by K. E. Brower and Andy Johnson, 219–237. Grand Rapids: Eerdmans, 2007.

Mattingly, Harold. *Roman Coins from the Earliest Times to the Fall of the Western Empire*. Chicago: Quadrangle Books, 1960.

McCarthy, Dennis J. *Treaty and Covenant: A Study in Form in the Ancient Oriental Documents and in the Old Testament*. New edition. Rome: Pontifical Biblical Institute, 1981.

Meadowcroft, T. J. *Aramaic Daniel and Greek Daniel: A Literary Comparison*. JSOTSup 198. Sheffield: Sheffield Academic Press, 1995.

Meadowcroft, T. J., and Nate Irwin. *The Book of Daniel: A Commentary on the New International Version*. Singapore: Asia Theological Association, 2004.

Meeks, Wayne A. "The Man from Heaven in Paul's Letter to the Philippians." In *The Future of Early Christianity: Essays in Honor of Helmut Koester*, edited by Birger A. Pearson, 329–36. Minneapolis: Fortress, 1991.

Mellor, Ronald, ed. *The Historians of Ancient Rome: An Anthology of the Major Writings*. New York: Routledge, 1998.

Moo, Douglas J. *The Epistle to the Romans*. NICNT. Grand Rapids: Eerdmans, 1996.

Moule, C. F. D. "Further Reflection on Philippians 2:5–11." In *Apostolic History and the Gospel: Biblical and Historical Essays Presented to F. F. Bruce on His 60th Birthday*, edited by W. Ward Gasque and Ralph P. Martin, 264–76. Exeter: Paternoster, 1970.

Mowinckel, Sigmund. *The Psalms in Israel's Worship*. Grand Rapids: Eerdmans, 2004.

Moyise, Steve. *Paul and Scripture*. London: SPCK, 2010.

Muraoka, T. *A Greek-English Lexicon of the Septuagint*. Rev. ed. Louvain: Peeters, 2009.

Murphy-O'Connor, J. *Paul the Letter-Writer: His World, His Options, His Skills*. Collegeville: Liturgical Press, 1995.

Nagata, Takeshi. "Philippians 2:5–11: A Case Study in the Contextual Shaping of Early Christianity." PhD Dissertation, Princeton Theological Seminary, 1981.

Nebreda, Sergio Rosell. *Christ Identity: A Social-Scientific Reading of Philippians 2.5–11.* FRLANT 240. Göttingen: Vandenhoeck & Ruprecht, 2011.

Nestle, Eberhard, Erwin Nestle, Barbara Aland, Kurt Aland, Iōan. D. Karavidopoulos, Carlo Maria Martini, Bruce M. Metzger, and Holger Strutwolf, eds. *Novum Testamentum Graece.* 28th ed. Stuttgart: Deutsche Bibelgesellschaft, 2012.

Nickelsburg, George W. E., and James C. VanderKam. *1 Enoch 2: A Commentary on the Book of 1 Enoch Chapters 37–82.* Edited by Klaus Baltzer. Hermeneia. Minneapolis: Fortress, 2012.

Nisbet, R. G. M. "Virgil's Fourth Eclogue: Easterners and Westerners." In *Vergil's Eclogues*, edited by Katharina Volk, 155–88. New York: Oxford University Press, 2008.

Niskanen, Paul. "Yhwh as Father, Redeemer, and Potter in Isaiah 63:7–64:11." *Catholic Biblical Quarterly* 68, no. 3 (2006): 397–407.

Oakes, Peter. "Made Holy by the Holy Spirit: Holiness and Ecclesiology in Romans." In *Holiness and Ecclesiology in the New Testament*, edited by K. E. Brower and Andy Johnson, 167–83. Grand Rapids: Eerdmans, 2007.

———. *Philippians: From People to Letter.* SNTSMS. Cambridge, UK: Cambridge University Press, 2007.

———. "Re-Mapping the Universe: Paul and the Emperor in 1 Thessalonians and Philippians." *Journal for the Study of the New Testament* 27, no. 3 (2005): 301–22.

O'Brien, Peter Thomas. *The Epistle to the Philippians: A Commentary on the Greek Text.* NIGTC. Grand Rapids: Eerdmans, 1991.

O'Collins, Gerald G. "Crucifixion." *Anchor Bible Dictionary*, vol. 1, edited by edited by David Noel Freedman, 1207–8. New Haven: Yale University Press, 2008.

Oswalt, John. *The Book of Isaiah: Chapters 40–66.* NICOT. Grand Rapids: Eerdmans, 1998.

———. *The Holy One of Israel: Studies in the Book of Isaiah.* Eugene: Cascade Books, 2014.

Oxford English Dictionary. 2nd ed. Oxford: Oxford University press, 2001.

Ovid. *Metamorphoses, Volume I: Book 1–8.* Translated by Frank Justus Miller. Revised by G. P. Goold. Loeb Classical Library 42. Cambridge, MA: Harvard University Press, 1916.

———. *Metamorphoses, Volume II: Book 9–15.* Translated by Frank Justus Miller and G. P. Goold. Loeb Classical Library 43. Cambridge, MA: Harvard University Press, 1984.

Park, M. Sydney. *Submission within the Godhead and the Church in the Epistle to the Philippians: An Exegetical and Theological Examination of the Concept of Submission in Philippians 2 and 3.* LNTS 361. London: T & T Clark, 2007.

Pate, C. Marvin. *Communities of the Last Days: The Dead Sea Scrolls, the New Testament & the Story of Israel*. Leicester: Apollos, 2000.

Paul, Shalom M. *Isaiah 40–66: Translation and Commentary*. Grand Rapids: Eerdmans, 2012.

Perriman, Andrew C. "The Pattern of Christ's Sufferings: Colossians 1:24 and Philippians 3:10–11." *Tyndale Bulletin* 42, no. 1 (1991): 62–79.

Peterlin, Davorin. *Paul's Letter to the Philippians in the Light of Disunity in the Church*. Leiden: Brill, 1995.

Peterman, Gerald W. *Paul's Gift from Philippi: Conventions of Gift-Exchange and Christian Giving*. SNTSMS 92. Cambridge, UK: Cambridge University Press, 1997.

Petronius, Seneca. *Satyricon. Apocolocyntosis*. Translated by Michael Heseltine. Rev. ed. Loeb Classical Library 15. Cambridge, MA: Harvard University Press, 1997.

Philo. *The Embassy to Gaius*. Translated by Francis Henry Colson. Loeb Classical Library 379. Cambridge, MA: Harvard University Press, 2004.

Piage, T. "Holy Spirit." In *Dictionary of Paul and His Letters*, edited by Daniel G. Reid, Gerald F. Hawthorne, and Ralph P. Martin, 404–13. Downers Grove: InterVarsity Press, 1993.

Pilhofer, Peter. *Philippi Band 1: Die Erste Christliche Gemeinde Europas*. Tübingen: Mohr Siebeck, 1995.

———. *Philippi Band 2: Katalog der Inschriften von Philippi*. Tübingen: Mohr Siebeck, 2009.

Pleket, H. W. "An Aspect of the Emperor Cult: Imperial Mysteries." *Harvard Theological Review* 58, no. 4 (1965): 331–47.

Portefaix, Lilian. *Sisters Rejoice: Paul's Letter to the Philippians and Luke Acts as Seen by First Century Philippian Women*. Stockholm: Almqvist & Wiksell, 1988.

Porter, Stanley E. "Holiness, Sanctification." In *Dictionary of Paul and His Letters*, edited by Daniel G. Reid, Gerald F. Hawthorne, and Ralph P. Martin, 397–402. Downers Grove: InterVarsity Press, 1993.

———. "Paul Confronts Caesar with the Good News." In *Empire in the New Testament*, edited by Stanley E. Porter, and Cynthia Long Westfall. Eugene: Pickwick, 2011.

Posner, Raphael, Uri Kaploun, and Shalom Cohen, eds. *Jewish Liturgy: Prayer and Synagogue Service through the Ages*. Jerusalem: Keter Publishing House, 1975.

Powell, Mark Allan. *What Is Narrative Criticism?* Minneapolis: Fortress, 1990.

Poythress, Vern S. "'Hold Fast' Versus 'Hold Out' in Philippians 2:16." *Westminster Theological Journal* 64, no. 1 (2002): 45–53.

Price, S. R. F. *Rituals and Power: The Roman Imperial Cult in Asia Minor*. Cambridge, UK: Cambridge University Press, 1984.

Raaflaub, Kurt A. "The Political Significance of Augustus' Military Reforms." In
Augustus, edited by Jonathan C. Edmondson, 203–28. Edinburgh: Edinburgh
University Press, 2009.

Rad, Gerhard von. *Holy War in Ancient Israel*. Translated by Marva J. Dawn. Grand
Rapids: Eerdmans, 1991.

Rapske, Brian. *The Book of Acts and Paul in Roman Custody*. The Book of Acts in
Its First Century Setting 3. Grand Rapids: Eerdmans, 1994.

Reed, Jeffrey T. "Philippians 3:1 and the Epistolary Hesitation Formulas: The
Literary Integrity of Philippians, Again." *Journal of Biblical Literature* 115, no.
1 (1996): 63–90.

Remus, Harold. "Persecution." *Handbook of Early Christianity: Social Science
Approaches*, edited by Anthony J. Blasi, Jean Duhaime, and Paul-André
Turcotte, 431–52. Lanham, MD: Rowman & Littlefield, 2002.

Rendtorff, Rolf. *The Covenant Formula: An Exegetical and Theological Investigation*.
Edinburgh: T & T Clark, 1998.

Resseguie, James L. *Narrative Criticism of the New Testament: An Introduction*.
Grand Rapids: Baker Academic, 2005.

Reumann, John Henry Paul. *Philippians: A New Translation with Introduction and
Commentary*. AYBRL. New Haven: Yale University Press, 2014.

Roberts, J. J. M. "Isaiah in Old Testament Theology." *Interpretation* 36, no. 2
(1982): 130–43.

Roberts, Jimmy J. M. *First Isaiah: A Commentary*. Edited by Peter Machinist.
Hermeneia. Minneapolis: Fortress, 2015.

Schaller, B. "Βῆμα." In *Exegetical Dictionary of the New Testament*, vol. 1, edited by
Horst Balz and Gerhard Schneider, 215–16. Grand Rapids: Eerdmans, 1990.

Schneider, G. "Ἀγάπη." In *Exegetical Dictionary of the New Testament*, vol. 1, edited
by Horst Balz and Gerhard Schneider, 8–12. Grand Rapids: Eerdmans, 1990.

Schramm, Brooks. "Exodus 19 and Its Christian Appropriation." In *Jews,
Christians, and the Theology of the Hebrew Scriptures*, edited by Alice Ogden
Bellis, 334–43. Atlanta: SBL Press, 2000.

Schultz, Richard L. "Nationalism and Universalism in Isaiah." In *Interpreting
Isaiah: Issues and Approaches*, edited by David G. Firth and H. G. M.
Williamson, 122–44. Nottingham: Apollos, 2009.

Schweizer, Edward. *Lordship and Discipleship*. London: SCM Press, 1960.

Scott, James M. "Covenant." *Eerdmans Dictionary of Early Judaism*, edited by John
J. Collins and Daniel C. Harlow, 491–94. Grand Rapids: Eerdmans, 2010.

Seifrid, Mark A. "Romans." In *Commentary on the New Testament Use of the Old
Testament*, edited by G. K. Beale and D. A. Carson, 607–94. Grand Rapids:
Baker Academic, 2007.

Sellew, Philip. "'Laodiceans' and the Philippians Fragments Hypothesis." *Harvard
Theological Review* 87, no. 1 (1994): 17–28.

Sève, Michael, and Patrick Weber. "Un Monument Honorifique Au Forum De Philippes." *Bulletin de correspondance hellénique* 112 (1988): 467–79.

Shaw, David A. "Apocalyptic and Covenant: Perspectives on Paul or Antinomies at War?" *Journal for the Study of the New Testament* 36, no. 2 (2013): 155–71.

Shultz, Richard L. "Nationalism and Universalism in Isaiah." In *Interpreting Isaiah: Issues and Approaches*, edited by David G. Firth and H. G. M. Williamson, 122–44. Nottingham : Apollos , 2009.

Shum, Shiu-Lun. *Paul's Use of Isaiah in Romans: A Comparative Study of Paul's Letter to the Romans and the Sibylline and Qumran Sectarian Texts.* Tübingen: Mohr Siebeck, 2002.

Silva, Moisés. "Philippians." In *Commentary on the New Testament Use of the Old Testament*, edited by G. K. Beale and D. A. Carson, 835–40. Grand Rapids: Baker Academic, 2007.

———. *Philippians.* 2nd ed. BECNT. Grand Rapids: Baker Academic, 2005.

Skarsaune, Oskar. *In the Shadow of the Temple: Jewish Influences on Early Christianity.* Downers Grove: InterVarsity Press, 2002.

Smith, Gary. "Spiritual Blindness, Deafness, and Fatness in Isaiah." *Bibliotheca Sacra* 170, no. 678 (2013): 116–78.

Stanley, Christopher D. *Arguing with Scripture: The Rhetoric of Quotations in the Letters of Paul.* New York: T & T Clark, 2004.

———. *Paul and the Language of Scripture: Citation Technique in the Pauline Epistles and Contemporary Literature.* Cambridge, UK: Cambridge University Press, 1992.

Stanton, Graham. *Jesus and Gospel.* Cambridge, UK: Cambridge University Press, 2004.

Strabo. *Geography: Books 6–7.* Translated by Horace Leonard Jones. Loeb Classical Library 182. Cambridge, MA: Harvard University Press, 2001.

Stowers, Stanley Kent. *Letter Writing in Greco-Roman Antiquity.* Letters of Early Christianity 5. Philadelphia: Westminster, 1989.

Stromberg, Jakob. *An Introduction to the Study of Isaiah.* New York: T & T Clark, 2011.

Stuart, Douglas K. *Exodus.* NAC. Nashville: Broadman & Holman Publishers, 2006.

Suetonius. *The Lives of Caesars, Volume I: Julius. Augustus. Tiberius. Gaius. Caligula.* Translated by J. C. Rolfe. Rev. ed. Loeb Classical Library 31. Cambridge, MA: Harvard University Press, 1997.

Sweeney, Marvin A. "Eschatology in the Book of Isaiah." In *The Book of Isaiah: Enduring Questions Answered Anew: Essays Honoring Joseph Blenkinsopp and His Contribution to the Study of Isaiah*, edited by Joseph Blenkinsopp and Richard J. Bautch, 179–95. Grand Rapids: Eerdmans, 2014.

Swift, Robert C. "The Theme and Structure of Philippians." *Bibliotheca Sacra* 141, no. 563 (1984): 234–54.

Syme, Ronald. *The Roman Revolution*. London: Oxford University Press, 1939.

Synman, A. H. "A Rhetorical Analysis of Philippians 1:27–2:18." *Verbum et Ecclesia* 26, no. 3 (2005): 783–809.

Tacitus. *Histories: Books 4–5. Annals: Books 1–3*. Translated by Clifford H. Moore, John Jackson. Loeb Classical Library 249. Cambridge, MA: Harvard University Press, 1931.

Talbert, Charles H. "The Problem of Pre-Existence in Philippians 2:6–11." *Journal of Biblical Literature* 86, no. 2 (1967): 141–53.

Tan, Kim Huat. *The Zion Traditions and the Aims of Jesus*. Cambridge, UK: Cambridge University Press, 2005.

Tanner, J. Paul. "The New Covenant and Paul's Quotations from Hosea in Romans 9:25–26." *Bibliotheca Sacra* 162, no. 645 (2005): 95–110.

Tellbe, Mikael. *Paul between Synagogue and State: Christians, Jews, and Civic Authorities in 1 Thessalonians, Romans and Philippians*. Stockholm: Almqvist & Wiksell International, 2001.

Thekkekara, Mathew. "A Neglected Idiom in an Overstudied Passage (Phil 2:6–8)." *Louvain Studies* 17, nos. 2–3 (1992): 306–14.

VanderKam, J. C. "The Righteous One, Messiah, Chosen One, and Son of Man in 1 Enoch 37–71." In *The Messiah: Developments in Earliest Judaism and Christianity*, edited by James H. Charlesworth, 169–91. Minneapolis: Fortress, 1992.

Vermes, Geza. *The Complete Dead Sea Scrolls in English*. Rev. ed. New York: Penguin Books, 2004.

Vincent, Marvin R. *The Epistles to the Philippians and to Philemon*. Edinburgh: T&T Clark, 1897.

Virgil. *Eclogues. Georgics. Aeneid: Books 1–6*. Translated by H. Rushton Fairclough. Rev. ed. Loeb Classical Library 63. Cambridge, MA: Harvard University Press, 1999.

Vollenweider, Samuel. "Der 'Raub' Der Gottgleichheit: Ein Religionsgeschichtlicher Vorschlag Zu Phil 2.6(–11)." *New Testament Studies* 45, no. 3 (1999): 413–33.

Wagner, J. Ross. *Heralds of the Good News: Isaiah and Paul in Concert in the Letter to the Romans*. Leiden: Brill, 2003.

———. "Working Out Salvation: Holiness and Community in Philippians." In *Holiness and Ecclesiology in the New Testament*, edited by K. E. Brower and Andy Johnson, 257–74. Grand Rapids: Eerdmans, 2007.

Wallace, Daniel B. *Greek Grammar beyond the Basics: An Exegetical Syntax of the New Testament*. Grand Rapids: Zondervan, 2008.

Walton, John H., Victor Harold Matthews, and Mark W. Chavalas. *The IVP Bible Background Commentary: Old Testament*. Downers Grove: InterVarsity Press, 2000.

Wanamaker, C. A. "Philippians 2:6–11: Son of God or Adamic Christology?" *New Testament Studies* 33, no. 2 (1987): 179–93.

Wansink, Craig S. *Chained in Christ: The Experience and Rhetoric of Paul's Imprisonments*. Sheffield: Sheffield Academic Press, 1996.

Ware, James P. "Law, Christ, and Covenant: Paul's Theology of the Law in Romans 3:19–20." *Journal of Theological Studies* 62, no. 2 (2011): 513–40.

———. *Paul and the Mission of the Church: Philippians in Ancient Jewish Context*. Grand Rapids: Baker Academic, 2011.

———. *Paul's Theology in Context: Creation, Incarnation, Covenant, and Kingdom*. Grand Rapids: Eerdmans, 2019.

Watson, Duane Frederick. "A Rhetorical Analysis of Philippians and Its Implications for the Unity Question." *Novum Testamentum* 30, no. 1 (1988): 57–88.

Watson, Lindsay C. *A Commentary on Horace's Epodes*. Oxford: Oxford University Press, 2003.

Watts, John D. W. *Isaiah 34–66*. 2nd ed. Word Biblical Commentary 25. Nashville: Thomas Nelson, 1999.

Watts, Rikk E. "Isaiah in the New Testament." In *Interpreting Isaiah: Issues and Approaches*, edited by David G. Firth and H. G. M. Williamson, 214–33. Nottingham: Apollos, 2009.

Webster's Third New International Dictionary of the English Language. Chicago: Merriam-Webster, 1986.

Wildberger, Hans. *Isaiah 1–12*. Minneapolis: Fortress, 1991.

———. *Isaiah 13–27*. Minneapolis: Fortress, 1991.

Wilk, Florian. "Isaiah in 1 and 2 Corinthians." In *Isaiah in the New Testament*, edited by Steve Moyise and M. J. J. Menken, 133–58. London: T & T Clark, 2005.

William, William C. "כרע." *New International Dictionary of Old Testament Theology and Exegesis*. Vol. 2, edited by Willem A. VanGemeren, 727. Grand Rapids: Zondervan, 1997.

Williamson, H. G. M. *Isaiah 1–5: A Critical and Exegetical Commentary*. ICC. London: Bloomsbury, 2014.

Williamson, H. G. M. *Variations on a Theme: King, Messiah and Servant in the Book of Isaiah*. Carlisle: Paternoster, 1998.

Wise, Michael Owen, Martin G. Abegg, and Edward M. Cook. *The Dead Sea Scrolls: A New Translation*. Rev. ed. San Francisco: HarperSanFrancisco, 2005.

Witherington III, Ben. *Paul's Letter to the Philippians: A Socio-Rhetorical Commentary*. Grand Rapids: Eerdmans, 2011.

———. *Paul's Narrative Thought World: The Tapestry of Tragedy and Triumph.* Louisville: Westminster John Knox, 1994.

———. *The Acts of the Apostles: A Socio-Rhetorical Commentary.* Grand Rapids: Eerdmans, 1998.

Wojtkowiak, Heiko. *Christologie Und Ethik Im Philipperbrief: Studien Zur Handlungsorientierung Einer Frühchristlichen Gemeinde in Paganer Umwelt.* FRLANT 243. Göttingen: Vandenhoeck & Ruprecht, 2012.

Wright, Christopher J. H. "Covenant: God's Mission through God's People." In *The God of Covenant: Biblical, Theological and Contemporary Perspectives*, edited by Jamie A. Grant and Alistair I. Wilson, 54–78. Leicester: Apollos, 2005.

Wright, N. T. "Jesus Christ Is Lord: Philippians 2:5–11." In *The Climax of the Covenant: Christ and the Law in Pauline Theology*, 56–98. Edinburgh: T & T Clark, 1991.

———. *The New Testament and the People of God.* Minneapolis: Fortress, 1992.

———. *Paul and the Faithfulness of God.* Minneapolis: Fortress, 2013.

———. "Paul's Gospel and Caesar's Empire." In *Paul and Politics: Ekklesia, Israel, Imperium, Interpretation: Essays in Honor of Krister Stendahl*, edited by Richard A. Horsley, 160–83. Harrisburg: Trinity Press International, 2000.

———. "Ἁρπαγμός and the Meaning of Philippians 2:5–11." *Journal of the Theological Studies* 37, no. 2 (1986): 321–52.

Yinger, Kent L. *Paul, Judaism, and Judgment According to Deeds.* Cambridge, UK: Cambridge University Press, 1999.

Zanker, Paul. *The Power of Images in the Age of Augustus.* Ann Arbor: University of Michigan Press, 2002.

Index of Names

B
Baltzer, Klaus 47
Barclay, John 152
Bauckham, Richard 183
Bloomquist, L. Gregory 7–8
Bockmuehl, Markus 122, 157, 171, 180
Bryan, Christoper 151

C
Casey, P. M. 169

D
Dunn, James D. G. 169

F
Fowl, Stephen 6–7, 10–11, 200, 229, 232

H
Heen, Erik M. 191
Hellerman, Joseph H. 10
Hooker, Morna 4, 9, 207
Hurtado, Larry W. 5, 9, 178, 195

J
Justnes, Årstein 59, 60, 64

K
Käsemann, Ernst 3–5, 9, 168, 175, 207
Kim, Seyoon 130, 150

Koperski, Veronica 212
Kreitzer, Larry J. 2

L
Lipka, Michael 90
Lohmeyer, Ernst 156

M
Martin, Ralph P. 4, 157, 175
Meeks, Wayne A. 200

N
Nagata, Takeshi 176
Nebreda, Sergio Rosell 11

O
Oakes, Peter 8, 135, 142, 153, 168, 188
O'Brien, Peter T. 202

P
Park, M. Sydney 10, 11, 244–245
Price, Simon R. F. 90

W
Wagner, J. Ross 76
Wojtkowiak, Heiko 12, 140
Wright, N. T. 11, 153, 180

Y
Yinger, Kent L. 77

Index of Scripture

OLD TESTAMENT

Genesis
12:3 39
15:6 85
28:13–22........................ 44
28:14 39
28:18–22........................ 43

Exodus
15:11 22
15:16 LXX 225, 227
15:18 71
19:3–6............. 21, 23, 42
19:5 .... 21, 22
19:5–6........................... 29
19:6 ....39, 83–84
19:6 LXX 203
20:2–7 22
23:20–22 172
32:1–35......................... 29
32:7–10......................... 25

Leviticus
16:1–34...................... 42
26:12 21

Deuteronomy
2:23 LXX 227
4:39 22
7:8 53
11:25 LXX 227

21:22–23..................... 186
32:5 152
32:5 LXX 144, 224, 227

2 Samuel
7:12–16...................... 84

2 Kings
24:13–17...................... 25

2 Chronicles
36:15–21...................... 25

Psalms
2:7 159
6:5 24
17:50 LXX 79
22:27–29...................... 24
30:9 24
47:3 22
47:8 22
47:9 22
67:4–5........................... 22
72:10 51
75:8 73
82:1–7........................... 22
88:10–12...................... 24
93:1–5........................... 22
95:3 22
95:6–11........................ 25

96:4 22
97:1 22
97:5 22
97:7–9............................ 22
101:8 73
103:19 22
103:20 24
109:1 LXX............. 82, 186
110:1 65
115:4–6.......................... 41
115:17 24
116:1 LXX 79
119:119........................ 73
148:2 24

Proverbs
16:12 65
25:5 65

Isaiah
1–2 .... 30, 35
1:4 25
1:10–15.................... 25, 35
1:16–20........................ 42
1:21–23.................... 29, 41
1:21–31........................ 36
1:24–25........................ 26
1:24–31.................... 30, 41
1:25–27........................ 30
1–39 38

2:2 36	24:1–13 41	44:24 .... 53, 54
2:2–4 ....23, 32–33,	24:1–16 30	44:24–45:8 47
36–38, 49	24:5 43	44:24–45:25 .... 47, 49,
2:3 30	24:14–16 .... 32, 34	53, 55
2:5 33	24:21 26	44:28 .... 47, 50
2:6–11 41	24:21–23 37	44:28–45:3 50
5:16 40	25:6–8 32	44:28–45:13 38
6:1 186	26:19 24	44:28–45:25 48
6:1–5 37	30:7 73	45:1 47
6:1–6 40	30:27 172	45:1–8 50
6:3 24	32:1–5 38	45:1–13 48
6:3–5 40	33:5–6 37	45:3–4 48
6:5 38	33:17 37–38	45:4 54
6:9–10 41	33:17–24 52	45:5 49
7:14 .... 38, 110	33:20–22 37	45:5–6 50
9:1–7 38	33:22 38	45:8 .... 50, 61
10:5–19 41	37:23–29 41	45:9–11 51–52
11:1 65	40:1–11 37	45:9–13 47
11:1–9 .... 27, 52	40:9 .... 41, 148	45:11–12 48
11:1–10 38	40:10–11 25	45:11–13 51
11:2 39	40–55 ....34, 37–38,	45:12 50
11:6–9 .... 36, 110	47–48, 52, 54, 67	45:13 ....50–51, 54
11:9 65	41:8–9 39	45:14 ....48, 50–51
11:10 LXX 79, 81	41:10 41	45:14–16 54
13:11 41	41:13 41	45:14–17 47
13–23 33	42:1–7 38–39	45:15 ....49, 53–54
14:9 82	42:6 .... 30, 44	45:16 53
14:10 82	42:6 LXX 226	45:17 50
14:11 82	42:17–20 41	45:18 .... 48, 50
14:12–23 41	42:19–25 39	45:18–25 .... 47, 50
16:5 38	43:1 41	45:19 52
16:16 41	43:3 50	45: 20 53
18:1–7 33	43:5 41	45:20 ....37, 48, 71, 73
18:3–6 30	43:8 41	45:20–21 49
18:7 .... 32, 42	43:10 37	45:20–24 54
18:9 24	43:15 39	45:20–25 .... 178, 196
19:1–19 33	44:2 41	45:21 ....30, 49, 54
19:14–17 30	44:5 39	45:21–22 61
19:16 LXX 227	44:6 39	45:21–23 183
19:19–25 32	44:6–8 37	45:22 .... 48, 53
19:25 .... 43, 54	44:8 41	45:22–23 .... 11, 51
23:1–9 41	44:9 41	45:22–24 .... 14, 162
23:1–18 33	44:9–20 ....22, 37, 48	45:23 .... 15–16, 57–62,
23:17–18 .... 24, 42	44:17–18 41	68–71, 74–76, 80,
23:18 32	44:18–20 41	86–87, 168, 174, 249

45:23–24.....32, 34, 42, 44,
46, 48, 55,
61, 160, 183
45:23–24 LXX 149,
161–162, 177, 249
45:23 LXX........47, 78–79,
157, 171–172, 176
45:24 175
45:24 LXX................... 184
45:28 51
46:1–2........................... 37
46:1–13......................... 48
49:1–6...................38–39
49:3 39
49:6 .... 30, 44
49:6 LXX 226
49:11 LXX 79
49–55............................ 39
50:1 54
50:4–9........................... 38
50:10 39
51:13 41
52:7 148
52:7–10..........25, 162, 185
52:7–12......................... 42
52:13 186
52:13–53:12 ..... 27, 38, 42,
160, 162–163,
185, 197
52:13 LXX........... 163, 186
52–53.......................... 186
53:12 LXX........... 163, 185
54:10 43
56:1–7.........32, 34–35, 42,
53–54
56:3 43
56:4–6........................... 44
56:6 24
56:10 41
56–66................. 34, 37, 40
58:1–59:21.............. 42, 53
59:15–20....................... 37
60:1 .... 61, 64
60:1–3........................... 38
60:1–9........................... 34

60:1–16......................... 40
60:3–8........................... 42
60:5–7........................... 24
60:6–8........................... 32
60:7 24
60:9 24
60:10–14....................... 63
60–62............................ 40
61:1–3.................... 40, 148
62:11 .... 61, 64
64:4 41
65:12 41
65:17–25.................. 36, 62
66:14–16....................... 30
66:15–17....................... 62
66:15–18....................... 26
66:15–21....................... 34
66:15–24....................... 38
66:18–24....................... 36
66:20 .... 24, 26
66:20–24.................. 32, 35
66:21 24
66:22–23....................... 62
66:22–24..........25, 34, 36,
49, 55, 62
66:23 23
66:23–24....................... 26

Jeremiah
1:1–11 29
1:5–31 30
3:6–11 29
3:6–18........................... 30
3:17 30
4:1–2 30
10:2–10......................... 22
12:14–16....................... 25
16:14–20 LXX 30
16:19–20....................... 30
23:5–6........................... 27
24:7 31
25:4–11......................... 25
31:31–33.................. 25, 67
31:33 31
32:39 .... 31, 66

39:1–10......................... 25

Ezekiel
11:19 .... 31, 66
12:1–28......................... 25
16:30–33....................... 25
20:1–32......................... 29
20:8 25
20:13 25
20:13–24....................... 29
20:21 25
20:23 25
20:31 25
20:33–38....................... 30
20:33–44....................... 25
20:41 .... 24, 26
22:1–12......................... 29
34:23–24....................... 27
36:26–28....................... 31
36:27 31
38–39............................ 26
44:6–8........................... 29
44:9 24

Daniel
3:12 28
3:14 28
3:17 28
6:17 28
6:21 28
7:9 80
7:9–10........................... 24
7:9–12........................... 26
7:13–14..............27–28, 87
7:18 28
7:22 .... 26, 28
7:28 28
12:2 24
12:3 LXX........... 149, 226

Hosea
2:1–13........................... 29
2:23 25

Joel
2:28–32................25–26
2:30–32.........................30
3:5 26
3:5 LXX 184
4:1–16.........................26

Amos
2:6–7 29

Micah
2:2 29
4:1–4...........................23
4:11–13........................26
5:2–5 27

7:1–6..............................29

Zephaniah
1:2–6 29
1:4–13..........................26
2:8 26
2:11 25–26
3:1–4...........................29
3:8–9 31
3:8–13..........................30
3:9 25

Haggai
2:6–9...........................24
2:22–23.........................27

Zechariah
2:1–15.........................23
7:1–16.........................29
9:9–10.........................27
14:1–15........................26
14:9 ....25, 71
14:16 ....23, 26
14:20–21.......................30

Malachi
1:6–8 25
1:6–11.........................29
3:1–4...........................30

NEW TESTAMENT

Acts
1:27 134
2:25 134
2:32–33.......................189
2:33 186
3:20 134
4:15 134
5:31 186
13:14–52......................166
16:11 131
16:11–40..... 131, 133–134
16:12 131–132
16:13 133–134
16:13–14......................134
16:14 135
16:16 134–135
16:19 131
16:19–20......................131
16:19–24......................140
16:20–22......................143
16:21 131
16:22–24......................143
16:27–34......................135
16:37–39......................129
18:3 135
19:10 165
22:22–29......................129

25:10–12......................129
28:30 130

Romans
1:3 ....84, 158
1:3–4..............81, 138, 159
1:7 ....136, 138
1:8–15..........................77
1:9 241
1–11 85
1:16–17.................80, 138
2–3 84
2:16 ....82, 184
2:28 238
2:28–29........................83
2:29 ....239, 241
3:24 83
3:24–25.......................186
4 85
4:25 163
8 85
8:3 ....159, 239
8:3–8..........................239
8:4–6..........................239
8:4–13..........................83
8:15 241
8:19–23.......................193

8:34 82
9:4 84–85
9:4–5.............81, 240–241
9:5 81
9–11 85
10:9–13.......................184
11:4 171
11:27 84
12:16 83
13:1–7.........................150
14:1–6.........................194
14:1–15:13........78–83, 85
14:4 ....78, 81, 184
14:6 81
14:7–9..........................81
14:7–12.........................81
14:8 81
14:8–12.......................174
14:9 80
14:10 80
14:10–11......................249
14:10–12.....78, 80, 82–83,
                87, 175–176,
                184, 194, 204
14:11 ....14, 16, 32, 46, 57,
            75, 79, 81, 86–87,
            157, 167, 178, 184

14:13 78
14:15 84
14:17 .... 80, 83
15:1 78
15:1–2 78
15:2–3 84
15:5 84
15:5–6 184
15:6 ....78–79, 84, 87
15:6–11 79
15:7 .... 78, 84
15:7–12 81
15:8–9 84
15:9 79
15:12 81
15:15–21 80
15:22–16:23 122
15:22–24 78
15:22–33 77

1 Corinthians
1:2 136
1:23 186
1:24 205
3:17 136
6:1 151
9:26 153
11:1 243
15:1–4 138
15:3 .... 163, 186
15:3–4 .... 159, 210
15:4–8 189
15:20–28 .... 137, 160
15:39–42 246
16:1–12 122

2 Corinthians
1:22 242
3:6 184
5:5 242
5:10 82
8:1–2 135
8:1–4 131
13:11 123

Galatians
1:13–15 76
1:15–16 189
4:4 158

Ephesians
1:13–14 242
1:20–21 172
3:14 171
4:30 242

Philippians
1:1 .... 127, 194
1:1–3:1 121
1:3 15
1:3–11 ....123, 125, 201,
                    251, 253
1:4 15
1:5 .... 137, 159
1:5–6 .... 137–139, 251
1:5–7 205–206,
             208–209, 229
1:5–8 125
1:6 ...... 126, 175, 195, 203,
          217, 232–234,
                  251–252
1:7 ...... 125, 129–130, 137,
        140–141, 199–203,
                  230, 251
1:9 15
1:9–11 ....202, 208, 238
1:10 203
1:10–11 .... 14, 126,
          175–176, 194, 198,
          209, 217, 226, 232,
                  234, 250–252
1:11 .... 184, 239
1:12 131
1:12–14 .... 129, 141
1:12–18 .... 131, 149
1:12–26 .... 126, 149–151
1:13 207
1:14 226
1:17 129
1:18 129

1:18–20 149
1:19 .... 129, 131, 151, 204,
             229–230, 242
1:20–22 129
1:21 129
1:21–24 130
1:24–26 129
1:25 151
1:25–26 129
1:25–27 125
1:26 .... 137, 250
1:27 ....4, 137–138,
          140–141, 148–149,
          152, 159, 195, 207,
          220, 223, 250, 252
1:27–2:4 .... 6, 221
1:27–2:18 .... 11, 14, 16,
             124–126, 199,
          206, 222, 232–233,
             235, 250–253
1:27–28 .... 220, 230
1:27–28 ....12, 131, 142,
                  229, 242
1:27–30 ....10, 149, 151,
          219, 223–224, 229,
          232, 235, 250, 252
1:28 ....13, 139, 177,
             226–228, 231, 233
1:29 ....221, 231, 239
1:29–30 .... 130, 137,
                  140–141
1:30 ....129, 140, 143
2:1 .... 125, 230
2:1–4 .... 10, 143, 220,
             223, 232, 235
2:2 .... 137, 225
2:2–4 ....4, 151–152,
                  225, 252
2:3 225
2:3–4 .... 140–141, 220
2:5 ....4, 7, 14, 159, 167,
        199–200, 202, 206, 220,
          225, 229, 251–252
2:5–6 201

2:5-11 .....5, 146, 209, 221, 232, 234, 246
2:5-12 236
2:6 .... 159, 191
2:6-8 ....2, 6, 9-10, 13, 130, 140, 182, 187, 193, 195, 197, 206, 225, 240, 243
2:6-11 .... 1, 3-4, 6, 8, 10-13, 16, 124, 138, 151, 155-160, 163-164, 177, 199, 202, 205-206, 223, 242, 252-253
2:7 163
2:7-8 .... 191, 225
2:7-9 185
2:8 ....185, 221, 225
2:8-9 243
2:8-11 209
2:9 .... 10-11, 13, 182, 186-187, 189, 195, 198, 230
2:9-11 .... 2, 6-7, 12-14, 140, 168
2:10 .... 170, 173
2:10-11 ....9, 13-16, 32, 57, 126, 137, 149, 157, 161, 167-168, 171, 173, 175-178, 183, 187-188, 196, 198-199, 201, 203, 205, 209, 217, 221, 223, 232-234, 249, 251-253
2:10-14 244
2:11 ....46, 148, 151, 167-168, 178
2:12 .... 195, 207, 221-222, 225
2:12-12 252
2:12-13 ....201, 228
2:12-14 ....4, 151-152, 168, 221, 225, 231
2:12-15 232
2:12-16 ....198, 231
2:12-18 .....7, 10, 129, 168, 223, 227, 232-234, 252

2:13 ....195, 231, 233, 251-252
2:14 226
2:14-16 .... 226, 251-252
2:15 ....12, 140, 144, 148, 152, 207, 224, 241
2:15-16 137
2:15-18 168
2:16 ....14, 129, 141, 176, 203, 228, 233-234, 252
2:16-17 126
2:17 .... 4, 15, 129-130, 137, 227
2:17-18 222
2:18 ....137, 235, 250
2:19-24 4
2:19-30 ....11, 123, 126, 234, 236
2:22 129
2:25 148
2:25-30 4
3:1 ....123, 125, 235
3:2 ....125, 140, 145, 236, 250
3:2-3 124
3:2-4:4 ....16, 124-125, 199, 234, 250-252, 254
3:2-6 252
3:2-9 236
3:2-9 .... 134, 145
3:2-21 .... 121, 234-238, 248
3:3 ....15, 184, 230, 238, 253
3:4-6 236
3:4-6 ....76, 194
3:4-8 236
3:4-11 11
3:4-14 .... 209, 236, 238, 243
3:4-15 ....146, 217, 236
3:7-8 ....135, 237, 243
3:7-11 237
3:7-15 252

3:8 .... 130, 205, 210
3:8-11 ....217, 236, 238
3:8-14 245
3:8-21 4
3:9 .... 194, 203, 239, 253
3:9-11 251
3:10 .... 7, 125, 129-130, 244-245
3:10-11 .....7, 13, 126, 129, 194, 210, 229, 239, 243, 245, 251, 253
3:11 .... 7, 8, 245
3:12-14 .... 209, 217, 236, 242
3:12-15 195
3:15 .... 167, 199-200, 209, 236-237, 251
3:15-17 11
3:17 .... 225, 236, 242, 252
3:17-18 ....237, 240
3:18 ....12, 145, 237
3:18-19 152
3:18-19 .... 7, 250, 252-253
3:18-21 .... 151, 229
3:19 ....200, 237, 240
3:20 ...... 13, 129, 136-137, 146, 148
3:20-21 ....7-9, 11, 13, 126, 139, 152, 193, 203, 229, 235, 237, 245-246
3:21 .... 5, 195, 244-245, 253
4:1 .... 137, 149, 152, 235
4:1-4 .... 235-236, 238
4:1-9 121
4:1-19 126
4:2 143
4:2-3 .... 151-152, 250
4:3 ....137, 141, 143
4:5 126
4:5-9 234
4:7 193

4:7–9 147
4:9 225
4:10 200
4:10–20 .... 121–123, 138
4:11–12 129
4:13 244–245
4:14 .... 137, 140–141
4:15 .... 125, 148
4:15–16 123
4:15–18 135
4:18 .... 15, 139, 228
4:21–23 121
4:22 131
7–11 242
10–11 187–188

1 Thessalonians
1:6 243
2:2 ....131, 140, 143
4:1 123

Hebrews
1:4 172

Revelation
2:18 135
5:13 175

Index of Other Ancient Literature

JEWISH WRITINGS

1 Enoch
10:20–22 30
10:21–22 26
37–71 28
46:1–4 28
47:3 80
48 173
48:2–3 28
48:4 30
48:5 ....26, 28, 82, 173
48:5–10 80
48:7 31
48:8–10 .... 28, 31
48:10 .... 28, 30
52:4 28
61:8–9 26
61:8–11 24
62:1–16 80
62:9 26
90:29–33 26
90:33 24

Aleinu 16, 68, 70–72, 74, 80, 82,
                          85–86, 167, 249

Amidah 68–69, 72–74

Philo
   Legatio ad Gaium 149–50 95

Psalms of Solomon
17:22, 26–28 30
17:22, 29 30
17:26–27 30
17:31 .... 24, 30

Qumran Texts
1QIsa 163
1QIsaa 58, 65
1QIsaa 45:23 61
1QIsab 58
1QM 63, 67
1QpHab 67
1QS 67
1QSa 67
4Q161–5 63
4Q215 .... 58, 80
4Q215a 16, 30, 57–58, 61–66, 72, 82,
                          85–86, 167, 249
4Q215a frg. 1ii 59
4Q215a frg. 1ii 7–8 61
4Q252 65
4Q416 66
4QD 63, 67
IQS 63

Rosh Hashanah 68, 72

Sibylline Oracles
3:720 30
3:721–23 30
3:788–95 110

Targum of Isaiah 27

Tobit
13:11 30
14:6–7 30

CLASSICAL AND HELLENISTIC WRITINGS

Hesiod
    Works and Days 113
    Works and Days 109–201   106
    Works and Days 168–173   107
Homer
    Odyssey 5.561–69 106
Horace
    Carmen Saeculare 112
    Carmen Saeculare 67–68   113
    Epodes 16.1 107
Ovid
    Metamorphoses 15.758–61 103
    Metamorphoses 15.758–859 115
Seneca
    Apocolocyntosis 103
Suetonius
    Divus Augustus 13 192

Tacitus
    Annales 1.10 192
Virgil
    Aeneid 6.789–97 114
    Eclogue 4 .... 113, 114
    Eclogue 4.4–52 108
    Eclogue 4.7 109
    Eclogue 4.8–9 110
    Eclogue 4.15–17 110
    Eclogue 4.18–21 110
    Eclogue 4.23–35 110
    Eclogue 4.31–36 110
    Eclogue 4.37–39 110
    Eclogue 4.40–45 110
    Eclogue 9.45–50 108
    Georgic 1.25–42 189

Langham Literature, with its publishing work, is a ministry of Langham Partnership.

Langham Partnership is a global fellowship working in pursuit of the vision God entrusted to its founder John Stott –

to facilitate the growth of the church in maturity and Christ-likeness through raising the standards of biblical preaching and teaching.

Our vision is to see churches in the Majority World equipped for mission and growing to maturity in Christ through the ministry of pastors and leaders who believe, teach and live by the word of God.

Our mission is to strengthen the ministry of the word of God through:
• nurturing national movements for biblical preaching
• fostering the creation and distribution of evangelical literature
• enhancing evangelical theological education
especially in countries where churches are under-resourced.

Our ministry

Langham Preaching partners with national leaders to nurture indigenous biblical preaching movements for pastors and lay preachers all around the world. With the support of a team of trainers from many countries, a multi-level programme of seminars provides practical training, and is followed by a programme for training local facilitators. Local preachers' groups and national and regional networks ensure continuity and ongoing development, seeking to build vigorous movements committed to Bible exposition.

Langham Literature provides Majority World preachers, scholars and seminary libraries with evangelical books and electronic resources through publishing and distribution, grants and discounts. The programme also fosters the creation of indigenous evangelical books in many languages, through writer's grants, strengthening local evangelical publishing houses, and investment in major regional literature projects, such as one volume Bible commentaries like the *Africa Bible Commentary* and the *South Asia Bible Commentary*.

Langham Scholars provides financial support for evangelical doctoral students from the Majority World so that, when they return home, they may train pastors and other Christian leaders with sound, biblical and theological teaching. This programme equips those who equip others. Langham Scholars also works in partnership with Majority World seminaries in strengthening evangelical theological education. A growing number of Langham Scholars study in high quality doctoral programmes in the Majority World itself. As well as teaching the next generation of pastors, graduated Langham Scholars exercise significant influence through their writing and leadership.

To learn more about Langham Partnership and the work we do visit **langham.org**

Lightning Source UK Ltd.
Milton Keynes UK
UKHW022255051121
393429UK00007B/186